The English Tree of Roots
And Words from around the World

Horace G. Danner, Ph.D.
Professor of Communications
University of Maryland University College
Adelphi, Maryland

and

Roger Noël
Chairperson, Department of Modern Foreign Languages
Georgia College and State University
Milledgeville, Georgia

Imprimis Books
Occoquan, Virginia
2004

Other books by the authors
Discover It! A Better Vocabulary the Better Way
A Thesaurus of Medical Word Roots
(published by Imprimis Books)
A Thesaurus of Word Roots of the English Language
(published by University Press of America)

CONTENTS

DEDICATION

Dr. Danner dedicates his efforts in this book
to his six grandchildren,
Nathan, Alissa, Margaret, Donna, Susan, Madelline.

Dr. Noël dedicates his efforts in this book
to his wife,
Cookie.

ACKNOWLEDGMENTS

Although the book is a joint effort of both Roger Noël and me, its actual production took place in Virginia, where I live. Consequently, I wish to acknowledge the work of Chris Cruz, one of my students at University of Maryland University College, who set up the original document. Chris laid the foundation for the book and has continued to advise me, even after he was no longer my student.

The book could not have been produced without the help of Ric Clark, a dear friend, and who has his own company, Trinity Rivers Publishing. Ric set up the running header and the headwords, which was no easy job. He also advised me on numerous aspects of the book's production, coordinating work between the book designer and the printer. His knowledge of both book production and computers kept the project on schedule.

Steve and Gwynn Fuchs, a husband and wife designer team, took my basic ideas of a book cover and turned them into a work of art. They were a wonderful couple to work with, and I am grateful for their attention to design.

A book of this scope has never been attempted before, and it is encouraging to have someone of Jim Wallace's stature put his imprimatur on the book. Jim is president of SPELL (Society for the Preservation of English Language and Literature), and he graciously consented to writing the foreword. Until his retirement, Jim was an editor with the *Atlanta Journal-Constitution*, and is now editor of SPELL/Binder, the newsletter of SPELL. Jim and his wife, Marietta, live in Hoschton, Georgia.

I would also like to thank Marcel Southern and Julie Good, my contacts at Sheridan Books of Fredericksburg, Virginia, for their guidance throughout the final phase of the production process.

Before going to press, Kathy Clark did a final edit. I am grateful for her attention to detail.

Finally, Roger and I acknowledge you, the readers, for using the book. We hope it is even more than you bargained for. Please let us know what you think of it and how you plan to use it. I can be reached at words@imprimis-books.com.

FOREWORD

When I learned that Horace Danner and Roger Noël were producing this monumental work, the first thing that popped into my head was a vision of a radish. Very strange, I thought. What does a vegetable have to do with words? Then I remembered that a radish is not only a vegetable but also a root. The word *radish* comes from the Latin word *radix*, meaning *root*. From there, my mind jumped to recollections of my undistinguished studies in high school mathematics, where the concept of *radicals* had me stumped until the teacher explained that the word simply meant *roots*—the bases of number systems.

The authors, logophiles of the first order, have given us an invaluable tool in using, studying, teaching, and understanding the English language. The book fills a void and makes me wonder: Why hasn't anybody done this before? *The English Tree of Roots* can be used by almost everyone—students, school teachers—from elementary to high school, college teachers, home-school teachers, linguists, adults learning English as a second language, even crossword puzzle enthusiasts. Even a slight familiarity with the book's contents should guarantee a higher score on the verbal part of a senior's college board exams.

Although the authors are notably erudite scholars (Dr. Danner being a philologist who's had a lifelong fascination with words and their origins, and Dr. Noël, a language expert who speaks French, Flemish, Dutch, Spanish, and Italian as well as English and is proficient in Latin and Greek), this book is not arcane and esoteric. It's a practical reference guide that meets a real need for people who are educated or want to be.

The authors' process of "shredding out" the roots proved salutary; this effort, in effect, closes the circle of the roots, their variations, their close kin, and their descendants in what we call the English language. An example is Greek *gam*, the root for "marriage" which, in combination with numerous prefixes, yields "bigamy," "cleistogamy," "monogamy," "polygamy," and at least 20 other "-gamy" words. These words, in turn, have their own variations: the adjective forms such as "bigamous," "monogamous," and "polygamous," for example. The word lover could spend hours devouring the amazing information that results.

Foreword

After learning that *nasturtium* comes from roots meaning *nose* and *twist*, I can clearly picture someone sniffing that flower and reacting to its scent with a twist of the nose. English is an immensely adaptive and adaptable language, with by far the world's richest vocabulary—much of it borrowed from languages that don't share cognates with English (*ketchup*, for example, being derived from two Chinese characters for "fish sauce") and from those languages that do share our cognates (one-of-a-kind words such as *hooky*, from the Dutch word for "hide and seek," *hoeckje*, meaning to hide around the corner or "play hooky").

I was surprised to learn that many common words in English are derived from Arabic; for example, *mattress* originally meant "something thrown on the floor," and *chimney*, both Latin and Greek for "a burning chamber."

English is a fascinating language, and this book adds to the fascination by putting the map of our language's heritage at our fingertips. It joins my "must-have" list of books about English.

James J. Wallace
President
Society for the Preservation of
English Language and Literature

PREFACE

When I first learned to use the dictionary seriously as a teenager, I was bewildered by the many cross-references. Sometimes, it took as many as four jumps, so to speak, before finding the root meaning of a word. But it also proved exciting, because as I jumped from here to there, and back again, I picked up exciting bits of information, information that would serve me well as a writer and in teaching writing. For many years, I have toyed with the idea of sorting out the dictionary, placing the substantive words into families that share a common element. After Roger and I finally completed revising *Discover It!, A Better Vocabulary, A Better Way*, we set out to do just that. After classifying the words into root families, we further separated them in different forms of the root. For example, under *gam*, **marriage or sexual reproduction**, we placed the words ending with the adjective suffix *–gamous* together, and those ending in the noun suffix *–gamy* together. You will find twenty-four words ending in *–gamy*, for example, *bigamy, cleistogamy, deuterogamy, digamy, dichogamy, cleistogamy, polygamy, xenogamy*.

After going through the dictionary word by word, we then consulted the master word search engine: www.onelook.com, for words we may have overlooked as well as for many medical and scientific words not included in *Webster's New World Dictionary of American English*, Third College Edition. We tried not to include words that were esoteric, out of date, archaic, or obsolete. Consequently, the list should prove to be useful to students of all ages as well as all lovers of the English language.

Roger and I have enjoyed compiling this list of mainly Latin and Greek roots. There were many interesting words, however, that don't belong in any family. They are one-of-a-kind words, most of them adopted from other countries to fill a void where there was no equivalent in English. Who would have thought that *cotton, mattress*, and *sherbet*, for example, are from Arabic? Or that *hooky* is from Dutch? *Jungle* and *dungaree* from Hindi? For those types of words, we listed them in SMALL CAPS in the alphabetical list. Only the individual words are defined, and even then, just enough to give you an idea of the original meaning. Some words didn't need defining inasmuch as they are household words, such as COFFEE, TALC, SYRUP; for those words, we gave only the language of origin. At the end of the first segment of the root's listing, we have given words that have altered spellings that include the base element. We have indicated those words as [variant forms]. Phrases using the root under consideration were also placed in [straight brackets]. There were times when we couldn't resist giving the background of interesting words; we have enclosed those words in {curly brackets}. In addition, we have indicated with NB (the abbreviation for Latin *nota bene*, **note well**) words that may appear to belong in the list, but in fact are unrelated. In certain instances, we have given the Spanish equivalent, inasmuch as Spanish is now the secondmost spoken language in the United States.

The second part of the book—English to Roots—gives the combined list of roots for English words. For example, for *before*, we have listed *ante-, fore-, pre-, prim-e, pro-*.

We felt there was a need for this compilation. For example, eight of the ten words most often missed on a recent State of Virginia Standards of Learning test at the high-school level were of Latin origin. Teachers of high school students, especially those who are college-bound, should be able to use the list to its maximum potential. Motivated students themselves will find it a gold mine. We envision that homeschool parents will find the list invaluable.

Words of two or more roots are placed in their respective families. For example, *introspection* is listed under *intro-*, **within**, **inward** and under *spec*, **to see**. When the words had similar meanings, they were placed together, e.g., *act* and *agent*, both come from the same root that means "to do."

We have used the symbol ≈ to indicate a word or set of words beginning with the root under consideration. If this root is followed by another root, we have indicated this by placing a hyphen after the element's line heading. Where the root under consideration comes at the end of the word, we have indicated that with a hyphen (-) before the element. We have also used the symbol ≈ to break up long lists of words with the same element; for example, the prefixes *de-, dis-, pre-, pro-*, and the elements *–logy* and *–scopy* are considerably long. Where the number of words in family were small, we did not shred them out; rather, we separated the different forms with a semicolon, e.g., hysteria; hysterectomy; hysterotomy.

We have some suggestions as to how the book can best be used, although we have found in all our published works that readers devise other quite creative uses. First of all, check the list to find those elements about whose meaning you are positive; at the same

Preface

time, check words in that particular family to see if you are certain of their meanings, noting those that you think you would like to learn. Next, check the elements that yield the most words and commit those elements to memory. Certainly, we would suggest beginning with the prefixes, such as a-, ab-, acro-, ad-, an-, ana-, allo-, ante-, anti-, apo-, bi-, cata-, circum-, com-, de-, deutero-, di-, dis-, dys-, en-, ecto-, endo-, epi-, eu-, ex-, exo-, hetero-, homo-, hyper-, hypo-, in-, inter-, intra-, iso-, macro-, mal-, meta-, micro–, mono-, ne-, neg-, ortho-, pan-, para-, per-, peri-, poly-, pre-, pro-, pseudo-, quad-, re-, sub-, super-, syn-, tetra-, trans-, tri-, and uni-, taking note of their assimilations, truncations, and variants. For example, in *ad-*, **to**, **toward**, the "d" assimilates to the letter that begins the root, such as in the following: to *c-*: *accord, accredit*; to *f-*: *affect, affair*; to *g-*: *aggravate, aggrieve*; to *r-*: *arrest, arrive*; to *t-*: *attest, attune*. Assimilations, truncations, and variations make the word easier to say; linguists often call assimilation "the ease-of-pronunciation" rule. For example, it would be difficult to pronounce *adcord, adcredit; adfect, adfair; adgravate, adgrieve; adrest, adrive; adtest, adtune.*

After working through the prefixes, you could take one of the prefixed words and attempt to determine its meaning. For example, take *project*. Knowing that the prefix *pro-*, means "before," "forward," or "in front of," you could pair that meaning with *ject*, "to throw." You might surmise that the word, used as a verb, literally means "to throw forward." A check with the dictionary confirms that the verb meaning is "to throw or hurl forward." Its use as a noun is simply an extension of the verb's meaning, i.e., a proposal of something to be done; a plan; a scheme. We have purposely not given the definitions of words, leaving that to the excitement of the reader. We also had to keep in mind that the book is primarily a list of roots. A good dictionary is a necessity for confirming the meaning of words derived from roots. Often, combined elements need to be "massaged" in order to arrive at their actual meaning. For example, *pre-*, **before**, and *amble*, from *ambulare*, **to go**, yields *preamble*, literally, **going before**. The Preamble to the United States Constitution gives the reasons for the Constitution and its purpose. And indeed, the Preamble *does* go before the Constitution itself.

As you peruse the list of words, you will notice certain words that may surprise you. For example, under *carn*, **meat**, **flesh**, we have listed *carnation*. This is not a mistake, because *carnations* were originally "flesh-colored," but through permutation, they have evolved into a variety of colors. You might find it unusual that both *orphan* and *robot* share their heritage. Both come from Czeck *robota*, meaning "forced labor." In times past, orphans, bereft of their parents, were often forced to work for their room and board. Of course, a *robot* performs the work of its operator.

In addition, we think that the variant forms of certain words will prove interesting and exciting. In our book *Discover It!, A Better Vocabulary the Better Way*, we called these altered forms "words with disguised roots." For example, under *alt*, **high**, **height**, you will find not only *altitude* and *altimeter*, but also the variant forms *enhance*, *oboe*, and *haughty*, as well as *Terre Haute*, IN. Another example is *infantry*, which is placed in the same family as *infant*. Literally, *infant* means "one who is unable to talk," and extended to mean "one who is young or inexperienced." Thus, in the Middle Ages, young men, or infants, who did not own a horse were not permitted to join the cavalry and had to enlist in the infantry as a foot soldier, one who cleared the way for the cavalry.

Though English is a Germanic language, the main lexicon of English is Latin and French, with a sizable portion of Greek. In fact, the vast majority of medical words are derived from Greek. But English has a nice sprinkling of words from around the world. For example, most words used in music, such as *decrescendo*, *ritardando*, *piano*, and *subito*, are Italian, because of the Renaissance in music having its beginnings in Italy. We are also blessed with some very colorful words from Arabic, mainly because the Moors of Egypt conquered Spain and occupied the country for almost 1,000 years; consequently, most words in English of Arabic derivation came to us through Spanish. Examples of these words are *admiral*, *albacore*, *algebra*, *magazine*, *spinach*.

And we have *samovar* from Russian; *tea* and *ketchup* from China; *tomato*, *chili*, and *chocolate* from Mexico; *dungaree* and *bungalow* from Hindi. We have *askance*, *brandy*, *cookie*, *dollar*, *easel*, *hooky* as well as many others from Dutch. Most words in English beginning with *sk-* are Norse, for example, *skitter*, *skittish*, *skoal*, *skull*, *sky*. On and on the catalog of borrowings from other languages branches out, like a tree. The roots, trunk, limbs, branches, and leaves of the English tree fit together to yield the most versatile language in the world.

In conclusion, make this listing of roots work for you. We would be happy to hear how you used it. Please email any comments to comments@imprimis-books.com. I will immediately pass them on

Preface

to Roger. Certainly if you find errors or have suggestions for improving the list, we would like to hear from you. We want the list to be one that you can benefit from—and enjoy.

Part One

Roots List

A

ab-: **off**, **away**; sometimes, an
intensive
≈ab: abaxial, abdicate, abducent,
abduct, aberrant, aberration,
abhor, abhorrence, abhorrent,
abject, abjure
≈ablactation, ablate, ablaut,
abluent, ablution, abnegate,
abolish, abnormal, abomasum,
abominate, aboriginal,
aborigine, abort, abound,
abrade, abrasion, abreaction,
abrogate, abrupt, abruption
≈absent, absolute, absolution,
absolve, absorb, absorbent,
absorption, abstriction, absurd,
abundant, abuse, avocation
≈abs-: abscess, abscise, abscissa,
abscission, abscond, abstain,
abstemious, abstention,
absterge, abstinence, abstract,
abstracted, abstruse
≈a-: truncation of *ab-*: abate,
amanuensis, amusia, apriority,
aversion, avert
[variant forms: advance,
advantage]
[phrases: a posteriori,
a priori]
ABACAS: from Greek *abax*; lit.,
counting board; in architecture, a
slab forming the uppermost part of
the capital of a column
abb: Aramaic: **father**
abba, abbacy, abbatial, abbé,
abbess, abbot
ABET: from Old French: lit., to bait;
to incite, sanction, help, esp. in
wrongdoing
ABEYANCE: from Old French:
expectation; temporary suspension
ABILENE, TX: has only one known
source: Luke 3:1, in reference to
Lysanitas as the tetrarch of
Abilene

able: **to have**, **to hold** [see hab-it]
≈able: able; ability
- able: disable, disabled,
disenable, enable, unable
- ability: disability, inability
ACADEMIC: from Greek *Akademia*,
the estate of Akademos, who
encouraged Plato and other
Athenian philosophers to discuss
important issues at his retreat
acanth-o: **thorn**
≈acanth: acanthaceous,
acanthous, acanthus
≈acanth-: acanthoid, acanthoma
≈acantho-: acanthocarpous,
acanthocephalan, acanthocyte,
acanthophyllous
- acanth: coelacanth, cystacanth,
heteracanth, tragacanth
acar-o: **mite**
≈acar: acarian, acariasis, acarid
≈acar-: acaroid
≈acari-: acaricide, acariosis
≈acaro-: acarology, acarophilous,
acarophobia, acarotoxic
ac-ea: **to heal**; **medicine**
autacoid, panacea
{word note: panacea: with *pan-*, all,
a supposed remedy, cure, or
medicine for all diseases or ills; a
cure-all}
ac-er: **needle**, **pointed**
≈acer: acerate, acerose—one
meaning
≈acicul: acicula, pl., aciculae,
aciculate, aciculum, pl., acicula,
or aciculums
≈acu: acuate, acuation; aculeate,
aculeus; acumen, acuminate,
acute
≈aci-: aciform
≈acu-: acupuncture
≈acuo-: acuology
≈acut-: acutangular
- acute: hyperacute, peracute,
subacute, superacute

[variant forms: acnode, aglet,
  ague, aiguille, aiguillette,
  ocrea, mediocre, eglantine]
{word notes: acnode: an isolated
  point on the graph of an equation;
  mediocre: lit., middle of the peak}

acerb: bitter, sharp
≈acer: acerbate, acerbic, acerbity
- acerbate: exacerbate
≈acrim: acrimonious, acrimony
≈acr-: acrolein [acrid + olere, to
  smell]
≈acrid: acrid, acridine
  [variant forms: acerose—one
  meaning; vinegar]
≈acryl: acrylate, acrylic

acerv: a heap; cluster
acervate, acervative,
coacervation: growing in clusters

acet-o: vinegar
≈acet: acetate, acetic, acetous
≈acet-: acetabulum, acetamide
≈aceto-: acetolysis, acetometer

acid: sour, sharp
≈acid: acid, acidic, acidism,
  acidize
≈acidul: acidulate, acidulous
≈acid-: acidosis, acidosteophyte
≈acidi-: acidific, acidify
≈acido-: acidocyte, acidogenic,
  acidolysis, acidophilic
- acid: diacid, hexacid, monoacid,
  subacid, tetracid, triacid
- acidic: diacidic, monoacidic,
  nonacidic
- acidity: anacidity, hyperacidity,
  hypoacidity, inacidity,
  peracidity, subacidity,
  superacidity
  [variant forms: accipiter, alegar,
  eager, edge; paragon]
{word note: paragon: a model or
  pattern of perfection or
  excellence}

acin: grape; grape-shaped gland
≈acin: acinose, acinous, acinus

≈acini-: aciniform
≈acino-: acinotubular
ACINACIFORM: in botany, shaped like
  a scimitar

aco: following
acolyte; anacoluthon

acoust-o: hearing
≈acoust-ics: acoustic, acoustical,
  acoustics
≈acou-: acouesthesia
≈acousto-: acoustogram
- acoustic: optoacoustic
≈acusis: acusis—normal hearing
- acusia: bradyacusia, diplacusia,
  hypacusia, hyperacusia
- acusis: with prefixes: anacusis,
  diplacusis, dysacusis,
  hypacusis, hyperacusis,
  paracusis, pseudacusis
- acusis: with combining forms:
  nosoacusis, odynacusis,
  osteoacusis, presbyacusis

acr-o: pointed, highest, topmost
≈acr-: acromion, acronym
≈acro-: acrobat, acrobatics,
  acroblast, acrocarpous,
  acrocentric, acrocephaly,
  acrogen, acrolith, acromastitis,
  acromegaly, acropetal,
  acrophobia, acropolis,
  acrosome, acrospire, acrostic
  [second root is stichos]

act: to do, to act [see ag-og]
≈act: act, actable, action,
  activate, active, actor, actuary
- act: coact, counteract, enact,
  epact, exact, inexact, react,
  redact, retroact, transact
- act-: enactment, exacting,
  exactitude, exactly
- action: coaction, exaction,
  inaction, interaction,
  retroaction, transaction
- activate: deactivate, inactivate,
  reactivate, transactivate

- active: enactive, hyperactive,
   inactive, interactive, proactive,
   radioactive, retroactive
- agem: stratagem
≈agend: agendum, pl., agenda
≈agent: agent, agentive
- agency: interagency
≈agi: agile, agitate, agitation
- agulate: coagulate
- amin-e: examination, examine
- eg-y: strategic, strategy
- ig: indefatigable; prodigal
- igate: castigate, fatigate,
   fumigate, fustigate, levigate,
   litigate, mitigate, navigate
- igency: exigency
- igent: exigent, intransigent
- igeration: verbigeration
- iginous: vertiginous,
   vortiginous
- igu-e: disambiguate, fatigue;
   ambiguity
- iguous: ambiguous, exiguous
   [variant forms: ambassador,
   cogent, cogitate; quail— one
   meaning; remiges, squat]
   [compounds: auto-da-fé, entr'acte]
actin-: ray
≈actin: actinal, actinic, actinium
≈actin-: actinoid
≈actini-: actiniform
≈actino-: actinogen, actinograph,
   actinology, actinometer,
   actinomorphic, actinomycete,
   actinomycin, actinomycosis,
   actinouranium, actinozoan
- actinic: photoactinic
acus: see acoust-o
acute: see ac-er
ad-: to, toward
≈ad-: adage, adapt, adaxial, add,
   addend, addendum, address,
   addict, addition, address,
   adduce, adduct, ademption,
   adept, adequate

≈adhere, adherent, adhesion,
   adhesive, adhibit, adjacent,
   adjective, adjoin, adjourn,
   adjudge, adjudicate, adjunct
≈administer, admire, admit,
   admix, admonish, adnexa,
   adopt, adore
≈adscititious, adscript, adsorb,
   adulate, adumbrate, aduncate
≈advent, adverb, adversary,
   adverse, advice, advocate
≈ab-: assimilation of *ad-*:
   abbreviate, abbreviation
≈ac-: assimilation of *ad-*: accede,
   accelerant, accent, accept,
   access, accident, acclaim,
   acclimate, acclivity, accolade,
   accommodate, accompany,
   accomplice, accomplish,
   accord, accost, accouchment,
   account, accouplement,
   accouter, accredit, accrete,
   accrue, acculturate, accumbent,
   accumulate, accurate,
   accursed, accuse, accustom
≈ac-: variant of *ad-*: acquaint,
   acquiesce, acquire, acquisition,
   acquit
≈af-: assimilation of *ad-*: affable,
   affair, affect, afferent, affiance,
   affidavit, affiliate, affine,
   affinity, affirm, affix, afflatus,
   afflict, affluent, afflux, afford,
   afforest, affranchise, affricate,
   affront, affusion
≈ag-: assimilation of *ad-*:
   agglomerate, agglutinate,
   aggrade, aggrandize,
   aggravate, aggregate,
   aggression, aggrieve
≈al-: assimilation of *ad-*: allay,
   allegation, allege, allegiance,
   alleviate, alliterate, allocate,
   allocution, allot, allow, alloy,

allude, allure, allusion,
alluvion

≈an-: assimilation of *ad-*: annex,
annihilate, annotate, announce,
annul, annunciate,
annunciation

≈ap-: assimilation of *ad-*: appall,
appanage, apparatus, apparel,
apparent, apparition, appeal,
appear, appease, appellate,
appellation, append, appendix,
appetite, applaud, applicant,
apply, appoint, apportion,
apposite, appraise, appreciate,
apprehend, approach,
appropriate, approve,
approximate

≈ar-: assimilation of *ad-*: arraign,
arrange, array, arrears, arrest,
arrive, arrogant, arrogate

≈as-: assimilation of *ad-*: assail,
assault, assemble, assent,
assert, assess, asset, asseverate,
assiduity, assiduous, assign,
assimilate, assist, assize,
associate, assonance, assort,
assuage, assume, assumption,
assure

≈as-: variant of *ad-*: ascend,
ascendant, ascender, ascension,
ascent, ascertain

≈at-: assimilation of *ad-*: attach,
attack, attain, attaint, attempt,
attend, attention, attenuate,
attest, attire, attorn, attorney,
attract, attribute, attrition,
attune

≈a-: truncation of *ad-*: abeyance,
abut, amass, ameliorate,
amenable, amentia, amerce,
amoral, amortize, amount,
amuse, apart, aplomb, apostil,
apropos, ascent, ascribe,
ascription, aspect, aspire, avail

add: see dat-e

ADDIS ABABA: Amharic for "new
flower"; capital of Ethiopia

adelph: brother; in botany, number
of stamens

≈adelph: adelphia, adelphous

≈adelpho-: adelphogamy

- adelphia: Philadelphia, MS, PA

- adelphous: diadelphous,
monadelphous, pentadelphous,
polyadelphous, triadelphous

aden-o: gland

≈aden-: adenitis, adenectomy,
adenoid, adenoma

≈adeno-: adenoblast, adenocele

AD HOC: Latin: lit., for this; for a
special case only, as an ad hoc
committee

adip-o: fat

≈adip-: adipectomy, adipoid,
adipose, adiposity

≈adipo-: adipocere, adipochrome

≈adipos-: adiposuria

AD LIB.: for *ad libitum*, at liberty; a
musical direction meaning "at
one's pleasure"; *ad-lib*, coming
from the same source, means "to
improvise, extemporize"

ADMIRAL: Arabic: high leader

ADOBE: Arabic and Coptic: the brick

ADONIS: from Greek mythology; a
very handsome young man

AD REM: to the matter; to the point or
purpose

advantage: see ante-

AEGIS: Greek: shield of Zeus;
goatskin: a protection

aer-o: air

≈aer: aerate, aerial, aerie

≈aero-: aerobacter, aeroballistics,
aerobatics, aerobe, aerobic,
aerobiology, aerodonetics,
aerodrome, aerodynamics,
aerodyne, aeroelastic,
aeroembolism

≈aerogel, aerogram, aerography,
aerology, aeromechanics,
aeromedicine, aerometer,

aeronautical, aeroneurosis,
aeronomy
≈aeropause, aerophagia,
aerophobia, aerophore,
aeroplane, aerosat, aeroscope,
aerosol, aerospace, aerostatics,
aerotherapeutics
- aero-: anaerobe, anaerobic
≈ari-a: aria, arietta, or, ariette
- aria: malaria
[variant forms: eyrie, or eyry]
{word note: aerie: the nest of an
eagle or other bird of prey that
builds in a high place; a house or
stronghold on a high place; from
Latin *ager*, field, but spelling and
meaning influenced by *aer*, air,
and Middle English *ei*, egg}
aesth: to perceive [see esth]
≈aesth: aesthesia, aesthete,
aesthetic, aesthetics
- aesth: with prefixes: alloesthesia,
anaesthesia, apaesthesia,
dysaesthesia, panaesthsia,
paraesthesia, synaesthesia
- aesth: with combining forms:
acanthesthesia, cryaesthesia, or
cryesthesia, photesthesia
- aesthet-: anaesthetic,
anaesthetist
AFFENPINSCHER: German; lit.,
monkey terrier; a breed of small
dogs with a monkeylike
expression
AFTERMATH: *after* + obsolete *math*,
cutting or mowing of grass; a
second growth after the first
mowing; a result of consequences,
especially an unpleasant one
ag: I say; a thing said
- ag-: adage
- ig: prodigious, prodigy
AGHAST: from Old English *ghost*:
feeling great horrow or dismay;
horrified, terrified
agar: fungus
agaric, agariciform, agaricoid

AGATHOLOGY: the study of the
concept and nature of good
AGNUS DEI: lit., Lamb of God; a
representation of Christ as a lamb,
often holding a cross or flag
ag-og: to do, act, lead [see act]
- ag-e: choragus, anagoge
- agogic: hypnagogic, pedagogic
- agogue: copragogue,
demagogue, emmenagogue,
galactagogue, mystagogue,
pedagogue, sialagogue,
synagogue
- agogy: pedagogy
- egesis: diegesis, eisegesis,
exegesis, epexegesis
- eget-e: exegete, exegetic,
exegetical, exegetics
[variant form: pedant: from
pedagogue]
agon: to do, act; struggle
≈agon: agon, agonal, agonist,
agonistic, agony
- agon: glucagon
- agon-: antagonism,
antagonistic, antagonize
- gonist: antagonist, protagonist
agora: marketplace, assembly
≈agora: agora
≈agora-: agoraphilia,
agoraphobia
- agoria: phantasmagoria; also,
phatasmagory
- egoric-: categorical, categoric,
paregoric
- egory: allegory, category
- egyric: panegyric
{word note: agora: in addition to
listed meaning, *agora* is a
monetary unit of Israel, equal to
1/100 of a shekel}
agra: to seize; in some words, gout
anconagra, arthragra, chiragra,
dactylagra, glossagra, gonagra,
melagra, pellagra, podagra,
proctagra, tenontagra

agr-i: field, **country**
≈agr: agrarian, agrestic,
  agrimony
≈agri-: agribusiness, agriculture
≈agrio-: agriology
≈agro-: agrobiology,
  agrochemical, agrology,
  agronomy
≈agrosto: agrostology: grasses
- ager: onager
- egrin: peregrinate, peregrinator:
  pilgrim
  [variant forms: acre, aerie;
  pilgrim]
  [see aer-o for derivation of aerie]
AIKIDO: Japanese: lit., the art of
  matching the opponent's spirit; a
  Japanese system of self-defense
ailuro: **cat**
  ailuromancy, ailurophile,
  ailurophobia
AKIMBO: Middle English: *in
  kenebowe*, in a keen bow; a
  posture of having the hands on
  one's hips in a show of defiance or
  frustration
al: **to grow up** [see al-i]
  coalesce, coalition
  [variant forms: adolescent,
  obsolescent, obsolete]
al-: **the** (Arabic)
  albacore, albatross, alcaide,
  Alcatraz, alcazar, alcohol,
  alcove, alembic, alfalfa,
  algarroba, algebra, Algol,
  algorism, Alhambra, alidade,
  alizarin, alkali, alkanet
ALACRITY: liveliness, eagerness
alam: **poplar tree**; **cottonwood**
  alameda, Alameda, CA; Alamo
  (in San Antonio, TX), Los
  Alamos, NM; Alamogordo,
  NM
  {word note: Alamogordo, NM: lit.,
  big poplar: site of testing range
  where first atomic bomb was
  tested in 1945}

ala-t: **wings**
≈ala-t: alary, alate
≈ali-: aliform, aliped
- alate: dealate
  [variant forms: aileron, aisle]
alb: **white**
≈alb: alb, alba, albatross, albedo,
  albescent, albino, albite,
  albugineous, album, albumen,
  albumin, albus
≈album-: albumblatt
≈albumin: albuminuria
  [variant forms: aubade, daub]
ALBACORE: Arabic; lit., the young
  camel; tuna
ALBUQUERQUE, NM: after the Duke
  of Albu*r*querque, viceroy
  (1702-11) of New Spain
ALCAIDE: Spanish; from Arabic *al
  qadi*, the judge; the mayor of a
  Spanish or Spanish-American
  town, with certain judicial powers
ALCATRAZ: after Spanish *Isla de
  Alcatraces*, Island of Pelicans: site
  of federal prison (1934-63)
ALCAZAR: Spanish; from Arabic *al
  qasr*, the castle; a palace or
  fortress of the Moors in Spain
ALCOVE: Arabic: *al-qubba, the arch*;
  vault, dome
ALEATORIC, ALEATORY: pertaining to
  chance, or gambling
alex: **to defend**
  phytoalexin—an antibiotic
  produced by a plant in response to
  the intrusion of a disease-
  producing agent, esp. a fungus
ALFALFA: Arabic: *al fisfisa*, fodder in
  the freshest state
ALFRESCO: Italian: lit., in the cool;
  outdoors; open air, as *to dine
  alfresco*, or *an alfresco café*
ALGEBRA: Arabic; *al jabara*; lit., the
  reunion of broken parts
alg-o[1]: **cold**
≈alg: algid
≈alge-: algefacient
≈algo-: algogenic, algoscopy

alg-o^2: pain
≈alg: algesia
≈algo-: algolagnia, algometer
- algesia: analgia, analgesia
- algia: adenoalgia, artraglia,
  brachiaglia, cardialgia,
  causalgia, cephalgia, coxalgia,
  enteralgia, gastralgia,
  gingivalgia, glossalgia,
  gnathalgia, gonalgia,
  metralgia, myalgia, nephralgia,
  neuralgia, nostalgia,
  oophoralgia, orchialgia
alg-o^3: algae
  algae; algology
ali^1: garlic
  aliaceous, alicin
ali^2: other, else
≈ali-en: alias, alibi, alien,
  alienable, alienage; alienate,
  alienee, alienor, aliunde (law
  term)
≈ali-: aliquant, aliquot
- alienable: inalienable
  [abbreviations: et al., for *et*
  alibi: and elsewhere; for *et*
  alii: and others]
al-i: to nourish [see al]
≈al: altricial, alumna,
  pl., alumnae,
  alumnus, pl., alumni
≈ali: aliment, alimentary,
  alimony
  [variant form: prolific]
  [phrase: alma mater—
  nourishing mother]
allant: sausage
  allantoid, allantosis;
  chorioallantosis
all-o: other, strange [see alter]
≈all-: allonym
≈allo-: allocentric, allochthon,
  allochromatic, allogamy,
  allomorph, allogenic, allograft,
  allomerous, allomorphy,
  allopathy, allophone,

allosaurus, allotrophic,
  allotropic
≈allele: allele
≈allelo-: allelomorphic,
  allelotropic
- alla-: diallage; parallactic
- allel-: diallel, parallel
- allax: parallax
- allaxis: morphallaxis,
  parallaxis, trophallaxis
≈allotri-o: allotriodontia;
  allotriogeustia
ALMANAC: Coptic: calendar
ALOPECIA: baldness; loss of hair
ALPHABET: *alpha* + *beta*, the first two
  letters of the Greek alphabet
alter: other [see all-o]
≈alter: alter, alterable, alteration,
  alterative, altercate, altercation,
  alterity
≈alternat-e: alternate, alternation,
  alternative, alternator
- alterable: inalterable
- altern: subaltern, superaltern
- alternate: subalternate
  [variant forms: altruism,
  altruistic, adultery]
  [phrases: alter ego, alter idem]
alt-i: height, high
≈alt: altar, altitude, alto
≈alt-: altazimuth
≈alti-: alticamelus, altigraph,
  altiloquence, altimeter,
  altimetry, altiplano, altiscope,
  altithermal
≈alto-: altocumulus, altostratus
- alt-: exalt, exaltation; contralto
  [variant forms: enhance;
  oboe; haughty; Terre Haute,
  IN; hautboy—oboe]
  [phrases: haut monde haute, haute
  couture, haute cuisine, hauteur,
  haute vulgarisation]
{word note: Terre Haute: lit., high
  land; highest point on the Wabash;
  it is not the highest point in
  Indiana, however}

alveol-o: **cavity**; **gum socket**

≈alve-ol: alveolar, alveolate, alveolus, pl., alveoli; alveus

≈alveol-: alveolalgia, alveolectomy

≈alveolo-: alveolotomy

AM: in *radio*, stands for <u>a</u>mplitude <u>m</u>odulation; see FM

amar: **bitter**

amarelle, amaretto

marasca—sour cherry, maraschino

AMARILLO, TX: Spanish; lit., yellow; probably named after nearby Amarillo Creek, whose subsoil is yellow

AMARYLLIS: a shepherdess' name in poems by Virgil and Theocritus; a flower

amat: **love** [see am-i]

≈amat: amateur, amative, amatory

≈amor: amorist, amorous

- amor: enamor, inamorata
  [variant forms: French: amenity, amour, paramour; Italian: amore; Spanish: amor]
  [phrases: amor patriae; amour-propre]

amaur: **dark**; **blind**

amaurosis, amaurotic, amaurornis

amb[1]: **to walk**

≈amb-ul: amble, ambulacrum, ambulance, ambulate, ambulatory

- amble: preamble

- ambulate: circambulate, funambulate, noctambulate, perambulate, somnambulate
  [variant form: alley]

amb[2]: **around, both** [see amphi-]

≈am-: amphora, amplexicaul, amputate

≈amb-: ambage, ambagious, ambassador [second root is *act*]

≈ambien: ambience, ambient
[second root is *it*]

≈ambig: ambiguity, ambiguous
[second root is *act*]

≈ambit: ambition, ambitious

≈ambi-: ambidextrous, ambilateral, ambisexual, ambiopia, ambisinister, ambivalent, ambiversion

≈ambo-: amboceptor, ambosexual

≈an-: variant of *ambi-*: ancipital, anfractuous

- ambi-: circumambient [last root is from *it*]

- ambig-: disambiguate [last root is from *act*]
  [variant forms: andante, embassy, ombudsman—Swedish for "a deputy; representative"]

{word note: amphora: *amphi-*, around + *pherein*, to bear; a tall jar with a narrow neck and base and two handles, used by the ancient Greeks and Romans}

AMBER: from Arabic *anbar*; a yellow translucent fossil resin

ambly-o: **dull, blunted**

≈ambly-: amblyacousia, amblychromasia, amblyopia

≈amblyo-: amblyoscope

AMEER: variation of *emir*, which see

AMENITY: a pleasant quality; anything that adds to a person's comfort; related to *amare*, to love

ament: **thong, strap**

≈ament: ament—one meaning, amentaceous

≈amenti-: amentiferous, amentiform

am-i: **friend** [see amat]

amiable, amicable, amity
[variant forms: Spanish: amigo; French: ami (masculine); amie (feminine), Bon Ami®, enemy— lit., not a friend, enmity, inimical]
[phrase: amicus curiae]

amin-e: ammonia
amine; transamination;
rhodamine
amni-o: embryo; from "lamb"
amnion; amniocentesis,
amniochorial, amniogenesis,
amnioscopy, amniotomy
amoeba: change, amoeba
≈amoeba: amoeba, amoebaean
≈amoeb-: amoeboid
≈amoebo-: amoebocyte
amour: see amat
AMP: the basic unit of electrical
intensity, is named after André
Ampère (1775-1836), French
mathematician and physicist
AMPERSAND: the sign & — and: *and*
per se (by itself) *and*: used on
early slate boards when reciting
the alphabet and numbers
amphi-: around [see ambi-]
≈amphi-: amphiarthrosis,
amphiaster, amphibian,
amphibiotic, amphibacillus,
amphibious, amphibole,
amphibolite, amphibology,
amphibrach
≈amphichroic, amphicoelous,
amphictyon, amphictyony,
amphimacer, amphimixis,
amphipod, amphiprostyle
≈amphistylar, amphitheater,
amphithecium, amphitropous
≈amphis-: amphisbaena
[variant forms: ampul, ampulla]
AMOK: Malay: attacking furiously
AMONTILLADO: from Montilla, town
in Spain; a sherry
ampl-: large, spacious; from "to
contain"
≈ampl-e: ample, amply;
amplitude
≈ampli-: amplidyne,
amplification, amplify
AMULET: French; a charm; talisman;
worn on the body because of its
supposed magical powers

**amygd-al: almond, almond-
shaped; tonsil**
≈amygd-al: amygdala,
amygdalase, amygdalic,
amygdalin, amygdule
≈amygdal-: amygdalectomy,
amygdaloid
amyl: starch
≈amyl: amylase, amylum
≈amyl-: amyloid
≈amylo-: amyloclast, amylogen,
amylometer, amylophagia,
amylosynthesis
AMETHYST: lit., not to be drunk; a
purple or violet variety of quartz,
used in jewelry; the Greek
believed that the stone prevented
intoxication
an-: negative: not, without
≈an-: anacoluthon, anaerobe,
anaerobic, analcime, analgesia,
analgesic, anarchy, anarthria,
anastigmatic
≈anecdote, anemia, anencephaly,
anergy, anesthesia, anestrus,
aneurysm
≈anhedonia, anhydrous,
aniseikonia
≈anomaly, anorexia, anorthite,
anorthosite, anosmia,
anovulation, anoxemia, anoxia
≈a-: truncation of *an-*: abiotic,
abulia, abyss, acaudal,
acephalous, agnostic, amnesia,
amnesty, aneroid, anomie,
apathy, aphasia, aphonia,
aphotic, apnea, apod,
apolitical, aporia, apraxia,
apteral, apterygial, apteryx,
apyretic, atheist, atrophy
**ana-: again, against, up, according
to, backward**
≈ana: anabaena, anabas,
Anabaptist, anabasis, anabatic,
anabiosis, anabolism,
anabranch

11

≈anachronism, anaclastic,
  anaclitic, anacrusis, anadem,
  anadiplosis, anadromous
≈anaglyph, anagram, analects,
  analemma, analeptic, analogy,
  analysis
≈anamnesis, anamorphism,
  anamorphosis, anapest,
  anaphase, anaphora,
  anaphylaxis, anaplastic,
  anaptyxis
≈anasarca, anastomosis,
  anastrophe, anatase, anathema,
  anatomy, anatropous
≈an-: truncation of *ana*-: anagoge,
  anchorite, anion
ANACONDA: Sinhalese; lit., lightning
  stem; a snake of Sri Lanka
ANAPEST: lit., struck back; so called
  from reversing the dactyl; a
  metrical foot of three syllables
ANCHOVY: from Portuguese
ancill: **servant, helper**
  ancilla, ancillary
andr-o: **man, stamen, anther**
≈andr-: androecium
≈andro-: androgen, androgenous,
  androgynous, androsterone
- andro-: gynandromorphy
- androus: with prefixes:
  anandrous, decandrous,
  diandrous, dodecandrous,
  enneandrous, heptandrous,
  monandrous, octandrous,
  oligandrous, pentandrous,
  polyandrous, protandrous
- androus: with combining form:
  gynandrous
- andry: gynandry, misandry,
  monandry, polyandry
  [variant form: philander]
anem-o: **wind**
≈anem: anemone
≈anem-: anemosis
≈anemo-: anemograph,
  anemology, anemometer,
anemometry, anemophilous,
  anemoscope
angel: **messenger**
≈angel: angel, angelic, angelus
- angel-: evangel, evangelical,
  evangelism
- evangelism: televangelism
anger: see anxi-o
angi-o: **vessel**
≈angi-: angiectomy, angioma
≈angio-: angiogram,
  angiography, angiology,
  angioplasty, angiosarcoma,
  angiosperm, angiotensin,
  angiotrophic
- angea: hydrangea
- angi-: hemangioma,
  telangiectasis
- angium: with prefixes:
  macrosporangium,
  megasporangium,
  microsporangium
- angium: with combining forms:
  gametangium, sporangium,
  zoosporangium
{word note: hydrangea: from *hydro*-,
  water + *angeion*, vessel: a flower;
  so named for the cup-shaped seed
  pods}

ang-le: **hook, to bend, angle**
≈angl: angle, angler
- angle: quadrangle, pentangle,
  quadrangle, rectangle, triangle
≈angul: angular, angularity,
  angulate
- angular: equiangular,
  hexangular, multangular, also,
  multiangular, pentangular,
  rectangular, triangular
- angulate: triangulate
  [variant form: ancon]
ANGUILLIFORM: in the form of an eel
anim-a: **life, spirit**
≈anima-l: anima, animal,
  animalculum, animalism,
  animality, animalize

≈anim-at-e: animate, animated,
    animation, animatism,
    animato, animator, animism,
    animosity, animus
≈anim-: animadversion
- animate: exanimate, inanimate,
    reanimate
- animation: inanimation,
    reanimation, transanimation
- animity: equanimity,
    longanimity, magnanimity
- animous: magnanimous,
    pusillanimous, unanimous
anis-o: unequal; from *an-*, not +
    iso, same
≈anis-: aniseikonia
≈aniso-: anisogamete,
    anisomerous, anisometric,
    anisometropia, anisotropic
ANKH: Egyptian: life, soul; a cross
    with a top loop; an ancient
    Egyptian symbol of life
ankyl-o: crooked
≈ankyl-: ankylosis
≈ankylo-: ankylocheilia,
    ankylodactylia, ankyloglossia,
    ankylosaur, ankylostoma
    [variant forms: anchor; ankle,
    anklet]
ann-i: year
≈ann-u: annals, annual, annually,
    annuity
≈anni-: anniversary
- annual: biannual, circannual,
    semiannual, triannual
- annuate: superannuate
- enar-y: millenarian, millenary
- enn-: decennary, perennate
- ennial: biennial, centennial,
    decennial, octennial, perennial,
    postmillennial, quadrennial,
    quadricentennial,
    quindecennial, quinquennial,
    semicentennial, septennial,
    sesquicentennial, triennial

- ennium: millennium,
    quadrennium
    [variant form: solemn]
    [phrases: annus mirabilis,
    per annum]
ann-u: ring, anus
≈ann-u: annelid; annular,
    annulate, annulet, annulus
- annular: penannular
- annulate: biannulate
    [variant forms: anal, anus]
ANORAK: Greenlandic Eskimo for a
    heavy jacket with a hood; parka,
    which see
anser: goose
≈anser: anserine, anserated,
    anserous
≈anseri-: anseriform
- anser: merganser
{word note: merganser: with *mergus*,
    diver (waterfowl), from *mergere*,
    to dip, plunge, a fish-eating,
    diving duck}
ante: before
≈ante: ante, anterior
≈ante-: antebellum, antecede,
    antecedent, antechamber
≈antedate, antediluvian, antefix,
    antemeridian,
    ante meridiem (a.m.),
    antemortem
≈antenatal, antenuptial,
    antepartum, antependium,
    antepenult
≈anteroom, antetype,
    anteversion, antevert
≈anti-: variant of *ante-*:
    anticipant, anticipate,
    anticipation; antipasto
    [variant forms: ancestor,
    ancient, antic, antiquated,
    antiquary, antique, antiquity,
    antler, advance, advantage,
    disadvantage; vanguard, vantage]
    [phrases: status quo ante, penny
    ante]
anthem: see ant-i and phon-e

anth-o: **flower**

≈anth: anthemion, anthesis,
    anthodium
≈antho-: anthocarpous,
    anthocyanin, anthologize,
    anthology, anthophore,
    anthozoan
≈anther: anther, antheridium
≈anthero-: antherozoid
- anth-em: perianth; exanthem;
    chrysanthemum
- anthous: ananthous, epanthous,
    oliganthous, monanthous,
    polyanthous, rhizanthous
- anthus: acroanthus,
    amphanthus, helianthus
    {word note: anthology: orig., a
    garland of flowers; then, a
    collection of poems; now, a
    collection of poems, stories,
    songs, etc., chosen by the
    compiler}

anthrac-o: **coal, carbuncle**

≈anthrac: anthracine, anthracite,
    anthracnose
≈anthrac-: anthracoid,
    anthracosis
    [variant form: anthrax]

anthrop-o: **man**

≈anthrop-: anthropoid
≈anthropo-: anthropocentric,
    anthropogenesis,
    anthropography, anthropology
≈anthropometry,
    anthropomorphism,
    anthropopathy,
    anthropophagus,
    anthroposophy
- anthropist: misanthropist,
    philanthropist
- anthropic: neoanthropic,
    philanthropic, therianthropic
- anthropo- paleoanthropology
- anthropus: Pithecanthropus
- anthropy: lycanthropy,
    philanthropy, zoanthropy

ant-i-: **against**

≈ant-: antagonist, antalkali,
    antarctic, anthelion, anthelix,
    anthelmintic, antonym
≈anti-: antibacterial, antibaryon,
    antibiosis, antibiotic, antibody,
    antichrist, anticlimax,
    anticlinal, anticlinorium
≈antidepressant, antidote,
    antidromic, antifebrile,
    antihelix, antihero,
    antihistamine, antilithic,
    antilogy, antimere, antinode,
    antinomian, antinomy
≈antipathy, antiperistalsis,
    antipersonnel, antiperspirant,
    antiphlogistic, antiphonal,
    antiphrasis, antipode,
    antipyretic, antirachitic
≈antiscorbutic, antisepsis,
    antiseptic, antispastic,
    antistatic, antistrophe,
    antithesis, antithetical,
    antitoxic, antitussive, antitype,
    antiviral
    [variant form: anthem]
antique: see ante- [variant forms]
ANTRUM: cave; in anatomy, a cavity,
    especially one within a bone, as
    either of a pair of sinuses in the
    upper jaw

anxi-o: **to choke; narrow**

anxiety, anxious; anxiolytic
    [variant forms: anger, angina,
    angry, angst, anguish, anguished]
APAREJO: Southwestern Spanish: a
    kind of packsaddle made of a
    stuffed leather pad

apat: **to deceive**

apathetic—serving to mislead
    potential attackers: said of an
    animal's protective coloring;
    apatite

aper: **open**

aperient, aperitif, aperture—see
    opercul

[variant forms: April, overture, pert]

{word notes: <u>aperient</u>: a laxative; <u>overture</u>: Middle English: an opening; an introductory proposal or offer; musical introduction to an opera, introducing the motifs}

APERÇU: French: a discerning perception; insight; also, a short outline or summary

api: bees

≈api: apian, apiarian, apiary

≈api-: apiculture, apiphobia, apivorous

apic-o: a point [see aps-e]

≈apic: apical, apices—plural of *apex*, apiculate

≈apico-: apico-alveolar, apicodental

apo-: away, from

≈apo-: apoapsis, apocalypse, apocarpous, apochromatic, apocope, apocrine, apocrypha

≈apodictic, apodosis, apogamy, apogee, apology, apomict, apomixis

≈aponeurosis, apophyge, apophysis, apoplectic, apoplexy

≈aposematic, aposiopesis, apospory, apostasy, apostate, apostle, apostrophe

≈apothecary, apothecium, apothegm, apothem, apotheosis

ap-: a truncation of *apo-*: aphelion, aphersis, aphorism

{word note: aphorism: with horizein, to bound, a short, concise statement or principle}

APOPHYGE: in architecture, the concave curve where the end of the column spreads into its base or capital; phyge: to flee

aps-e: to fasten, a point, an arch
[from *haptein*, to fasten]

≈aps: apse, apsidal, apsis

- apse: synapse
- apsis: apoapsis, parasynapsis, periapsis, synapsis
- aptic: synaptic

apt-i: to grasp, fasten; suitable

≈apt: apt, aptitude

- apt: adapt, periapt, unapt
- apt-: adaptability, adapter, adaption, adaptive, inaptitude, maladapted
- aptation: adaptation, coaptation, maladaptation, preadaptation
- ept-: inept, ineptitude
[variant forms: attitude, copula]

aqu-a: water

≈aqu-a: aqua, aquacade, aquarelle, aquarist, aquarium, aquatic, aqueous

≈aqua-: aquamarine, aquaphobia, aquavit

- aquatic: semiaquatic

≈aque-: aqueduct

- aqueous: nonaqueous, subaqueous, terraqueous

≈aqui-: aquifer
[variant forms: aqua vitae, ewer, sewer, sewage; Spanish: agua; Italian: gouache]

aquil: eagle

aquilegia (see columbine), aquiline
[variant form: eagle]

ARABLE: from *arare*, to plow; suitable for plowing; hence, for producing crops

arachn: spider

≈arachn: Arachne, arachnia, arachnid

≈arachn-: arachnoid

≈arachni-: arachnifer, arachnivorous

≈arachno-: arachnodactyly, arachnography (computer term)

arbit-r: to judge

arbiter, arbitrage, arbitrament, arbitrary, arbitrate

arbor: tree
   arbor, arboreal, arboreous,
   arborescent, arboretum
   [phrase: arbor vitae]
   [Arbor Day: a tree-planting day,
   observed individually by the
   States in the US]
ARCANE: hidden; secret: understood
   by only a few
ar-c-h: **a bow**; **curved**
≈ar-: arbalest
≈arc-ul: arc, arcade, arch, arco,
   arculate
≈arci-: arciform
- arch: inarch
{word note: arbalest: with *ballein*, to
   throw, a medieval crossbow}
arch: **to rule**
- arch: with prefixes: eparch,
   exarch—one meaning, monarch,
   tetrarch, trierarch
- arch: with combining forms:
   chiliarch, gymnasiarch,
   heresiarch, matriarch, oligarch,
   patriarch, symposiarch
- archate: exarchate
- archy: with prefixes: anarchy,
   autarchy, diarchy, dyarchy,
   heptarchy, monarchy,
   pentarchy, tetrarchy, triarchy
- archy: with combining forms:
   gynarchy, hagiarchy,
   hierarchy, matriarchy,
   oligarchy, patriarchy,
   trierarchy
- arky: autarky
archa: **ancient**, **beginning**, **chief**,
   first, **primary**
≈arch: archaic, archaism
≈arch-: archangel, archbishop,
   archdeacon, archdiocese,
   archduchy, archenteron
≈arche-: archegonium
- arch: endarch, exarch— one
   meaning, menarche, mesarch,
   xerarch

≈archae-: archaebotany,
   archaecyte, archaefauna,
   archaelatry, archaelithic,
   archaeornis
≈archaeo-: archaeoastronomy,
   archaeology, archaeopteryx
≈archive: archive
≈archi-: archiblast, archicarp,
   archidiaconal, archipelago,
   architect, architectonic,
   architrave, archivolt
≈archo-: archoplasm
COARCTATE: to press together;
   constricted, narrowed, or
   compressed, as a segment of a
   blood vessel
ard: **to burn**
   ardent, ardor, arduous
   [variant forms: arson; ash]
AREA: Latin for a vacant place,
   courtyard, a threshing floor;
   possibly from *arere*, to be dry
aren-a: **sand**
≈arena: arena, arenaceous,
   arenarious, arenite
≈areni-: arenicolite, arenicolous
arg: **work**
   lethargic, lethargy; argon—*a-*,
   not + *ergon,* work
argent-i: **silver**
≈argent: argent, argentic,
   Argentina, argentous
≈argent-: argentite
≈argenti-: argentiferous
- arge: litharge
argill: **clay**
≈argill: argillaceous; argillite
≈argilli-: argilliferous
≈argillo-: argillocolous
AGUARDIENTE: Spanish; lit., fiery
   water; any of various common
   alcoholic liquors of Spain, Latin
   America, etc.
argu-e: **to make clear**
   argue, argument,
   argumentative

ARGYLE: a clan tartan of Argyll, Scotland; argyles: socks with Argyle pattern

ARIA: an air or melody in an opera, cantata, or oratorio, esp. for solo voice with instrumental accompaniment

ARID: from *arere*, to be dry; lacking enough water for things to grow; dry and barren; not interesting; a related word is *aril*, next entry

aril-l: covering
aril—see *arid*; arillode

aristo: the best
aristocracy, aristocrat, aristocratic

arithm: art of measurement
arithmetic, arithmetician; arithmancy, arithmometer; logarithm

ARIZONA: little springs; from Papago, the language of an Indian people living in what is now Arizona

arm-a: shield, protection
≈arm: armada, armadillo, armament, armature, armor, armorial, armoire, armory, arms, armure, army
≈armi-: armiger, armigerous, armistice
- arm-: alarm, disarm, disarmament, disarming, unarmed
- arme: gendarme
[variant forms: alarum, ambry]

aroma: sweet spice
aroma, aromatic; aromatherapy

arp: harp
arpeggiate, arpeggio
[variant form: harp]

ARRAS: from Arras, city in France, where it was first made; an elaborate kind of tapestry; a wall hanging, especially of tapestry

ARROW: from *arc*, in the sense of belonging to the bow

ARROWROOT: a plant used by the American Indians to draw the poison from arrow wounds

ARROYO: Spanish; a dry gully; also, a small stream

ARSIS: to lift up; omission

ars-en: arsenic
arsenic, arsenical, arsenide; arsine

ARSENAL: from Arabic *dar assinaia*, wharf, workshop; a place for making or storing weapons and other munitions; a store or collection, as *an arsenal of facts*

arter-io: artery
≈arter-y: arterial, arteriole, artery
≈arterio-: arteriogram, arterioplasty, arteriosclerosis, arteriostenosis, arteriotomy
- arteritis: periarteritis

arthr-o: joint
≈arthr: arthrous
≈arthr-: arthralgia, arthritis, arthrodynia
≈arthro-: arthrocele, arthrocentesis, arthrogram, arthromere, arthropod, arthroscope, arthrospore
- arthria: anarthria, dysarthria
- arthritis: coxarthritis, gonarthritis, holarthritis, monoarthritis, oligoarthritis, osteoarthritis, polyarthritis
- arthrosis: diarthrosis, enarthrosis, synarthrosis

art-ic: joint; to join, fit together
≈art: art, artisan, artist, artistic, artistry, artless
≈artic: article, articulate
≈arti-: artifact, artifice, artificial
- articulate: biarticulate disarticulate, inarticulate
- artistic: inartistic

artio: even
artiodactyl—any hoofed mammal having an even number

of toes, including swine,
hippopotamuses, and all ruminants

asc: to exercise; train for athletic competition
ascesis, ascetic, asceticism

asc-o: bag, bladder
≈ascid: ascidian, ascidium
≈ascidi-: ascidiform
≈asco-: ascobolus, ascocarp,
ascicentrum, ascogonium,
ascomycete, ascospore

ascar: intestinal worms
ascariasis, ascarid
ASHLAR: or, ashler: a square-cut
building stone
ASKANCE: lit., how if; with a side-
ways glance; with suspicion

as-i: ass, donkey
asinine, asininity; ass
[variant form: easel]

asper: rough
≈asper: asper, asperate, asperity
- asperat-: exasperate—two
meanings; exasperation
ASSASSIN: from Arabic *hemp*

aster: inferior
poetaster—a would-be poet
ASTHMA-TIC: Greek; a panting for
breath

astragal: anklebone, vertebra, architectural molding
astragal, astragalus

astr-o: star
≈astra: astral, astration
≈astro-: astrodome, astrolabe,
astrology, astronaut,
astrometry, astronomical,
astronomy, astrosphere
- astrous: disastrous
≈aster: aster, asteriated, asterisk,
asterism
≈aster-: asteroid, asterope
- aster: amphiaster, diaster,
disaster, verticillaster
{word note: disaster: lit., the falling
apart of the stars}

ASTUTE: endowed with cunning;
showing a clever or shrewd mind
ATASCADERO, CA: Spanish; lit.,
mudhole; a city between Los
Angeles and San Francisco

ather-o: awn, chaff, grainy
≈ather: atherectomy, atheroid,
atheroma, atherosis
≈athero-: atherogenesis,
atherogenic, atherosclerosis

athlet-e: to struggle
≈athlet-e: athlete, athletic
- athlete: triathlete
- athlon: biathlon, decathlon,
heptathlon, pentathlon,
triathlon
ATLANTA, GA: after Western and
Atlantic Railroad, of which
Atlanta was the eastern terminus
ATLAS: in Greek mythology, a Titan
compelled to support the heavens
on his shoulder; in lower case, a
book of maps, the original of
which depicted Atlas with the
world on his shoulder

atmo: vapor
atmometer, atmophile,
atmosphere

atom: atom; from a-, not + tom, to cut; hence, not able to be cut
further, as the Greeks thought
≈atom: atom, atomic, atomicity,
atomics, atomism, atomistic,
atomize, atomizer, atomy
- atomic: heptatomic, hexatomic,
interatomic, monatomic,
pentatomic, polyatomic,
preatomic, subatomic,
tetratomic, triatomic
ATONE: from Middle English *at
onen*, at one; thus, to become
reconciled; from the verb is the
noun *atonement*

atr-a: fierce, cruel; from "black"
atrocious, atrocity; atrabilious
ATRIUM: central court, chamber,
cavity; pl., atria or atriums

ATTIC: from Attica (Athens), Greece; orig., a low wall or story above the cornice of a classical façade; the room or space just below the roof of a house; garret

auct: to increase
≈auct-ion: auction, auctioneer, auctorial
≈augment: augment, augmentation
≈augur: augur, augury
≈august: august
- augurate: inaugurate
≈author: author, authority, authorize
- author: coauthor
≈aux: auxesis, auxiliary, auxin
≈auxo-: auxochrome, auxocyte, auxotrophic
- auxis: onychauxis
[variant forms: auteur, octroi]

aud-i-o: to hear
≈aud-io: audible, audience, audile, audio
≈audio-: audiology, audiometer
≈audit: audit, audition
≈audit-: auditorium
≈auditor: auditor, auditory
- audition: subaudition
[variant forms: obedient, disobedient, obeisance, obey, disobey, oyez]
[phrase: oyer and terminer]

audac: to dare, bold
audacious, audacity

aul: tube, pipe
≈aulo-: aulophobia, aulophyte
- aulic: hydraulic
AULD LANG SYNE: Scottish; lit., old long since; old times; the good old times of one's youth, etc.

aur-i: gold
≈aur: aureate, aureole, auric, aurous, aurum
≈auri-: auriferous, aurify
[variant forms: eyrir, oriole]

auri-c: ear
≈aur-ic: aural, auricle, auricula, auricular, auriculate
≈auri-: auriform, aurilave
- aural: binaural, monaural
- auricular: subauricular
- auriculate: biauriculate

auscult: to listen
auscultation
[variant form: scout]

auster: harsh
austere, austerity

austral: south
austral, Australia

aut-o-: self
≈aut: autistic
≈aut-: autarchy, authentic, autoecious, autopsy
≈auto-: autocephalous, autochthon, autoclave, autocracy, autocrat
≈autodidact, autodyne, autogamy, autogenesis, autogenous, autograph, autologous, autolysis, automatic, automobile, autonomy
≈autophobia, autophyte, autoplasty, autosome, autotelic, autotomy, autotoxin, autotrophic
- auto-: photoautotrophic
- authentic: inauthentic
[variant form: effendi]
AUTOBAHN: German; *automobile* + *bahn*, a course, highway; in Germany and Austria, an expressway

avar: greed, greedy
avarice, avaricious
[variant forms: avid, avidity]
AVATAR: Sanskrit *ava*, down + *tarati*, he crosses over; in Hinduism, a god appearing on earth in bodily form; incarnation of God; any incarceration or embodiment

AVE: Hail!; from *avere*, be, or fare
well, as in *Ave Maria*, the first
words of the angel Gabriel,
addressing the Virgin Mary
(Luke 1:28)

avi: **bird**

≈avi-a: aviary, aviation, avis

≈avi-: aviculture, avifauna

- avis: rara avis—rare bird
  [variant forms: auspex, auspice,
  auspicious, inauspicious, ocarina,
  ostrich]
  [phrase: par avion—by airmail]
  {word note: ostrich: orig., *avis
  struthio*; lit., ostrich bird}

AVOIRDUPOIS: French: lit., to have
weight [*pois* from Latin *pensum*,
weight]

AVUNCULAR: orig., maternal uncle;
grandfather; ancestor

ax: **axis**

≈ax: axial, axil, axis, axle

≈axio-: axiobuccal, axiolabial

- axial: axonadaxial, abaxial,
  adaxial, biaxial, coaxial,
  epaxial, equiaxial, hemiaxial,
  heteraxial, homaxial, hypaxial,
  monaxial, multiaxial,
  neuraxial, nonaxial, paraxial,
  periaxial, postaxial, preaxial,
  semiaxia, subaxial, transaxial,
  triaxial, uniaxial

- axle: transaxle

axill: **armpit**

axilla, axillar, axillary

axio-m: **worthy** [from "act"]

axiology, axiom, axiomatic

AZALEA: from Greek *azaleos*, dry;
adopted to indicate "the dry
plant," or one that thrives in dry,
or well-drained soil

AZIMUTH: Arabic; *as-sumat*, lit., the
way, path; an angular measurement used to locate an object, star,
etc.

AZURE: Persian; sky blue, or any
similar blue color; old poetic for
"the blue sky"

B

bacc-i: **berry**

≈bacca: bacca. baccate

≈bacci-: bacciferous, bacciform,
baccivorous
[variant forms: bagasse, bagatelle]

bacill-i: **rod**, **staff**

≈bacill: bacillary, bacillus

≈bacill-: bacillemia, bacillosis

≈bacilli-: bacillicide, bacilliform

≈bacillo-: bacillomyxin,
bacillophobia

- bacillus: lactobacillus,
  pneumobacillus

≈bacter: bacterium, pl., bacteria,
bacterize

≈bacteri-: bactericide

≈bacterio-: bacteriology,
bacteriolysis, bacteriophage

- bacterial: antibacterial

- bacterium: mycobacterium

≈baculi-: baculiform
[variant forms: debacle, imbecile,
imbecility]

BADINAGE: light, playful talk; banter

BADMINTON: a game in India brought
to England and played at
Badminton Castle, on the estate of
the Duke of Beaufort

BAGEL: Yiddish *beygl*; orig., ring

bail: **to keep in custody**, **deliver**

bail, bailee, bailey, bailiff,
bailie, bailiwick, bailment,
bailor, bailsman

BAKSHEESH: in Egypt and India, a tip

bal-l: **to throw**

≈ball: ball, the dance; ballad,
ballade, ballet, ballista,
ballistics, balloon, ballot,
ballotement

- balest: arbalest [see note under
  ar-c-h]

- ballistic: aeroballistic,
  antiballistic

- bol-: symbol, symbolist

- bola: hyperbola, parabola
- bole: amphibole, hyperbole
- bolectomy: embolectomy
- bolic: with prefixes:
  ametabolic, amphibolic,
  catabolic, diabolic, ecbolic,
  embolic, epibolic, hyperbolic,
  metabolic, parabolic, symbolic
- bolic: with combining form:
  galactobolic, thrombolic
- bolism: aeroembolism,
  anabolism, catabolism,
  embolism, hyperbolism,
  metabolism, symbolism
- bolize: parabolize, symbolize
- boloid: hyperboloid, paraboloid
- bology: amphibology,
  symbology
- bolous: paurometabolous
- bolus: amphibolus, embolus
- boly: emboly, epiboly
- ble: parable
- blem: emblem, periblem,
  problem
- blematic: emblematic,
  problematic
  [variant form: Spanish: bola]
  {word note: parable: a story that is
  "thrown beside" to illustrate a
  moral or religious lesson}
BALAUSTINE: pertaining to the
  pomegranate
balne: baths
  balnea; balneology
BAMBOO: from Malay *bambu*
BANANA: from Mande, an African
  language
BANAUSIC: practical; merely
  mechanical
BANDANNA: from Hindi; originally
  meant "a method of dyeing"; a
  large, colored handkerchief,
  usually with a figure or pattern
BANE: from Old English *bana*,
  murderer; has come to mean "the
  cause of death, ruin, or harm";
  adjective: baneful: pernicious

BANGLE: Hindi *bangri*, glass
  bracelet; a decorative bracelet,
  armlet, or anklet
ban-n: to call, summon
≈ban: ban, banal, bandit, banns
- band: abandon, abandoned,
  contraband
BANNOCK: from Gaelic *bannach*:
  Scottish for a thick, flat cake made
  of oatmeal or barley meal baked
  on a griddle
BANSHEE: from Irish *bean sidhe*; lit.,
  a woman fairy; in Celtic folklore,
  a female spirit; a wailer
BANTAM: from Bantam, Java; a small
  domestic fowl; small but
  aggressive person; as an adjective,
  describing such a person
bapt: to immerse
≈bapt: baptism, Baptist,
  baptistery, baptize
- baptism: pedobaptism
- baptist: Anabaptist
barb: beard
  barbate, barbel, barbellate,
  barber, barbet; rebarbative
  {word note: barber: originally called
  a "bearder"}
BARBARIAN: from *barbar*, used for
  unintelligible speech of foreigners
bar-i: heavy
≈bari: barite, barium; baritone, or
  barytone
≈bar-o-: barogram, barograph,
  barometer, baroscope
- bar-ic: isobar; centrobaric,
  hyperbaric, hypobaric
≈bary-: baryon; barysphere,
  barytone, or baritone
- baryon: antibaryon
bar-k: small boat
  bark; debark, embark,
  disembark
  [Spanish: barcarolle, embarcadero:
  a loading wharf]
BAR MITZVAH: Hebrew: son of the
  commandment; see bath mitzvah

BARN: lit., barley-room

BAROQUE: French: irregular; imperfect pearl; style of art, architecture, and music [see *rococo*]

bar-r: **bar, barrier**

≈bar-r: bar, barrier, barrister

- bar-go: debar, disbar, embargo

- barrass: embarrass, disembarrass

 [French phrase: *embarras de richesses*, having too much to choose from]

{word note: barrister: in England, a defense attorney}

BARRACK: orig., cabin, mud hut

BARTER: Old French; orig., to cheat; related words: barrator, or barrater; barratry

bary- words: see bar-i

bas-e¹: **low**

 base—one meaning; bass, bassoon; abase

bas-e²: **to go, base**

≈bas-e: base—one meaning, basement, basidium, basilar, basion, basis, pl., bases

≈basic: basic, basicity

≈basi-: basicranial, basifacial, basification, basifolia, basilateral, basinasal, basipetal

≈baso-: basophil, basoplasm

- base: diabase, rheobase, surbase

- basic: monobasic, polybasic, tetrabasic, tribasic, ultrabasic

- basis: anabasis, catabasis

- bat: acrobat

- bate: stereobate, stylobate

- batic: acrobatic, aerobatic, anabatic, adiabatic

 [variant forms: amphibaena, anabaena, diabetes]

BASENJI: Bantu; lit., monkey; so named because of its monkeylike tail and face; an African breed of dog that does not make a true barking sound

basil: **royal, king**

 basil, basilic, basilica, basilisk

 {word note: basil: orig., *basilikon phyton*, lit., royal plant; a plant of the mint family}

BATH MITZVAH: Hebrew: daughter of the commandment; see bar mitzvah

bath-o: **depth** [see benthos]

≈bath: bathetic, bathos

≈batho-: batholith, bathometer, bathophobia

- bath: eurybath, isobath, stenobath

≈bathy-s: bathyal, bathysmal

≈bathy-: bathycardia, bathygraph, bathymetric, bathypelagic, bathyphyll, bathypnea, bathyscape, bathyscaphe, bathysphere

 [variant forms: abyss, abysmal]

BATON ROUGE, LA: French for "red stick"; translation of Choctaw *itu-uma*, red pole, a boundary mark; probably between the hunting grounds of two tribes

bat-t: **to strike, beat**

≈batt: battalion, battement, batter, batterie, battery, battle, battlement, battue

- bat-: combat, combatant, combative, debatable, rabat, rabato

- bate-: abate, abatement, debate, rebate

- batt-: abattoir, embattle

 [variant forms: rabbet, bascule]

 [phrase: hors de combat]

bauch: **beam, tree trunk**

 debauch, debauchee, debauchery

BAYONET: a military dagger; first made in Bayonne, France

BAZAAR: Persian: a market

beau: see bell for *beauty*

BEAUCOUP: French: very much; very many

BEDLAM: dialectal pronunciation of *Bethlehem*, from Hospital of St. Mary of Bethlehem, an old insane asylum in London, known for its noise and confusion

BEDOUIN: from Arabic *badawin*, plural of *badawi*, desert dweller; an Arab of any of the nomadic desert tribes of Arabia, Syria, or North Africa; any wanderer or nomad

BEGONIA: after M. Bégon (1638-1710), French governor of Santo Domingo and patron of science; a clustered, showy flower

BEGUINE: a native dance of Martinique: from French for infatuation; fancy

BEHEMOTH: Hebrew *behema*, beast; an unidentified huge animal (Job 40:15-24); any animal or thing that is huge or very powerful

BEIJING, China: Chinese for "northern capital"; capital of China

BELFRY: orig. meaning: protector of the peace; a movable tower

BELIE: from Old English *beleogan*, to deceive by lying; to give a false idea of

bell: beautiful

≈bella: belladonna

- bell-: embellish, embellishment

≈beau-ty: beau, beautician, beautiful, beauty
[variant forms: bauble, belle, bibelot]
[phrases: bel canto; belles-lettres]

belli: war

≈belli: bellicose

≈belli-: belligerent

- bel-l: rebel, rebeldom; rebellion, rebellious

- bellum: antebellum, postbellum
[variant forms: revel, revelry; duel]
[phrase: casus belli]

BELLWETHER: orig., a male sheep with a bell tied around its neck, that led the flock; a leader; anything suggesting the general tendency of events, style, etc.

ben-e: good, well

≈ben: benign, benignant, benignity

≈bene-: benedicite, benediction, benefaction, benefactor, benefice, beneficence, beneficent, beneficial, beneficiary, benefit, benevolence, benevolent
[variant form: benison]
[phrase: nota bene— note well; abbreviated NB]

BENELUX countries: acronym for <u>Bel</u>gium, <u>Net</u>herlands, <u>Lux</u>embourg

benthos: depth of the sea
[see bath-o]
benthos, archibenthos, epibenthos, mesobenthos

BERCEUSE: French: to rock: a lullaby

BERSERK: also, beserker; from Old Norse *berserkr*, warrior clothed in bearskin; from *bera*, bear + *serkr*, coat; one of a group of early Norse warriors known for their ferocity in battle; one who is like a berserker; *berserk* can be used as an adjective or adverb: in or into a state or violent or destructive rage or frenzy; see *amok*

best: beast
bestial, bestiality, bestialize
[French phrase: bête noire: lit., black beast; anything greatly feared or disliked]

BEWILDER: orig., to cause to be lost, as in a wilderness

bezzle: to destroy
embezzle, embezzlement
{word note: embezzle: to steal money entrusted to one's care}

bi-: two
≈bi-: biannual, biannulate, biathlon, biauriculate, also, biauricular, biaxial

≈bicameral, bicapsular, bicentennial, bicephalous, biceps, bicipital, bicultural, bicuspid, bicycle

≈bidentate, biennial, bifacial, bifarious, bifid, bifilar, bifurcate, bigamy, bigeminy, bigeneric

≈bijugate, bilabial, bilateral, bilingual, bilocular

≈bimanous, bimanual, bimestrial, bimodal, bimolecular, bimorphemic

≈binational, binomial, binucleate

≈biparous, bipartite, biped, bipedalism, bipetalous, bipinnate, bipod, bipolar

≈biramous, bireme, bisect, biserrate, bisexual, bisulcate, bivalence

≈bin: binary, binate

≈bin-: binaural, binocular

- bin-e: combine, combination, recombinant

≈bis-: bisaxillary, biscotti, biscuit, bissextile, bistort
  [variant form: balance]
  {word note: balance: *lanx* is a scale-pan, two of which were hung from a bar, with a particular weight on one and the desired commodity on the other until there was a "balance"; the plural of *lanx* is *lance*}

bib-e: to drink

≈bib: bib, bibulous

- bib-e: imbibation, imbibe
  [variant forms: beer, imbrue, pourboire—a tip, gratuity]

bibl-io: book

≈bibl-e: Bible, biblical, biblicist, bibliotics

≈biblio-: bibliography, biblioklept, bibliolatry, bibliology, bibliomancy, bibliomania, bibliopegy, bibliophile, bibliopole, bibliotheca
  [Spanish: biblioteca—library]

BIKINI: after Bikini, Marshall Islands, atomic testing site; suggests the explosive effect on the viewer; a two-piece bathing suit for women

bil: strong
  debilitate, debility

bil-e: bile

≈bil-e: bile, bilious

≈bili-: bilirubin, biliverdin

- bilious: atrabilious

BILLINGSGATE: after London fish market, notorious for foul language; foul, vulgar, abusive talk

bi-o: life

≈bi-o: biome; biotic

≈bio-: bioactive, biocatalyst, biochemistry, biogenesis, biography, bioherm, biology, biospshere

- b-: enterobiasis, rhizobium

- be: aerobe, microbe

- bic: aerobic, anaerobic, microbic, polymicrobic, polysaprobic, saprobic

- biology: aerobiology, agrobiology, exobiology, cryobiology, photobiology, radiobiology

- biont-: eobiont, symbiont

- biosis: with prefixes: allobiosis, anabiosis, antibiosis, parabiosis, symbiosis

- biosis: with combining form: aerobiosis, necrobiosis

- biotic: with prefixes: abiotic, antibiotic, endobiotic, macrobiotic, prebiotic

- biotic: with combining forms: photobiotic, xenobiotic

BIT: computer term: coalescence of *binary* + *digit*; equivalent to a 0 (zero) or a 1 (one); a single digit in a binary number system

BIVOUAC: lit., by watch; orig., a night guard; a temporary military encampment; from French; orig., German

BIZARRE: orig. from Basque; beard; came to mean very odd; grotesque; fantastic

blanc: **white, blank**
blanch, blank, blanket, blanquette, blancmange
[points of interest: Blanca Peak, CO; Mont Blanc—highest peak of the Alps, France]
[phrases: blanc fixe, carte blanche; blanc de blancs—white of whites, a white wine]

BLARNEY: from a stone near Blarney Castle, Ireland; smooth talk used in flattering or coaxing

BLASÉ: French: sickened from excess

blasph: **to speak evil of**
blaspheme, blasphemous, blasphemy

blast-o: **shoot, sprout**
≈blast: blastema, blastic, blastula
≈blast-: blastoid, blastoma
≈blasto-: blastocarpous, blastocele, blastocyst, blastocyte, blastoderm, blastogenesis, blastomere, blastomycosis, blastophore, blastosphere, blastotomy
- blast: with prefixes: archiblast, ectoblast, entoblast, epiblast, hypoblast, mesoblast, parablast
- blast: with combining forms: erythroblast, fibroblast, gymnoblast, hematoblast, idioblast, lymphoblast, melanoblast, myeloblast, neuroblast, odontoblast, osteoblast, statoblast, trophoblast
- blastic: amphiblastic, diploblastic, heteroblastic, holoblastic, meroblastic, protoblastic, triploblastic

- blastoma: neuroblastoma, retinoblastoma
- blastula: amphiblastula

BLEACHERS: so called from effects of exposure; a section of seats, usually bare benches, for spectators at outdoor sporting events

blephar-o: **eyelid**
blepharitis, blepharoncus; blepharoplasty

BLINTZ: Yiddish; from Russian *blinyets*, diminutive of *blin*, pancake; a thin pancake rolled with a filling of cottage cheese, fruit, etc.

BLITHE: from German *blithia*, light, bright; thus, lighthearted

BLITZKRIEG: German: *blitz*, war + *krieg*, war; thus, lightning war; sudden, swift, large-scale offensive warfare intended to win a quick victory; any sudden, overwhelming attack

BOCA RATON, FL: Spanish, Rat's Mouth (inlet); from nearby Lake Boca Raton; hidden rock that frays ships' cables, with reference to the lake's outlet to the sea

bogue: see bucca for disembogue

BOISE, ID: French: covered with trees; capital of Idaho

bol-e: see bal-l for hyperbole, metabolism

bomba: **cotton**
bombast, bombastic, bombastical

bon-a: **good**
≈bon: bonanza, bonito, bonny, bonus
≈boni-: bonification, boniform
- bon-: debonair, embonpoint
[variant forms: beatific, beatification, beatitude, boon, bounty]
[phrases: bona fide, bona fides, Bon Secour, AL; commune bonum, summum bonum, cui bono? to whose good?]

{word note: bonanza: from Spanish; orig., fair weather at sea}

BONESET: a plant of eastern North America; so named because it supposedly helped knit broken bones

BONFIRE: lit., bone fire; orig., designated the burning of bodies after a fire or epidemic; later referred to burning of heretics; now, an open-air fire for a public celebration

BONSAI: Japanese *bon*, basin or pot + *sai*, to plant; potted plant

BOOMERANG: native Australian; a flat, curved stick that can be thrown so that it will return to a point near the thrower; also, something that goes contrary to one's expectations

BOONDOCKS: WWII slang, from Tagalog *bundok*, mountain; any remote rural or provincial region; Tagalog is one of the three official languages of the Philippines, the others being English and Spanish

BOOTY: Germanic: orig., distribution, sharing; spoils of war

borea-l: north wind

boreal, Boreas, god of the north wind; hyperborean
[phrase: aurora borealis]

BORSCHT, or borsch: Russian *borscht*, beet; a beet soup

BORZOI: Russian for swift: a breed of dog

BOSS[1]: Dutch *baas*, master

BOSS[2]: French *bosse*, a bump, swelling; a raised part or protruding ornament on a flat surface; term also used in architecture, geology, mechanics

BOSSA NOVA: Portuguese; lit., new bump, new tendency; a jazz samba music originating in Brazil, with a light, flowing line

botan-i: a plant

≈botan-y: botanica, botanical, botanist, botanize; botany

- botany: ethnobotany, geobotany
[related words: proboscis, proboscidean]

BOUGAINVILLEA: after Louis Antoine de Bougainville, French navigator and explorer; a woody tropical vine with bright flowers

BOULDER: from Swedish *bullersten*, lit., noisy stone; Boulder, CO, from the large number of rocks, or boulders, there

BOURBON: from *Bourbon* County, KY; an American whiskey

bov: ox, cow

bovid, bovine [*proboscis, proboscidean* may be related; see *botan-i*]
[variant forms: beef, buccinator, bucolic, buffalo, bugle, bulimia]
{word note: bulimia: abnormal hunger}

BOXER: from German *boxen*; a dog known for its aggressiveness; it begins a fight with its paws similar to a pugilist, or professional boxer

brace: arm

brace, bracelet
embrace—one meaning
[variant forms: brassard, brassiere]
[phrase: brace and bit]

brachi-o: arm

≈brach: brachial, brachiate, brachium, pl., brachia, brachialis
≈brachi-: brachialgia
≈brachio-: brachiocrural, brachiopod, brachioradial, brachiosaurus, brachiotomy
[Spanish: brazo, Brazos River]

brachy: short

≈brachy-: brachybacteria, brachybasia, brachyblast, brachycardia, brachycephalic, brachyceral, brachycranial, brachydactylic, brachylogy, brachypterous, brachyuran

- brach: amphibrach, dibrach,
  tetrabrach, tribrach
bract-eo: **modified leaf**; from thin
  metal plate
  bract, bracteate; bracteolate
brady: **slow**
  bradyacusia, bradycardia,
  bradyglossia, bradykinetic,
  bradylexia, bradylogia
branch-io: **gills**
≈branch: branchia, pl., branchiae,
  branchiate
≈branchi-: branchioma
≈branchio: branchiomotor,
  branchiopod
- branch: elasmobranch,
  lamellibranch, lophobranch,
  nucleobranch, nudibranch
- branchiate: with prefixes:
  abranchiate, dibranchiate,
  tetrabranchiate, unibranchiate
- branchiate: with combining
  forms: caducibranchiate,
  cryptobranchiate,
  dermobranchiate,
  zygobranchiate
brand: **to burn**
  brand, brandish, brandling,
  brandy
BREAD: from an Indo-European root
  that means "to ferment"; *brew* is
  from the same base
BREN (GUN): a submachine gun used
  by the British in WWII; after
  B̲rno, Czechoslovakia, where first
  made + E̲nfield, England, where
  manufactured for the British army
brev-i: **short, brief**
≈brev-e: breve, brevet, breviary,
  breviate, brevity
≈brevi-: brevibacillus,
  brevicalyx, brevirostrate
- breviate: abbreviate
  [variant forms: brief; debrief,
  abridge, unabridged; merriment,
  merry]

{word note: merry: akin to Old High
  German *murgi*, short; from IE
  base *mreghu-*, short; yields Greek
  brachys and Latin *brevis*, short;
  basic sense: lasting a short time;
  seeming brief}
BRICK: from Middle Dutch *breken*, to
  break, in the sense "piece of baked
  clay"; Brick, NJ (orig., where
  bricks were made)
BRIDAL: lit., bride-ale; marriage feast
BRISKET: the breast of an animal;
  meat cut from this part
BROGUE[1]: from Irish *brog*, a shoe;
  orig. from Old Norse *broc*, leg
  covering; *brogan*, a heavy work
  shoe, is from the same source
BROGUE[2]: from Irish *barrig*, a hold
  on the tongue; pronunciation
  peculiar to a dialect
broil[1]: **to cook by explosing to
  flame**
  broil, broiler
broil[2]: **to quarrel**
  embroil; imbroglio—Italian;
  from embroil
BROKER: orig., one who broached, or
  tapped, a cask of wine; a wine
  dealer; later, the word came to
  mean any retailer; still later, a
  middleman
bronch-o: **windpipe**
≈bronch: bronchial, bronchus
≈bronch-: bronchitis
≈broncho-: bronchopneumonia,
  bronchoscope, bronchospasm
- bronchial: endobronchial,
  prebronchial, tracheobronchial,
  transbronchial
bronto: **thunder**
  brontograph, brontology,
  brontometer, brontophobia,
  brontosaurus, brontotherium
BROWSE: orig., a bud or shoot, which
  animals nibble on; thus, a
  browsing room of a library
BRUSQUE: orig., a butcher's broom;
  abrupt, curt

brut: beast
brut, brutal, brutality, brutalize,
brute, brutish
BRYN MAWR, PA: Welsh for "big
hill"
bry-o: to swell, be full
- bryo-: embryo, embryonic
- bry-: embryectomy
- bryo-: embryogeny,
embryology, embryophyte
NOTE: *bry-o* and *bryo* are related,
both coming from Greek *bryein*, to
sprout
bryo: moss
bryology, bryophyte, bryozoan
bucca: mouth, cheek
≈bucca: buccal
≈bucco-: buccoaxial,
buccocervical, buccoclusion,
buccodistal, buccogingival,
buccolabial, buccolingual
- bogue: disembogue
- bouch-: debouch, débouché,
debouchment, embouchure
[variant forms: buckle; rebozo,
saltimbocca, Spanish: boca]
BUDGET: orig., a bag, pouch, in
which recurring expenses were set
aside; related to *budget* is *bulge*
BUFFALO, NY: one authority says it
is a translation of the name of an
Seneca Indian who lived there;
other authorities say that it may
have come from French *beau
fleuve*, beautiful river, referring to
the Niagara River
bul: to will; determination
≈bul: bulesis
- bulia: abulia, dysbulia,
hyperbulia, hypobulia,
parabulia
bull[1]: to boil; bubble
ebullient—overflowing
[variant forms: boil, parboil,
bouillabaisse, bouillon]
{word note: bouillabaisse: French:
lit., to boil and lower; a fish stew}

bull[2]: a seal, anything round;
knob
bull, bulla, bullate, bullet,
bulletin, bullion—one meaning
{word note: bulletin: from *bulla*, a
seal; thus, *bull*, an official edict, or
decree; a *bulletin* was originally a
brief official statement}
BUNGALOW: lit., "Bengalese"; Hindi
for thatched house
BUREAU: French for writing table;
orig., coarse cloth used as a table
cover
BURGLAR: orig., a house servant;
then, one who broke into a
building at night to steal; now, one
who breaks into a building or
home at any time to steal
BURROW: orig., to defend, to take
refuge; from Middle English
burgh, from which is derived
borough
burs-e: bag
≈burs-e: bursa, bursar, burse,
≈burs: bursectomy, bursitis
≈bursi-: bursiform
≈burso-: bursopathy, bursotomy
- burs-e: disbursal, disburse,
disbursement, reimburse
[variant form: purse]
{word notes: bursar: a treasurer of a
college—one who holds the purse;
reimburse: lit., to put back in the
pocket; to pay back money spent}
bus-h: woods
ambuscade, ambush
[variant forms: boscage; Spanish:
bosque]
BUSHEL[1]: orig., from Gaul *bostia*,
handful; further from *bosta*, palm
of hand; a unit of dry measure for
grain, fruit, etc., equal to 4 pecks
or 32 quarts; a container for
holding one bushel; a weight
equivalent to one bushel
BUSHEL[2]: prob. from German
bossein, to patch up, repair; to
repair, renovate, or alter,
especially garments

but: end
abut, abutment, abuttals,
abutter
BUTLER: Old French for cupbearer;
orig., bottle bearer
but-t: **to thrust, push**
butt; rebut, rebuttal, rebutter
butry: **butter**
butryaceous, butryric, butryrin
[variant forms: butter, buttery]
{word note: butter: lit., cow cheese;
from Greek *bous*, cow + *tyros*,
cheese}
byss: **linen, flax**
≈byss: byssus
≈byssi-n-: byssiferous, byssinosis
(brown lung disease)

C

CABAL: French; from Hebrew
kabala: intrigue, junta
CABOOSE: from Dutch *kubuys*: cabin
house; the trainmen's car on a
freight train, usually at the rear;
British for a ship's galley
cac-o: **bad**
≈cac-: cachexia, caconym
≈caco-: cacodemon, cacoepy,
cacoethes, cacogenics,
cacography, cacophemism,
cacophony, cacotrophy
≈kakisto-: kakistocracy—
government by the least qualified
or most unprincipled citizens
cad-e: **to fall**
≈cad: cadaver, cadaverous,
cadence, cadenza
≈cadu: caducity, caducuous
- cad-e: decadence, decadent,
cascade—double use of root
≈casual: casual, casualty
≈cas-: cascade—double use of root
≈casuist: casuist, casuistic,
casuistry

- casion-: occasion, occasional,
occasionalism, occasionally
[variant forms: case—one
meaning, caesura; chance, cheat,
decay, escheat]
[phrase: casus belli—case for war]
CADUCEUS: the staff of an ancient
herald; especially, the winged staff
with two serpents coiled about it,
carried by Mercury; a symbol of
the medical profession
CAIRN: Gaelic: a group of stones
used as a monument
CAJOLE: French for "to chatter like a
jay in a cage"; to coax
calamus: **reed**
calamus; calamiferous
[variant forms: chalumeau,
shawm—an early reed instrument
resembling the oboe]
calamity: see clast
calc-i: **limestone; to account**
≈cal-c: calcareous, calcium,
caliche
≈calci-: calcicole, calciferous,
calcifuge, calcify
≈calcul-us: calculable, calculate,
calculated, calculus
- cal: pedocal (pedo: soil)
- calcul-: incalculable,
miscalculate, precalculate,
recalculater
[variant form: causeway: see
word note, next entry]
cal-c: **heel of the foot**
≈cal-: caltrop—interesting word
≈calc: calcaneus, calcar
- cal-c-: decal; recalcitrant
[variant forms: calque, calx,
caulk; causeway; inculcate]
{word note: causeway: orig., a raised
footway or embankment over
marshy ground; the base of the
word is from *calc-*, which has two
meanings: the "heel of the foot"
and "limestone"; some sources say
that a causeway is made solid by
being continually stamped by the

heel, while others declare it comes from the limestone used as a base; at any rate, the causeway over Lake Ponchartrain, in New Orleans, is 24 miles long; it is the longest bridge in the world}

calc: **shoe**
calceolate; calceiform; discalced—barefooted, as members of certain religious orders
[variant form: chaussure]

cald: **warm, hot**
≈cald: caldarium, caldera, caldron
≈cale: calenture, calescent
≈cale-: calefaction, calefactory
- calent: transcalent, intranscalent
- calescence: decalescence, incalescence, recalescence
≈calor: caloric, calorie, calorize
≈calori-: calorific, calorimeter
[variant forms: callant, caudle, cauldron, chafe, chaldron, chauffer, chowder, nonchalance, nonchalant, réchauffé, scald]

calend: **to call out, to announce solemnly** [see clam]
≈calend: calendar, calends, calendula
- calary: intercalary
- calate: intercalate
[variant forms: nomenclator, nomenclature]
CALICO: from Calicut, India, where it was first obtained; a white cotton fabric

call: **hardened, insensitive**
callosal, callose, callosity, callous, callus

calli: **beautiful**
≈calli-: calligraphy, calliope, calliopsis, callipygian
≈cali-: calisthenics
≈calo-: calomel, caloyer
[variant form: kaleidoscope]
{word notes: callipygian: having

shapely buttocks; calisthenics: with *sthenos*, strength, beautiful strength}

CALM: from Greek *kauma*, heat, esp. of the sun; orig., the heat of the day: a time of rest; compare siesta

calumn: **trickery, slander**
calumniate, calumnious, calumny
[variant forms: cavil, challenge]

calv: **bald**
calvities; calvarium; Calvary: skull
[variant form: callow]

calyptr-o: **to cover, cover; cup**
≈calyptra: calyptra
≈calyptro-: calyptrogen
- calyp-se: apocalypse, apocalyptic, eucalyptus
[variant forms: calyculus, calypter, calix, calyx, epicalyx, chalice; kylix]
CALYPSO: probably from Trinidad patois *kaiso*, town crier, who gave news in rhythm and doggerel; a sea nymph in Homer's *Odyssey*

camb: **to change, barter**
cambist, cambium; procambium
[variant forms: change, exchange, interchange, interchangeable; Spanish: cambiar—to change]
CAMELLIA: named after G. J. Kamel (1661-1706), Moravian missionary in the Far East; state flower of Alabama

camer-a: **room**
≈camer-a: camera, camerlingo
- cameral: bicameral, tricameral, unicameral
≈camar: camaraderie, camarilla
[variant forms: cabaret; chamber, chamberlain; antechamber; chum, comrade, chimney]
[phrases: in camera, camera obscura; robe de chambre]

camis: **shirt**
camisado, camise, camisole

[variant forms: chemise,
chemisette; Spanish: camisa]
{word note: camise: orig. from
Arabic *qamis*}

camp: **field** [see champ]
≈camp: camp, campaign,
campestral, campo, campus
- camp: decamp
[variant forms: scamper, campo
santo; Spanish: campesino]
{word note: scamper: with *ex-*, out,
lit., originally, to get out of the
field (of battle)}

campan-o: **bell**
campanile, campanula,
campanulate; campanology

campylo: **bent, crooked, arched**
campylobacter,
campylocarpum,
campylocentrum,
campylorhynchus,
campylotropous
[variant form: camber]

can: **dog** [see cyn-o-s]
canaille, canary, canicula,
canine
[variant forms: chenille, kennel]
[phrases: Canis Major, Canis
Minor; cave canem]

cancel: **to strike out**
≈cancel-l: cancel, cancellation,
cancellous
≈chancel-l: chancel, chancellery,
chancellor, chancery: lattice;
from "cancel"

canc-r: **crab, cancer**
cancer; cancroid; precancerous
[variant forms: canker, chancre;
chancroid]

can-d-el: **to shine, glow**
≈can: canescent
≈cand: candescent, candle,
candor
≈candel: candela, candelabrum
≈candid: candid, candidate
- candescent: incandescent

- cendiary: incendiary
≈cense: cense, censer
- cens-e: incense; accensor,
incensor, precensor
- centor: precentor
[variant forms: chandelier,
chandelle, chandler,
chandlery; Old Norse kindle]
{word notes: candidate: in Roman
times, a candidate wore a white
toga, either to identify him as
such, or to symbolize his purity;
chandler: orig., a maker or seller
of candles; a retailer}

CANDY: from Sanskrit *khanda*, a
piece of sugar

can-e: **a reed, groove, channel**
≈can-e: canasta, cane, canella,
canister, canyon
≈canal: canal, canaliculated,
caniculus, canalization
≈cane-: canephoros
≈cann: canna, cannelloni,
cannoli, cannon, cannula
≈canon: canon, cañon, canonic,
canonical, canonize
[variant forms: caramel; channel]

can-t: **to sing**
≈can-t: canorous, cant, cantabile,
cantata, cantalina, cantatrice,
cantus
≈canti: canticle, Canticles,
cantillation
≈canto: canto, cantor
- cant-: descant, incantation,
recant
≈canzon-e: canzone, canzonet,
canzoni
- cent-: accent, accentual,
accentuate; concent; incentive
[variant forms: chant, chanter;
enchant, enchanting,
enchantment, disenchant;
chanterelle, chanteuse,
chantey, chantry; chanticleer;
chanson, chansonnier, charm,
hen, oscine]

[phrases: cantus firmus, bel canto; chanson de geste]

CANTER: contraction of *Canterbury gallop*, from pace at which the pilgrims rode to Canterbury, as in Chaucer's *Canterbury Tales*

cant-h: edge, rim, corner

≈cant: canteen, cantle, canton

≈canthus: canthus

≈canti-: cantilever

- cant: decant, decanter

- canthus: epicanthus, syncanthus, telecanthus

CANVASS: probably from use of a canvas for sifting; to try to get votes; to poll opinions; canvas: from "hempen cloth"

cap: to seize, take, hold

≈cap: capable, capacious, capacity, capacitance, capacitor, capias, capsule, capstan

- cap-: incapable; incapacious, incapacitate, incapacity

- capsul-: bicapsular, encapsulate, microencapsulation

≈capt: caption, captious, captivate, captive, captor, capture

- capt-: mercaptan, recapture

≈cas-e: case—one meaning, casement

≈cass: cassation, cassette

- ceipt: receipt

- ceit-: conceit, deceit, deceitful

- ceive: apperceive, conceive, deceive, misconceive, perceive, preconceive, receive

- ceivable: receivable

- ceiver: conreceiver, perceiver, receiver, transceiver

- ceps: forceps

- cept-: accept, concept, except, excepting, incept, intercept, percept, precept

- ceptacle: conceptacle, receptacle

- ceptance: acceptance, susceptance

- ceptible: conceptible, deceptible, perceptible, receptible, susceptible; susceptibility; insusceptible

- ception: apperception, conception, contraception, deception, exception, inception, interception, intussusception, perception, preconception, reception

- ceptional-: exceptional; exceptionalism

- ceptive: conceptive, deceptive, exceptive, imperceptive, inceptive, perceptive, preceptive, receptive, susceptive

- ceptor: with prefixes: acceptor, interceptor, interoceptor, preceptor, receptor

- ceptor: with combining forms: photoreceptor

- ceptual: conceptual, perceptual; interperceptual

- chase: enchase, purchase

- cipal: principal, municipal

- cipant: anticipant, participant

- cipate: anticipate, emancipate, participate

- cipation: anticipation, emancipation, participation

- cipative: anticipative, participative

- cipe: recipe

- cipience: incipience, percipience, recipience, or, recipiency

- cipient: excipient, incipient, percipient, recipient

- ciple: disciple, manciple, participle, principle

- ciplin-e: indiscipline,
  multidisciplinary
- cup-: occupancy, occupant,
  occupy, preoccupied
- cupat-: nuncupative,
  occupation, preoccupation
- cuperate: recuperate
  [variant forms: aperçu; cable,
  cash, cashier—one meaning;
  caitiff, case—one meaning,
  casket, cater, catch, chase,
  chassis, corporal—one meaning,
  prince; recover—one meaning]
  [phrase: ad captandum]
  {word note: aperçu: a discerning
  perception; insight; also, a short
  outline or summary}

capill: hair

≈capill: capillaceous, capillature,
  capillarity, capillary
≈capilli-: capilliflora, capilliform

cap-it: head

≈cap: cap, capsize, captain,
  capuche
≈capit: capitate, capitation,
  capitol
≈capital: capital, capitalism,
  capitalist, capitalization,
  capitalize, capitally
≈capitul: capitular, capitulate,
  capitulation, capitulum
≈capo: capo, caporal
≈cap-e: caparison, cape, capote,
  cappelletti: cape, hooded cloak;
  protection
- cap-e-: escapade, escape,
  inescapable, escapement
- capit-: decapitate; recapitulate
≈capri: caprice, capriccio,
  capricious
- ceps: biceps, quadriceps, triceps
≈chap-e: chape, chapeau, chapel,
  chaperon, chaplain, chaplet
≈chief: chief, chieftain
- chief: kerchief, handkerchief,
  mischief

- chieve-: achieve, achievement
- cip-: precipice; precipitancy;
  precipitant; precipitate;
  precipitous
- cipital: ancipital, bicipital,
  occipital
- ciput: occiput, sinciput
  [variant forms: cabbage,
  cabotage, cadet, caddie,
  cattle, caudillo, cauliflower,
  chapter, chattle, chamfron, chape,
  chapeau, chapel, chaplain, chef;
  cope—one meaning; muscovado;
  scapegoat]
  [phrases: cap-a-pie, da capo]

capn-o: smoke; carbon monoxide

≈capno-: capnomancy
- capnia: acapnia, hypercapnia,
  hypocapnia, isocapnia

car: dear

  caress, caruncle
  [variant forms: charity, cherish]
CARAVAN, CARAVANSARY: Persian; a
  company of travelers traveling
  together

carb: carbon

≈carbon: carbon, carbonado,
  carbonate, carbonize
≈carbon-: carbonuria
≈carboni: carboniferous
≈carbo-: carbocylic,
  carbohydrate
≈carbur: carburet, carburetor,
  carburize
  [variant form: carbuncle]

carcin-o: cancer

  carcinoma, carcinomatosis,
  carcinogen

**cardin: principal; from "door
  hinge"**

  cardinal, incardinate
{word note: cardinal: lit., that on
  which a thing turns; thus, of chief
  importance, as cardinal points;
  also, a chief leader of the church, a
  member of the Pope's council;
  from this meaning, denotes the

color of the cardinal's cassock, a
bright red; has come to denote the
name of a kind of redbird}

cardi-o: heart

≈cardiac: cardiac

≈cardi-: cardialgia, cardiodynia,
cardioid

≈cardio-: cardiocele,
cardiocentesis, cardiogram,
cardiolysis, cardiophony

- cardia: acardia, bathycardia,
bradycardia, dextrocardia,
exocardia, leptocardia,
megalocardia, tachycardia

- cardial: endocardial, exocardial

- carditis: endocarditis,
myocarditis, pericarditis

- cardium: endocardium,
epicardium, myocardium,
pericardium

CARAT: from carob seed; a unit of
weight of four grains in weighing
precious stones and gems

CARET: a one-word Latin sentence: It
is lacking, indicated by the sign ∧

carn-i: meat, flesh

≈carn: carnage, carnal,
carnassial, carnation, carnelian

≈carni-: carnify, carnival
carnivorous

- carn-: encarnalize, incarnation,
incarnadine, reincarnation

- carnate: discarnate, incarnate
[variant forms: chili con carne,
charnel]

caroten: carrot

carotene; carotenoid
[variant form: carrot]

CAROTID: Greek; plural *carotids*
designates the two great arteries of
the neck; to plunge into a deep
sleep or stupor: so called because
compression of these was believed
to cause unconsciousness; a
carotid artery

carp: wrist; from "to turn"
carpal, carpus; metacarpal

[variant form: varve]

carp-o: fruit; to pluck

≈carp: carpel, carpet

≈carpo-: carpogonium,
carpology, carpophagous,
carpophore

- carp: with prefixes: archicarp,
endocarp, epicarp, exocarp,
mesocarp, pericarp, procarp,
pseudocarp, schizocarp

- carp: with combining forms:
podocarp, sarcocarp, sporocarp

- carpellary: monocarpellary,
polycarpellary, tricarpellary

- carpic: isocarpic, monocarpic,
pericarpic, pleurocarpic,
polycarpic, schizocarpic

- carpous: with prefixes:
acrocarpous, apocarpous,
oligocarpous, polycarpous,
pseudocarpous, syncarpous

- carpous: with combining forms:
anthocarpous, rhizocarpous

- carpus: podocarpus

- carpy: parthenocarpy
[variant forms: excerpt; scarce]
[phrase: carpe diem—seize the
day]

cartilag-e: gristle

· cartilage, cartilaginous

cart-o: card, chart, map

≈cart: cartel, carton, cartoon,
cartouche, cartridge, cartulary

≈carto-: cartogram, cartographer,
cartomancy, cartophily
[variant forms: card, discard;
chart, charter, chartist, chartulary]
[phrases: a la carte, carte blanche,
carte du jour; Magna Carta,
Magna Charta]

cas: house

casino, casita
[variant forms: chalet; Spanish:
casa]

case: cheese

≈case: casein, caseose, caseous

≈case-: casefy

≈caseino-: caseinogen
[variant forms: cheese; Spanish: quesadilla, queso]

CASHMERE: from Kashmir, located between Afghanistan and Tibet; a fine carded wool from goats of Kashmir and Tibet

CASSANDRA: from Cassandra, a prophetess cursed by Apollo so that her prophecies, though they were true, were fated never to be believed; a prophet of doom

CASSOCK: from Russian *kozak*, Cossack, nomad, adventurer; in allusion to their usual riding coat; worn as an outer garment or under the surplice by clergymen, choristers, etc.

CASTANETS: lit., chestnuts, so named from the shape

cast: to make pure

≈cast-e: caste, castigate, castrate, castrato

≈chast: chaste, chasten, chastise, chastity
[variant forms: incest, incestuous]
{word note: castigate: lit., to purify; to punish or rebuke severely}

castell: castle
castellan, castellany, castellated
[variant form: castle]

cat-a-: down, away, completely

≈cat: cation

≈cat-: catechesis, catechism, catechumen, category, cathedra, cathedral, catheter, cathexis, cathode, catholic, catoptrics

≈cata-: catabasial, catabolism, catachresis, cataclastic, cataclysm, catacomb, catadromous, catafalque, catkinetic, catalectic, catalepsy, catalogue, catalysis, catalyst, cataphyll, cataplasia,

cataplasm, catapult, cataract, catarrh, catarrhine, catastasis, catastrophe, catatonia

- cathode: photocathode
[variant forms: cadastre, scaffold]

CATAMARAN: from Tamil *kattu*, tie + *maram*, log, tree; a two-hulled racing sailboat; a *trimaran* has three hulls

caten: link of chain
catena, catenary, catenate, catenulate; concatenate
[variant forms: chain, chignon]

cathar: pure
cartharsis, cathartic; Catherine

cathedra-l: chair [see hedr; cata-]
cathedra, cathedral; procathedral; ex cathedra
[variant forms: chair, shay]
{word note: cathedral: the main church of a bishop's see, containing the cathedra, the throne of the bishop}

CATKIN: Dutch *kattechin*, lit., small cat; from resemblance to a cat's tail; a drooping, deciduous spike of unisexual flowers without petals, as in poplars, walnuts, and birches

CAUCUS: prob. of Algonquian extraction; orig., council; may also be from Greek *kaukos*, drinking cup

caud[1]: tail

≈caud: caudad, caudal, caudate

- caudal: acaudal, bicaudal, unicaudal
[variant forms: queue; coda, coward, cowardice, cue—one meaning]
{word note: queue—orig., a pigtail; a line or file of persons; a stored arrangement of computer data}

caud[2]: tree trunk, log, stem

≈caud: caudex

≈caul: caulescent, caulicle

- caul-: acaulescent, amplexicaul

cauli: cabbage; orig., head; see cap
cauliflower

[variant forms: cole, coleslaw,
kale, kohlrabi]

caus-e: a cause, reason
≈caus-e: causable, causal,
causation, causative, cause,
causerie
- cus-: excusable, inexcusable;
accusative
- cusatory: accusatory,
excusatory
- cuse: accuse, excuse, recuse
[phrase: cause célèbre]

caus-t: to burn; fever, heat
≈caustic: caustic, causticize
≈caus-: causalgia
- caust-ic: encaustic, holocaust,
hypocaust
≈cauter: cauterant, cauterize,
cautery
- cautery: cryocautery
[variant forms: ink; calm]
{word note: ink: from Greek *en-*, in
+ *kaiein*, to burn; lit., to burn in}

caut: to be on one's guard
caution, cautionary, cautious;
incautious, precaution
[variant forms: caveat, cavil;
Spanish: cuidado—be careful]
[phrases: caveat emptor—let the
buyer beware; cave canem]

caval: horse
≈caval: cavalcade, cavalier,
cavalla, cavalry
≈chivalr-y: chivalric, chivalrous,
chivalry
[variant forms: Spanish: caballero;
chevalier: knight; from "horse"]
[phrase: cheval-de-frise]

cav-e: hollow, cavern
≈cav-e: cavatina, cave, cavetto,
cavitation, cavity
- cav-e: concave, concavity,
excavate; excavation;
excavator
- cava: postcava, precava
≈cavern: cavern, cavernous

≈cavi- cavicorn
[variant forms: cage, jail, caul:
membrane]
[phrase: vena cava]
CCCP: translitration of Russian
initials for USSR
CECUM: blind [see ciego]

cede: to yield, to go
≈cede: cede
- cede: accede, antecede,
concede, intercede, precede,
recede, retrocede, secede
- cedence: antecedence,
precedence
- cedency: antecedency
- cedent: antecedent, decedent,
precedent, succedent
- cedur-e: procedural, procedure
- ceed: exceed, proceed, succeed;
exceeding, proceeding;
exceedingly; proceeds
≈cess: cessation, cession
- cess: abscess, access, excess,
precess, process, recess,
success
- cess-: accessible, incessant,
inaccessible, necessarily,
necessary, necessitarianism,
necessitate, necessitous,
necessity
- cession: accession, concession,
intercession, precession,
procession, recession,
secession, succession
- cessional: processional,
recessional
- cessive: concessive, excessive,
recessive, successive
- cessor-y: antecessor,
intercessor, predecessor,
successor; accessory
[variant forms: ancestor; cease;
decease, deceased, predecease]
cedium: grief, funeral rites
epicedium—a funeral ode or
hymn; dirge

ceil: **to cover**
≈ceil: ceil, ceiling
≈ceilo-: ceilometer
[variant forms: clandestine;
conceal, color (see separate
entry); Spanish: cielo]

cele: **tumor, hernia**
- cele: with prefixes: entocele,
exocele, metacele
- cele: with combining forms:
adipocele, aerocele, amniocele,
arthrocele, blastocele,
cardiocele, cephalocele,
cystocele, enterocele,
gastrocele, glossocele,
gonocele, gonycele, hydrocele,
orchiocele, osteocele,
rectocele, varicocele

celebr: **honor**
celebrant, celebrate, celebrity;
concelebrate

celer: **swift**
≈celer: celerity
- celer-: accelerant, accelerator,
deceleron
- celerate: accelerate, decelerate
- celeration: acceleration
{word note: deceleron: *decelerate +
aileron*: an aileron used to slow
down an aircraft in flight; speed
brake}
celery: see petro

celest: **heaven**
celesta, celestial
[variant form: chintz]

celib: **unmarried**
celibacy, celibate

cel-l: **to rise, project**
excel, excelsior, excellence,
excellent
[phrase: Gloria in excelsis (Deo):
glory (to God) in the highest:
Luke 2:14]

cell-o: **small room**
≈cell-ar: cell, cella, cellar,
cellarage, cellaret

≈celli-: celliferous, celliform
≈cello-: cellophane
≈cellul-e: cellular, cellule
≈cellul-: cellulitis, cellulose
- cellular: intercellular,
intracellular, unicellular
CELSIUS, Anders, 1701-1744:
Swedish scientist; inventor of the
Celsius thermometer
CEMETERY: lit., a sleeping place;
from Greek *koiman*, to put to
sleep; akin to *keimai*, to lie down
CENACLE: dining room; capitalized,
the room in which Jesus and his
disciples ate the Last Supper; a
coterie, as of writers; Spanish for
evening meal: cena

cen-o[1]: **new, recent**
≈ceno-: cenogenesis, Cenozoic
- cene: Eocene, Holocene,
Miocene, Oligocene,
Paleocene, Pleistocene,
Pliocene
[variant forms: encaenia, recent,
rinse]

cen-o[2]: **common**
≈ceno: cenobite, cenocyte,
cenogamy, cenogenesis,
cenospecies
- cene: epicene
≈coen-o: coenurus; coenocyte,
coenosarc

ceno: **empty**
cenophobia, cenotaph; kenosis

cens: **to tax, judge, value**
≈censor: censor, censorious,
censorship
≈censur-e: censurable, censure
≈census: census
- cension: recension

cent: **one hundred**
≈cent: cent, centavo, centime,
centum, centurion, century
≈cent-: centenarian, centenary,
centennial; Centenary College,
Shreveport, LA

- cent-: percent, percentage,
  percentile
- centenary: quincentenary,
  tercentenary
- centennial: bicentennial,
  quadricentennial, tricentennial
- cento: quattrocento
≈centu-: centuple, centuplicate
**centesis: to center, point,
  puncture**
≈centesis: centesis
- centesis: amniocentesis,
  arthrocentesis, cephalocentesis,
  enterocentesis,
  pneumonocentesis
centi-: one hundredth
  centigrade, centigram,
  centiliter, centimeter,
  centipede, centipoises,
  centistoke
centr: center
≈centr: central, centric, centriole,
  centrum
≈centri-: centrifugal, centripetal
≈centro-: centrobaric, centrocyte,
  centromere, centroplasm,
  centrosome, centrosphere
- centra-: concentrate,
  concentration, decentralize,
  dicentra
- centric: with prefixes: concentric,
  eccentric, exocentric,
  heterocentric, homocentric
- centric: with combining forms:
  androcentric, anthropocentric,
  egocentric, ethnocentric,
  heliocentric, phallocentric,
  theocentric
- centrism: ethnocentrism,
  polycentrism
- center: concenter, decenter,
  epicenter, hypocenter,
  metacenter, orthocenter
cephal-o: head
≈cephal: cephalic, cephalous

≈cephalo-: cephalopod
- cephal-: rhizocephalan,
  rhynchocephalian
- cephalic: with prefixes:
  acrocephalic, macrocephalic,
  megacephalic, mesocephalic,
  nanocephalic, orthocephalic,
  pachycephalic, plagiocephalic,
  procephalic
- cephalic: with combining forms:
  brachiocephalic, cynocephalic,
  dolichocephalic, eurycephalic,
  hydrocephalic
- cephalous: acephalous,
  autocephalous, bicephalous,
  dicephalous, leptocephalous
- cephaly: acrocephaly,
  autocephaly, leptocephaly,
  macrocephaly, microcephaly,
  oxycephaly
cer-a: wax
≈cer-e: ceraceous, cerate,
  cerated, cere, cereus, cerotic
≈ceru: cerumen, ceruse
≈ceri-: ceriferous
≈cero-: ceroplastics
- cer-e: adipocere, ozocerite
  [variant form: ciré]
ceram: pottery
  ceramic, ceramist
cer-at: horn [see kerat-o]
≈cera: cerastes
≈cerat: ceratopsian, ceratoid,
  ceratodus
- cera-n: chelicera, cladoceran
- cerat-: triceratops
- ceros: Monoceros, rhinoceros
cerc: tail
≈cerc: cercaria, cercus
- cercal: cephalocercal,
  diphycercal, heterocercal,
  homocercal
- cercus: cysticercus
cerebr-o: the brain
≈cereb: cerebellum

38

≈cerebr: cerebral, cerebrate,
   cerebrum
≈cerebr-: cerebroside
≈cerebro-: cerebrospinal
- cerebrate: decerebrate
   [variant forms: cernuous, saveloy]
ceremony: awe, **reverent rite,**
   ceremony
   ceremonial, ceremonious,
   ceremony, unceremonious
CERMET: coalescence of *ceramic*
   metal, a bonded mixture of
   ceramic material and a metal
cert: to contend, **contest**
   concert, concerted; disconcert,
   preconcert
cert-i: to separate, **sift, judge**
   ≈cert: certain, certiorari—a legal
   term, certitude
   ≈certi-: certificate, certify
- certain-ty: ascertain, uncertain,
   uncertainty
- certi-: decertify, incertitude
- cern: concern, discern, secern,
   unconcern
- cern-: indiscernible;
   concerning, discerning
- cernment: concernment,
   discernment
- cree: decree
- creet: discreet, indiscreet
- crement: excrement, recrement
- crementitious: excrementitious
- cret-: decretal, secret, secretary,
   secretaire, secretin; excreta
- crete: discrete, excrete,
   indiscrete, secrete
- cretion: discretion, excretion,
   indiscretion
- cretory: decretory, excretory,
   secretory
- crimin-: discriminable,
   discriminant, discriminating,
   discriminative, discriminator,
   discriminatory

- criminate: discriminate,
   indiscriminate
- crimination: discrimination,
   indiscrimination
- crine: apocrine, autocrine,
   eccrine, ectocrine, endocrine,
   exocrine, holocrine, merocrine
- crinology: endocrinology
≈cris: crisis, pl., crises
- crisy: hypocrisy
≈crit: criterion, critique; critic,
   critical, criticism, criticize
- crit-e: hematocrit, hypocrite
- critic: diacritic, epicritic,
   hypercritic, hypocritic
- critical: acritical, diacritical,
   hypercritical, hypocritical,
   precritical, supercritical
- criticism: metacriticism
   [see crim-in for incriminate]
   [variant forms: crayon, cretaceous]
CERULEAN: sky-blue, azure; from
   "heaven"
CERVEZA: Spanish for beer, from
   Ceres, Roman goddess of
   agriculture and grain
cervic: neck, or **cervix**
   ≈cervi: cervical, cervix
   ≈cervic-: cervicitis
   ≈cervico-: cervicobrachial,
   cervicobuccal, cervicofacial,
   cervicoplasty, cervicotomy
cest: ribbon
   cestode; cestoid
cet-o: whale
   cetacean; ceticide, cetology;
   spermaceti
chaet-o: hair, bristles
   ≈chaeta: chaeta
   ≈chaeto-: chaetognath, chaetopod
- chaete: oligochaete, polychaete
- chet-e: spirochete, spirochetosis
CHAGRIN: from French; noun: grief,
   sorrow, vexation; verb: to cause to
   feel chagrin; embarrass and annoy
chair: see hedr

chalc-o: **copper, brass**
≈chalcid: chalcid
≈chalco-: chalcocite,
   chalcography, chalcolithic,
   chalcopyrite
CHALYBEATE: containing salts of
   iron; tasting like iron; from
   Chalybes, name of a people in
   Pontus noted for their steel
cham: **earth, ground**
   chameleon, chamomile
CHAMBRAY: a fabric first made in
   Cambrai, France
champ: **field, flat land** [see camp]
   champagne, champaign,
   champerty, champignon,
   champion
   [variant form: campus]
chao: **space, disorder**
   chaos, chaotic
character: **an engraving**
   instrument
   character, characteristic,
   charactery
charg-e: **to load a wagon, car**
≈charge: charge, charger
- charge: discharge, encharge,
   precharge, recharge,
   supercharge, surcharge,
   turbocharge
   [variant forms: car, cargo,
   caricature, carry, cart, supercargo;
   chariot, charioteer]
char-isma: **grace, beauty,**
   kindness
≈charisma: charisma, charismatic
- charist-ic: Eucharist, eucharistic
≈charit-y: charity, charitable
- charitable: uncharitable
charm: **to sing, bewitch**
   charm, charmer, charmeuse
CHARY: orig. from *care*; wary,
   disinclined
chas-m: **yawning, hollow, gulf**
   chasm; chasmogamy;
   monochasium

[variant form: casemate]
chaste: see cast-e
CHATOYANT: having a changeable
   color or luster; also, a gem, such
   as the cat's-eye; from "cat"
CHAUVINISM: from Nicolas Chauvin,
   a French soldier extremely
   devoted to Napoleon; blind
   enthusiasm for military glory
check: Persian; **means of restraint,**
   control
   check, checked, checker,
   checkmate
   [variant forms: chess, exchequer]
CHEDDAR: a cheese first made in
   Cheddar, England
CHEETAH: Hindi; *chiti*, leopard
CHEF MENTEUR: lit., big, or chief
   liar; a major thoroughfare in New
   Orleans, LA
cheim: **winter**
   cheimophobia; isocheim
chela: **claw**
≈chela: chela, chelate
≈chel-: cheloid, or keloid
≈cheli-: chelicera, cheliferous,
   cheliform
CHELONIAN: pertaining to a turtle
chem-o: **chemistry**; orig., to pour
≈chem: chemistry
≈chem-: chemurgy
≈chemo-: chemosphere,
   chemotaxis
chess: see check
chevr-e: **goat**
   chevre, chevron, chevrotain
   [variant forms: caper, capricorn,
   caprine, capriole]
chevelure: see hevel
chiasm: **crosswise**
   chiasma, chiasmus;
   chiasmapexy
chicane: **to arrange, bring about**
   chicane, chicanery
   {word note: chicanery: the use of
   clever but tricky talk or action to
   deceive, evade, etc.; deception}

CHICORY: from Greek *kikhora*

CHIHUAHUA: a breed of dog first bred in Chihuahua, Mexico

CHILI: from Nahuatl, the language of the Aztecs (Mexico); a very hot seasoning

chili: one thousand [see kilo]

≈chili: chiliad, chiliasm

≈chili-: chiliarch

≈chilo-: chilogram, same as kilogram

chilo: lip

≈chil-: chiloma

≈chilo-: chiloplasty, chilopod

CHIMNEY: from Latin *camera* and Greek *kaminos*, a chamber for burning

CHINQUAPIN: Algonquian; a nut tree of the beech family

CHINTZ: from Hindi *chhint*, bright; a brightly colored cloth

CHIPMUNK: American Indian *achitamo*, squirrel

chir-o: hand

≈chir: chiral

≈chiro-: chirognomy, chirography, chiromancy, chiropody, chiropractor, chiropter

- chiridion: enchiridion [variant form: surgeon] {word note: enchiridion: lit., in hand; a rare word for handbook or manual}

CHIT: Hindi; *chitthi*, letter, note; a voucher of a small sum owed for drink, food, etc.

chivalry: see caval

chlamy-do: cloak, coat

≈chlamyd: chlamydate, chlamydeous, chlamydia

≈chlamyd-: chlamydemia

≈chlamydo-: chlamydophilia, chlamydosaurus chlamydospore

- chlamydeous: achlamydeous, dichlamydeous,

homochlamydeous, monochlamydeous

chlor-o: green

≈chlor: chloral — chloro + alcohol, chlorate, chlorella, chlordane, chlorine

≈chlor-: chloroma, chlorosis

≈chloro-: chloroform, chlorophyll, chlorophyte, chloroplast

- chloride: tetrachloride

choat-e: to hitch, hold

inchoate, inchoation, inchoative

CHOCOLATE: from Nahuatl, the language of the Aztecs (Mexico)

chol-era: bile, jaundice

≈cholera: cholera

≈chol-: cholemia

≈chole-: cholecyst, cholecystitis, cholelith, cholesterol

- chol-: hypercholesterol, melancholia; melancholy

chondr-o: cartilage, grain

≈chondr-: chondrectomy, chondrite, chondroma

- chondr-o: achondrite, enchondroma, hypochondria, hypochondriac, mitochondrian, perichondrium; achondroplasia

CHOPSTICKS: Pidgin English for Chinese *k'wai-tsze*, the quick ones

chor: country, place; to retire

anchorite, enchorial, isochor

chord: cord, string

≈chord: chord, chordate

- chord: with prefixes: heptachord, hexachord, monochord, octachord, tetrachord

- chord: with combining forms: cephalochord, clavichord, harpsichord, notochord [variant form: cordillera]

chor-eo: orig., dance; then, singers to accompany dancers in a Greek drama

≈chor: choral, chorale, choric,
  chorus
≈chor-: choragus, choriamb
≈choreo-: choreography
- chorea-n: orchichorea,
  terpsichorean
  [variant forms: choir, antechoir]
chori: apart
  choripetalous—same as
  polypetalous, having separate
  petals
chori-on: fetal membrane
  chorion, chorioallantosis
CHORTLE: a portmanteau word, one
  that combines two words in form
  and meaning; *chortle* comes
  probably from *chuckle* and *snort*;
  smog, from *smoke* and *fog*
chresis: to use
≈chresto-: chrestomathy
- chresis: catachresis— incorrect
  use of a word or words, as by
  misapplication of terminology or
  by strained or mixed metaphor
**chris-m-a: anointing oil, unction;
  anointed**
≈chris-m: chrism, chrismatory,
  chrisom
≈christ: Christ, christen,
  christening, Christian
≈christ-: Christmas
chromat: color
≈chrom: chromate, chromatic,
  chromium
≈chromato-: chromatograph,
  chromatolysis, chromatophore
≈chromo-: chromogen,
  chromomere, chromonema,
  chromophil, chromophore,
  chromoplast, chromosome,
  chromosphere
- chroic: amphichroic
- chroism: dichroism,
  pleochroism, trichroism
- chromatic: achromatic,
  apochromatic, dichromatic,

heterochromatic,
  homochromatic, isochromatic,
  monochromatic,
  orthochromatic, panchromatic,
  polychromatic, trichromatic
- chromatin: euchromatin,
  heterochromatin
- chromatism: metachromatism
- chromatosis: hemochromatosis
- chrome: with prefixes:
  auxochrome, monochrome,
  polychrome
- chrome: with combining forms:
  Kodachrome®, phytochrome
- chromic: dichromic,
  photochromic
- chroous: isochroous
- chrosite: rhodochrosite
chron-o: time
≈chron: chronic, chronicle
≈chrono-: chronogram,
  chronology, chronometer,
  chronoscope
- chrone: isochrone
- chronic: achronic, diachronic,
  monochronic, polychronic,
  subchronic, synchronic
- chronism: anachronism
- chronograph: photochronograph
- chronology: geochronology
- chronous: anachronous,
  anisochronous, asynchronous,
  dyschronous, geosynchronous,
  heterochronous,
  homochronous, isochronous,
  metachronous, orthochronous,
  plesiochronous, synchronous,
  tautochronous
chrys-a: gold
≈chrys: chrysalis
≈chrys-: chrysanthemum,
  chrysarobin, chryselephantine
≈chryso-: chrysoberyl,
  chrysoderma, chrysolite,
  chrysoprase

chthon: the earth
≈chthon: chthonian, chthonic
≈chthono-: chthonophagia
- chthon-ous: autochthon;
  heterochthonous
CHURCH: from Greek *kyriake (oikia)*,
  the Lord's (house)
CHURLISH: rude, vulgar, surly; from
  churl, orig., peasant, freeman; a
  surly, illbred person; boor
CHUTNEY: from Hindi *chatni*; a relish
CHUTZPAH, or chutzpa: Yiddish for
  shameless audacity
chyl-o: fluid, juice
≈chyle: chyle
≈chyli-: chyliferous
≈chylo-: chylocyst, chylology
- chylia: dyschylia, euchylia,
  hyperchylia, hypochylia
chym-o: juice, humor, chyle
≈chyme: chyme
≈chymi-: chymiferous
≈chymo-: chymogen,
  chymopapain, chymotrypsin
- chyma: parenchyma,
  proenchyma, sclerenchyma
- chyme: mesenchyme
- chymosis: ecchymosis
CIAO: Italian; altered from Lombard
  schiavo, slave; used to translate
  Austrian *servus*, for "your
  obedient servant"; can mean either
  "hello" or "goodbye"
cicatr: scar
  cicatricle, cicatrix, cicatrize
cid-e: to fall, cut, split, kill
to fall
- cid-: decidua, incidentally,
  loculicidal, recidivist
- cide: coincide
- cidence: incidence, coincidence
- cident: accident, incident,
  occident
- cidental: accidental,
  coincidental, incidental,
  occidental

- ciduous: deciduous,
  indeciduous, prociduous,
  succiduous
to cut
- cide-: decide, excide, undecided
- cinn-: concinnate, concinnity,
  concinnous, inconcinnity
- cis: précis
- cise: abscise, circumcise,
  concise, excise—one meaning,
  incise, precise
- cision: circumcision, concision,
  decision, indecision, incision,
  precision, recision,
  uncircumcision
- cisive: decisive, incisive,
  indecisive
- cisor: incisor
to kill
- cide: deicide, fratricide,
  germicide, herbicide,
  homicide, insecticide,
  mariticide, matricide,
  parricide, patricide, pesticide,
  sororicide, spermicide, suicide,
  taeniacide, tyrannicide,
  uxoricide, vermicide, virucide
  [variant forms: cement, chisel,
  comma, coupon, decoupage]
  [phrase: stare decisis]
ciego: blind [see cecum]
  Spanish: pichiciego—a blind
  armadillo
cili-o: eyelid, eyelash
≈cili: ciliary, cilium, ciliolate
- ciliary: interciliary, superciliary
- cilious: supercilious
  [variant form: seel]
  [NB: conciliary]
{word note: supercilious: in
  reference to facial expression with
  raised eyebrows; disdainful or
  contemptuous; haughty}
cinc-t: to gird, encircle, a belt
≈cinc-t: cinch; cincture
- cinct: precinct, succinct

≈cingul: cingulum
- cingle: surcingle
  [variant forms: enceinte—*en*-
  has two opposite meanings in
  this word; shingle—one
  meaning, shingles]
cine: **movies** [see kine]
  cinema; cinephile;
  cinematography
  [Spanish: cine]
ciner: **ashes**
≈ciner: cineraria, cinerarium,
  cinereous
- cinerat-e: incinerate, incinerator
cinque: **five**
  cinquecento, cinquefoil
circ-a: **circle, around**
≈circ-a: circa, circinate
≈circl-e: circle, circlet
≈circu-l: circular, circulate,
  circus
≈circ-: circambulate
≈circa-: circadian
- circle-: circumcircle, encircle,
  encirclement, semicircle
≈circuit: circuit, circuitous,
  circuitry, circuity
≈circum-: circumboreal,
  circumcise, circumference,
  circumflex, circumfluent,
  circumfuse, circumjacent,
  circumlocution,
  circumnavigate,
  circumnutation, circumpolar,
  circumrotate, circumscribe,
  circumspect, circumstance,
  circumvallate, circumvent,
  circumvolution
  [variant forms: search, research;
  recherché]
cirr: **a curl**
≈cirr: cirrate, cirrus
≈cirri-: cirriform, cirriped
≈cirro-: cirrocumulus,
  cirrostratus

CIRRHOSIS: tawny, orange-yellow; a
  condition of the liver
CIRSOID: enlargement of a vein
cis-: **this side of**
  cislunar, cismontane, cisplatin;
  Cismont, VA
CISSOID: in mathematics, a curve
  converging into a pointed tip;
  opposite of *sistroid*
cit-e: **to summon, call forth**
≈cit-e: cite, citation
- cit-: excited, excition, solicit,
  solicitous, solicitude
- cita-: recital, recitative
- citan-: oscitancy, oscitant
- citate: resuscitate
- citation: excitation, recitation,
  resuscitation
- cite: with prefixes: excite, incite,
  miscite, recite
- cite: with combining form:
  plebiscite
- citor: excitor, solicitor
  [variant form: insouciant]
  [phrase: loco citato]
citr-o: **citrus, citric acid**
  citrate, citreous, citrine; citron,
  citronelal, citronella; citrus
civ-il: **town, city**
≈civ-il: civic, civil, civilian,
  civility, civilization, civilize
- civil: uncivil
- civility: incivility, uncivility
≈cit-y: citadel, city, citizen
clad-o: a **branch, shoot**
≈clasist: cladist, cladistics
≈clado-: cladogenesis,
  cladogram, cladophyll,
  cladoptosis, cladosporium
clam: **to shout, cry out**
≈clam: clamant, clamor
- clamation: acclamation,
  declamation, disclamation,
  exclamation, proclamation,
  reclamation

- clamatory: declamatory,
  exclamatory
≈claim: claim, claimant, claimer
- claim: acclaim, counterclaim,
  declaim, disclaim, exclaim,
  proclaim, quitclaim, reclaim
- claimable: irreclaimable
- claimer: disclaimer
  [variant forms: chamade, clatter,
  réclame]
clandestine: see ceil
clar-i: clear, bright
≈clar: claret, clarinet, clarion,
  clarity, claro
≈clari-: clarification, clarify
- clar-e: declaration, declarative,
  declare, declaredly, declarer
  [variant forms: clear, chanticleer,
  chiaroscuro, clairvoyant,
  clerestory, éclair; glair]
  [phrase: en clair]
clast: to break, divide
≈clast: clastic
- clast: iconoclast, osteoclast
- clastic: with prefixes: anaclastic,
  cataclastic
- clastic: with combining forms:
  cryptoclastic, iconoclastic,
  proteinoclastic, pyroclastic
≈class: class, classic, classical,
  classicism; classis
- clase: clinoclase, euclase,
  oligoclase, orthoclase,
  plagioclase
- clasis: with prefixes: aclasis,
  anaclasis, autoclasis,
  cataclasis, diaclasis
- clasis: with combining forms:
  cytoclasis, erythroclasis,
  hemoclasis, hymneoclasis,
  lipoclasis, onychoclasis,
  osteoclasis, trichoclasis
- clasm: biblioclasm, cataclasm,
  iconoclasm
- class-: déclassé, declassify,
  superclass

- classic: neoclassic, postclassic,
  pseudoclassic, semiclassic
  [variant forms: calamitous,
  calamity]
CLATHRATE: latticelike—in botany,
  resembling latticework; reticu-
  lated; term also used in chemistry
claus-e: to close
≈claus-e: clausal, clause
≈claustral: claustral
≈claustro-: claustrophobia
≈clos-e: close, closet, closure
- close: disclose, enclose,
  foreclose, inclose, reclose
- closion: eclosion
- closure: disclosure, enclosure,
  exclosure, foreclosure
- clude: conclude, exclude,
  include, occlude, preclude,
  seclude
- cluding: concluding, excluding,
  including
- clus-e: exclusivity, occlusal;
  recluse
- clusion-ist: conclusion,
  exclusion, inclusion,
  malocclusion, occlusion,
  preclusion, reclusion,
  seclusion; exclusionist
- clusive: conclusive, exclusive,
  inclusive, inconclusive,
  preclusive, seclusive
- clusivity: exclusivity
- clusory: conclusory, exclusory,
  reclusory
  [variant forms: cloisonné, cloister,
  cloture, sluice; cleistogamous,
  cleistogamy]
  [phrase: mare clausum]
clav-i-[1]: club
  clavate; clavicorn, claviform,
  clavigerous—one meaning
clav-i-[2]: key
≈clavi: clavicle, claviuclar,
  clavier, claviger, clavis

≈clavi-: clavichord,
 clavigerous—one meaning
- clave-: autoclave, conclave,
 enclave, exclave
- clavicle: interclavicle
 [variant forms: clef, ophicleide;
 Spanish: llave]
clemen: merciful, mild
 clemency, clement;
 inclemency, inclement
cler: clergy, priest
 clergy, cleric, clerisy, clerk;
 anticlerical
clesia: church; with *ec-*, out +
 kalein, to call; thus, to call out;
 orig., a Greek assembly
≈ecclesia: ecclesia, Ecclesiastes,
 ecclesiastic, ecclesiastical,
 ecclesiasticism
≈ecclesio-: ecclesiology
 [variant form: paraclete]
clim: to lean, slope
≈clim-ate: climacteric, climactic,
 climate, climax
≈climato-: climatograph,
 climatology, climatotherapy
- climate: acclimate,
 mesoclimate, macroclimate,
 microclimate
- climax: anticlimax, disclimax
≈clin-e: cline, clinic, clinical
≈clino-: clinometer
- clin-: inclination, inclined,
 reclinate, recliner
- clinal: isoclinal, monoclinal,
 synclinal
- clination: declination,
 inclination, disinclination
- clinable: declinable, inclinable,
 indeclinable
- cline: with prefixes: anticline,
 decline, disincline, incline,
 isocline, microcline,
 monocline, pericline, recline,
 syncline

- cline: with combining forms:
 geosyncline, halocline,
 helicline, pycnocline,
 thermocline
- clinic-: policlinic, polyclinic,
 triclinic; preclinical
- clinium: triclinium
- clinometer: inclinometer
- clinorium: anticlinorium,
 synclinorium
- clinous: declinous, diclinous,
 monoclinous; matriclinous
≈clit: clitoris
- clite: heteroclite
- clitic: anaclitic, enclitic,
 heteroclitic, proclitic, synclitic
- clivitous: acclivitous,
 declivitous
- clivity: acclivity, declivity,
 proclivity
 [variant forms: client, clientele;
 declension]
 {word note: client: the basic meaning is one who leans on another
 for protection, healing}
CLINQUANT: spangled, tinseled
CLIQUE: from Old French *cliquer*, to
 make a noise; a coterie of
 snobbish people
CLOACA: a cesspool; from *cluere*, to
 clean; term also used in zoology
CLOAK: from "clock," which was
 originally "bell," because of the
 similarity of shapes; as a verb, to
 conceal, disguise, as to cloak
 one's anger with a smile; a
 cloakroom was a feature in old
 classrooms, where coats, hats, and
 umbrellas were left temporarily
clon-e: twig; from "to break"
≈clon-e: clone, clonic, cloning
- clonal: biclonal, monoclonal,
 oligoclonal, polyclonal
clonus: spasm; from "turmoil"
 clonus; blepharoclonus,
 myoclonus, opsoclonus,
 synclonus

clysm: to wash
  cataclysm—a great flood;
  deluge; any great upheaval that
  causes sudden and violent change,
  as an earthquake or war
CLOY: to surfeit, satiate
CNIDARIAN: any of a phylum of
  invertebrate animals including the
  jellyfishes, characterized by
  stinging cells
**cocc-id: a kernel, seed, berry-
  shaped bacteria**
≈cocc-id: coccid, coccus
≈cocci-: coccigenic
≈coccidi-: coccidiosis
- coccal: gonococcal
- coccus: with prefixes:
  diplococcus, megacoccus,
  micrococcus
- coccus: with combining forms:
  blastococcus, coprococcus,
  enterococcus, meningococcus,
  pneumococcus,
  staphylococcus, streptococcus
cochl: snail, snail shell
  cochlea, cochleate
  [variant form: cockle]
COCKROACH: from Spanish
  cucaracha; an insect with long
  antennae and a flat, soft body
coc-t: to cook, mature
- coc-: precocial, precocious,
  precociousness, or precocity
- coct: concoct, decoct; concocter
- coction: concoction, decoction
- coctive: concoctive
  [variant forms: apricot, culinary,
  kiln, kitchen, pumpkin, quittor,
  ricotta; cuisine]
  [phrases: terra cotta, haute cuisine]
  {word note: pumpkin: orig., cooked
  by the sun, the inferred meaning
  that the gourd was not fit to be
  eaten until turning in color}
cod-e: tablet of laws
≈cod-e: code, codex, pl., codices,
  codicil

≈codi-: codify
≈codico-: codicology
- code: decode, encode
coel-o: hollow, body cavity
≈coelom: coelom
≈coel-: coelacanth, coelenteron
- coele: astrocoele, blastocoele,
  enterocoele, epicoele,
  gastrocoele, hematocoele,
  hydrocoele, mesocoele,
  metacoele, myelsocoele,
  myocoele, neurocoele,
  optocoele, rhabdocoele,
  schizocoele, splanchnocoele
- coelous: amphicoelous
  [variant form: celiac]
coelo: sky, heavens
  coelostat—an optical system
  consisting of two mirrors with a
  moving mirror mounted on an axis
  parallel to the earth's axis of
  rotation and driven by clockwork
  so as to reflect the same portion of
  the sky continuously or to track
  the sun
  [Spanish: cielo]
COFFEE: from Arabic qahwa: may be
  after Kaffa, area in Ethiopia,
  where the plant was first grown
cogitat-e: to ponder; from com-,
  together + agitate
  cogitate, cogitative; excogitate
  [phrase: cogito ergo sum]
COGNAC: from Cognac, France; a
  French brandy
cognition: see gn
col: to strain
  colander; percolate, percolator
  [variant forms: coulee, coulisse,
  couloir; portcullis]
  [phrase: piña colada]
col-e: to dwell, inhabit
≈colon: colonial, colonialism,
  colonist, colonize, colony
- cole: calcicole
- colous: arenicolous, nidicolous,
  saxicolous, silvicolous,

stercoricolous, terricolous
[variant forms: cult, inquiline]
cole-o: **sheath**, **womb**, **vagina**
≈coleus: coleus
≈coleo-: coleopteran, coleoptile,
    coleorhiza
≈colp-: colpitis
≈colpo-: colposcope
COLISEUM: COLOSSAL: from
    Colossus, a giant statue of Apollo,
    set at the entrance to the harbor of
    Rhodes around 200 B.C. Soon
    after its completion, it was
    destroyed by an earthquake.
COLESLAW: from Dutch *kool*,
    cabbage + *salade*, salad
col-l: **neck**
≈col-l: col, collar, collet
≈col-: colporteur
- col-: accolade, machicolate
- coll-: decollate, décolletage,
    décolleté, torticollis
{word note: accolade: lit., to the
    neck; orig., an embrace formerly
    used to confer knighthood; now,
    anything done or given as a sign
    of great respect, approval,
    appreciation, etc.}
coll-a: **paste**, **glue**
≈coll: collage
≈coll-: collenchyma, collodion,
    colloid
≈colla-: collagen
≈collo-: collotype
- col: protocol
    [phrase: papier collé]
col-on: **colon**, the lower part of
    large intestine
≈col: colic, colon
≈col-: colitis
≈colono-: colonogram,
    colonometer, colonoscope,
    colonoscopy
- colitis: enterocolitis
colon: **column**, **pillar**
    colonel, colonnade; column,
    columnist; intercolumniation

color-i: **color**, **hue**
≈color: color, colorado,
    Colorado, colorant, coloration,
    coloratura
≈colori-: colorimeter
- color-: decolorize, discoloration
- color: discolor, tricolor
colp: see cole-o for colpitis
colubr: **snake**
    colubrid, colubrine
COLUMBINE: pertaining to a dove;
    also, a flower, perhaps from the
    resemblance of the spurs of its
    flowers to the beak of a dove
com-: **with**, **together**; **intensive**
≈com-: combat, combatant,
    combination, combine,
    combustion
≈comfort, comfrey, comitia
≈command, commeasure,
    commence, commend,
    commensal, commensurate,
    comment, commerce,
    commination, commingle,
    commissary, commiserate,
    commission, commit,
    committee, commix,
    commode, common,
    commotion, commove,
    commune, commute
≈compact, compadre,
    companion, compare, compart,
    compass, compassion,
    compatible, compatriot,
    compeer, compel,
    compendious, compendium,
    compensate, compete,
    competent, compile
≈complacent, complain,
    complaisant, complement,
    complete, complex,
    complexion, complicate,
    complicity, compliment,
    complot, comply, component,
    comport, compose, compound,

comprehend, compress,
comprise, compromise,
compulsion, compunction,
compurgation, compute

≈co-: truncation of *com-*: coact,
coadjutor, coadunate, coalesce,
coaptation, coarctate, coauthor,
coaxial, coerce, coetaneous,
coeval, cogent, cognition,
cohabit, cohere, cohesion,
cohort, coincide, coition,
colatitude, copolymere, co-
relation, cosine, costar,
cotenant, covariance

≈cog-: variant of *com-*: cognate,
cognomen

≈col-: assimilation of *com-*:
collaborate, collapse, collate,
collateral, collation, colleague,
collect, college, collide,
colligate, collimate, collinear,
collision, collocate, collogue,
colloquial, colloquy, collude,
colluvium

≈con-: assimilation of *com-*:
connate, connect, connive,
connote, connubial

≈con-: variant of *com-*:
concatenate, concave, conceal,
concede, conceit, conceive,
concelebrate, concent,
concenter, concentrate,
concentric, concept,
conceptacle, concern, concert,
concession, concierge,
concinnity, concise, conclave,
conclude, concoct,
concomitance, concord,
concourse, concrescence,
concrete, concubinage,
concupiscence, concur

≈condemn, condense,
condescend, condign,
condiment, condition, condole,

condominium, condone,
conduce, conduct

≈confabulate, confarreation,
confection, confederate,
confer, confess, confetti,
confide, confidant, confident,
configure, confine, confirm,
confiscate, conflagrant,
conflict, confluence, conform,
confound, confraternity,
confront, confuse, confute

≈congeal, congener, congenial,
congenital, congest,
conglobate, conglomerate,
conglutinate, congratulate,
congregate, congress,
congruence

≈conjecture, conjoin, conjoint,
conjugal, conjugate, conjunct,
conjure

≈conquer, conquest

≈consanguinity, conscience,
conscious, conscript,
consecrate, consecution,
consensual, consensus,
consent, consequence,
conserve, consider, consign,
consist, consistent, consociate,
consolation, consolidate

≈consonant, consort, conspecific,
conspectus, conspicuous,
conspire, constant, constellate,
consternate, constipate,
constitute, constrain, constrict,
construct, construe,
consubtantiate, consult,
consume, consummate,
consummation, consumption

≈contact, contactor, contagion,
contagious, contain,
contaminate, contemplate,
contemporary, contempt,
contend, content,
conterminous, contest, context,
contiguous, continence,

continent, contingent,
continue, contort, contour,
contract, contribute, contrite,
contrive, contumacy, contuse
≈conurbation, convalesce,
convection, convene, convent,
conventicle, converge,
converse, convert, convex,
convey, convict, convince,
convivial, convocation,
convoke, convolute, convoy,
convulse
≈cor-: assimilation of *com*-:
corrade, correct, correlate,
correspond, corrigible,
corroborate, corrode,
corrosion, corrugate, corrupt
com: to revel
≈com: comedian, comedic,
comedienne, comedy, comic
- comi-: encomium, encomiast,
encomiastic
com-a: hair
coma[1], comate, comatulid,
comet, comose
coma-t: deep sleep
coma[2], comatose
comb: tomb
catacomb—an underground tomb
combustion: see ust-ul
comit: to accompany; from *com*-,
with + *itere*, **to go**
concomitance, concomitancy,
concomitant
COMITY: courteous behavior; polite-
ness; civility; from *comis*, polite
con: service
deacon, diaconal, diaconate
conat: to undertake, attempt
conation, conative, conatus
conch: a shell
≈conch: conch, concha
≈conch-: conchoid, conchoidal
≈conchi-: conchiferous,
conchiform

≈concho-: conchology,
conchomancy, conchometer
[variant forms: congius; coquille,
coquina]
concil-e: to call [see sul-t]
≈concil: conciliar, conciliate,
conciliatory
- concil-e: reconcile,
reconciliation, irreconcilable
[variant forms: council, counsel,
consult]
cond: to hide
abscond, incondite, recondite
[variant forms: sconce—one
meaning, ensconce, scoundrel;
Escondido, CA]
CONDOM: from Italian *guanto*, a
glove
con-e: cone, wedge, peak
≈con-e: cone, conic, conical
≈con-: conodont, conoid
≈coni-: conifer, coniferous
- con-ic: obconic, keratoconus
cone: rabbit
coney; Coney Island
conidi-o: dust
≈conid: conidial, conidium
≈conidio-: conidiophore
- coniosis: pneumoconiosis
cont-r-ar: against, opposite
≈contr: control, contrast
≈contrar: contrarian, contrariety,
contrarious, contrary
≈contr-: contralto
≈contra-: contradict,
contradictory, contraposition,
contrapositive, contrapuntal,
contravallation, contravene
≈contre-: contrecoup,
contredanse, contretemps
≈contro-: controversial,
controversy, controvert
≈counter-: counteract,
counterattack, counterchange,
countercharge, countercheck,
counterclaim,

counterespionage, counterfeit,
countermand, countermeasure,
counterpart, counterpoint,
counterpoise,
counterrevolution,
counterscarp, countersign,
countervail
- counter: encounter, reencounter
[variant form: country]
[phrases: au contraire, per contra]
COOKIE: from Dutch *koekje*,
diminutive of *koek*, a cake
COOLIE: from Hindi *quli*, hired
servant; an unskilled native
laborer, especially, formerly in
India, China, etc.; a person doing
heavy labor for little pay

cop: abundance
copious, copy; cornucopia

cope: to strike, cut
- cope: apocope, pericope,
syncope
- copate: apocopate, syncopate,
syncopation
COPENHAGEN, Denmark: lit.,
protected harbor; capital of
Denmark
COPRA: Hindi; *khopra*, dried coconut
meat, the source of coconut oil

copro: dung, excrement
≈copr: copragogue, copralalia
≈copro-: coprolite, coprology,
coprophagous, coprophilia

copul: to unite, couple
[from *co-apere*, to fasten together]
≈copul: copula, copulate
≈coupl-e: couple, couplet,
coupling
- couple: accouplement, decouple
[variant form: cobbler]
{word note: cobbler: orig., one who
puts together, as a shoe cobbler;
then, the dessert, a deep-dish fruit
pie, where a mixture is put
together}

cor: pupil of eye
≈cor-: corectasis

≈coreo-: coreoplasty
≈coro-: coroplasty
- coria: isocoria

corac: raven
coraciiform, coracoid
[variant forms: corbel, cormorant,
corvine]

coral-l: small stone
≈coral-l: coral, coralline
≈corall-: coralloid
≈coralli-: coralliform

cord: chord, cord, rope
cordage, cordelle, cordillera,
cordite, cordon, corduroy
[phrases: cordon bleu, cordon
sanitaire]

cord-i: heart
≈cord: cordate, cordial
≈cordi-: cordiform
- cord: accord, concord, discord,
disaccord, record; misericord
- cord-: accordant, according,
concordat, obcordate
- cordance: accordance,
concordance
- cordant: concordant, discordant
≈courage: courage, courageous
- courage: discourage, encourage;
discouraging, encouraging
- couragement: discouragement,
encouragement
[variant form: core]
[phrase: cri de Coeur: lit., cry from
the heart; an impassioned plea]
CORGI: Welsh *corr*, dwarf + *gi*, dog;
lit., dwarf dog

cor-i: leather, hide, skin
≈cor-a: coracle, coriaceous,
corium
- coriate: excoriate
≈cort: cortex, cortical
≈cortici-: corticifugal
- cortical: epicortical, infracortical
[variant forms: cork, cuirass,
currier, quarrel—one meaning;
scourge]

cor-n: **crown**

≈corn: cornice, corniche

≈coron: corona, coronal,
coronary, coronation, coroner
[variant forms: corolla, corollary;
crown, curb, curve, curvet]

{word notes: <u>corniche</u>: a roadway
that winds along a cliff or steep
slope; <u>corollary</u>: orig. money paid
for a garland; hence, a gift,
gratuity; a proposition that follows
from another that has been
proved}

corn-i: **horn; upper part of the
body; head**

≈corn-i: corn [on foot], cornea,
corner, cornet, corniculate

≈cornu: cornu, cornuted

≈cornu-: cornucopia

- corn: with prefixes: tricorn,
unicorn

- corn: with combining forms:
capricorn, cavicorn, clavicorn,
longicorn, lamellicorn
[variant forms: cairn, hornet]

CORONACH: Irish and Gaelic; lit., to
weep together; weeping; in
Scotland, a dirge, sung or played
on bagpipes

corp-or: **body**

≈corpor: corporal—one meaning,
corporeal, corporation

≈corpo-: corposant

≈corps-e: corps, corpse

≈corpu-s: corpulent, corpus,
corpuscle

- corpor-: incorporable,
incorporate, incorporeal,
incorporeity

≈corse-t: corselet, corset,
corsetiere, corsetry
[variant forms: corsage;
leprechaun]
[phrases: Corpus Christi, corpus
delicti, corpus juris, esprit de
corps; Corpus Christi, TX]

{phrase note: esprit de corps: lit.,
spirit of the body; group spirit;
sense of pride, honor, etc., shared
by those in the same group or
undertaking}

CORROBOREE: Australian; from
korobra, dance; in Australia, a
dance festival held at night by
Aborigines to celebrate tribal
victories

CORUSCATE: to glitter; to give off
flashes of light; glitter; sparkle

cosm-os: **world, universe**

≈cosm: cosmesis, cosmetic-s,
cosmetician, cosmic, cosmos

≈cosmeto-: cosmetology

≈cosmo-: cosmogony,
cosmography, cosmology,
cosmonaut, cosmopolitan

- cosm: macrocosm, microcosm

cost: **rib, side; coast**

≈cost: costa, costal, costrel

- cost: accost

- costal: infracostal, intercostal,
sternocostal, subcostal

- costate: tricostate, unicostate

≈coast: coast, coaster

- coastal: intercoastal,
intracoastal; Intracoastal
Waterway
[variant forms: cutlet, entrecôte,
Spanish: chuleta, cuesta; Costa
Rica]

{word note: accost: lit., to bring side
by side; to approach and speak to;
greet first, before being greeted,
esp. in an intrusive way; to solicit
for sexual purposes}

COTTON: Arabic *qutan*

cotyl-edon: **cavity, hollow**

≈cotyledon: cotyledon

≈cotyl-: cotyloid

- cotyl: epicotyl, hypocotyl

- cotyledon: acotyledon,
dicotyledon, monocotyledon,
polycotyledon

- cotylous: dicotylous

- cotylus: hectocotylus

COUGAR: from Portuguese *cuçuarana*, a translation of Tupi Indian name, *susuarana*, false deer, so named from the cougar's color; the Tupis are from Brazil, where the educated speak Portuguese

count[1]: to reckon, to tell

≈count: count—one meaning, countless

- count: account, discount, recount—one meaning

[variant form: raconteur]

count[2]: companion

[from *com-*, with + *itere*, to go]

count—one meaning, countess, county

[variant form: constable]

coup: a blow, to strike

coup; contrecoup, recoup

[variant forms: coupe, coupé, cope—one meaning, coppice, copse]

[phrases: coup de grâce, coup de main, coup de maître, coup d'état]

court: an enclosed place

≈court: court, courteous, courtesan, courtesy, courtier, courtly

- court-: discourteous, discourtesy

[variant forms: cohort, cortege, curtesy, curtilage, curtsy, horticulture, orchard]

[phrase: court-martial]

couter: to sew, outfit

couture, couturier

accouter, accouterment

cover: to hide, cover

≈cover-t: cover, coverage, covert, coverture

- cover-y: discover, discovery, recover—one meaning

- coverable: recoverable, irrecoverable

- covert: discovert

[variant forms: curfew, kerchief, handkerchief; occult, occultation, occultism]

{word notes: <u>curfew</u>: from Old French *covrefeu*, lit., cover the fire; the signal to extinguish the town fire and secure the area before retiring; <u>kerchief</u>: lit., that which covers the head}

covet: desire

covet, covetous

CORVINE: like a crow

cox: hip

coxa, coxalgia

[variant form: cuisse]

crac-y: to rule; strength

- cracy: with prefixes: autocracy, kakistocracy

- cracy: with combining forms: aristocracy, democracy, gerontocracy, gynecocracy, meritocracy, mobocracy, ochlocracy, plutocracy, stratocracy, technocracy, theocracy

- crat: aristocrat, autocrat, democrat, physiocrat, plutocrat, theocrat

- cratic: with prefixes: autocratic, mesocratic

- cratic: with combining forms: aristocratic, autocratic, democratic, physiocratic, plutocratic, theocratic

- cratium: pancratium

CRAG: from Celtic; a steep, rugged rock that rises above others or projects from a rock mass

crani-o: skull, head

≈crani: cranial, craniate, cranium

≈cranio-: craniology, craniometry, craniotomy

- crania: hemicrania— migraine

- cranial: dolichocranial, ectocranial, encranial, entocranial, epicranial,

extracranial, intracranial,
mesocranial, neurocranial,
pericranial, postcranial
- cranium: endocranium,
  entocranium, epicranium,
  macrocranium, osteocranium,
  otocranium, pericranium
- cranon: olecranon

crapul: drunkenness
  crapulence, crapulent,
  crapulous

cras: tomorrow
  procrastinate — lit., to put
  forward until tomorrow; to put off
  doing something unpleasant or
  burdensome until a future time;
  especially, to postpone such
  actions habitually

crass: thick
  crass; incrassate

crater: a mixing
  crater, cratering
  [variant forms: dyscrasia,
  idiosyncrasy]

CRAVAT: French; a dialectal form of
  Croatian *Hrvat*, a neckerchief,
  scarf, or necktie; used by the
  French in reference to scarves
  worn by Croatian soldiers

creas: flesh
≈creo-: creosote
- creas: pancreas
- creatic-n: pancreatic, pancreatin
- creat-: pancreatalgia,
  pancreatectomy
- creatitis: pancreatitis

cred-it: to believe
≈cred: credence, credenda,
  credential, credenza, credible,
  credo
≈credit: credit, creditable,
  creditor
- credible: incredible
- credit: accredit, discredit,
  disaccredit, microcredit
- creditable: discreditable

≈credul: credulity, credulous
- credulity: incredulity
- credulous: incredulous
  [variant forms: creed, grant;
  miscreant, recreant]

cren: notched, scalloped
  crenate, crenation, crenel,
  crenulate
  [variant form: cranny]

crep[1]: to rattle
≈crep-e: crepe, crêpe, crepitate,
  crepitation
- crep-it: decrepit, decrepitate,
  decrepitude; discrepancy
  [variant forms: crape, craven,
  crevasse, crevice, crisp]

crep[2]: dark
  crepuscular, crepuscule

cresc: to grow, increase
≈cresc: crescendo, crescent
- creant: procreant
- crease: decrease, increase
- creasingly: decreasingly,
  increasingly
≈creat-e: create, creation,
  creative, creature
- create: increate, procreate,
  recreate, re-create
- creative: procreative
- crement: decrement, increment
- crescence: concrescence,
  excrescence; decrescendo
- crescent: decrescent,
  excrescent, increscent
- crete: accrete, concrete
- cretion: accretion, concretion
  [variant forms: accrue, croissant,
  cereal, Creole, crew, critter,
  recruit]

CRICOID: circle, ring, curl

crim-in: offense
≈crim-e: crime, criminal,
  criminate
≈crimino-: criminology
- criminate: incriminate,
  recriminate

[phrase: particeps criminis]
[see cert-i for discriminate]

crin[1]: **lily**
crinoid; encrinite

crin[2]: **hair**
≈crini-: criniculture, crinigerous
≈crino-: crinoline

critical: see cert-i

CRISSCROSS: from Middle English *Christcros*, Christ's cross

CROMLECH: Welsh, *crom*, bent + *llech*, flat stone; a Neolithic monument of megaliths, such as Stonehenge, in England

cros: **a hook**
crosier; lacrosse
[variant forms: encroach, encroachment]

crot: **pulse, to strike**
dicrotic, tricrotic
[variant form: anacrusis]

CROUPIER: orig., one who rode on the croup, or rump, of a horse; thus, an inferior assistant; a person who rakes in the chips at a gambling table

cruci: **cross**
≈cruci: crucial, cruciate
≈cruci-: crucifer, crucifix, crucifixion, cruciform, crucify
- crucian: Rosicrucian
- cruciat-e: excruciate, excruciating
[variant forms: cruise, crusade; crux; cruzado; Santa Cruz, Bolivia; Veracruz, Mexico]
[phrases: Croix de Guerre, crux ansata, crux capitata]

crud-e: **bleeding, rough, raw**
crude, crudités, crudity;
recrudesce, recrudescence
[variant forms: cruel, cruelty, ecru]
{word note: crudités: raw vegetables served as hors d'oeuvres}

crusis: see crot for anacrusis

crust: **crust, shell**
≈crust: crust, crusty, crustacean
- crust-: encrust, encrustation, encrusted
[variant forms: croustade, crouton, custard]
[phrase: en croûte—wrapped in pastry and baked: said especially of meat, as pâté en croûte]

cry: **to cry, wail**
cry; decry, descry
[phrases: cri de coeur, dernier cri]

cryo: **extreme cold; crystal**
≈cry-: cryonic, cryonics
≈cryo-: cryobiology, cryocautery, cryogenics, cryohydrate, cryophile, cryophyte, cryoscopy, cryostat, cryosurgery, cryotherapy
≈crystal-l: crystal, crystalline, crystallite, crystallize
≈crystall-: crystalloid
≈crystalli-: crystalliferous
≈crystallo-: crystallography
- cryst: metacryst, phenocryst, xenocryst
- crystal: quasicrystal

crypt-o: **secret, hidden**
≈crypt: crypt, cryptic
≈crypt-: cryptesthesia, cryptorchidism
≈crypto-: cryptobiosis, cryptoclastic, cryptogam, cryptogenic, cryptogram, cryptography, cryptology
- crypt: decrypt, encrypt
- cryptic: incryptic, procryptic
- cryption: encryption
- crypha-l: Apocrypha, apocryphal

cten-o: **scales, teeth**
ctenoid, ctenoidean;
ctenophore, ctenosaura

cton: **to kill**
rhizoctonia—a type of fungus which causes various diseases of many garden vegetables and ornamental plants

cub-e: **to lie down**; **a bed**
≈cub-e: cube, cubation, cubatory,
   cubature, cubic, cubiculum,
   cubicle, cubit
≈cub-: cuboid
- cubat-e: incubate, incubation,
   incubator
- cubin-e: concubinage,
   concubine
- cubus: incubus, succubus
- cumb: accumb, decumb,
   procumb, recumb, succumb
- cumbent: accumbent,
   decumbent, incumbent,
   procumbent, recumbent
   [variant forms: couch, couchant,
   couchette, couvade, covey,
   covin, accouchement;
   incunabula]

cul: **posterior, bottom, anus,**
buttocks
   culet, culotte; sans-culotte
   [variant form: recoil]
   [phrase: cul-de-sac—lit., bottom
   of the bag]

culmin: **peak, summit**
   culminant, culminate,
   culmination

culp-a: **guilt, blame**
≈cul-: culprit
≈culpa: culpa, culpable
- culpable: exculpable, inculpable
- culpate: disculpate, exculpate,
   inculpate
- culpation: disculpation,
   exculpation, inculpation
- culpatory: disculpatory,
   exculpatory, inculpatory
   [phrase: mea culpa]
   {word note: culprit: contraction of
   prosecutor's phrase *culpable, prit*
   a averer nostre billet: guilty, ready
   to prove our case}

cult-i: **to care**
≈cult: cult, cultivate, cultivator,
   culture

≈culti- cultigen
- cult: incult
- cultural: bicultural,
   intercultural, multicultural,
   sociocultural, transcultural
- culturate: acculturate,
   enculturate
- culture: with prefixes:
   counterculture, interculture,
   monoculture, subculture
- culture: with combining forms:
   agriculture, horticulture,
   mariculture, sericulture,
   silviculture, viniculture

cultr: **knife, plowshare**
   cultrate—sharp-edged; pointed
   [variant forms: colter, cutlass,
   cutler, cutlery]

cumb: **obstruction, barrier**
≈cumber: cumber, cumbersome
≈cumbr: cumbrance, cumbrous
- cumber: encumber,
   disencumber
- cumbrance: encumbrance
CUMMERBUND: Hindi and Persian
   kamar, loins + band; loin band

cumul: **to amass**
≈cumul: cumulate, cumulation,
   cumalative, cumulous,
   cumulus
≈cumuli-: cumuliform
- cumulat-e: accumulate,
   accumulation, accumulative
- cumulus: cirrocumulus
CUNCTATION, CUNCATIVE: delay,
   hesitate, linger

cune: **wedge**
≈cune: cuneal, cuneate
≈cunei-: cuneiform
≈cuneo-: cuneonavicular
   [variant form: coin]
CUNNING: from Middle English
   cunnen, to know; sly, crafty

cup: **tub, cup**
   cup, cupola, cupping, cupulate,
   cupule

[variant form: cuvette]

cupid: **desire**

≈cupid: cupid, cupidity
- cupis-: concupiscence
  [variant form: covet]

cupr: **copper**

≈cupr: cupreous, cupric, cuprite, cuprous
≈cupr-: cupremia
≈cupri-: cupriferous, cupriuria

cur: **to run**

≈cur: curule—interesting word!
≈corr: corral, corrida, corridor
≈cors: corsair—a pirate ship
≈cours-e: course, courser, coursing
≈curren-t: currency, current
≈curric: curricle, curriculum
- cor: succor—to give aid
- course: concourse, discourse, intercourse, recourse
- cur: concur, incur, occur, recur
- currence: concurrence, incurrence, intercurrence, occurrence, recurrence
- current: with prefixes: concurrent, decurrent, excurrent, intercurrent, recurrent, undercurrent
- current: with combining form: photocurrent
- curricular: cocurricular, extracurricular
≈curs-e: curse, cursive, cursor, cursorial, cursory
- cursion: decursion, excursion, incursion, recursion
- cursive: decursive, discursive, excursive, incusive, recursive
- cursor-y: precursor, precursory
- cursus: concursus, excursus
  [variant forms: coarse; scour—one meaning]
  [phrases: curriculum vitae; hors concours; au courant, coureur de bois]

cur-e: **to care, cure** [see sur-e]

≈cur: curable, curate, curative, curator, curio
≈cure: cure, curé, curet, curettage
- cur-: accuracy, incurable, procurator; pococurante
- curate: accurate, inaccurate
- cure: with prefixes: procure, secure, insecure, sinecure
- cure: with combining forms: manicure, pedicure
≈curio: curious, curiosity
- curious: incurious
- curity: security, insecurity
  [variant forms: proxy, scour—one meaning, sure]
  [phrases: amicus curiae, per curiam]

CURMUDGEON: surly, ill-mannered person

CURRANT: from Anglo-French *raisins de Corauntz*, raisins of Corinth; orig., currants were imported from Corinth

CURRY: from Tamil *kari*, sauce; Tamil is a language of India

curt: **short**

curt, curtail, curtal, curtate
[variant forms: kirtle, shirt, short, skirt]
[phrase: tout court]

curv-e: **bent**

≈curv-e: curvaceous, curvature, curve, curvet, curvity
≈curvi-: curvicaudate, curvicostate, curvidentate, curviform, curvilinear, curvinervate, curvirostal
- curve: decurve, outcurve
- curvate: incurvate, recurvate
  [variant forms: curb; Spanish: curva—curve]

cus-e: **to strike** [see cuss-]

- cus-: incus, recusant, irrecusable
- cuse: incuse, recuse
  [variant forms: rescue, ruse]

cusp: point, pointed end, spear
≈cusp: cusp, cuspate, cuspid, cuspidate
- cuspid: bicuspid, tricuspid
  [NB: cuspidor—from Portuguese *cuspir*, to spit]
cuss: to shake, strike [see cus-e]
- cuss: concuss, discuss, percuss
- cuss-: discussable, discussant
- cussion: concussion, discussion, percussion, repercussion
- cussive: concussive, percussive
  [variant form: cashier, as a verb]
custod: a guard, keeper
custodial, custodian, custody
custom: to become accustomed
≈custom: custom, customs, customary, customer
- custom: accustom, accustomed, disaccustom
≈consuetud-e: consuetude, consuetudinary
  [variant form: costume]
cut: skin
≈cut: cutaneous, cuticle, cutis
≈cutin: cutin, cutinization
- cutaneous: intracutaneous, percutaneous, subcutaneous, transcutaneous
cyan: blue
≈cyan: cyan, cyaneous, cyanide
≈cyan-: cyanosis
≈cyano-: cyanoderma
- cyanin: anthocyanin, betacyanin, cholecyanin, hemocynanin, urocyanin
cycl-e: circle, cycle
≈cycl-e: cycle, cyclic, cyclone
≈cycl-: cycloid, cyclopean, Cyclops, cyclorama
≈cyclo: cyclobranchiate, cyclometer, cycloplegia, cyclostome, cyclothymia
- cycle: autocycle, bicycle, biocycle, epicycle, hemicycle,

motorcycle, pericycle, recycle, tricycle, unicycle
- cyclic: acyclic, concyclic, dicyclic, endocyclic, encyclic, epicyclic, exocyclic, heterocyclic, isocyclic, macrocyclic, monocyclic, polycyclic, tricyclic
- cyclical: encyclical
- cycline: tetracycline
- cycloid: epicycloid
- cyclo-: encyclopedia
cylind-r: to roll; cylinder
cylinder, cylindrical; cylindroid
cym: sprout; something swollen; a wave [see kym]
≈cym-e: cyma, cymatium, cyme, cymose
≈cym-: cymoid
≈cymo-: cymogene, cymograph, cymophobia, cymotrichous
cymb: boat, bowl
cymbal, cymbalom, cymbidium
cyn-o-s: dog [see can]
cynic, cynical, cynicism; cynosure—lit., dog's tail
cyn-th: moon
Cynthia; apocynaceous; apocynthian, pericynthian
cyst-i: sac, bladder
≈cyst: cyst, cystic
≈cyst-: cystitis, cystoid, cystectomy
≈cysti-: cysticercoid, cysticercus
≈cysto-: cystoblast, cystocarp, cystocele, cystolith, cystoscope, cystotomy
- cyst-: with prefixes: encyst, macrocyst, polycystic
- cyst: with combining forms: dacryocyst, nematocyst, oocyst, otocyst, sporocyst, statocyst, trichocyst

cyt-o: a cell
≈cyto: cyton
≈cyto-: cytobiology, cytoblast,
  cytochrome, cytocyst,
  cytogenesis, cytogenetics,
  cytokinesis, cytology,
  cytolysis, cytoplasm,
  cytotaxonomy, cytotoxic
- cyt-: polycythemia; syncytium
- cyte: with prefixes: amphicyte,
  endocyte, epicyte, macrocyte,
  microcyte, monocyte
- cyte: with combining forms:
  acanthocyte, auxocyte,
  blastocyte, erythrocyte,
  granulocyte, hemocyte,
  histocyte, leukocyte,
  lymphocyte, megakaryocyte,
  melanocyte, myelocyte,
  osteocyte, phagocyte,
  reticulocyte, solenocyte,
  spermatocyte, thrombocyte
- cytosis: endocytosis,
  exocytosis, monocytosis,
  phagocytosis
CZAR: from *Caesar*, title of the
  emperor of Rome; the title of any
  of the former emperors of Russia;
  an autocrat; see kaiser

D

dacry-o: a tear
≈dacry-: dacryadenitis,
  dacryagogue, dacryocystitis,
  dacryoma
≈dacryo-: dacryocele,
  dacryocyst, dacryocystitis,
  dacryocyte, dacryogenic,
  dacryolith, dacryostenosis
dactyl-o: finger, toe
≈dactyl: dactyl, dactylate,
  dactylic
≈dactyl-: dactylagra, dactylalgia

≈dactylo-: dactylogram,
  dactylography, dactylology,
  dactylomancy
- dactylous: adactylous,
  anisodactylous, artiodactylous,
  brachydactylous, didactylous,
  discodactylous,
  heterodactylous,
  leptodactylous,
  macrodactylous,
  microdactylous,
  monodactylous,
  orthodactylous,
  pachydactylous,
  polydactylous, pterodactylous,
  syndactylous, tridactylous,
  zygodactylous
- dactyl: with prefixes: adactyl,
  anisodactyl, antidactyl,
  pentadactyl, perissodactyl,
  polydactyl, syndactyl
- dactyl: with combining forms:
  artiodactyl, leptodactyl,
  pterodactyl, zygodactyl
- dactyly: ectrodactyly,
  heptadactyly, hexadactyly,
  hyperdactyly, hypodactyly,
  leptodactyly, macrodactyly,
  oligodactyly, syndactyly
  [variant form: date, the fruit]
  {word note: dactyl: a metrical foot of
  three syllables—one long and two
  short—corresponding to the three
  joints of the index finger}
DAHLIA: from A. Dahl, 18th-c.
  botanist; a showy flower
DAISY: lit., day's-eye; a flower
dam: woman, lady
  dame, damsel, madam,
  madame
damant: to subdue
  adamant, adamantine
  [variant form: diamond]
DAMASK: after the city of *Damascus*,
  capital of Syria, where the fabric
  was first made

dam-ni: **to damn**, **harm**
≈dam-n: damage, damn,
  damnable, damnation,
  damnatory, damned
≈damni-: damnify
- demn-: condemn,
  condemnation, condemnatory,
  indemnity
- demni-: indemnification,
  indemnify
dar: **wood**
  deodar—lit., tree of the gods; a
  tall Himalayan cedar
DARLING: from Old English *dearling*,
  diminutive of *deore*, dear; a
  person much loved by another; as
  an adjective, very dear; beloved
DASHIKI: said to be of Yoruba origin,
  but probably a coined word: a
  loosefitting, usually brightly
  colored, robe or tunic modeled
  after an African tribal garment
DASTARD: a sneaky, cowardly
  evildoer
dat-e: **to give**
≈dat-e: datary, dative, datum, pl.,
  data, date
- dand: deodand
- date: with prefixes: antedate,
  postdate, predate
- date: with combining form:
  mandate
- datatory: mandatory
- dit-: edit, editor, editorial
- dition: edition, perdition,
  rendition, tradition
≈don: donate, donation, donor
- don-e: condone, condonation,
  pardon
≈dos-e: dosage, dose
≈dosi-: dosimeter
- dos-e: apodosis, isodose
≈dot: dot—one meaning, dotation
- dotal: anecdotal, sacerdotal
- dote: anecdote, antidote,
  epidote

≈dow: dowager, dower, dowry
- dow-: endow, endowment,
  disendow
  [variant forms: add, addendum,
  superadd, perdu, perdue, render,
  rendezvous, rent, surrender,
  tradition, traitor, treason]
  [phrase: editio princeps]
  {word note: anecdote: orig., not
  given out; not published}
DAUGHTER: prob. from Sanskrit
  duhitár, one who milks the cows;
  "similarly" spelled in many of the
  Indo-European languages: *Tochter*
  (German); *dauhtar* (Gothic);
  thugater (Greek)

de-: **down**, **away**, **off**; sometimes,
  an intensive
≈de-: debacle, debar, debark,
  debate, debilitate, debouch,
  debridement, debrief, debris,
  debut
≈decadent, decamp, decant,
  decapitate, decease, deceive,
  decelerate, decenter, deception,
  decerebrate, decertify, decide,
  deciduous, declaim, declare,
  declension, decline, declivity,
  decoct, decode, decollate,
  decrease, decree, decrepit,
  decrescent, decry, decumbent,
  decurved
≈deduce, deface, defalcate,
  defame, default, defeasance,
  defeasible, defeat, defecate,
  defect, defend, defer,
  defervescence, defiant,
  defibrillate, deficient, defilade,
  define, definite, deflate,
  deflect, defoliate, deform,
  defray, defunct
≈dégagé, degauss, degenerate,
  deglutition, degrade, degree,
  degression, dégustation
≈dehisce, dehumidify, dehydrate,
  deject

≈delay, delectable, delegate,
  deliberate, delicate, delight,
  delineate, delinquent, delirious,
  delirium, deliver, delude,
  deluge
≈demand, demarcate, dement,
  demerit, demise, demolish,
  demonstrate, demulcent,
  demur, demure, demurrer
≈denature, denigrate,
  denominate, denote, denounce,
  denude
≈depart, depend, depilate,
  deplete, deplore, deploy,
  deport, depose, deposit, depot,
  deprave, deprecate, depreciate,
  depress, deprive, depute
≈deracinate, derange, derelict,
  deride, derisive, derive,
  derogate, derogatory
≈descend, describe, desecrate,
  desert, deserve, desiccate,
  desiderate, design, desire,
  desist, desolate, despair,
  despise, despondent, destine,
  destitute, destroy, desultory
≈detach, detail, detain, detect,
  deter, detergent, determine,
  deterrent, detersive, detest,
  detonate, detour, detract,
  detriment, detrude, detruncate
≈devastate, deviate, devoid,
  devolve, devote, devour
≈di- variant of *de*-: diminish,
  distill, diverticulum
DEARTH: from Middle English *deore*,
  precious, costly, beloved, dear;
  therefore, scarcity, lack

deb-t: to owe
≈deb-it: debenture, debit, debt,
  debtor
- debt-: indebted, indebtedness
  [variant forms: devoir, due,
  duteous, dutiable, dutiful,
  duty, endeavor]
debilitate, debility: see bil

dec: ten
≈dec: decade, decanal, decile
≈dec-: decathlon, decennial
≈deca-: decagon, Decalogue,
  decapod, Decameron,
  decamerous [second root in
  previous two words is *hemera*],
  Decapolis
≈decem: December
≈decem- decemvir
- decennial: quindecennial
- decimo: octodecimo
≈decu: decurion, decussate
≈decu-: decuple
≈den: denarius
- denum: duodenum
≈deci: decimal; decigram,
  decimate: tenth
  [variant forms: dean, dicker,
  dime, doyen, doyenne, dozen,
  duodenum; Spanish: dinero]

dece: to befit
≈dec: decency, decent
≈décor: décor, decorate,
  decoration, decorous, decorum
- decent: indecent
- décor-: indecorous, indecorum
DECOY: from Dutch *de kooi*, the
  cage; as a verb, to lure or be lured

dect: to accept
  pandect; synecdoche—a figure
  of speech; a whole for the part

deed: to do
  deed, indeed
deem: see emp-li for redeem

dei: god, God, deity
≈dei: deism, deist, deity
≈dei-: deicide, deific, deification,
  deiform, deify
≈deo: deodand, deodar
  [variant forms: diet—an assembly;
  divination, divinity,divine;
  French: adieu; Spanish: adios]
  [variant forms: Deo volente—God
  willing; deus ex machina; Deo
  Volente, MS; prie-dieu]

delic: **to make manifest**
  psychedelic—of or causing
  extreme changes in in the
  conscious mind, as hallucinations,
  delusions of awareness and
  sensory perception
del-e: **to blot out**, **erase**, **destroy**;
  from *de-*, from + *linear*, to daub
  dele, delete, deletion; indelible
DELETERIOUS: injurious, destructive
DELPHINIUM: the larkspur, a flower;
  from *dolphin*, because of the
  resemblance of the nectary to the
  dolphin
delt: **delta**; from Greek Δ, orig.,
  door; equivalent to English "d"
  delta, deltaic; deltoid
demi: **half**, **small**
  demitasse, demimondaine,
  demimonde, demisemiquaver,
  demivolt
NB: demijohn
DEMIJOHN: a corruption of French
  dame Jeanne, Lady Jane; a
  narrow-necked bottle in wicker-
  work, from the fancied similarity
  of form
dem-o: **people**
≈dem: demotic
≈dem-: demagogue
≈demo-: democracy, democrat,
  democratic, demographics
- demic: endemic, epidemic,
  esodemic, exodemic,
  homodemic, pandemic
≈demi: demigod, demiurge
- demi-: epidemiology
demon: **devil**; also, divine spirit
≈demon: demon, demoniac,
  demonism, demonize
≈demono-: demonolatry,
  demonology
- demon-: pandemonium;
  eudemonia
≈daemon: daemon
- daemon-: eudaemonia,
  eudaemonism

dendr-o: **tree**
≈dendr: dendrite, dendrous
≈dendr-: dendroid
≈dendri-: dendriform
≈dendro-: dendrochronology,
  dendrolatry, dendrology,
  dendrophagous, dendrophilia,
  dendrophobia, dendrotoxin
- dendron: philodendron,
  rhododendron
- dendrum: epidendrum
DENIM: orig., serge *de Nîmes*; from
  Nîmes, France, where the fabric
  was first made
dens-e: **thick**, **compact**
≈dens-e: dense, density
- dens-e: condense, condensation,
  condenser
dent-i: **tooth**
≈dent: dent—one meaning, dental,
  dentate, dentation, denticulate,
  dentil, dentist, dentition,
  dentulous, denture
≈dent-: dentoid
≈denti-: dentiform, dentifrice,
  dentigerous
- dent: indent, trident
- dent-: indentation, indention,
  indenture, indentured,
  interdental
- dentate: bidentate, curvidentate,
  edentate, multidentate,
  octodentate tridentate
  [variant form: dandelion]
  [phrase: al dente]
desm: **to bind**
≈desm: desmid
≈desm-: desmoid
≈desmo-: desmosome
- desis: syndesis
- desmosis: syndesmosis
- dem: anadem, diadem
≈deonto-: deontology
- detic: syndetic
- deton: asyndeton, polysyndeton

derm: **skin, covering**
≈derm: dermad, dermal, dermis
≈dermat-: dermatalgia,
   dermatitis, dermatodynia
≈dermato: dermatocyst,
   dermatography, dermatology,
   dermatopathy, dermatophyte
- derm: with prefixes: ectoderm,
   endoderm, hypoderm,
   mesoderm, periderm
- derm: with combining forms:
   blastoderm, melanoderm,
   pachyderm, phelloderm
- derm-: epidermis, epidermoid,
   intradermal, taxidermy
- derma: epiderma, erythroderma,
   melanoderma, pyoderma,
   scleroderma, xeroderma
- dermatous: pachydermatous,
   sclerodermatous
- dermia: leukodermia
- dermic: endermic, hypodermic,
   pachydermic, transdermic
- dermous: leptodermous,
   malacodermous,
   pachydermous, sclerodermous
des: **to divide**
   geodesic, geodesy, selenodesy
DES MOINES, IA: from French *la*
   rivière des Moines, the river of the
   monks; the river flows through the
   city
DETERIORATE: to make worse
DETROIT, MI: from French *détroit*,
   strait, which was first applied to
   the river that flows through the
   city
deuter-o: **second, secondary**
≈deuter: deuterium
≈deuter-: deuteragonist,
   deuteranopia
≈deutero-: deuterogamy,
   deuterogenesis, deuteroplasm,
   deuteronomic, Deuteronomy,
   deuteropathy, deuteroplasm,
   deuteroscopy, deuterosome

dex: **to point out**; from "to speak"
   index, indexation, indexical;
   indicia
dext-r: **right**
≈dexter: dexter, dexterity,
   dexterous
≈dexio-: dexiotropic
≈dextr-a: dextrin, dextral,
   dextran, dextrose, dextrous
≈dextra-: dextrarotation,
   dextrarotatory
≈dextro-: dextrocardia,
   dextrogram, dextro*rse*; second
   root is from ve*rsus*
- dextral: sinistrodextral
- dextrous: ambidextrous
   [variant form: destrier]
di-: **two, twice**
≈di- diacid, diadelphous,
   diandrous, diarchy, diatom,
   dibasic, dibranchiate
≈dicentra, dichroism,
   dichromate, dichromatism,
   dichromic, dichroscope,
   diclinous, dicotyledon,
   dicrotic, didynamous
≈digamy, digastric, digenesis,
   diglot, dihedral, dilemma
≈dimeter, dimetric, dimity,
   dimorphism, diode, dioecious,
   dioxide
≈dipetalous, diphase, diphthong,
   diphycercal, diphyletic,
   diphyllous, diphyodont,
   diplegia, dipnoan, dipody,
   dipteral, dipterous, diptych
≈distich, distome, disyllable,
   ditheism, divalent
- di-: hendiadys
{word note: hendiadys: from Greek
   hen dia dyoin, one thing by means
   of two: a figure of speech in which
   two nouns joined by *and* are used
   instead of a noun and a modifier,
   e.g., *deceit and words* for *deceitful*
   words}

dia-: across, through
≈dia-: diabase, diabetes, diabetic,
    diabolic, diachronic, diacritic,
    diacritical
≈diadem, diadromous,
    diagenesis, diageotropism,
    diagnose, diagnosis, diagonal,
    diagram
≈diakinesis, dialect, dialectic,
    dialogue, dialysis, diameter
≈diapason, diapause, diapedesis,
    diaphanous, diaphone,
    diaphoresis, diaphragm,
    diaphysis, diapositive
≈diarrhea, diastase, diastem,
    diastema, diastole,
    diastrophism, diatessaron,
    diathermancy, diathesis,
    diatonic, diatribe, diatropism
≈di-: truncation of *dia-*: diallage,
    diapophysis, diarthrosis,
    dieresis, diestrus, diopter,
    diuresis
- dia-: epidiascope
dia: day
≈dia: diary
- dian: circadian, meridian,
    postmeridian, quotidian
- dio-: eudiometer
≈diet: diet, dietary, dietetic,
    dietetics, dietician: daily
    allowance
    [variant form: dismal]
    [phrases: carpe diem, per diem,
    Dies Irae, dies non, sine die]
    {word note: circadian: designating or
    of behavioral rhythms associated
    with the 24-hour cycles of the
    earth's rotation}
DIAPER: orig., an ornamental cloth;
    from *jasper*
dic: justice, to show, prove
≈dic: dicast
- dic-: syndic, syndicalism,
    syndicate
- dictic: apodictic, epidictic

≈deic: deictic
- deictic: epideictic
dicha: in two, asunder
≈dicha: dichasium
≈dich-: dichoptic
≈dicho-: dichogamy,
    dichotomous, dichotomy
dict: to say, word [see dex, digit]
≈dict: dictate, dictator,
    dictatorial, diction, dictionary,
    dictum
- dic-: benedicite, dedicated,
    fatidic, indicator, predicament,
    predicatory, veridical
- dicable: predicable, vendicable
- dicant: abdicant, indicant,
    predicant
- dicate: abdicate, dedicate,
    indicate, predicate, vindicate
- dication: dedication, indication,
    predication, vindication
- dicative: indicative, predicative
- dict: with prefixes: addict,
    contradict, edict, indict,
    interdict, predict, retrodict
- dict: with combining form:
    verdict
- dictable: indictable,
    contradictable, predictable
- diction: with prefixes: addiction,
    benediction, contradiction,
    indiction, interdiction,
    malediction, prediction
- diction: with combining forms:
    jurisdiction, valediction
- dictious: contradictious
- dictive: addictive, predictive,
    vindictive
- dictment: indictment
- dictorian: valedictorian
- dictory: contradictory,
    valedictory
- dition-: condition, conditional,
    conditioned, precondition,
    unconditional, unconditioned

[variant forms: benison, dight,
ditto, ditty, indite, judge,
paradigm, policy—one meaning;
see another *policy* under *polis*;
preach, preacher, token]
[phrases: obiter dictum; voir dire,
ipsi dixit, mirabile dictu]

didac-t: to teach
Didache, didactic; autodidact

didym: two, twin; testicles
≈didym: didymium, didymous,
didymus
≈didym-: didymalgia, didymitis,
didymodynia
≈didymo-: didymospore
- didymis: epididymis
- didymus: gastrodidymus

DIESEL: from Rudolph Diesel
(1858-1913), who invented the
diesel engine

digit: finger, toe; from *dicere*, to
say, to point out [see dex, dict]
≈digit: digit, digital, digitalis,
digitate, digitize
≈digiti-: digitiform, digitigrade,
digitinervate, digitipartite,
digitipinnate
- digitat-e: interdigitate,
prestidigitation
{word note: digitalis: the flower
foxglove; so named from its
thimblelike flowers, after the
German name *Fingerhut*, thimble}

dign-i: worthy, deserving, fitting
≈digni: dignitary, dignity
≈digni-: dignified, dignify
- dign-: condign, indignant,
indignation, indignity
[variant forms: dainty, deign;
disdain, disdainful]
[phrase: infra dig]

dim: to put, do
condiment: lit., to put together; a
seasoning or relish for food, as
pepper, mustard, sauces, etc.
dine: see jejun

DINGHY: Hindi *dingi*; a rowboat

dino[1]: rotation
dinoflagellate: lit., swirling, or
rotating flagella: a class of single-
celled algae

dino[2]: terrible
dinosaur, dinothere
diocese: see ec-o

dipl-o: double, two, twin
≈diplo: diploe, diploma,
diplomacy, diplomat,
diplomate
≈dipl-: diploid, diplopia, diplosis
≈diplo-: diploblastic,
diplococcus, diplopod
- diplosis: anadiplosis

dipso: thirst
dipsomania, dipsomaniacal,
dipsotherapy

dis-: apart, away; general negative
≈dis-: disable, disabuse,
disaccredit, disadvantage,
disaffect, disaffiliate,
disaffirm, disafforest,
disaggregate, disagree,
disallow, disambiguate,
disappear, disappoint,
disapprove, disarm, disarrange,
disarray, disarticulate,
disassemble, disassociate,
disaster, disavow
≈disband, disbar, disbelief,
disburden, disburse
≈discalced, discard, discarnate,
discern, discharge, disciple [see
word note], disclaim,
disclamation, disclose,
discolor, discomfit,
discommend, discommode,
discompose, disconcert,
disconfirm, disconformity,
disconnect, disconsolate,
discontent, discord, discount,
discourage, discourse,
discourteous, discover,
discovert, discredit, discreet,

discrepant, discretion,
discriminate, discursive,
discuss
≈disdain, disease, disembark,
disembarrass, disembogue,
disemployed, disenable,
disenchant, disendow,
disenfranchise, disengage,
disentail, disequilibrate,
disestablish, disesteem
≈disfavor, disfeature, disfigure,
disfranchise
≈disgorge, disgrace, disguise,
disgust
≈dishabille, dishevel
≈disillusion, disinclination,
disinfect, disinflation,
disinformation, disingenuous,
disinherit, disintegrate,
disinter, disinterested,
disinvestment, disinvite
≈disjoin, disjoint, disjunct
≈dislocate, disloyal
≈dismantle, dismay, dismember,
dismiss, dismount
≈disobey, disoblige,
disoperation, disorder,
disorganize, disorient
≈disparage, disparate, disparity,
dispassionate, dispatch, dispel,
dispensary, dispensation,
dispense, displace, display,
displease, disport, dispose,
dispossess, dispraise, disprize,
disproof, disproportion,
disprove, dispute
≈disqualify, disquiet, disquisition
≈disrate, disregard, disrelish,
disrepair, disrepute, disrespect,
disrobe, disrupt
≈dissatisfy, dissect, disseize,
dissemble, disseminate,
disseminule, dissension,
dissent, dissepiment,
dissertation, disserve, dissever,

dissident, dissilient, dissimilar,
dissipate, dissolution, dissolve,
dissonant, dissuade,
dissymmetry
≈distain, distemper, distend,
distinct, distinguish, distort,
distract, distrain, distraught,
distrust, disunion, disvalue
≈de-: variant of *dis*-: debauch,
defy, depart
≈di-: truncation of *dis*-: digest,
dilapidate, dilate, diligent,
dilute, dimension, dimerous,
dimidiate, direct, diriment,
disperse, distal, distance,
distress, distinction,
distinguish, district, divagate,
divaricate, diverge, diverse,
divert, divest, divide, division,
divisor, divulge
≈dif-: assimilation of *dis*-: differ,
difference, difficile, difficult,
diffident, diffract, diffuse
[variant forms: dine, dinner]
{word note: disciple: some
authorities place this word in the
cern family, that is, a learner;
others indicate that it comes from
dis- + *capere*, to hold; a pupil or
follower of any teacher, esp. of
Jesus; an apostle}
disc: **disc**; orig., a table
≈disc: disc, discus
≈disc-: discoid
≈disco-: discography, discophile,
discothèque
[variant forms: desk, dish, disk]
diurn: **day**; see jour-nal
diurnal, terdiurnal, tridiurnal
DIVAN: Turkish for bundle of written
sheets; a sofa
doche: see dect for synecdoche
doc-t: **to teach**; **belief**
≈doc: docent, docile, doctor
≈doctrin-e: doctrinaire, doctrine
- doctrinate: indoctrinate

≈document: document,
documentary, documentation
≈doxo-: doxology
- dox: heterodox, orthodox,
paradox
[German: privatdocent]
dodeca: twelve [*duo*, 2 + *deca*, 10]
dodecagon, dodecahedron,
dodecaphonic, dodecasyllable
dogma: to think true
dogma, dogmatic, dogmatics
DOLABRIFORM: in the form of a
pickax, as certain leaves
DOLDRUMS: equatorial ocean regions
noted for dead calms; hence, *in the
doldrums*; the blahs
dol-e: pain, grief
≈dolor: dolor, dolorous
≈dole-: doleful
- dol-e: condole, condolence,
indolence, indolent
[music terms: con dolore;
doloroso]
{word note: indolent: lit., not
causing pain, as *an indolent cyst*;
slow to heal, as *an indolent ulcer*;
also, lazy; disliking work, as
though work would cause pain}
DOLERITE: a coarse, crystalline
variety of basalt; from *doleros*,
deceptive, because of its close
resemblance to diorite
dolicho: long
≈dolich-: dolichonyx
≈dolicho-: dolichocentrum,
dolichocephalic, dolichoceric,
dolichocolon, dolichocranic,
dolichofacial, dolichohieric,
dolichomorphic,
dolichopodous, dolichosaurus,
dolichouranic
dollar: see thal
DOLOMEN: from Breton *taol*, table +
men, stone: a monolithic tomb or
monument consisting of a large,
flat stone laid across upright
stones; a cromlech, which see

dom-e: house
≈dom-e: domain, dome, domical,
domicile
≈domest: domestic, domesticate
≈domin: dominant, dominate,
domineer, domineering,
dominical, dominie, dominion,
domino
- dome: astrodome, interdome,
lithodome, macrodome
- dominant: predominant,
subdominant
- dominate: predominate
- dominium: condominium
- domitable: indomitable
[variant forms: belladonna,
dame, damsel, danger, daunt,
daunting, dauntless, demesne,
duenna, madam, madame,
madonna, major-domo; despot,
Spanish: don, doña]
donet: to shake
aerodonetics—the science of
soaring in a glider
DONNYBROOK: from Donnybrook
Fair, held annually in Donnybrook, near Dublin, Ireland, where
there was much brawling and
rowdiness; a rough, rowdy fight;
often used figuratively
dor-a: a gift
Dorothy, Pandora, Theodore,
Thermidor
[variant form: pandurate]
dorm: sleep
dormant, dormer, dormer
windows; dormitive,
dormitory; dormouse
{word note: dormouse: a small
rodent that appears sleepy or
drowsy}
dors: the back
≈dors: dorsad, dorsal, dorsum
≈dorsi-: dorsiduct, dorsiflexion,
dorsispinal, dorsiventral
- dorsal: cervicodorsal,
mediodorsal, ventrodorsal

67

- dorse-: endorse, endorsee,
  endorsement
  [variant forms: doss, dosser,
  dossier, do-si-do; extrados,
  intrados, reredos]
DOTE, DOTAGE, DOTARD, DOTTY:
  from Middle English; influenced
  by Middle Dutch *dotten*, to be
  insane
DOUGHTY: brave, courageous, valiant
DRACONIAN: rigorous, severe; after
  Draco, the name of a severe
  Athenian jurist

drama-t: an action, drama
≈drama: drama, dramatic,
  dramatize
≈dramat-: dramaturge,
  dramaturgy
- drama: melodrama, monodrama
  [variant form: drastic]
  [phrase: dramatis personae]
DRAWING ROOM: orig., withdrawing
  room; a place to which dinner
  guests might retire, or "withdraw,"
  for conversation and coffee
DREADNOUGHT, or dreadnaught: a
  British warship that "dreaded
  naught"; also, a coat made of a
  thick woolen cloth
DRESDEN: from Dresden, Germany,
  on the Elbe, where first made: a
  fine porcelain
dress: see rect
droit: see rect

drom-e: to run
≈drom: dromedary
- drome: with prefixes:
  palindrome, prodrome,
  syndrome
- drome: with combining forms:
  aerodrome, hippodrome,
  lampadrome, loxodrome
- dromic: antidromic, palindromic
- drometer: hemodrometer
- dromous: amphidromous,
  anadromous, antidromous,
  catadromous, diadromous,

heterodromous, homodromous,
oceanodromous, prodromous

dub: doubting, to waver in
  opinion; root may be related to
  du-o, two
≈dub: dubiety, dubious, dubitable
- dubitable: indubitable
≈doubt: doubt, doubtful,
  doubtless
- doubtable: redoubtable
  [see next family for redoubt]
  [see du-o]

duc: to lead
≈duc-e: ducal, ducat, duce
- duc-: educate, education,
  educator, irreducible;
  traducianism; conducive
- ducable: educable, ineducable
- duce: adduce, conduce, deduce,
  educe, induce, introduce,
  produce, reduce, reproduce,
  seduce, traduce, transduce
- ducent: abducent, adducent
≈duct: duct, ductile
- duct: with prefixes: abduct,
  adduct, conduct, deduct, educt,
  induct, misconduct, product
- duct: with combining forms:
  aqueduct, dorsiduct
- duct-: conductivity, inductee,
  inductile
- ductance: conductance,
  inductance, transconductance
- duction: adduction, conduction,
  induction, introduction,
  production, reduction,
  reproduction, subduction,
  transduction
- ductive: with prefixes:
  conductive, deductive,
  eductive, inductive,
  productive, reductive,
  reproductive, seductive
- ductive: with combining form:
  photoconductive

- doctor-y: conductor, inductor, introductory
- due: endue, subdue
- dux: redux
  [variant forms: conn, conduit, dossil, douche, duchess, duchy, duke, redoubt]
  [phrase: reductio ad absurdum]
DUDELSACK: German: bagpipe
DUFFEL: Dutch; from Duffel, a town in Belgium; a durable fabric
dul: trickery
  sedulity, sedulous
dulc-i: sweet
≈dulc: dulcet
≈dulci-: dulcify, dulcimer
- dulcorate: edulcorate
  [French: douceur]
dul-e: slave
  dulia; hierodule; hyperdulia
  [variant form: doula: female servant]
dulg-e: to yield to or satisfy a desire [orig. meaning of root obscure]
  indulge, indulgence, indulgent
  [variant form: indult]
DULUTH, MN: named after Daniel G. Du Lhut (1636-1710), French explorer
DUNCE: after John Duns Scotus (c. 1265-1308); his followers, called Dunsmen, Dunses, Dunces, were regarded as foes of Renaissance humanism; thus, dunce cap, a cone-shaped hat that children slow at learning were formerly forced to wear in school
DUNGAREE: Hindi *dungri*; a coarse cotton fabric; specifically, blue denim [see denim]
DUNGEON: orig., an underground earthen cellar for storing fruits; later, a dark underground cell, vault, or prison; may have originally been covered with dung; or, may have come from *donjon*, keeper of the castle

du-o: two
≈du: dual, dualism, duet, duo
≈du-: duple, duplex, duplicate, duplicity
- duplicate: reduplicate
≈duo-: duologue, duopoly
≈duum-: duumvir, duumvirate
  [variant forms: deuce; double, doublet; redouble; dozen; double-entendre, dub—one meaning; dyad, dyarchy]
  [*doubt* may be from this root; see dub]
duodec: twelve
≈duodec: duodecimal, duodecimo
≈duoden: duodenal, duodenary, duodenum
{word note: duodenum: a section of the small intestines that Roman physicians approximated to be the length of the width of 12 fingers}
dur-e: hard, lasting
≈dur: durable, dural, duramen, durance, duration, duress, during, duro, durum
- dur-: endurance, enduring
- durable: endurable, nondurable, perdurable, undurable
- dural: epidural, extradural, intradural, peridural, subdural, transdural
- durate: indurate, obdurate
- dure: endure, perdure
  [variant forms: dour, Duron®]
  [medical term: dura mater]
{word note: dour: from Gaelic *dur*, rough and rocky land; thus, severe; stubborn, obstinate}
dus: to put on
- dusium: indusium
- dyma: ependyma
- dys: ecdysis, ecdyson
{word note: indusium: lit., undergarment, tunic; in anatomy and zoology, any covering membrane}

dyna-m: **power, strength**
≈dyn-e: dynast, dynasty, dyne
≈dynam: dynamic, dynamics,
   dynamism, dynamite, dynamo
- dynamous: didynamous,
   homodynamous, isodynamous,
   tetradynamous, tridynamous
- dynamic: isodynamic,
   photodynamic, telodynamic,
   thermodynamic
- dynamics: aerodynamics,
   geodynamics, hemodynamics,
   photodynamics,
   thermodynamics
- dyne: aerodyne, anodyne,
   autodyne, heterodyne

dys-: **bad, ill, abnormal**
≈dyscalculia, dyscrasia,
   dysentery, dysfunction,
   dysgenic, dysgraphia,
   dyskinesia, dyslexia,
   dyslogistic, dysmenorrhea
≈dyspareunia, dyspepsia,
   dyspeptic, dysphagia,
   dysphasia, dysphonia,
   dysphoria, dysplasia, dyspnea,
   dysprosium, dysrhythmia,
   dystonia, dystopia, dystrophic,
   dystrophy, dysuria

dyt: **to go in**
- dytum: adytum
- dyte: troglodyte

E

EASEL: from Dutch *ezel* and German
   esel, diminutive of ass, donkey; a
   tripod for holding artwork
eas-e: **lying nearby**
   ease, easy; disease
   [variant forms: malaise, adjacent]
ebri: **drunk**
   inebriate, inebriated, inebriety
   [variant form: sober]

EBURNATION: from *ebur*, ivory; an
   abnormal condition of bone or
   cartilage in which it becomes very
   dense and smooth like ivory
e-ch: **to hold**
- e-ch: entelechy; epoch
- exia: cachexia
- exis: cathexis [habit; from *echein*,
   to hold]
   [variant forms: hectic, epoch]
   {word note: hectic: orig. referred to a
   permanent condition or habit of
   the body; then, of a fever accom-
   panying wasting diseases, such as
   tuberculosis; thus, its present
   meaning: characterized by
   confusion, rush, excitement, etc.}

echin-o: **prickly, spiny**
   echinus; echinoid, echinosis;
   echinochrome, echinoderm
ech-o: **to cry out, to sound**
≈echo: echo
≈echo-: echogram
- ech-: catechesis, catechetical,
   catechism, catechumen
- echoic: anechoic

ec-o: **home, environment**; from
   oikos, a house
≈ec: ecesis
≈eco-: ecology, economy,
   ecospecies, ecosphere,
   ecosystem, ecotype
- ecology: synecology
- economics: geoeconomics,
   macroeconomics
- oecium: androecium,
   gynoecium
- oecious: autoecious, dioecious,
   heteroecious, homoecious,
   monoecious, synoecious,
   trioecious
≈ekistics: ekistics
- oky: euroky, stenoky
   [variant forms: diocese,
   ecumenical, parish, parochial,
   vicinity, village; -ville of place
   names]

ectasis: a stretching out
  atelectasis, corectasis,
  telangiectasis
ecto-: outside, external
≈ect-: ectorganism
≈ecto-: ectobiology, ectoblast,
  ectocardia, ectocolon,
  ectocommensal, ectocornea,
  ectocranial, ectocrine, ectocyst,
  ectoderm, ectogenesis,
  ectogenous, ectogony,
  ectomere, ectomorph,
  ectomorphic, ectonuclear,
  ectoorganism, ectoparasite,
  ectoplacenta, ectoplasm,
  ectoproct, ectosarc, ectosphere,
  ectothermal, ectothrix,
  ectotoxin, ectotrophic,
  ectozoon
-ectomy: surgical removal; lit., a
  cutting out [from Greek *ek-*, out +
  temnein, to cut + *-y*, action of]
≈ amygdalectomy,
  appendectomy, embolectomy,
  gastrectomy, hepatectomy,
  hysterectomy, jejunectomy
≈laryngectomy, lipectomy,
  lobectomy, mastectomy,
  nephrectomy, neurectomy,
  oophorectomy, orchidectomy,
  ovariectomy
≈pancreatectomy, pneumectomy,
  prostatectomy, pylorectomy,
  salpingectomy, splenectomy,
  vasectomy
ed[1]: to sing
  comedy; ode
ed[2]: to eat
≈ed: edacious, edacity, edible
- edible: inedible
≈esc: escarole (endive), esculent
- es-e: comestible, obese
≈esur: esurient
  [variant form: etch]
EDAPHIC: of the soil

EDELWEISS: lit., noble white; the state
  flower of Germany before WWII
EDEMA: a swelling; tumor
edi: to build, construct
  edifice, edify
  [variant form: aedile—in ancient
  Rome, an official in charge of
  buildings, roads, sanitation,
  public games, etc.]
edra: see hedr
EERIE, or eery: from Middle English
  eri, filled with dread
EGGNOG: nog: a strong ale
ego: I, self
≈ego: ego, egoism, egoistic,
  egotism, egotist
≈ego-: egocentric, egomania
  [phrase: alter ego]
eid-o: shape, what is seen [see oid]
  eidetic, eidolon
  kaleidoscope
elasmo-: metal plate
  elasmobranch, elasmosaurus,
  elasmothere
elastic: to spring back
≈elastic: elastic, elasticity
- elastic: aeroelastic, inelastic
- elasticity: photoelasticity
electr: electric, amber
≈electr: electric, electrician,
  electrition, electricity, electrum
≈electr-: electrode, electron
≈electri-: electrification, electrify
≈electro-: electrolysis,
  electrocute (electro- + execute)
ELECTUARY: a medicine made by
  mixing drugs with honey or syrup
  to form a paste; from *ek-*, out +
  leichein, to lick
element: first principle
  element, elemental, elementary
ELEEMOSYNARY: alms, charity
elephant: elephant, ivory
  [see eburn]
  elephant, elephantiasis,
  elephantine; chryselephantine

ELEUTHEROMANIA: a mania or frantic zeal for freedom

EL PASO, TX: orig., *El Paso del Norte*, the north pass (of the river)—the Rio Grande

EL SOBRANTE, CA: Spanish: leftover; when the ranchos on the East Bay were parceled out, this area was "left over"; a city near San Francisco

elytron: **covering, sheath**
elytron; hemelytron

EMBLEMENTS: in law, cultivated growing crops which are produced annually; the profits from such crops

EMBROCATE: to moisten and rub a part of the body with an oil, liniment, etc.; the noun is *embrocation*

embryo: see bry-o

eme: **to vomit**
emesis, emetic

emer: see hemer

-emia: see hemia

EMIR: also, ameer; Arabic *amir*; from *amara*, to command; in Muslim countries, a ruler, prince, commander; *admiral* is from the same root

emp-li: **to buy, take**
- empl: exemplar, exemplary, exemplum
- empli-: exemplification, exemplify
- empt-: exempt, preemptive, peremptory
- emption: ademption, exemption, redemption
 [variant forms: diriment, example, irredentist, prompt, impromptu, premium, ransom, redeem, redeemer, irredeemable, sample, sampler]
 {word note: premium: lit., that which is taken before; a reward or prize bonus; as an adjective, at a value or price higher than usual}

emulat-e: **equal, excel**
≈emul-ate: emulate, emulative, emulator, emulous
≈imit-at-e: imitable, imitate, imitation, imitative
- imitable: inimitable

en-[1]: **not**
enemy—second root is *amicus*, friend; entire—from *integer*, whole, untouched, undiminished

en-[2]: **in**
≈en-: enable, enact, enamel, enamor, enantiomorph, enarthrosis
≈encaenia, encage, encamp, encapsulate, encarnalize, encaustic, encephalon, enchain, enchant, enchase, enchilada, enchiridion, enchondroma
≈enchorial, encircle, enclave, enclitic, enclose, encode, encomium, encompass, encounter, encourage, encrinite, encroach
≈encrust, encrypt, enculturate, encumber, encyclical, encyclopedia, encyst
≈endear, endeavor, endemic, endorse, endow, endue, endure, enema, energy, enfeeble, enfeoff, enfilade, enforce, enfranchise
≈engage, engender, engine, engird, engorge, engraft, engrail, engrain, engram, engrave, engross, engulf
≈enhance, enharmonic, enjambment, enjoin, enjoy
≈enlace, enlarge, enlighten, enlist
≈ennoble, enphytotic, enrage, enregister, enroll, enroot, ensanguine, ensconce, ensemble, ensign, ensilage, ensue, ensure

≈entablature, entablement, entail,
  entangle, entasis, entelechy,
  entente, enthalpy, enthrall,
  enthusiasm, enthymeme,
  entice, entomb, entrap, entreat,
  entreaty, entrench, entropy
≈enuresis, envelope, envenom,
  envious, environ, envisage,
  envoy, enzootic, enzyme
≈em-: variant of *en*-: embalm,
  embargo, embattle, embellish,
  embezzle, emblem,
  emblements, embolus,
  embrace, embrocate, embryo,
  emmenagogue, emmetropia
≈empathy, empennage, emperor,
  emphasis, emphysema, empire,
  empirical, emplace, employ,
  emporium, empyema,
  empyreal
encephal-o: brain; from *en*-, on +
  cephalos, head
≈encephal: encephalic
≈encephal-: encephalitis
≈encephalo-: encephalogram,
  encephalograph,
  encephalometer
- encephalon: with prefixes:
  deutencephalon, diencephalon,
  epencephalon, exencephalon,
  mesencephalon,
  metencephalon,
  micrencephalon,
  neoencephalon,
  proencephalon, telencephalon
- encephalon: with combining
  forms: myelencephalon,
  rhombencephalon,
  thalamencephalon
- encephaly: anencephaly,
  hydrocephaly, hyperencephaly
ENDIVE: probably a variation of an
  Egyptian word for *January*, when
  endive is said to grow in Egypt;
  see escarole under ed[2]

endo-: within
≈end-: endodontics, endosmosis,
  endosteum, endostosis
≈endo-: endobiotic, endoblast,
  endocardial, endocardium,
  endocarp, endocentric,
  endocommensal, endocranium,
  endocrine, endocytosis
≈endoderm, endogamy, endogen,
  endolymph, endometrium,
  endomixis, endomorph,
  endoparasite, endophyte,
  endoplasm
≈endoscope, endoskeleton,
  endosperm, endospore,
  endothecium, endothelium,
  endothermal, endotoxin,
  endotracheal
ENGLAND: orig., *Angleland*, land of
  the Angles; later, *Engleland*
enigma: speaking in riddles
  enigma, enigmatic
enn: see ann for biennial
ENNEAD: a group or set of nine
  (books, gods, etc.)
ennui: see odi
eno: see oeno
ENSIFORM: sword-shaped, as an iris
  or a gladiolus leaf; xiphoid
enter: see intra-
enter-: between
  enterprise, enterprising,
  entertain, entertaining,
  entertainment
enter-o: intestine
≈enter: enteric
≈enter-: enteritis
≈entero-: enterobiasis,
  enterocele, enterocentesis,
  enterostomy, enterovirus
- enter-: exenterate, parenteral
- enteritis: gastroenteritis
- enteron: archenteron,
  coelenteron, mesenteron
-entery: dysentery, mesentery
  [variant form: entrails]

ento-: within
  entoblast, entophyte, entoproct,
  entozoon
entom: cut into; from *en-*, in + *tom*,
  cut
≈entom: entomostracan
≈entomo-: entomology,
  entomophagous,
  entomophilous: insect (because
  the insect is "cut into" sections)
entrails: see inter-
entrance: see *intra-* for "entryway";
  see *it-* for "to fill with wonder"
entre-: between
  entrechat, entrecôte, entremets,
  entresol, entrepreneur
  [French: entre nous, entrepôt]
enter, entrée, entry: see intra-
EOLIAN: also, aeolian: carried,
  formed, eroded, or deposited by
  the wind, as sand dunes, sediment,
  etc.
eor: a hovering in the air [see
  meteor]
  meteor, meteoric, meteorite
**eo-sin-o: early, early part of a
  period**
  eobiont, eolith, eosin;
  eosinophil
epaulet: see spatul
epee: see spatul
epeiro: mainland
  epeirogeny—also, epirogeny—
  movements or uplift of the earth's
  crust and producing continents,
  ocean basins, etc.
epheb-e: a young man; from *epi-*,
  upon + *hebe*, early manhood
≈epheb-e: ephebe, ephebus
≈ephebo-: ephebophilia
**ep-i-: anterior, beside, on, on the
  outside, over, upon**
≈epi-: epibenthos, epiblast,
  epiboly, epicalyx, epicanthus,
  epicardium, epicedium,
  epicene, epicenter, epicotyl,
  epicranium, epicritic, epicycle

≈epideictic, epidemic,
  epidendrum, epidermis,
  epidiascope, epididymis,
  epidote, epidural
≈epifauna, epifocal, epigastric,
  epigeal, epigene, epigenesis,
  epigenous, epiglottis, epigone,
  epigram, epigraph, epigynous
≈epilepsy, epilimnion, epilogue,
  epimere, epimysium, epinasty,
  epineurium, epiphany,
  epiphenomenon, epiphysis,
  epiphyte, epiphytotic
≈episcia, episcopal, episode,
  episome, epistasis, epistaxis,
  epistemic, episternun, epistle
≈epitaph, epitasis, epitaxy,
  epithalamium, epithelium,
  epithet, epitome, epitope,
  epizoic, epizoon
≈ep- truncation of *epi-*:
  epencephalon, ependyma,
  epenthesis, epexegesis,
  ephemeral, ephor, epoch,
  epode, eponym, epoxy
EPICUREAN: from Epicurus, who held
  that the main goal of man was the
  life of calm pleasure; thus, given
  to luxury
episio: pubic region
  episiotomy—an incision of the
  perineum, often performed during
  childbirth to prevent injury to the
  vagina
ep-o: word
  epic, epopee, epos; orthoëpy
epoch: see e-ch and ep-i
ept: from *apisci*, **to attain, pursue**
  adept: highly skilled; expert
equ-a: equal, level, even, flat
≈equ-al: equable, equal, equality
≈equat-e: equate, equation,
  equator
≈equ-: equanimity
- equal-: inequality; unequal
- equate: adequate, inadequate

≈equit: equitable, equity

≈equi-: equiangular, equilateral, equilibrium, equinox, equivocate

- equi-: disequilibrate, inequitable, inequity, inequivalve

  [variant forms: Ecuador; egalitarian; égalité; iniquitous, iniquity]

equ-i: horse

  equerry, equestrian; equine; equitant, equitation, equites; equisetum

ERA: orig., counter for calculating; now, a basis for calculating or reckoning the years from some important occurrence or given point of time

erc: to confine, enclose

  coerce, coercive, exercise, exerciser, exercitation

  [variant forms: arcane, arcanum]

eremite: see hermit

eresis: to take, grasp

  dieresis, syneresis

ergo: work

≈ergo-: ergograph, ergometer, ergonomics

- ergetic-s: energetic, energetics, hyperenergetic, inergetic, synergetic

- ergonic: exergonic

- ergu-e: exergue, energumen

- erg: energid, synergid; energize, Energizer®; synergism; hypergolic—hyper- + erg + ol

- ergon: parergon

- ergy: allergy, anergy, energy, synergy

- ure: inure

- urge: demiurge

- urgy: chemurgy, dramaturgy, liturgy, metallurgy, theurgy, zymurgy

  [variant forms: argon: from *a-*,

negative + *ergon*, work; hors d'oeuvre, surgeon, surgery]

ergot: plant disease; orig., rooster's spur

  ergot, ergotism

ERIE, PA: Huron for "place of the long-tailed wildcat"

ERISTIC: strife; controversial, wrangling

ero-t: sexual love

≈erot: erotic, erotica, eroticism

≈ero-: erogenous

≈eroto-: erotogenic, erotomania

- erotism: autoerotism, heteroerotism, homoerotism

  [variant form: pederasty]

err: to wander

≈err: err, errancy, errant; erroneous, error

≈errat: erratic, erratum, pl., errata

- errable: inerrable

- eration: aberration

- errant: aberrant, inerrant

ERRAND: messenger, mission, news

errant: see **it**, as in *itinerant*

ERSATZ: German: substitute, esp., something inferior, as oleomargarine for butter

ert: skill, art

  inert, inertia

erythr-: red

≈erythr: erythron; erythema, erythrism

≈erythr-: erythrite, erythroid

≈erythro: erythroblast, erythroblastosis, erythrocyte, erythroderma, erythromycin, erythropoiesesis, erythropoietin, erythrosine

≈erysi-: erysipelas, erysipeloid

escadrille: see quad

escalade: see scal-e

ESCARGOT: French: snail, especially, an edible snail

escence: process of beginning or becoming

  adolescence, obsolescence;

adolescent, obsolescent

eschar: scar
  eschar, escharotic
  [variant form: scar]
ESCHATOLOGY: study of last things,
  that is, death, resurrection,
  judgment, immortality
escort: see rect-i
escutcheon: see scu

esis: to throw, set in motion
  paresis, synesis

eso-: within, into
≈eso: esoteric, esoterica
≈eso-: esoneural, esotropia
espadrille, esparto: see spir
esquire: see scu

essen: to be
≈essen-tial: essence, essential,
  essentially, essentialism
- essence: quintessence
- essential: inessential,
  nonessential, quintessential
- entity: nonentity
- ent-ee: absent, absentee
≈interest: interest, interested,
  interesting
- interest-: disinterest,
  disinterested, uninterested,
  uninteresting
  [variant forms: entity, presence,
  present, pride, prosit, proud]
  [phrases: in absentia, in esse]

est: to value, appraise
≈est-im: esteem; estimate,
  estimation, estimator
- esteem: disesteem
- estimable: inestimable
- estimate: overestimate,
  underestimate

esthe: feeling
≈esthe: esthesia, esthetics
≈esthesio-: esthesiometer
- esthesia: with prefixes:
  acroesthesia, anesthesia,
  hyperesthesia, paresthesia,
  synesthesia, telesthesia

- esthesia: with combining forms:
  algesthesia, baryesthesia,
  cryptesthesia, thermanesthesia,
  thermesthesia

estrus: gadfly, frenzy
≈ester: ester
≈estr: estrus, estrone, estrous
≈estro-: estrogen, estrogenic
- estrus: anestrus, anoestrus,
  diestrus, metestrus, proestrus
ESTUARY: lit., the tide; orig., a
  boiling; akin to *estival*; see ether
ÉTAGÈRE: French for a free-standing
  set of open shelves
ET AL.: abbreviates *et alii*, and others;
  often seen in the case of multiple
  authors, with a listing of the main
  author(s), followed by *et al.*

ether: to burn
  ether, ethereal, etherize;
  etherify
  [variant forms: ester, estival,
  estivate: summer]
ETHMOID: lit., shaped like a strainer;
  designating the perforated bone or
  bones of the nasal cavity

ethn-o: nation, people
≈ethnic: ethnic, ethnicity
≈ethno-: ethnobotany,
  ethnocentrism, ethnography,
  ethnolinguistics, ethnology,
  ethnomusicology
- ethnic: interethnic, multiethnic
- ethnology: paleethnology

eth-o: character, custom
≈ethic: ethic, ethical, ethicist,
  ethics
≈etho-: ethogram, ethology,
  ethonomics
ETIOLATE: to deprive of strength; in
  botany, to bleach or blanch by
  depriving of sunlight
ETIOLOGY: the assignment of a cause,
  or the cause assigned, as the
  etiology of bluegrass music, or the
  etiology of cancer
ETIQUETTE: ticket

etymo-n: **true sense of a word**
  etymon, etymography,
  etymology
eu-: **good, pleasant**
≈eu: eucalyptus, Eucharist,
  euchromatin, euclase,
  eudemonia, eugenics,
  eukaryote, eulogia, eulogy,
  euonymus
≈eupatrid, eupepsia, eupeptic,
  euphemism, euphonious,
  euphonium, euphoria,
  euphotic, euphuism, euplastic,
  euploid, eupnea, euthanasia
≈ev-: variant of eu-: evangel,
  evangelist
EUNUCH: from Greek *eune*, bed +
  echein, to have, hold; guardian of
  a bed
EUREKA: I have found it!
eur-y-: **wide, broad**
≈eur-: euroky
≈eury-: eurybath, eurycephalic,
  euryhaline, euryhygric,
  euryphagous, euryplastic,
  eurypterid, eurytherm,
  eurytopic
- eurysm: aneurysm
ev: **age**
- eval: coeval, longeval,
  medieval, primeval
- evity: longevity
  [variant form: coetaneous]
EWE: a female sheep; see *ovine*
ex-: **out, out of, away, beyond**
≈ex-: exacerbate, exact,
  exaggerate, exalt, examine,
  example, exanimate,
  exanthem, exarch, exasperate
≈ex cathedra, excavate, exceed,
  excel, excellent, excelsior,
  except, exception, excerpt,
  excess, exchange, excide,
  excipient, excise—two
  meanings, excite

≈exclaim, exclamation, exclave,
  exclosure, exclude, exclusion,
  excogitate, excommunicate,
  excoriate, excrement,
  excrescence, excreta, excrete,
  excruciate, exculpate,
  excurrent, excursus, excursion,
  excuse
≈execrable, execrate, execute,
  exedra, exegesis, exemplar,
  exempt, exenterate, exercise,
  exergue, exert, exeunt [second
  root is **it**]
≈exfoliate, exhale, exhaust,
  exhibit, exhilarate, exhort,
  exhume, exigent, exist, exit,
  exodontics, exodus, exonerate,
  exophthalmos, exorable,
  exorbitant, exorcise
≈expand, expanse, expatriate,
  expect, expectorate, expedient,
  expedite, expel, expend,
  expense, experience, expert,
  expiate, expire, explain,
  explant, expletive, explicit,
  explode, exploit, explore,
  exponent, export, expose,
  expound, express, expropriate,
  expulsion, expunge, expurgate
≈exquisite, exsanguine, exscind,
  exsect, exsert, exsiccate,
  exstipulate, exstrophy, extant,
  extemporaneous, extend,
  extenuate, exterminate, extinct,
  extirpate, extol, extort, extract,
  extradite, extricate, extrude,
  extubate, exuberant, exude,
  exult, exurb, exuviate
≈e-: truncation of *ex-*: ebullient,
  eclosion, ecru, edentate, editor,
  educate, egregious, egress,
  ejaculate, eject, elegant,
  eliminate, elocution, elope,
  eloquent, elucicate, elusion,
  elute, eluvial, eluviate

≈emaciate, emanate, emancipate,
  emarginate, emasculate,
  emend, emerge, emergency,
  emeritus, emigrate, eminent,
  emissary, emission, emit,
  emollient, emolument,
  emotion, emulsion, emunctory
≈enervate, enormity, enormous,
  enucleate, enumerate,
  enunciate, eradicate, eructate,
  erudite, erumpent, eruption
≈especial, establish, estate,
  evacuate, evade, evaginate,
  evaluate, evanesce, evaporate,
  evasion, evection, event, evert,
  evict, evident, evince,
  eviscerate, evocation,
  evolution, evolve, evulsion
≈ec-: assimilation of *ex-*: eccentric,
  ecchymosis, ecclesia, eccrine
≈ec-: variant of *ex-*: ecbolic,
  ecdysis, eclampsia, eclectic,
  eclipse, eclogue, ecstasy,
  ectopia, ectype
≈ef-: assimilation of *ex-*: efface,
  effect, effeminate, efferent,
  effervesce, effete, efficacious,
  efficacy, efficient, effigy,
  effloresce, effluent, effluvium,
  efflux, effort, effulgent,
  effusive
≈es-: variation of *ex-*: escape,
  escapee, escapement,
  escapism, escapist, escapology
exert: see s-er-t
exo-: outside, outer, outer part
≈exot: exoteric, exotic, exotica
≈exo-: exobiology, exocarp,
  exocentric, exocrine,
  exocytosis, exogamy,
  exogenous, exopathic,
  exoskeleton, exosphere,
  exospore, exotoxin
≈exter-n: exterior, exteriority,
  exteriorize; extern, external

≈extero-: exteroceptor
**extr-a-: additional, besides,
  beyond, more than, outside;**
  from *exo-*
≈extr-a: extra, extraneous,
  extreme, extremity, extremum,
  extrinsic
≈extra-: extracanonical,
  extracurricular, extrados,
  extragalactic, extrajudicial,
  extralegal
≈extramarital, extramundane,
  extramural, extranuclear,
  extraordinary, extrapolate,
  extrasensory, extrasystole
≈extraterrestrial, extraterritorial,
  extravagant, extravaganza,
  extravasate, extravascular
≈extro-: extroversion, extrovert
  [variant forms: strange, stranger,
  estrange]
  [phrase: in extremis]
expatiate: see spac-e

F

fab: to speak
≈fabl-e: fable, fabled, fabliau, pl.,
  fabliaux
≈fabul: fabular, fabulist, fabulous
- fable: affable, ineffable
- fabulate: confabulate
- face: preface
≈fam-e: fame, famous, famously
- fam-e: defamation, defamatory,
  defame, infamous, infamy
- fancy: infancy
- fant-: infant, infanta, infantile,
  infantilism, infantilize,
  infantine, infantry
- fanticide: infanticide
≈fat-e: fatal, fatalism, fatality,
  fatally, fate, fated, fateful
≈fati-: fatidic

- fess-: confess, profess
- fessed: confessed, professed
- fession: confession, profession
- fessional: confessional, professional
- fessor: confessor, professor
  [variant forms: fado, fay, fairy]
  [phrase: confessio fidei]

FABACEOUS: of the legume order of plants; leguminous

fabric: workman
  fabric, fabricate, fabrication
  [variant form: forge—one meaning]

fac-e: to do, make
≈fac-e: façade, face, facet
≈faci: facial, facies, facing
≈facil-e: facile, facilitate, facility
≈facul: facultative, faculty
- faceable: ineffaceable
- faceted: multifaceted
≈fac-: facsimile, factotum
- face: deface, efface, interface, surface, subsurface
- facial: with prefixes: bifacial, hemifacial, interfacial, trifacial
- facial: with combining forms: basifacial, brachyfacial, craniofacial, dentofacial, dolichofacial
- facient: febrifacient, parturifacient, rubefacient, stupefacient, tumefacient
≈fact: fact, facticity, faction, factional, factious, factitious, factitive
≈factor-y: factor, factory
≈factu: factual, facture
≈fact-: factoid
- faction: with prefixes: benefaction, malefaction
- faction: with combining forms: calefaction, lubrifaction, olfaction, patefaction, petrifaction, putrefaction,

satisfaction, stupefaction, tumefaction
- factor: benefactor, malefactor
- factory: calefactory, olfactory
- facture: manufacture
≈fashion: fashion, fashionable
≈feas: feasance, feasible
- feasance: defeasance, malfeasance, misfeasance, nonfeasance
- feasible: defeasible, infeasible, indefeasible
- feasor: tortfeasor
≈feat: feat, feature
- feat-: defeat, defeature, disfeature
≈feck: feckless, fecklessly, fecklessness
- fect: affect, confect, defect, disaffect, disinfect, effect, imperfect, infect, perfect, prefect
- fect-: effectuate, infectious, pluperfect
- fecta: superfecta, trifecta
- fectation: affectation
- fected: affected, defected, infected, perfected
- fectible: indefectible, perfectible
- fection: affection, confection, infection, perfection, refection, transfection
- fectionary: confectionary
- fective: affective, effective, infective, ineffective, perfective
- fector-y: effector; refectory
- fectual: effectual, ineffectual
- fectuate: effectuate
- fecture: prefecture
- feit: counterfeit, forfeit, surfeit
≈fetish: fetish, fetishism, fetishize: charm, sorcery
- fiable: falsifiable, verifiable

- fic: algific, beatific, calorific,
  deific, febrific, honorific,
  malefic, morbific, prolific,
  salvific, scientific, somnific,
  soporific, specific, sudorific,
  terrific, torporific, vaporific
- fic-: deficit, difficult, officer,
  officiant, officiate
- ficant: clarificant, significant,
  insignificant
- ficacy: efficacy, inefficacy
- ficacious: efficacious,
  inefficacious
- ficate: certificate, pontificate
- fication: gratification,
  magnification, mortification,
  nullification, pacification,
  personification, ramification,
  saponification, scarification,
  specification, stratification,
  verification, versification,
  vinification
- fice: with prefixes: benefice,
  office, suffice
- fice: with combining forms:
  edifice, orifice, sacrifice
- ficence: beneficence,
  magnificence, munificence
- ficent: beneficent, magnificent,
  maleficent, munificent
- ficial: artificial, beneficial,
  official, superficial
- ficiary: beneficiary, officiary
- ficiency: deficiency, efficiency,
  sufficiency
- ficient: deficient, efficient,
  proficient, sufficient;
  inefficient, insufficient
- ficies: superficies
- ficile: difficile
- ficious: officious, inofficious
- ficity: specificity
- fier: pacifier, versifier
- fit: benefit, comfit, discomfit,
  retrofit

- fiture: discomfiture
- fy: acidify, alacrify, amplify,
  beatify, calefy, carnify, casefy,
  certify, citify, clarify, classify,
  codify, crucify
≈damnify, deify, diversify,
  dignify, dulcify, edify,
  etherify, electrify, exemplify,
  falsify, fortify, fructify
≈gentrify, glorify, gratify,
  horrify, humidify, identify,
  indemnify, intensify, justify,
  lapidify, lignify, liquefy, lithify
≈magnify, metrify, modify,
  mollify, mortify, mystify,
  nidify, nigrify, notify, nullify,
  objectify, opsonify, ossify
≈pacify, personify, putrify,
  qualify, quantify, ramify,
  rarefy, ratify, rectify, reify,
  reunify, revivify, rigidify
≈salify, sanctify, saponify,
  satisfy, scarify, signify,
  silicify, simplify, solemnify,
  solidify, specify, stratify,
  stultify, stupefy, syllabify
≈tepefy, terrify, testify, torrefy,
  tumefy, typify, unify, verify,
  versify, vilify, vinify, vivify
  [variant forms: confetti, affair,
  fiat, parfait; Spanish: aficionado,
  hacienda]
  [phrases: facile princeps, fait
  accompli, au fait, prima facie;
  ex officio, ex post facto, ipso
  facto; laissez faire, savoir
  faire; de facto, scire facias, venire
  facias; quod erat faciendum]
FACETIOUS: joking or trying to be
  jocular, especially at inappropriate
  times; facetiae: rare for "witty
  sayings"
FACULAE: plural use; bright areas
  visible on the surface of the sun,
  especially near its edge; akin to
  facetious, which see

FAHRENHEIT: from Gabriel Daniel
Fahrenheit (1686-1736), a German
physicist resident in Holland
fail: see fall
fain: joyful, glad
fain; fawn—one meaning
faith: see fid
falc-i: sickle
≈falc: falcate, falcular, falchion
≈falci-: falciform
- falcate: defalcate
[Note: By folk etymology, *falcon* is
associated with this family
because of its curved beak and
talons.]
fall: to deceive
≈fall: fallacious, fallacy, fallible
- fallible: infallible
≈false: false, falsetto; falsehood
≈falsi-: falsifiable, falsify
≈fail: fail, failing, failure
≈fault: fault, faulty
- fault: default
≈fraud: fraud, fraudulent
- fraud: defraud
    [variant forms: faubourg, faucet,
    faux, frustrate]
    [phrases: faux-naïf, faux pas]
{word note: falsehood: orig., referred
    to an uneducated or lay person
    wearing the hood of the medical
    profession; an untruth, a lie}
FALLOPIAN tubes: after Gabriele
Fallopio, 16th-c. anatomist
falque: scaffold, wooden tower
    [see pulpit]
    catafalque—a wooden frame-
    work, usually draped, on which
    the body in a coffin lies in state
    during an elaborate funeral
    [variant forms: scaffold,
    scaffolding]
fam: hunger
    famine, famish
famil-y: family establishment
≈famil-y: familial, familiar,
    family

- familiar-: defamiliarize;
    unfamiliar
- family: subfamily, superfamily
    [variant forms: materfamilias,
    paterfamilias]
    [phrase: en famille]
fan: see phaner-o
fan-e: temple
≈fan: fan—one meaning, fane,
    fanatic, fanatical
- fan-e: profanation, profane,
    profanity
FARAD: from Michael Faraday,
    (1791-1867), English scientist; the
    basic unit of electric capacitance
farce: see frequen-t
FARDEL: from Arabic *fardah*, bundle;
    has come to mean "burden." "Who
    would *fardels* bear,/To grunt and
    sweat under a weary life."
    Shakespeare
farious: of divine law, possible
    bifarious, multifarious,
    nefarious, octofarious,
    omnifarious, plurifarious,
    quinquefarious, trifarious
farin: grain
    farina, farinaceous, farinose;
    farraginous, farrago;
    confarreation
fasc: a band, sash, bundle
    fasces, fascia, pl., fasciae, or
    fascias, fasciate, fasciation,
    fascicle, fasciulate, fasciculus,
    fascine, fascism, fascist
    [variant form: fess, or fesse]
fascin: to bewitch, charm, enchant
    fascinate, fascination,
    fascinator
fast: a loathing, disgust
    fastidious, fastuous
fastigi: a slope, roof
    fastigiate, fastigium
FATHOM: lit., stretched out; two arms
    outstretched to embrace; a unit of
    length (six feet) to measure the
    depth of water

fatig: to weary, tire
  fatigable, fatigue, fatigues;
  indefatigable
fatu: empty, foolish
  fatuity, fatuous; infatuate,
  infatuated
  [variant form: fade]
fauc: throat, gullet
  faucal, fauces
  [variant form: suffocate]
faun-a: animals of an area; from
  Latin Fauna, sister of Faunus,
  Roman god of animals and crops
  fauna; avifauna, epifauna,
  macrofauna, microfauna
  [variant form: fauvism]
fav-eol: honeycomb
  favella, faveolate, favus;
  faviform
fav-or: to favor
  favor, favorable, favored,
  favorite, favoritism; disfavor
  [variant form: favonian;
   Spanish: por favor]
febr: fever
≈febr: febricity, febrile
≈febri-: febrifacient, febriferous,
  febrific, febrifuge
- febrile: afebrile, antifebrile
  [variant form: fever;
   Spanish: fiebre]
fec: grounds, dregs
≈fec: fecal, feces
≈fecul: feculence, feculent
≈fecul-: fecaloid
- fecate: defecate
fecund: fertile
  fecund, fecundate, fecundation,
  fecundity
  infecund, superfecundation
fee: property
≈fee: fee; feoff, feoffe; fee
  simple, fee tail
≈feud: feud—one meaning,
  feudal, feudalism, feudality,
  feudatory

- feudation: infeudation
  [variant form: fellow]
{word note: fellow: from Old
  English *feolaga*, partner; lit., a
  laying down of wealth for a joint
  undertaking}
feeble: weak; orig., "to be wept
  over"
  feeble; enfeeble
  [variant form: foible]
feli: cat
  felid, feline
felic: happy
≈felicit-y: felicitate, felicitous,
  felicity
≈felici-: felicific
- felici-: infelicitous, infelicity
  [Spanish: feliz; feliz Navidad]
fellat-e: to suck
  fellate, fellatio, fellator,
  fellatrice
FELLUCA: from Arabic *fulk*, ship
felon: villain
  felon, felonious, felonry,
  felony
  [variant form: fell—one
  meaning]
fem-in: female
≈fem-in: female; feminine,
  feminism, feminize
- femin: effeminacy, effeminate
  [phrases: feme covert, feme sole,
   femme de chambre, femme fatale]
FEMUR: thigh; pl., femurs, or femora;
  the largest, longest, and heaviest
  bone in the body, extending from
  the hip to the knee
fend: to strike
≈fend: fend, fender
- fend: defend, offend
- fend-: defendant, defender,
  codefendant
- fense: defense, offense
- fenseless: defenseless,
  offenseless
- fensible-: defensible,
  indefensible, offensible

- fensive: defensive, offensive,
  inoffensive
  [variant form: fence]

fenestra: window
  fenestra, fenestrated,
  fenestration; defenestration

FENNEL: lit., little hay; diminutive of
  Latin *fenum*, hay

fer: wild
  feral, ferity, ferocity, ferocious
  [variant form: fierce]
  [phrase: ferae naturae]

fer-e: to bear, carry [see lat-e]
≈fere: feretory
≈fertil-e: fertile, fertility,
  fertilize, fertilizer
- fer-: Lucifer, offertory,
  preferment; sufferance
- fering: offering, suffering
- fer: with prefixes: confer, defer,
  differ, infer, offer, prefer,
  proffer, refer, suffer, transfer
- fer: with combining form: conifer
- fera: vinifera
- ferable: insufferable, preferable,
  sufferable
- ferate: proliferate, vociferate
- feree: referee
- ferendum: referendum
- ferent-: differentia,
  differentiate, indifferentism;
  differentiable
- ference: circumference,
  conference, difference,
  indifference, inference,
  preference, reference,
  teleconference, transference
- ferent: afferent, different,
  efferent, indifferent, referent
- ferential: deferential,
  differential, inferential,
  preferential, referential,
  transferential
- ferral: conferral, deferral,
  referral, transferral

- ferous: carboniferous,
  celliferous, cheliferous,
  coniferous, crystalliferous,
  cupriferous
≈febriferous, gemmiferous,
  graniferous, lactiferous,
  laniferous, luciferous,
  luminiferous
≈mammiferous, melliferous,
  metaliferous, muciferous,
  odoriferous, ossiferous,
  oviferous
≈piliferous, pestiferous,
  pomiferous, poriferous
≈saliferous, sebiferous,
  seminiferous, setiferous,
  siliciferous, somniferous,
  soniferous, soporiferous,
  spiriferous, splendiferous
≈umbelliferous, umbriferous,
  uriniferous, viniferous,
  vociferous
- fertile: antifertile, infertile,
  interfertile
  [variant form: furtive]
  [medical term: vas deferens]

fer-e: to strike
  interfere, interference;
  interferometer, interferon

ferment: to boil
  ferment, fermentation,
  fermentative

ferr: iron
≈ferr: ferreous, ferric, ferrite,
  ferritin, ferrous
≈ferri-: ferricyanic, ferriferous,
  ferriprive
≈ferru: ferruginous, ferrule
- fer-r-: pedalfer; nonferrous
  [variant form: farrier]

ferul: stick, whip, rod
  ferula, ferule

ferv: to glow, boil
≈ferv: fervency, fervent, fervid,
  fervor

- fervesc-e: defervescence,
  effervesce, effervescent
- fervid: perfervid
  [variant forms: comfrey, ferment]
fest: **to attack**
  infest, manifest
festin: **to hurry**
  festinate, festination
fest-iv-e: **joyful**
  festal, festoon
  festival, festive, festivity
  [variant forms: feast; fete, or fête,
  Italian: festa; Spanish: fiesta;
  French: fête champêtre]
FETID: stinking
fet-a: **slice, ribbon**
  feta; fettuccini
fet-e: **productive; fetus**
≈fet: fetal, fetus
≈feti-: feticide, fetiparous
≈feto-: fetology, fetoscope
- fet-e: effete, superfetation
  [variant form: fawn—one
  meaning]
FETTUCINE: Italian: lit., small
  ribbons; a form of pasta
feud: see fee
FIASCO: lit., flask; from Italian *far
  fiasco*, to make a bottle; complete
  failure, possibly from one's
  nipping the bottle excessively
fiber: **fiber**
≈fiber: fiber
- fiber: interfiber, microfiber,
  myofiber, neofiber, unifiber
≈fibr: fibrin, fibrinous, fibrous
≈fibr-: fibroid, fibrosis, fibroma
≈fibril: fibril, fibrilar, fibrillation
- fibril: myofibril, neurofibril,
  protofibril
- fibrillate: defibrillate
≈fibrino-: fibrinogenic,
  fibrinolysis
≈fibro-: fibroblast, fibrocyte
≈fimbria: fimbria, fimbriate,
  fimbriation

fict: **to form, mold, devise**
≈ficti: fictile, fictitious, fictive
≈fiction: fiction, fictional,
  fictionalize
- fiction: metafiction
≈figment: figment
≈figur-e: figural, figurant,
  figurative, figurine; figure
- figure: configure, disfigure,
  prefigure, transfigure
- figuration: configuration,
  prefiguration, transfiguration
- figy: effigy
  [variant forms: fainéant, faint,
  feign, feigned, feint, lady, traffic]
- fid: see fiss for bifid
fid: **to trust**
≈fide: fideism, fidelity
≈fiduci: fiducial, fiduciary
≈fiance-e: fiancé, fiancée
- fian-ce: defiance, defiant
- fid-e: affidavit, confidant,
  confidante, confide, confident,
  confidential, confiding,
  nullifidian, perfidious, perfidy
- fidel: infidel, infidelity
- fidence: confidence, diffidence,
  self-confidence
- fident: confident, diffident,
  overconfident
≈federa-l: federal, federate,
  federative
- feder-: confederacy, confederal,
  confederate, confederation,
  confederative
≈faith: faith, faithful, faithless
- faith: interfaith, unfaithful
  [variant forms: fealty, affiance,
  defy]
  [phrases: bona fide, bona fides, de
  fide, confessio fidei; auto-da-fe,
  Portuguese for "act of faith";
  Santa Fe, capital of New Mexico;
  semper fidelis: always faithful;
  motto of the United States
  Marine Corps]

fiend: **hate**; orig., to harm
  fiend, fiendish
figure: see fict
fil-e[1]: **line, thread**
≈fil: filament, filar, filaria,
  filature, filose, filum
≈fil-e: file—one meaning, filé,
  filet, or fillet (for some meanings)
- filade: defilade, enfilade
- filament: monofilament
- filar: bifilar, unifilar
- file: defile—one meaning,
  profile
≈fili-: filiform, filigree
≈filo-: filopodium
  [variant form: purfle]
fil-e[2]: **to make foul**
  file—one meaning, defile—one
  meaning
fili: **son, daughter**
≈fil: filial, filiation
- filial: unfilial
- filiate: affiliate, disaffiliate
  [phrase: fille de joie]
film: **membrane, foreskin**
  film, filmic, filmy, microfilm;
  film noir
filt-r: **to filter, strain**
  filter, filterable; filtrate;
  infiltrate
  [variant form: felt: the material;
  orig., used to strain or filter liquor]
fin-e: **to end, limit; boundary**
≈fin-e: finable, finance, financial,
  financier, fine, finely, finesse,
  fining
≈final: final, finale, finalist,
  finality, finalize, finally
≈fini: finial, finical, finicky
≈finis: finis, finish, finished
≈finit-e: finite, finito, finitude
- fin-: indefinable, refinance,
  infinitesimal
- fine: confine, define, refine,
  superfine

- fine-ry: confinement,
  refinement, refinery
- finish: refinish
- finite: definite, indefinite,
  infinite, transfinite
- finition: definition
- finity: affinity, infinity
- finitive: definitive, infinitive
- finitude: infinitude
  [variant forms: refiné, traffic]
  [phrases: ad finem, ad infinitum,
  in fin, fin de siècle, fines herbes,
  fini]
FINGERHUT: German; lit., finger hat;
  thimble
firm: **strong**
≈firm: firm, firmament
- firm: affirm, confirm, disaffirm,
  disconfirm, infirm
- firm-: confirmed, confirmation,
  confirmatory, infirmary,
  infirmity
  [variant forms: fermata, farm;
  Spanish: firma— signature]
  [phrases: cantus firmus, terra
  firma]
fisc: **money basket, public
  treasury**
  fisc, fiscal, fiscalist;
  confiscable, confiscate
fiss: **to cleave, split**
≈fiss: fissile, fission, fissure
≈fissi-: fissipalmate, fissiparous,
  fissiped
- fid: bifid, multifid, palmatifid,
  pentafid, quadrifid, quinquefid,
  octofid, septemfid, sexfid,
  trifid
  [variant form: vent—one meaning]
fistul: **pipe, tube, ulcer**
  fistula, fistulous
fix: **to fasten, attach**
≈fix: fix, fixate, fixation, fixative,
  fixed, fixer, fixity, fixture
- fix: affix, antefix, infix, prefix,
  suffix, transfix

[variant forms: dike, fibula, fichu,
microfiche, fishplate, soffit]
[phrases: idée fixe, prix fixe]
flabell: a fan; from "breeze"; from
"to blow"
flabellate, flabellum
[variant form: flageolet]
FLACCID: lacking force or firmness,
as flaccid muscles
flagell-i: **to whip**
≈flagell: flagellant, flagellate,
flagellation, flagellin,
flagellum
≈flagelli-: flagelliform
- flagellate: dinoflagellate,
hemoflagellate,
phytoflagellate, zooflagellate
[variant forms: flagitious, flail,
flog]
flagrant: see flam-e
FLAK: acronym for German
Fliegerabwehrkanone, antiaircraft
guns, lit., cannons
flam-e: **flame, to burn**
≈flam-e: flame, flaming
≈flamb: flambé, flambeau,
flamboyant
- flame: aflame, inflame
≈flamm: flammable
- flamm-: inflammable,
inflammation, inflammatory
≈flagr: flagrancy, flagrant
- flagr-: conflagrant,
conflagration, deflagrate
[phrase: in flagrante delicto]
FLAMENCO: Spanish; lit., Flemish;
the Spanish gypsy style of dance,
characterized by clapping,
dancing, or music very emotional
and mournful
FLAMINGO: Portuguese: lit.,
flamenco: a large tropical bird
with long legs, and bright pink or
red feathers; associated with _flame_
because of its color; see _flamenco_
flat-e: **to blow**
≈flat: flatulence, flatulent, flatus

- flat-: afflatus, inflated,
inflationary
- flate: conflate, deflate, inflate,
reflate, sufflate, insufflate
- flation: conflation, deflation,
disinflation, inflation, reflation
≈flavor: flavor, flavorful [an odor;
from "to blow"]
[variant forms: flageolate, flute,
soufflé]
FLAUNT: to make a gaudy,
ostentatious, conspicuous,
impudent, or defiant display;
see _flout_
flav-on: **yellow**
flavanone, flavescent, flavin,
flavine, flavone, flavonoid
flavor: see flat-e
flect: **to bend**
≈flect: flection
- flect-: inflectional; reflectance,
reflector
- flect: with prefixes: circumflect,
deflect, inflect, reflect
- flect: with combining form:
genuflect
- flection: deflection, inflection,
reflection
- flective: deflective, inflective,
reflective
≈flex: flex, flexible, flexile,
flexion, flexor, flexuous,
flexure
- flex-: circumflex, reflex,
retroflex
- flexed: deflexed, inflexed
- flexible: inflexible
- flexion: with prefixes:
anteflexion, circumflexion,
deflexion, hyperflexion,
inflexion, introflexion,
reflexion
- flexion: with combining form:
dorsiflexion, genuflexion
- flexive: reflexive

FLEDGE: to grow feathers necessary
for flying; to fit an arrow with
with feathers; FLEDGLING: a young
bird just fledged; a young,
inexperienced person

fletch: **arrow**
fletch, fletcher
[variant forms: flèche, fléchette]

flict: **to strike**
afflict, conflict, conflicted,
conflictual, inflict
[variant form: profligate]

floc-c: **wool**
floc, floccose, floccus;
flocculant, flocculate, floccule,
flocculent, flocculus
[variant forms: flock, floss]

flor: **flower** [from Flora, goddess of
flowers]
≈flor: flora, floral, florescence,
floriated, florid, Florida, florin,
florist, floristics
≈flori-: floribunda, floriculture,
floriferous, florigen,
florilegium
- flora: albiflora, grandiflora,
microflora, multiflora,
passiflora
- floresc-e: effloresce,
efflorescent, inflorescence
- florous: biflorous,
geminiflorous, noctiflorous,
radiciflorous, ramiflorous,
triflorous, tubuliflorous,
uniflorous
≈flower: flower, flowerage,
flowered, flowery
- flower: deflower
[variant forms: ferret—one
meaning; fioritura; fleur-de-lis,
enfleurage, flirt, flirtation,
flirtatious, flirty; flourish;
cauliflower]
{word note: Florida: in Spanish,
"abounding in flowers"; so named
by Ponce de Leon, who discovered
Florida during the springtime

while searching for the Fountain
of Youth}

FLOUT: orig., to play the flute; to
mock and scoff at; show scorn or
contempt; compare with *flaunt*

flot: **to float**
flotage, flotation, flotilla,
flotsam
[variant forms: fleet, float,
floater, floating]
[phrase: flotsam and jetsam]

flu-c: **to flow**
≈flu: fluctuate; fluency, fluent,
fluid, fluidics
- fluction: solifluction
- fluen-: confluence, influence,
influential, influenza
- fluent: affluent, confluent,
effluent, influent, profluent,
refluent
- fluous: mellifluous, superfluous
≈fluor: fluor, fluoresce,
fluorescence, fluorescent
- fluoro-: photofluorography
≈fluv: fluvial, fluviatile
- fluv-e: effluvium, interfluve
≈flux: flux, fluxion
- flux: afflux, conflux, efflux,
influx, reflux
[variant forms: flue, flume]

FLUMMERY: Welsh *llymru*, lit.,
soured oatmeal; any easily eaten
food; also, meaningless flattery or
silly talk

FM: in *radio*, stands for *frequency
modulation*; see AM

foc-us: **fireplace**; thus, the center
≈foc: focal, focus, pl., foci
≈foci-: focimeter
- focal-s: with prefixes: afocal,
bifocals, confocal, epifocal,
perifocal, trifocal, unifocal
- focal: with combining form:
matrifocal, parfocal, patrifocal,
varifocal
- focus-: autofocus, unfocused

[variant forms: foyer, fuel, fusil—
one meaning, fusilier, fusileer,
fusillade, curfew, locofoco]

fold: **to fold**
manifold, multifold

foli-o: **leaf**
≈foli: foliaceous, foliage, foliate,
foliation, folium
≈folio: folio, foliolate, foliose
- foliate: acutifoliate,
brevifoliate, defoliate,
exfoliate, infoliate, interfoliate,
perfoliate, trifoliate, unifoliate
- folio: portfolio
- foliolate: quinquefoliolate,
trifoliolate, unifoliolate
- folium: trifolium
[variant forms: foil—one of three
meanings; cinquefoil, counter-
foil, milfoil, quatrefoil, trefoil;
feuilleton, mille-feuille]

foll: **small bag, sac**; orig. "bellows,
windbag"
follicle, folly; fool

foment: **to keep warm**
foment, fomentation
fondue: see fuse²

for-: **away, apart**
forbear, forbearance, forbid,
fordo, fordone, forfend, forget,
forgive, forgo
≈for-: **intensive**
forlorn—from Old English
forleosan, to lose utterly;
abandoned or deserted; without
hope; desperate

for¹: **warm**
forceps—orig., smith's tongs;
from *formus*, warm + *capere*, to
take; tongs or pincers for grasping,
compressing, and pulling, used
especially by surgeons and
dentists

for²: **outdoors, outside** [see hors]
≈for: foreign, forensic, forest,
forum
≈for-: forfeit, forfeiture

- forest: afforest, deforest,
disafforest
[variant forms: faubourg,
foreclose, forejudge—one
meaning, hors d'oeuvre,
farouche]

fora¹: **a hole, opening; to bore**
≈fora: foramen
- forat-e: perforate, perforated,
perforation, perforative,
imperforate
- forium: triforium
[variant form: bore]

fora²: **fodder, food**
forage, foray

ford: **to further**
afford; affordable

fore: **before in time, place, order,
or rank**; also, **the front part**
forearm—two meanings,
forebear, forebode, foreboding,
forebrain, forecast, forecastle,
forecheck, foredoom,
forefront, forego, foregone,
foreground, forehand,
forehead, forejudge—one
meaning, foreknowledge,
foreman, forename, forenoon,
foreordain, foreplay, forerun,
foresail, foresee, foreshadow,
foresight, forespeak, forestall,
forestay, foretaste, foretell,
forethought, foretoken,
foretooth, foretop, forewarn,
foreword
[NB: foreclose—see for²]
forge: see fabric

form¹: **figure, form, image, shape**
≈form: form, formal, formalism,
formality, formalize, formant,
formless
≈format: format, formation,
formative
≈formul-a: formula, formulary,
formulate, formulism,
formulize

- form: with prefixes: conform,
  deform, inform, microform,
  multiform, reform, transform,
  triform, uniform
- form: with combining forms:
  acinaciform, anguilliform,
  celliform, cheliform,
  cumuliform, cuneiform,
  curviform, deiform, libriform,
  linguiform, moniliform,
  oviform, pelviform, piliform,
  pisiform, plexiform, ramiform,
  retiform, salverform,
  scalariform, scutiform,
  setiform, stelliform, stratiform,
  umbiliform, ursiform,
  variform, vermiform,
  vitriform, vulviform
- form-: conformable, informant,
  informative, informed,
  reformatory
- formal: conformal, informal
- formation: conformation,
  deformation, disinformation,
  information, malformation,
  preformation, reformation,
  transformation
- former: informer, reformer,
  transformer
- formity: conformity, deformity,
  disconformity, inconformity,
  unconformity, uniformity
  [variant form: firmer—a
  carpenter's tool]
  [phrase: pro forma]

form²: to accomplish, furnish
  perform, performance,
  performative
  [variant forms: furnish, furniture;
  veneer—see separate entry]
FORMICARY: an anthill or ants' nest
FORMIDABLE: dreadful

forni: sexual immorality; also, an
  arch, vault
  fornicate—two meanings,
  fornication, fornix

FORSYTHIA: after William Forsyth
  (1737-1804), English botanist; a
  bush with bright-yellow flowers,
  that blooms in early spring

fort-i: strong
≈fort: fort, forte, fortress
≈forti: fortis, fortissimo, fortitude
≈forti-: fortification, fortify
- fort: comfort, counterfort,
  discomfort, effort
- fortable: comfortable,
  discomfortable, uncomfortable
≈forc-e: force, forced, forceful,
  forcible
- force: deforce, enforce,
  perforce, reinforce
- forciant: deforciant
  [variant forms: forzando,
  sforzando—music terms]
  [phrases: a fortiori, force
  majeure]
{word note: comfort: to make strong;
  to strengthen much}
FORTNIGHT: a period of fourteen
  nights; two weeks

fortu: chance
≈fortu: fortuitous, fortuity
≈fortun-e: fortunate, fortune
- fortunate: unfortunate
- fortune: misfortune

foss-il-i: ditch, dig
≈foss: foss, fossa, fosse, fossette,
  fossorial; fossulate
≈fossil: fossil, fossilize
≈fossili-: fossiliferous
- fossil: macrofossil, microfossil,
  pseudofossil, subfossil
  [variant forms: fovea, foveola:
  small pit, hollow]

fount: a spring of water
  fount, fountain; font, fontanel
foyer: see foc-us

frac-t: to break
≈frac-t: fracas, fractal, fraction,
  fractional, fractionate,
  fractious, fracture, fractus

- fract-o-: anfractuous,
  refractometer
- fract: diffract, infract, refract
- fraction: diffraction, infraction,
  refraction
- fractory: refractory
≈frag: fragile, fragility, fragment,
  fragmental, fragmentate
- frag-: irrefragable, suffragan,
  suffragist; septifragal
- frage: ossifrage, saxifrage,
  suffrage
≈frang: frangent, frangible
- frangible: infrangible,
  refrangible, irrefrangible
- fring-e: infringe; refringent
  [variant forms: defray; frail,
  fricassee, frivol, frivolity,
  frivolous, osprey; refrain—
  one meaning, sassafras]
  [NB: *Fringe* itself is not in this
  family; the word comes from
  Latin *fimbriae*, shreds, fibers]
fragr: to smell
  fragrance, fragrant
  [variant form: flair]
frain: rein
  refrain—one meaning: to hold
  back; keep oneself (from doing
  something); abstain, forbear; see
  fract for another *refrain*
franch: free
  franchise; affranchise,
  disfranchise, enfranchise,
  disenfranchise
  [variant forms: frank, franklin,
  frankpledge]
frang: see frac-t for frangible
FRANTIC:frenetic:phrenetic
frater: brother
≈frater: frater, fraternal,
  fraternity, fraternize
≈fratri-: fratricide
- fraternity: confraternity,
  interfraternity
  [variant forms: confrere, friar,
  friary]

fraud: see fall
fray: from Germanic *frith*, peace
  affray [see frac-t for defray]
  [*af-* is derived from *ex-*, out of]
frenu-m: bridle
  frenulum, frenum
  [variant form: chamfron]
frenzy: see frenetic
frequen-t: to stuff, repeated
  frequency, frequent,
  frequentation, frequentative;
  infrequent
  [variant forms: farce, farceur,
  farcical; infarct]
fric: to rub
≈fric: fricative, friction
- fricate: affricate
- frice: dentifrice
- friction: affriction, antifriction
  [variant forms: frayed, frazzle;
  friable: crumbly]
FRIDAY: from Frigg, wife of Odin,
  and the Old Norse goddess of love
frig: cold
  frigid; frigorific; refrigerant,
  refrigerate, refrigerator
FRIGATE: Italian *fregata*; a sailing ship
fringe: see frac-t for infringe
FRISSON: French; a shudder or shiver,
  as of delight or excitement
frond: leaf
  frond, frondent, frondescence,
  frondose
front-i: forehead, front
≈front: front, frontage, frontal,
  frontier, frontlet, fronton
≈fronti-: frontispiece
≈fronto-: frontogenesis,
  frontolysis, frontopalatal,
  frontoparietal
- front-: affront, confront,
  effrontery, forefront, prefrontal
  [variant form: frons]
{word note: frontispiece: with
  specere, to look, the front of a
  church; orig., the first page, esp.
  the title page of a book; in

architecture, the main façade; a pediment over a door, window}

FRONT ROYAL, VA: During the Civil War, a sergeant, weary from trying to assemble the newly mustered troops, ordered them "to front the royal oak," which stood in the town square.

fruct-i: fruit, enjoyment

≈fruct: fructiculose, fructose, fructuous

≈fructi-: fructiferous, fructify, fructivorous

- fruct-: usufruct, usufructuary

≈frugi-: frugiferous, frugivorous
  [variant forms: frugal; fruit, fruitage, fruition, fruity; Spanish: disfrutar—to enjoy]

frument: grain

frumentaceous, frumentarious, frumentation, frumenty

frustu: a bit, piece

frustule, frustum

frut: shrub

≈frut: frutescent, fruticant, fruticose, fruticous

- fruticose: suffruticose

FUCHSIA: from L. Fuchs (1501-66), German botanist; a flower

[Note: Most names of flowers ending in –ia and –ea honor their discoverer. Known exceptions: azalea, hydrangea, petunia]

fug-e: to flee

≈fug: fugacious, fugal, fugitive, fugue

- fugal: axifugal, basifugal, calcifugal, centrifugal, corticifugal, febrifugal

- fuge: with prefixes: refuge, subterfuge

- fuge: with combining forms: aquifuge, arthrifuge, calcifuge, febrifuge, vermifuge

- fugous: nidifugous, somnifugous

- fug-: refugee, refugium

FULCRUM: bedpost, support

fulg-ur: to shine

≈fulg-ur: fulgent, fulgurate, fulgurating, fulgurous

- fulg-ent: effulgence; effulgent, refulgent
  [variant form: foudroyant]

FULIGINOUS: full of smoke or soot; dark, dusky

fulmin: lightning

fulminant, fulminate

fulv: yellow

fulvene, fulvous, fulvescent

fum-e: to blow, smoke

≈fum-e: fumarole, fume, fumitory

≈fumig-: fumigant, fumigate

- fum-e: perfume, perfumer, perfumery

- fumigate: suffumigate

funct-ion: to perform

≈funct: function, functional, functionalism, functionary

- funct-ion: defunct, malfunction

- functional: dysfunctional

- functory: perfunctory
  [variant form: fungible]

fund-a: bottom

≈fund: fund, fundament, fundamental, fundus—in anatomy, the base of a hollow organ

- fund: defund, refund—one meaning; profundity

≈found: found—one meaning, founder, founderous, foundation

- found: profound
  [variant forms: fond—one meaning; plafond]

funer: funeral

funeral, funerary, funereal

fung: fungus, mushroom

fungal, fungoid, fungus, pl., fungi

funic: cord, rope

funicle, funicular, funiculus

fur: rage
≈fur: furious, furor, fury
- furiate: infuriate
furc: fork
≈furc: furcate, furcula, furculum
≈furci-: furciferous
- furcate: bifurcate, trifurcate
  [variant forms: fork, forficate,
  carrefour, fourchette—the side
  strip of a finger a glove; in
  anatomy, a small fold of skin at
  the posterior end of the vulva]
  FURLOUGH: from Dutch *verlof*, lit.,
  for permission
furt: thief
  furtive; ferret—one meaning
fusc: dark, dusky
  fuscous; infuscate, obfuscate
fuse[1]: cord, tube, casing, spindle
  fuse—one meaning, fusee,
  fuselage; fusiform; defuse
fuse[2]: to pour, melt
≈fuse: fuse—one meaning, fusible,
  fusil—one meaning
≈fusion: fusion, fusionism
- fus-: infusible, infusionism,
  infusorian, perfusionist
- fuse: confuse, diffuse, effuse,
  infuse, interfuse, perfuse,
  profuse, refuse, suffuse,
  transfuse
- fusion: affusion, circumfusion,
  confusion, diffusion, effusion,
  infusion, profusion, transfusion
- fusionism: diffusionism
- fusive: confusive, diffusive,
  effusive, infusive, perfusive,
  profusive, suffusive,
  transfusive
≈fond: fondant, fondue
≈found: found—one meaning,
  foundry
- found: confound, confounded
- fund: refund—one meaning
- fund-: infundibuliform,
  infundibulum

[variant forms: font, funnel; futile,
  futility]
fusil-l: musket
  fusil—one meaning, fusilier,
  fusileer, fusillade
fust: a stick
  fustian, fustic, fustigate
fut-e: to strike, beat
- fute: confute, refute
- futable: refutable, irrefutable
- futation: confutation
futur-e: about to be
  future, futureless, futurism,
  futuristic, futurity, futurology

G

gag-e: to pledge
≈gage: gage
- gage: with prefixes: dégagé,
  engage, disengage
- gage: with combining form:
  mortgage
- gage-: engaged, engaging;
  engagement
  [variant forms: wage, wager]
  GAINSAY: Anglo-Saxon; lit., to say
  against; deny
galact-o: milk; stars [from a mass
  of stars appearing milky, as the
  Milky Way] [see lact]
milk
≈galact: galactic, galactose
≈galact-: galactagogue,
  galactoma, galactosis
≈galacto-: galactoblast,
  galactocele, galactogen,
  galactography, galactopexy,
  galactophagia, galactophagous,
  galactophore, galactopoietic,
  galactorrhea
stars
≈galac: galactic
- galactic: extragalactic,
  intergalactic, intragalactic

[variant forms: galaxy;
metagalaxy, protogalaxy]

galea: helmet
galea, galeate—wearing a
helmet; helmet-shaped

gall: merry, brave, heroic
gallant, gallantry, galliard,
gallivant
[variant form: gala]

gallin: hen, or **cock**; from "nesting
on the ground"
gallinacean, gallinaceous,
gallinule

GALORE: from Irish-Gaelic *go leor*,
enough; abundant, plentiful; used
postpositively, e.g., an orchard
with apples galore

**gam: marriage, sexual
    reproduction**
≈gam-ete: gamete, gamic
≈gamet-: gametangium
≈gameto-: gametogenesis,
gametophore, gametophyte
- gam: cryptogam, phanerogam
- gamete: with prefixes: agamete,
anisogamete, homogamete,
heterogamete, isogamete,
macrogamete, megagamete,
microgamete, progamete
- gamete: with combining forms:
oogamete, planogamete,
zoogamete
- gamic: agamic, anisogamic,
apogamic, autogamic,
epigamic, exogamic
≈gamo-: gamogenesis,
gamopetalous, gamophyllous,
gamosepalous
- gamous: with prefixes:
digamous, heterogamous,
monogamous, polygamous
- gamous: with combining forms:
cleistogamous, oogamous
- gamy: with prefixes: allogamy,
apogamy, autogamy, bigamy,
cenogamy, chasmogamy,

cleistogamy, deuterogamy,
digamy, dichogamy,
endogamy, exogamy,
heterogamy, homogamy,
hypergamy, isogamy,
monogamy, polygamy,
syngamy
- gamy: with combining forms:
adelphogamy, misogamy,
oogamy, opsigamy, xenogamy

gamb: leg
gamb, or gambe, gambado,
gambit, gambol, gambrel,
gammon
[variant forms: jamb, enjambment]

GAMBESON—of Germanic origin; a
quilted cotton garment worn under
medieval armor

ganglio-n: a swelling
ganglion; ganglioside;
postganglionic, preganglionic

GARDENIA: after Alexander Garden
(1730-91), U.S. botanist; a flower
gargle: see gorg-e
GARLIC: lit., spear-leek

gar-r: to protect
≈gar: garage, gardyloo, garment,
garnish, garnishee,
garnishment, garniture,
garrison
- gard-: regard, regardant,
regardful, regarding,
regardless, disregard
≈guard: guard, guardant,
guarded, guardian
≈ward: ward, warden, warder
≈ward-: wardrobe, wardroom,
wardship
- ward-: award, reward,
rewarding
≈war-e: ware, warehouse,
wareroom, warison
- ware: aware, beware
[variant forms: vanguard, warn,
warning, wary]
[phrase: en garde]

garrul: **to chatter**
  garrulity, garrulous
gastr: **stomach**
≈gastr: gastrea, gastric
≈gastr-: gastrectomy, gastritis
≈gastro-: gastrocele,
  gastroenteritis, gastrolith,
  gastronomy, gastropod,
  gastroscope, gastrotomy,
  gastrotrich, gastrovascular
≈gastrula: gastrula, gastrulation
- gastric: with prefixes:
  cacogastric, digastric,
  endogastric, epigastric,
  exogastric, intragastric,
  mesogastric, monogastric,
  trigastric
- gastric: with combining forms:
  enterogastric, hemogastric,
  hepatogastric, pneumogastric,
  urogastric
- gastrium: epigastrium,
  hypogastrium, mesogastrium
- gastrone: enterogastrone
GAUCHE; GAUCHERIE: awkward,
  warped; awkwardness
GAUCHO: a cowboy, usually of mixed
  Indian and Spanish ancestry,
  living on South American *pampas*,
  plains
gaud: **joyful**
  gaud, gaudery, gaudy
  [variant forms: joy; possibly, gay]
  [phrase: gaudeamos igitur]
GAUZE: from Arabic *kazz*, raw silk;
  orig., a light fabric; also, thin mist
gav: **to stuff**
  gavage, gavotte
GAZETTE: from Venetian dialect
  gazeta, a small coin; the price of a
  newspaper; part of the name of
  many newspapers
GEEK: Dutch; madman, fool
GEISHA: from Sino-Japanese *gei*, art
  (of dancing, singing) + *sha*,
  person; a Japanese woman trained
  in singing, dancing, the art of

conversation, etc., to serve as a
hired companion to men
gel-at-o: **to freeze**
≈gel-id: gel, gelid, gelidity;
  gelatin, gelatinize, gelation,
  gelato
- gel: aerogel, plasmagel
- gelation: congelation, regelation
  [variant forms: congeal, galantine,
  jelly]
GELDING: from Old Norse *gelda*, to
  castrate; a castrated male animal,
  especially, a horse
gemin: **twin**
  geminal, geminate, Gemini;
  bigeminal, trigeminal
gem-m: **a swelling, bud, precious
stone**
≈gem-m: gem, gemma
≈gemmu: gemmule,
  gemmulation
≈gemo-: gemology
≈gemmi-: gemmiferous,
  gemmiform, gemmiparous
GEMSBOK: Afrikaans; from German
  gemse, chamois + *bok*, buck; a
  large antelope of South Africa
gen-e: **birth, origin**
≈gen-e: gender, gene, genesis,
  genre, gens, gentry
≈genetic: genetic, genetics
- gender: engender, transgender
- geneic: allogeneic, autogeneic,
  coisogeneic, isogeneic,
  syngeneic, xenogeneic
- geneous: heterogeneous,
  homogeneous
- genetics: pharmacogenetics
- genial: congenial
- genious: ingenious [not to be
  confused with *ingenuous*]
- genism: eugenism,
  monogenism, polygenism
- genital: congenital
- genitive: philoprogenitive,
  progenitive

≈generic: generic

≈general: general, generalissimo,
  generalize

≈generat-e: generate, generation,
  generative, generator,
  generatrix

≈genero: generosity, generous

≈geni: genial, genie, genius

≈gen-: gendarme (gen + d'armes),
  genome (gene + chromosome)

≈genit: genital, genitalia,
  genitals, genitive

≈genu: genuine, genus, pl., genera

- genarian: octogenarian

- gen: with prefixes: acrogen,
  antigen, endogen, mutagen

- gen: with combining forms:
  androgen, calyptrogen,
  cryogen, halogen, histogen,
  hyalogen, ionogen, nitrogen,
  oxygen, oxyhydrogen,
  pathogen, phellogen,
  plasminogen, pyrogen,
  teratogen

- gene: with prefixes: epigene,
  hypogene, indigene, Neogene

- gene: with combining forms:
  oncogene, plasmagene,
  plastogene, pseudogene

- gener-: congener,
  intergenerational,
  turbogenerator

- generate: degenerate, regenerate

- generous: multigenerous,
  ungenerous

- genesis: with prefixes:
  autogenesis, deuterogenesis,
  digenesis, diagenesis,
  ectogenesis, epigenesis,
  henogenesis, metagenesis,
  monogenesis, neogenesis,
  palingenesis, pangenesis,
  paragenesis, polygenesis,
  syngenesis

- genesis: with combining forms:
  anthropogenesis,
  gametogenesis, gamogenesis,
  glycogenesis, hypnogenesis,
  morphogenesis, mutagenesis,
  oogenesis, orthogenesis,
  osteogenesis, parthenogenesis,
  pathogenesis, pedogenesis,
  petrogenesis, phytogenesis,
  psychogenesis, pyogenesis,
  schizogenesis,
  spermatogenesis,
  spermiogenesis, sporogenesis,
  thermogenesis, xenogenesis,
  zygogenesis, zymogenesis

- genic: with prefixes: dysgenic,
  eugenic, monogenic,
  transgenic

- genic: with combining forms:
  anthropogenic, cryogenics,
  cryptogenic, dacryogenic,
  hallucinogenic, lactogenic,
  myelogenic, myogenic,
  nephrogenic, neurogenic,
  pathogenic, photogenic,
  phylogenic, phytogenic,
  pyrogenic, radiogenic,
  rhizogenic, saprogenic,
  somatogenic, zoogenic,
  zymogenic

≈genito-: genitourinary

- genitor: primogenitor,
  progenitor

- geniture: primogeniture,
  ultimogeniture

≈geno-: genocide, genotype

- genous: with prefixes:
  autogenous, ectogenous,
  endogenous, epigenous,
  exogenous, heterogenous,
  homogenous, hypogenous,
  indigenous, isogenous

- genous: with combining forms:
  bacteriogenous, biogenous,
  caseogenous, collogenous,

erogenous, hematogenous,
ignigenous, keratogenous,
nitrogenous, terrigenous,
urogenous
≈gent: genteel, gentile,
gentilesse, gentility, gentle,
gentleman, gently
≈gentri-: gentrify
- genue: ingénue
- genuous: ingenuous,
disingenuous
- genus: nudigenus, subgenus
- geny: with prefixes: apogeny,
autogeny, dichogeny,
endogeny, polygeny, progeny
- geny: with combining forms:
androgeny, astrogeny, biogeny,
blastogeny, cosmogeny,
cytogeny, embryogeny,
epeirogeny, ethnogeny,
eugeny, geogeny, ontogeny,
orogeny, photogeny,
phylogeny, zoogeny
- gin-e: engine, engineer
- gn-: malign, malignant,
malignity
[variant forms: gin, jaunty, nevus]
[phrases: genius loci, sui generis]
GENIAL: pertaining to the chin
genic: knee, a joint
≈genicul: geniculate
≈genu-: genuflect
≈gon-: gonalgia
- gonid: pycnogonid
- gonum: polygonum
geo: earth
≈ge-: geanticline, geode, geoid;
georgic [second root: *ergon*,
work]
≈geo-: geobiology, geobotany,
geocentric, geochemist,
geochronology, geodesy,
geodynamics
≈geoeconomics, geogeny,
geognosy, geography, geology,

geomancy, geometric,
geometry, geomorphic
≈geophagy, geophone,
geophysics, geophyte,
geopolitics, geopressured
≈geoscience, geostationary,
geostrophic, geosynchronous,
geosyncline
≈geotaxis, geotectonic,
geothermal, geotropism
- geal: epigeal, hypogeal
- gee: apogee, perigee
- geotherm: isogeotherm
- geography: phytogeography,
zoogeography
- geology: hydrogeology,
photogeology
- geotropism: apogeotropism,
diageotropism
- geum: hypogeum
ger[1]: **to bear, to do**
≈ger: gerent, gerund, gerundial,
gerundive
- ger-: armiger; exaggerate;
congeries; vicegerency;
belligerent, vicegerent;
dentigerous
≈gest: geste, gestate, gestation,
gestic, gesticulate, gesture
- gest-: digester, egesta,
indigested
- gest: congest, digest, egest,
ingest, predigest, suggest
- gestational: progestational
- gestible: digestible,
indigestible, suggestible
- gestion: congestion,
decongestion, digestion,
indigestion, suggestion
- gestive: digestive, indigestive,
suggestive
- gist-: register, registered,
registrar, registration, registry,
enregister
[variant form: jest]

ger²: **old**
≈ger-: geriatrics
≈geronto-: gerontocracy,
    gerontology, gerontomorphosis
- ger-: progeria; erigeron
    [variant form: caloyer]
ger³: **crane**
    geranium, pedigree, crane (both
    the bird and the device)
{word notes: geranium: also known
    as cransbill, or crane's-bill; from
    Greek *geranion*, cranebill;
    diminutive of *geranos*, a crane;
    because of the resemblance; see
    pelargonium; pedigree: lit., foot of
    the crane, from the resemblance of
    an ancestral tree to the foot of a
    crane}
germ-i: **bud, shoot**
≈germ: germ, german, germane,
    germinal, germinate,
    germanative
≈germi-: germicide, germiparity
- germ: ovigerm
gest: see ger¹ for gesture, digest
GESTAPO: from German *Ge(heime)*
    Sta(ats)po(lizei), lit., secret state
    police; the secret police force of
    the German Nazi state; see KGB,
    MVD
gesture: see ger¹
GEYSER: Icelandic; lit., gusher; after
    the name of a certain hot spring in
    Iceland
ghast: **ghost**
    ghastly, aghast
GHOTI: George Bernard Shaw (1856-
    1950), British dramatist and critic
    (born in Ireland), suggested that
    fish be spelled as *ghoti*. Take the
    last two letters of *tough*, the
    second letter of *women*, and the *ti*
    sound of *exception*.
gib-b: **a swelling, bulge, hump**
    gib, gibbosity, gibbous
GIBRALTAR: named in honor of Arab
    general Tarik ibn Zaid, who
    captured the rock in A.D. 711.

Original name: *Jebel-al-Tarik*,
    Mountain of Tarik
giga-: **giant; one billion**
giant
≈gigant: gigantean, gigantesque,
    gigantic, gigantism
≈giganti-: giganticide
≈giganto-: gigantology,
    gigantomachy, gigantomastia
one billion
    gigabit, gigabyte, gigacycle,
    gigahertz, gigaliter, gigameter,
    gigaton, gigawatt, gigayear
    [variant forms: giant; Spanish:
    gigante]
gild: **gold**
    gild, gilder, gilding
GINGHAM: from Malay *ginggang*,
    striped cloth; a fabric
gingiv: **the gums** [see gum-m]
    gingival, gingivitis
gird: **to enclose, a circle**
    gird, girder, girdle, girdler;
    engird
    [variant forms: girth, yard]
glab-r: **bald**
    glabella, glabrate, glabrescent,
    glabrous
    [variant form: gabbro]
glac-io: **ice, shiny**
≈glac-e: glacé, glacial, glaciate,
    glacier, glacis
≈glacio-: glaciology
- glacial: englacial, interglacial,
    postglacial, subglacial
    [variant forms: glass, glaze,
    deglaze, verglas]
gladi: **sword**
    gladiate, gladiator, gladiatorial,
    gladiola, gladiolus
    [variant form: glaive]
glam: **enchantment**
    glamorize, glamorous,
    glamour—also, glamor,
    deglamorize
    [variant form: grammar]

gland: **gland**; from "acorn,"
  because of its shape
  gland, glanders, glandula, pl.
  glandulae, glandular, glandule,
  glandulous
  [variant form: glans; in full:
  glans penis]
glauc-o: **blue, bluish gray**
≈glauc: glaucous
≈glauc-: glaucoma
≈glauco-: glaucophane
≈glaucon-: glauconite
≈glaucos-: glaucosuria
GLEAN: from Old Irish *digleinn*, he
  gathers; to gather, learn, find out
gli-a: **glue**
≈gli-: glioma
≈glia: gliadin
≈glia-: gliacyte
- glea: mesoglea
- glia: ectoglia, neuroglia
- gloea: mesogloea, zoogloea
gliss: **to glide**
  glissade, glissando
glob-e: **globe, ball, sphere**
≈glob-e: global, globate, globe,
  globose, globous, globular,
  globule, globy
≈glob-: globoid
≈globi-: globiferous
- globate: conglobate, inglobate
- globin: hemoglobin,
  myoglobin, oxyhemoglobin
≈glomer: glomerate, glomeration,
  glomerulate, glomerule
≈glomule: glomule
- glomerat-e: agglomerate,
  conglomerate; conglomeration
GLOCKENSPIEL: German; to play
  with bells; a musical instrument
  with small bells that are struck
  with wooden mallets
glom: see glob-e for conglomerate
GLOM: from Gaelic *glaim*, to snatch,
  grab; to steal; to look over; view;
  see

glor-y: **great honor**
  glory, glorious; glorify;
  inglorious, vainglorious
gloss: **tongue**
≈gloss: glossa, glossal, glossary
≈gloss-: glossagra, glossalgia,
  glossectomy
≈glosso-: glossographer,
  glossolalia
- gloss-: hypoglossal, isogloss,
  odontoglossum
≈glott: glottal, glottis
- glot-: diglot, monoglot, polyglot
- glott-: epiglottis, proglottid
gluc-o: **sweet, sugar**
≈gluc: gluconate, glucose,
  glucoside
≈gluc-: glucagon
≈glycerine: glycerine
≈glyco-: glycogen, glycogenesis,
  glycolysis
- glycemia: hyperglycemia,
  hypoglycemia
  [variant form: licorice]
glut: **to swallow**
  glut, glutamate, glutton;
  englut, deglutition
  [variant form: goliard]
GLUTEUS: buttocks, rump
glutin: **glue**
≈glutin: glutinous
- glutinant: conglutinant
- glutinate: agglutinate,
  conglutinate
- glutinin: phytohemagglutinin
glyco: see gluc-o for hypoglycemia
glyph-o: **to carve**
≈glyph: glyph
≈glypho-: glyphography
- glyph: anaglyph, petroglyph,
  solenoglyph, triglyph
- glyphics: hieroglyphics
≈glypt: glyptic, glyptics
≈glypt-: glyptodont
≈glypto-: glyptography

gnath: jaw
≈gnath: gnathic, gnathite,
  gnathous
≈gnath-: gnathitis, gnathodynia
≈gnatho-: gnathography,
  gnathoplasty, gnathopod
- gnath: plectognath
- gnathous: hypognathous,
  metagnathous,
  opisthognathous,
  orthognathous, prognathous
gnom-e: **to know, knowledge**
≈gnom-e: gnome, gnomic,
  gnomon
- gnit-: cognition, cognitive,
  precognition, incognito
- gniz-: cognizable, cognizance,
  cognizant, incognizant
- gnize: cognize, recognize
- gno-: cognoscible, cognoscente,
  cognovit
- gnom-: pathognomonic;
  physiognomy
- gnor-e: ignoramus, ignorance,
  ignorant, ignore
≈gnos: gnosis, Gnostic
- gnose: diagnose, prognose
- gnosia: agnosia, prosopagnosia
- gnosis: diagnosis, prognosis
- gnostic: agnostic, diagnostic,
  prognostic
- gnosticate: prognosticate
- gnosy: geognosy,
  pharmacognosy
  [variant forms: quaint, acquaint,
   acquaintance; connoisseur,
   reconnaissance, reconnoiter]
  [phrases: terra incognito;
   ignoratio elenchi]
GOMPHOSIS: an immovable bodily
  joint; from a nail, bolt, tooth
gonalgia: see genic-
gon-io: **angle, corner**
≈gonion: gonion
≈gonio-: goniometer,
  goniopuncture

- gon: decagon, enneagon,
  heptagon, hexagon, octagon,
  orthogon, pentagon, perigon,
  polygon, quindecagon,
  tetragon, trimetrogon
- gonal: diagonal, isogonal,
  orthogonal, polygonal,
  tetragonal
- gonic: agonic, isogonic
- gono-: trigonometry
- gonous: trigonous
gon-o: **cell, procreation, offspring,**
  semen, seed, reproduction
≈gon: gonad, gonidium
≈gono-: gonococcus, gonocyte,
  gonophore, gonopore,
  gonorrhea
- gone: epigone
- gonic: dysgonic
- gonium: archegonium,
  ascogonium, carpogonium,
  epigonium, erythrogonium,
  oogonium, ovogonium,
  perigonium, pregonium,
  spermagonium,
  spermatogonium,
  spermogonium, sporogonium,
  syngonium
- gony: with prefixes: heterogony,
  isogony, telegony
- gony: with combining forms:
  cosmogony, schizogony,
  sporogony, theogony
gorg-e: **to swallow**
≈gorg-e: gorge, gorgeous,
  gorgerin, gorget
- gorge: disgorge, engorge,
  regorge
- gurgitat-e: regurgitate,
  regurgitation
  [variant forms: gargle, gargoyle,
   gurgle]
GOSPEL: lit., good story
GOUDA cheese: after Gouda,
  Netherlands, where originally
  produced

GOURMAND; GOURMET: both
   probably from French *gromet*,
   wine taster, servant. *Gourmand*
   came to mean "a glutton, epicure";
   gourmet, "one who is fond of fine
   food"

govern: orig., **to steer a ship**
≈govern: govern, governance,
   governess, government,
   governor
- govern-: misgovern,
   intergovernmental

grac-e: pleasing
≈grac-e: grace, gracile, gracious
- grac-e: disgrace, disgraceful;
   ungracious
- gree-: agree, disagree,
   disagreeable, disagreement
   [variant forms: engrail; grateful;
   Spanish: gracias; Italian: grazioso]
   [phrase: ars gratia artis]

grad-e: step
≈grad-e: gradate, gradation,
   grade, gradient, gradine
≈gradu-ate: gradual, graduate,
   graduation, gradus
- gradable: biodegradable,
   photodegradable
- gradation: degradation
- grade: with prefixes: aggrade,
   degrade, intergrade, retrograde,
   subgrade
- grade: with combining forms:
   centigrade, digitigrade,
   orthograde, palmigrade,
   plantigrade, pronegrade,
   saltigrade, tardigrade
- gredient: ingredient
- gree: degree
≈gress: gressorial
- gress: aggress, congress,
   digress, egress, ingress,
   progress, regress, retrogress,
   transgress
- gression: aggression,
   congressional, degression,

digression, introgression,
   progression, regression,
   transgression
- gressive: aggressive, digressive,
   ingressive, progressive,
   regressive
- gressor: aggressor, regressor,
   transgressor
   [variant forms: gradatim;
   grallatorial]

graft: shoot, bud; from "stylus"
≈graft: graft, graftage
- graft: allograft, autograft,
   engraft, heterograft, xenograft
GRAHAM cracker: from the Reverend
   Sylvester Graham (1794-1851),
   who advocated a whole grain diet

gram: to write [see glam]
≈gramm: grammar, grammatical
- grammatical: ungrammatical
- gram: with prefixes: anagram,
   diagram, engram, epigram,
   hexagram, isogram,
   monogram, pangram,
   pentagram, program, tetragram
- gram: with combining forms:
   aerogram, cladogram,
   ideogram, lipogram,
   myelogram, nephogram,
   nomogram, oscillogram,
   parallelogram, phonogram,
   phraseogram, pyelogram,
   scintigram, seismogram,
   sociogram, sonogram,
   sphenogram, sphygmogram,
   stereogram, thermogram
- grammetry: photogrammetry
≈graph: graph, grapheme,
   graphic, graphite
≈grapho- graphology
- graph: with prefixes: allograph,
   antigraph, autograph, digraph,
   epigraph, hectograph,
   homograph, micrograph,
   monograph, pantograph,

paragraph, polygraph,
telegraph, telephotograph,
trigraph
- graph: with combining forms:
  aerograph, angiograph,
  barograph, chirograph,
  hyetograph, hygrograph,
  lithograph, manograph,
  meteorograph, myograph,
  odograph, oleograph,
  oscillograph, phonograph,
  photograph,
  photochronograph,
  photolithograph,
  photomicrograph, pictograph,
  pneumograph, pyelograph,
  radiograph, scintigraph,
  seismograph, serigraph,
  spirograph, stereograph,
  stylograph, tachygraph,
  xylograph
- grapha: agrapha, hagiographa,
  pseudepigrapha
- grapher: biographer,
  hagiographer, lexicographer
- graphia: agraphia, dysgraphia,
  palingraphia, paragraphia
≈graphic: with prefixes:
  dysgraphic, heterographic,
  homographic
- graphic: with combining forms:
  calligraphic, cosmographic,
  iconographic, ideographic,
  orthographic, stylographic
- graphical: typographical
- graphy: with prefixes:
  autobiography, heterography
- graphy: with combining forms:
  aerography, angiography,
  anthropography, biography,
  chirography, cryptography,
  ethnography
≈glyphography, hydrography,
  hypsography, ichnography,
  iconography, ideography

≈logography, mammography,
  metallography, mythography,
  nomography, nosography
≈oceanography, organography,
  orography, orthography
≈paleography, paleontography,
  petrography, photography,
  photolithography,
  phototelegraphy,
  physiography,
  phytogeography, pictography,
  planography, polarography,
  pornography, prosopography,
  pyrography
≈selenography, sphygmography,
  stenography, stratigraphy,
  stylography
≈tachygraphy, technography,
  telegraphy, thermography,
  topography, typography
≈uranography, videography,
  xerography, zincography,
  zoography
[variant form: paraph]

gramin: grass
gramineous, graminoid;
graminivorous
[variant form: graze]

gran: grain
≈gran: granadilla, granary,
  grange, granola; granita,
  granite
≈grani-: graniferous, graniform,
  granivorous
≈grano-: granolith, granophyre
≈granul-e: granular, granulate,
  granule, granulite
≈granul-: granuloma, granulose
≈granulo-: granulocyte
- granuloma: lipogranuloma
- granate: pomegranate
  [variant forms: grain, grainy,
  engrain, ingrain, ingrained;
  corn, garner, garnet, filigree,
  grenade, grenadier, grenadine,
  grogram, kernel]

[phrase: cum grano salis—lit.,
with a grain of salt; not too
literally; with some reservation]

grand-i: great

≈grand: grand, grandee, grandeur

≈grandi: grandiose, grandioso

≈grandi-: grandiflora,
grandiloquent, grandisonant

- grandize: aggrandize,
aggrandizement

[phrase: grand prix; in full: Grand
Prix de Paris; lit., grand prize of
Paris; orig., an international horse
race; now, a long-distance auto
race]

graph: see gram

grat-i: pleasing, favor [see grac-e]

≈grat: gratis, gratitude,
gratuitous, gratuity

≈grati-: gratification, gratify

- grat-: congratulate,
congratulation, ingratiate,
ingratitude

[Spanish: gracias—thank you]
[phrase: ex gratia—as a favor]

grav-e: heavy

≈grav-e: grave—one meaning,
gravid

≈gravit: gravitas, gravitate,
graviton, gravity

- gravate: aggravate, aggravation

- gravity: hypergravity,
hypogravity, microgravity,
supergravity

[variant forms: grief, grieve,
grievous; aggrieve]

grave: stylus, engraving

≈gravure: gravure

- grav-e: engrave

- graving: engraving,
photoengraving

- gravure: heliogravure,
photogravure, pyrogravure,
rotogravure

greas-e: fat, thick

grease, greasy; degrease

greg: herd

≈greg: gregal, gregarine,
gregarinian, gregarious

- gregate: aggregate, congregate,
desegregate, disaggregate,
segregate

- gregation: congregation,
segregation

- gregious: egregious

gress: see grad for regression

griph: riddle; from *griphos*, fishing
basket

logogriph—a word puzzle

GRISLY: from Old English *grislic*, to
shudder; ghastly, repugnant

GRIZZLY: from Old French *gris*, grey;
GRIZZLY BEAR; influenced by
association with *grisly*, previous
entry

GROIN: probably from *abyss*,
depression; the hollow or fold
where the abdomen joins either
thigh; in architecture, the sharp,
curved edge formed at the junction
of two intersecting vaults; a
strong, low sea wall

gross: large, thick

gross; engross, engrossed,
engrossing

[variant forms: grocer, grocery,
grogram]

{word notes: grocer: orig., a dealer
in the gross, or in large quantities;
wholesaler; Gros Ventre, lit, big
belly: a member of a western tribe
of the Arapaho}

grot-to: cave

grotto, grotesque, grotty

gru: to fall; to agree in the sense of
"falling, or coming, together"

congruence; congruent,
incongruent; congruity,
incongruity; congruous,
incongruous

[variant form: ruin]

{word note: congruous: corresponding to what is right or reasonable}

GUANO: Spanish; from Incan Quechua *huanu*, dung; manure of sea birds, found especially on islands off the coast of Peru; also, bat manure

guard: see gar-r

GUERRILLA: lit., small war; member of a small defensive force of irregular soldiers, making surprise raids, esp. behind the lines of an invading enemy army; also spelled *guerilla*

GUILLOTINE: from Dr. J. I. Guillotin, French, (1738-1814), who improved the decapitation device that had already been used for centuries, by sharpening the blade and increasing its weight

guis-e: **way, manner**
guise; disguise, disguised

gulf: **gulf, gap**
gulf; engulf

gullet: see guttural

gum-m: **the gums** [see gingiv]
gum, gumma, gummite, gummosis, gummous

GUPPY: after R. J. L. Guppy, of Trinidad, who first provided specimens for the British Museum; a small fish native to Barbados, Trinidad, and Venezuela; it is often kept in aquariums because of its bright colors and easy care

gust: **taste**
gustation, gustatory, gusto; degustation, disgust
[variant forms: ragout; Spanish: gusta; Greek: hypogeusia]
{word note: ragout: lit., to revive the appetite of; a highly seasoned stew}

GUTEN TAG: German: good day; a greeting; see *salaam, shalom, skoal*

gutt: **a drop**
gutta, guttate, guttatim, gutter; guttiform

[variant forms: gout, gouty, guilloche]

guttur: **throat**
≈guttu: guttural, gutturalize
≈gutturo-: guttoronasal, gutturophony, guttorotetany
[variant forms: gular, gules, gullet]

gymn: **nude, naked**
≈gymn: gymnasium, gymnast, gymnastic
≈gymn-: gymnodont
≈gymnasi-: gymnasiarch
≈gymno-: gymnoblast, gymnocarpium, gymnocyte, gymnophilia, gymnophobia, gymnosophist, gymnosperm, gymnospore
- gymnist: chirogymnist

gyn: **woman, female, pistils**
≈gyn: gynaeceum
≈gyn-: gynandromorph, gynandrous, gynarchy
≈gyne-: gynephobia
- gyne: trichogyne
≈gyneco-: gynecocracy, gynecology, gynecomastia
≈gyno-: gynoecium, gynophore
- gynous: androgynous, epigynous, heterogynous, hypogynous, monogynous, perigynous, polygynous
- gyny: misogyny, monogyny, philogyny, polygyny

GYPSY: originally thought to have come from Egypt

gyr-o: **a circle, whirl**
≈gyr-e: gyral, gyrate, gyration, gyre, gyro, gyrous, gyrus
≈gyro-: gyrochrome, gyrocompass, gyrodactylus, gyrograph, gyromagnetic, gyroscope, gyrostat
- gyrate: levogyrate
≈gir: girandole; girasol
- giro: autogiro

H

HAHA: of uncertain background; a sunken fence

hab-it: to hold
≈habit: habit, habitable, habitant, habitat, habitation, habitual, habituate, habitude, habitué
- habit-: cohabit, inhabit, inhabitable, inhabitant
- habitat: microhabitat
≈habil: habile, habilament, habilitate
- habille: dishabille
- habilitate: rehabilitate
- hibit: adhibit, exhibit, inhibit, prohibit
- hibition-: adhibition, exhibition, inhibition, prohibition; exhibitionism
- hibitive: exhibitive, inhibitive, prohibitive
- hibitor-y: exhibitor, inhibitor; exhibitory
[variant forms: able, inability, unable, binnacle, debit, debt, prebend, prebendary]
[phrase: habeas corpus]

hach: ax
hachure—from Old French *hacher*, to chop; further from *hache*, *ax*; any of a series of short parallel lines, esp. in map-making, to represent a sloping or elevated surface
[variant forms: hash, hatchet, hatchment]

hadron: thick, strong
hadron, hadronic; hadrosaur

hagi-o: saint, sacred, holy
≈hagi-: hagiarchy
≈hagio-: hagiocracy, hagiographa, hagiographer, hagiolatry, hagiology, hagiophobia, hagioscope, hagiotherapy

HALBERD: from Middle High German *helmbarte*; from *helm*, handle + *barte*, an ax; a combination spear and battle-ax used in the 15th and 16th centuries

HALCYON: a legendary bird, identified with the kingfisher

hal-e: to breathe
exhalant, exhalation, exhale; inhalant, inhalation, inhale
[variant form: halitosis: bad breath]

hallucin-o: to wander mentally, rave
≈hallucinat-e: hallucinate, hallucination, hallucinatory
≈hallucin-: hallucinosis
≈hallucino-: hallucinogen

HALLUX: big toe; pl., halluces

HALO: from Greek *halos*, threshing floor; a ring of light around the sun or moon; light surrounding the head of a divine or sacred personage; see orchestra

hal-o: salt
≈hal: halide
≈halo-: halobiont, halochromism, halocline, halogen, halophile, halophilic, halophyte
- haline: euryhaline, hyperhaline, isohaline, stenohaline

HANDSCHUH: German; glove: lit., hand shoe

HANDSOME: originally, easily handled, handy, convenient

HANGAR: French; sometimes said to be derived from a place where gliders were "hung"; more probably from Middle Dutch *hamgaerd*, home guard; in French, means "shed"

h-apl-o: single
≈hapl-: haploid, haplont, haplosis
≈haplo-: haplology, haplopathy
- h-ap: aplite

HARA-KIRI: Japanese *hara*, belly + *kiri*, a cutting; a ritual suicide: belly-cutting

HARASS: originally, to set a dog on;
to trouble, worry, or torment, as
by cares, debts, repeated questions
HARBINGER: Frankish; shelter; an
advance representative, as robins
are harbingers of springtime
harmon: a fitting together
≈harmon: harmonic, harmonica,
harmonize, harmony
- harmon-: disharmony,
polyharmony, inharmonious
- harmonic: anharmonic,
enharmonic, philharmonic,
subharmonic
HARVEST: lit., a time of cutting
HASTATE: having a triangular shape,
as some leaves; from Latin *hasta*,
a spear
haust: to draw, drain
≈haust: haustellum, haustorium
- haust-: exhaust, exhaustion,
exhaustive; exhaustible,
inexhaustible
haute [see alti]
HAVOC: possibly from Old French
haver, to hook; great destruction,
as the tornado wreaked havoc on
the coast; *cry havoc*: to give an
army the signal for pillaging
hears-e: to harrow
hearse, rehearsal, rehearse
HEATHEN: orig., a heath dweller;
interpreted as a pagan; a related
word is *hoyden*: a bold, boisterous
girl; tomboy
hebdomad: seven, week
[see hept-a]
hebdomad, hebdomadal,
hebdomadary
hebe: youth, young man
≈hebe: hebetic
≈hebe-: hebephile, hebephilia,
hebephobia, hebephrenia
- pheb-e: ephebe, ephebus
hebet: dull, blunt
hebetate, hebetative, hebetude,
hebetudinous

hect-o: one hundred
≈hect-: hectare
≈hecto-: hectocotylus,
hectogram, hectograph,
hectometer
≈hecatom: hecatomb [second root
from *bous*, ox]
hectic: see e-ch
hedon: pleasure
≈hedon: hedonic, hedonist,
hedonistic
≈hedono-: hedonophilia,
hedonophobia
- hedonia: anhedonia
h-edr: chair; to sit; also, side
- h-edr: cathedra, exedra,
Sanhedrin
- hedral: cathedral, dihedral,
hemihedral, rhombohedral,
tetartohedral, tetrahedral,
trihedral
- hedron: chiliahedron,
decahedron, deltahedron,
heptahedron, hexahedron,
icosahedron, octahedron,
pentahedron, polyhedron,
rhombohedron, tetrahedron,
trisoctohedron
[phrase: ex cathedra]
{word note: Sanhedrin: from Talmud
Hebrew *synedrion*, assembly; the
highest court and council of the
ancient Jewish nation, having
religious and civil functions; it
was abolished with the destruction
of Jerusalem in A.D. 70}
hegemon: leadership, dominance
hegemonism, hegemony
HEINOUS: from Old French *hair*, to
hate; outrageously evil
heli-o: sun
≈heli: heliacal, helium
≈heli-: helianthus
≈helio-: heliocentric, heliolatry,
heliometer, Heliopolis,
heliosphere, heliostat,

heliotaxis, heliotherapy,
heliotrope, heliotropism,
heliozoan
- hel-: isohel, parhelic
- helio-: pyrheliometer
- helion: anthelion, aphelion,
  parhelion, perihelion
helic-o: spiral
≈helic: helical, helicon, helictite
≈heli-: heliclin
≈helic-: helicoid
≈helico: helicopter
≈helix: helix, pl., helices
- helix: antithelix, or anthelix
{word note: helicopter: lit., spiral-
  wing}
HELMET: from a Frankish word that
  means *covering*; thus, a protective
  covering for the head; originally,
  the headpiece in full-body armor
helminth-o: worm
≈helminth: helminth,
  helminthiasis, helminthic
≈helmintho-: helminthology
- helminth: nemathelminth,
  platyhelminth, pseudohelminth
- helmintic: anthelmintic
helot: serf, slave
helot, helotism, helotry
hemat-o: blood
≈hema: hemal, hematal, hematic,
  hematin
≈hem-: hemangioma
≈hemat-: hematoma, hematuria
≈hemato-: hematoblast,
  hematocrit, hematogenous,
  hematology, hematophagous,
  hematopoiesis, hematozoon
≈hemo-: hemochromatosis,
  hemocyanin, hemocyte,
  hemodynamics,
  hemoflagellate, hemoglobin,
  hemoglobinuria, hemolymph,
  hemolysis, hemophile,
  hemoptysis, hemorrhage,

hemorrhoid, hemostasis,
  hemostatic, hemotoxin
- hem-: phytohemagglutinin
- h-emia: **blood condition**: with
  prefixes: anemia, anoxemia,
  anoxyemia, hyperemia,
  hyperglycemia, hypoglycemia,
  polycythemia
- h-emia: **blood condition**: with
  combining forms: acidemia,
  cholemia, glycemia, ischemia,
  ketonemia, leukemia,
  pachyhemia, pyemia,
  sapremia, thalassemia,
  toxemia, uremia
h-emer: day
≈hemer-: hemeralopia
- hemera-l: ephemera, ephemeral,
  ephemerid, ephemeris,
  ephemeron
- emeron: Decameron,
  hexaemeron
{word note: Decameron: a collection
  of a hundred tales by Boccaccio
  (published 1353), presented as
  stories told by a group of
  Florentines to while away *ten* days
  during a plague}
hemi-: half
hemiaxial, hemicephaly,
  hemichordate, hemicrania,
  hemicycle, hemihedral,
  hemihydrate, hemimorphic,
  hemiola, hemiparasite,
  hemiplegia, hemisphere,
  hemistich, hemitrope,
  hemizygous
[variant form: migraine]
hendeca: eleven [*hen*—1 +
  deca—10]
hendecagon, hendecahedron,
  hendecasyllabic
hen-o: one
hendiadys, henogenesis,
  henotheism
[variant forms: enosis, hyphen]

hent: to prepare, achieve
authentic — lit., one who does
things himself/herself; from *auto-*,
self + *hentes*, to prepare, achieve;
thus, genuine
hepa-t-o: liver
≈hepa: heparin, hepatic,
hepatica — a liver-shaped flower
≈hepat-: hepatectomy, hepatitis
hept-a-: seven [see hebdoamad]
≈hept: heptad
≈hept-: heptarchy, heptathlon,
heptose
≈hepta-: heptachord,
heptachromic, heptadactylism,
heptagon, heptahedron,
heptamerous, heptameter,
heptastich, Heptateuch
herb-i: grass, herb
≈herb: herb, herbaceous,
herbage, herbal, herbalist,
herbarium, herbed
≈herbi-: herbicide, herbiferous,
herbivorous
here: to stick
- here: adhere, cohere, inhere
- herence: adherence, coherence,
incoherence
- herent: adherent, incoherent,
inherent
- hesion: adhesion, cohesion
- hesive: adhesive, cohesive
[variant forms: hesitancy,
hesitant, hesitate, hesitation]
her-ed: to inherit
≈heredit-y: hereditament,
hereditarian, hereditary,
heredity
≈herit: heritable, heritage
- herit: disinherit, inherit
- herit-: inheritable, inheritance
[variant forms: heir, heirloom,
heirship]
heres-i: to take
≈heres: heresy
≈heresi-: heresiarch

≈heretic-al: heretic, heretical
- h-eresis: apheresis, dieresis
hermeneut: to translate
hermeneutic, hermeneutics
hermit: desolate
hermit, hermitage
[variant forms: eremite,
eremitic, eremurus]
hernia: intestine
hernia, herniated
[variant form: yarn — from *haru-spex*, soothsayer; lit., intestine-
seer]
hero: hero [from Greek mythology:
a man of great strength and
courage
hero, heroic, heroin, heroine;
antihero
{word note: heroin: so called from
its euphoric effect, of making one
feel like a hero}
herp-eto: serpent; from "to creep"
herpes, herpetic, herpetology,
herpetotomy
hes: see heter for aphesis
hes: see here for adhesive
heta: companion
hetaera, hetaerism
heter: to send
- heter: catheter, catheterize
- hes: aphesis
heter-o: other
≈heter-: heteresthesia,
heterodont, heteroecious,
heteronym, heteronymous,
heterosis
≈hetero-: heteroatom,
heteroblastic, heterocercal,
heterochromatic,
heterochthonous, heteroclite,
heterocylic
≈heterodox, heterodyne
≈heterogamete, heterogamous,
heterogeneous, heterogenous,
heterogony, heterograft,
heterography, heterogynous

≈heterolecithal, heterologous,
  heterolysis
≈heteromerous,
  heterometabolism,
  heteromorphic
≈heteronomous, heterophil,
  heterophony, heterophyllous,
  heterophyte, heteroplasty,
  heteroploid, heteropterous
≈heterosexual, heterosphere,
  heterosporous
≈heterotaxis, heterothallic,
  heterotopia, heterotrophic
≈heterozygosis, heterozygote
heuristic: to discover
  heuristic, heuristics
  [variant form: Eureka: I have
  found (it)!: exclamation said to be
  uttered by Archimedes, when he
  discovered a way to determine the
  purity of gold by applying the
  principle of specific gravity]
hevel: hair; from "chevel"
  dishevel
  [variant form: chevelure]
hex-a-: six
≈hex: hexad
≈hex-: hexangular, hexosan,
  hexose
≈hexa-: hexachord, hexaemeron,
  hexagon, hexagonal,
  hexagram, hexahedron,
  hexahydrate, hexameter,
  hexapla, hexapod, hexastich,
  Hexateuch, hexavalent
  [variant form: samite]
hi: to gape
  hiatal, hiatus
  dehisce, dehiscent
HIBACHI: Japanese *hi*, fire + *bachi*,
  bowl; firebowl
hibern: winter
  hibernaculum, hibernal,
  hibernate; hibernoma
HICKORY: from American Indian
  pawcohiccora

hidr: sweat
≈hidr-: hidradenitis, hidrosis,
  hidrotic
≈hidro-: hidrocystoma
- hidrosis: hyperhidrosis,
  panhidrosis, parahidrosis,
  polyhidrosis
hier-o: holy
≈hier: hieratic
≈hier-: hierarchy
≈hiero-: hierocracy, hierodule,
  hieroglyph, hieroglyphics,
  hierology, hierophant
hil: scar, mark; from "little thing"
  hilum, hilus
hilar: glad
≈hilar: hilarious, hilarity; Hilary
- hilar-: exhilarant, exhilarate,
  exhilaration
{word note: hilarious: from an
  ancient Roman festival held in the
  spring to celebrate the renewal of
  life after the cold winter}
hipp-o: horse
  hippodrome, hippogriff, or
  hippogryph, hippopotamus;
  eohippus
HIRCINE: pertaining to a goat
HIRSUTE: hairy, shaggy, bristly
histo: tissue
≈histo-: histocyte, histogen,
  histogenesis, histology,
  histolysis, histopathology,
  histophysiology,
  histoplasmosis
- histamine: antihistamine
histor-ic: knowing, learned
≈histor: historian, historic,
  historical, historicism, history
- historic: ahistoric, prehistoric
≈historio-: historiography
  [variant form: story—an account
  or a level of a building recounting
  significant events]
histrion: actor
  histrionic, histrionics

h-izesis: to sit

synizesis— in *biology*, the
contraction of chromatin towards
one side of the nucleus during the
prophase of meiosis; in *linguistics*,
the union in pronunciation of two
adjacent vowels into one syllable
without forming a diphthong, e.g.,
el<u>ee</u>mosynary

h-od-e: road, way

≈odo-: odograph, odometer
- hod-e: method; cathode,
  photocathode
- od: with prefixes: period, synod
- od: with combining form:
  photoperiod
- od-: exodus, methodic,
  Methodist, methodize,
  methodology
- odaem: proctodaem,
  stomodaeum
- ode: with prefixes: anode, diode,
  episode, palinode, pentode,
  tetrode
- ode: with combining forms:
  nematode, photodiode
- odic-: episodic, periodic;
  periodical, periodically,
  periodicity
- odization: periodization

h-ol-o: whole, holy

≈hol-: holy, holistic, holiday,
  holily, holiness
≈hol-: holonymå
≈holo-: holoarthric, holoblast,
  holocaust, Holocene,
  holocephalic, holocrine,
  hologamous, hologamy,
  hologenesis, hologram,
  holograph, hologynic,
  holohedral, holometer,
  holomorphic, holophrastic,
  holophytic, holotype, holozoic
- hol-: catholic, catholicity
  [variant forms: halibut, halidom,
  Halloween, hemiola, hollyhock]

{word note: halibut: with *butt*, a
particular type of flounder; so
called because eaten on holy
days}

h-om: man

≈hom: homage, homager,
  homunculus
≈homi-: homicide
≈homin: hominid, hominize
≈homin-: hominoid
- omin-: abominable, abominate
  [variant forms: Spanish: hombre;
  omber, ombre]
  [phrases: argumentum ad
  hominen; ecce homo, novus
  homo; Homo sapiens]

homil: sermon

homiletic, homiletics, homily

h-om-o: same, equal, like

≈hom-: homonym, homonymous
≈homo-: homocentric,
  homocercal, homochromatic,
  homoecious, homoeroticism,
  homogamy, homogeneous,
  homogenous, homogenize,
  homograph
≈homolecithal, homologate,
  homologous, homomorphism
≈homoousian, homophile,
  homophobia, homophone,
  homophonic, homoplastic,
  homoplasy, homopolymer,
  homopteran
≈homosexual, homosphere,
  homosporous, homostyly,
  homotaxis, homothallic,
  homozygote
≈homeo: homeomorphism,
  homeopathy, homeostasis,
  homeothermal, homeotypic
≈homoi: homoiousian,
  homoiplasia
≈homolo: homolographic,
  homolosine
  [variant forms: anomalous,
  anomaly]

hon: **dignity**, **repute**, **esteem**
≈honest: honest, honesty
- honest: dishonest
≈honor: honor, honorable,
  honorably, honorarium,
  honorary
≈honori: honorific
- honor-: dishonor, dishonorable
  [Spanish: honesto]
HOOKY: from Dutch *hoeckje*, hide
  and seek; thus, to hide around the
  corner from school

h-opl: **to prepare**; **weapon**
  hoplite, panoply
{word note: hoplite: a heavily armed
  foot soldier of ancient Greece}
HORDE: from Turkish *ordu*, a camp; a
  nomadic tribe; swarm; from the
  same root is Urdu, the language of
  Pakistan

hor-iz: **to divide**, **mark off**
≈horiz: horizon, horizontal
- horis: aphorism; aphoristic
  [variant forms: aorist, diorite]

hormone: **impulse**
≈hormone: hormone
≈hormono-: hormonology,
  hormonoprivia
- hormone: antihormone,
  ectohormone, neurohormone,
  phytohormone
  [variant form: pheromone]

horo: **hour**
  horologe, horologist, horology,
  horoscope
  [variant forms: hour, ephor]

horr-i: **to bristle**, **to shudder**
≈horr: horrendous, horrent,
  horrible, horribly, horrid,
  horror
≈horri-: horrific, horrify,
  horripilate, horripilation
- hor-r-: abhor, abhorrence,
  abhorrent
  [variant form: ordure—dung, filth,
  manure, excrement]

hors: **outside** [see for²]
  hors concours, hors de combat,
  hors d'oeuvre

hort: **to urge**
  hortatory, exhort, exhortation,
  exhortatory

horti-: **a garden**
≈horti-: horticulture—the art or
  science of growing flowers, fruits,
  vegetables, and shrubs, especially
  in gardens and orchards
- hort: cohort
  [variant form: orchard]
{word note: cohort: originally, an
  ancient Roman military unit of
  300-600 men, constituting one
  tenth of a legion; any group or
  band; an associate, colleague, or
  supporter}
HOSANNA: from Hebrew *hoshrah
  nna*, save, we pray; an exclamation to give praise to God

hosp: **host**, **guest**, **stranger**, **enemy**
≈hosp: hospice
≈hospit: hospitable; hospital,
  hospitality, hospitalization,
  hospitalize
- hospitable: inhospitable
≈host: host, hostage, hostel,
  hosteler, hostess, hostile,
  hostility, hostler
  [variant forms: hotel, hotelier]
HOUSTON, TX: after Samuel Houston
  (1793-1863), US general and
  statesman; president of Republic
  of Texas (1836-38)
HOWITZER: from Czech *houfnice*, a
  short cannon; originally, a sling

hum: **moist**
≈humid: humid, humidity,
  humidor
≈humidi-: humidification,
  humidify
- humid: semihumid
- humidify: dehumidify
≈humor: humor, humoral,
  humoresque, humorist

human-e: human, man
≈human-e: human, humane,
humanism, humanist,
humanitarian, humanities,
humanity, humanize, humanly
- human-e: inhuman, infrahuman,
preterhuman; inhumane;
inhumanity; dehumanize
hum-e: earth, ground, soil
≈hum: humble, humus
- hume: exhume, inhume,
transhume
- humance: transhumance
- humation: exhumation
[variant forms: humiliate,
humility: small, slight; akin
to earth, ground, soil]
HUMERUS: the shoulder
HURRICANE: from Spanish *huracán*; a
West Indian word for a violent
tropical cyclone
HUSBAND: Anglo-Saxon; lit., house-
dweller; to manage economically;
conserve; husbandman: a farmer
HUSK: from Middle Dutch *huus*,
house; the dry outer covering of
various fruits and seeds
HUSKY: altered from *Eskimo*: a breed
of sled dog
HUSSY: contraction of *housewife*; a
woman of low morals
hyal-o: glass, glassy, transparent
≈hyal: hyalescence, hyalin,
hyaline
≈hyal-: hyalite, hyaloid
≈hyalo-: hyalogen, hyaloplasm,
hyalopterous
hydr-o: water
≈hydr: Hydra, hydrant, hydrate,
hydrous
≈hydr-: hydrangea, hydraulic,
hydroid
≈hydro-: hydroacoustics,
hydrobranchiate, hydrocele,
hydrocephaly, hydrocyst,
hydrofoil, hydrogen,
hydrogeology, hydrography,

hydrolysis, hydropathy,
hydrophilic, hydrophobia,
hydrophone, hydrophyte,
hydroscope, hydrosphere,
hydrostatics, hydrotropism
- hydrate: carbohydrate,
cryohydrate, dehydrate,
hemihydrate, hexahydrate,
monohydrate, trihydrate
- hydric: dihyric, endohydric,
exohydric, hexahydric,
isohydric, mesohydric,
monohydric, polyhydric
- hydrogen: oxyhydrogen
- hydrous: anhydrous, enhydrous
[variant form: dropsy]
{word notes: hydrangea: lit., water
cell; a flower; hydraulic: from
hydraulis, lit., water tube, pipe}
hyet-o: rain
≈hyeto-: hyetograph,
hyetography, hyetology,
hyetometer, hyetophobia
- hyet: isohyet
hygiene: health
hygiene, hygienic, hygienics,
hygienist; hygeiolatry
hygr-o: moisture
≈hygro-: hygrograph, hygrology,
hygrometer, hygroscope,
hygrothermal
- hygric: euryhygric, stenohygric
hylo: wood, matter
≈hylo: hylomorphism,
hylophagous, hylozoism
- (h)yla: pteryla
hymen: membrane
≈hymen: hymen, hymeneal
≈hymen-: hymenectomy,
hymenitis, hymenoid
≈hymeno-: hymenopterous
**hyper-: beyond, excessive, more
than the normal, over**
≈hyperacidity, hyperactive,
hyperbaric, hyperbola,

111

hyperbole, hyperbolic,
hyperborean
≈hypercritical, hyperdulia,
hyperemia, hyperesthesia,
hypereutectic
≈hypergamy, hyperglycemia,
hypergolic, hyperkeratosis,
hyperkinesis
≈hyperopia, hyperostosis,
hyperparasite, hyperploid,
hyperpnea, hyperpyrexia
≈hypersensitive, hypersexual,
hypersonic, hypersthene
≈hypertension, hypertext,
hyperthermia, hyperthyroid,
hypertonic, hypertrophy,
hyperventilation

hypn: sleep
≈hypn-: hypnagogic, hypnosis,
hypnotic
≈hypno-: hypnobate,
hypnogenesis, hypnology,
hypnophobia, hypnoscope
- hypnotic: posthypnotic

hyp-o: below, under
≈hyp-: hyphen, hyphenate;
hyponym, hypoxia
≈hypo-: hypoblast, hypocaust,
hypocenter, hypochondria,
hypochondriac, hypocotyl,
hypocrisy, hypocrite,
hypocritical
≈hypoderm, hypodermic,
hypoeutectic, hypofunction
≈hypogastrium, hypogeal,
hypogene, hypogenous,
hypogeum, hypogeusia,
hypoglossal, hypoglycemia,
hypognathous, hypogynous
≈hypokinesis, hypomania,
hyponasty, hypophysis,
hypoplasia, hypoploid
≈hypostasis, hypostatize,
hypostyle, hypotaxis,
hypotenuse, hypothalamus,

hypothecate, hypothermal,
hypothesis, hypothetical
- hypo- neurohypophysis
{word note: hyphen: lit., under one;
together; in one}
HYPOCORISTIC: orig., calling by
endearing names; of or being a pet
name or a diminutive or a term of
endearment

hyps-: height
≈hyps-: hypsodont
≈hypsi-: hypsicephalic
≈hypso-: hypsography,
hypsometer, hypsometry
HYSTERESIS: from *hysterein*, to be
behind; in *physics*, a lag of effect
when the forces acting on a body
are changed

hyster-o: womb, uterus
≈hyster: hysteria, hysterical
≈hyster-: hysterectomy
≈hysteri-: hysteriform
≈hystero-: hysterotomy
HYSTRICOMORPHIC: lit., in the form
of a porcupine; designating a
group of rodents, including the
porcupines and chinchillas

I

IAMB: a metrical foot consisting in
English of an unaccented syllable
followed by one accented one,
e.g., *to strive, to seek, to find, and
not to yield*; the example is *iambic
pentameter*, or five feet of iambs

iatr-o: healing
≈iatr: iatric, iatrics
≈iatro-: iatrogenics, iatrology
- iastric-s: geriatrics, pediatrics,
psychiatric
- iatrician: geriatrician,
pediatrician, physiatrician
- iatry: podiatry, psychiatry
ICEBERG: Dutch: *ijsberg*, ice
mountain

ichno: footprint
ichnography, ichnology
ichthy-o: fish
≈ichthy: ichthyic, ichthyism
≈ichthy-: ichthyoid, ichthyosis,
  ichthyornis
≈ichthyo-: ichthyolatry,
  ichthyolite, ichthyology,
  ichthyophagous, ichthyosaur,
  ichthyotoxic
icon-o: image, symbol
≈icon: icon
≈icono-: iconocentric,
  iconoclasm, iconoclast,
  iconography, iconolatry,
  iconology, iconomania,
  iconophilia, iconostasis
- icon: orthicon
[variant form: aniseikonia]
ICOSAHEDRON: a solid figure with
  twenty plane surfaces
ide: idea, form, appearance, image
≈idea-l: idea, ideal, idealism,
  idealist, ideally
≈ideat-e: ideate, ideation
≈ideo: ideogeny, ideogram,
  ideography, ideokinetic,
  ideolect, ideology, ideomotor,
  idiopathic, ideophobia,
  ideophone
≈idol: idol, idolism, idolize,
  idiologize
≈ido-: idolater, idolatrize,
  idolatrous, idolatry [second root
  is *latris*, hired servant; worshiper]
≈idolo-: idoloclast, idolomancy
≈idyll: idyll, idyllic, idyllist
[variant form: eidetic]
[phrases: idée fixe, idée reçue]
ident-i: the same
identic, identical, identity;
identify
[variant form: idem]
[phrases: identical
  proposition, identity crisis,
  identity element]

idio: one's own
≈idio: idiocy, idiom, idiomatic,
  idiot, idiotic
≈idio-: idioblast, idiochromatic,
  idiocratic, idiogamist,
  idiographic, idiolalia, idiolatry,
  idiolect, idiomorphic,
  idiopathic, idioplasm,
  idiosyncrasy
[term: idiot savant]
ign: to set on fire
igneous, ignescent, ignite,
ignition; preignition
[term: ignis fatuus]
il-e: to wander
exile, exilic;
postexilic, preexilic
ilemma: covering
mucolemma, myolemma,
neurilemma, plasmolemma
ile-o: ileum, groin
≈ile: ileum
≈ile-: ileitis
≈ileo-: ileofemoral, ileostomy
imag-o: a likeness, image
image, imagery, imaginary,
imagination, imaginative,
imagine, imaging, imagism,
imago
imbric: overlapping; from "gutter
  tile"; from "rain"
imbricate, imbrication
imitate: see emulat-e
IMPROVE: to gain, to turn to
  advantage [not related to *approve*]
in-[1]: in
≈in-: inarch, inaugurate
≈incandescent, incarcerate,
  incarnate, incendiary, incense,
  incentive, inception, inchoate,
  incident, incinerate, incipient,
  incise, incision, incite, incline,
  include, income, incorporate,
  increase, increment,
  incriminate, incubate, incubus,

inculcate, inculpate,
incumbent, incur, incurrent,
incursion, incurvate, incuse
≈indebted, indeed, indent,
indenture, index, indicate,
indiction, indoctrinate, induce,
induct, indulge, indurate
≈infarct, infect, infer, infiltrate,
infix, inflate, inflect, inflict,
inflorescence, influence,
influenza, inform, infraction,
infringe, infuriate, infuscate,
infuse
≈ingeminate, ingenious,
ingenuous, ingest, ingratiate,
ingredient, ingress, ingurgitate
≈inhabit, inhale, inhere, inherent,
inherit, inhibit, inhume
≈initial, initiate, initiation,
initiative, inject
≈innate, innovate, innuendo
≈inoculate, inosculate
≈inquest, inquire, inquisition,
inquisitive
≈inscribe, inscription, insect,
insert, insidious, insignia,
insinuate, insist, insolate,
inspect, inspire, inspissate,
install, instant, instigate, instill,
instinct, institute, instruct,
instructor, instrument, insult,
insurgent, insurrection
≈intaglio, integument, intend,
intent, intimidate, intinction,
intonation, intoxicate, intricate,
intrigue, intrude, intubate,
intuition, intumesce
≈inunction, inundate, inure,
invade, invaginate, invective,
inveigh, invent, invert, invest,
investigate, inveterate,
invidious, invigilate,
invigorate, invite, invocation,
involucre, involute, involve

≈il-: assimilation of in-: illation,
illuminate, illusion, illustrate,
illuvium
≈im-: assimilation of in-:
immanent, immanentism,
immerge, immerse, immigrate,
imminent, immiseration,
immix, immolate, immure
≈im-: variant of in-: imbibe,
imbroglio, imbrue, imbue
≈impact, impale, impanation,
impanel, impassion, impaste,
impeach, impede, impediment,
impel, impend, impersonate,
impetigo, impetuous, impetus,
impinge, implacental, implant,
implead, implement, implicate,
implicit, implode, implosion,
imply, import, important,
impose, impound, impoverish,
imprecate, impregnate,
impress, imprest, imprimatur,
imprimis, imprint, imprison,
impromptu, impropriate,
improve, impugn, impulse,
impute
≈ind-: old prefix for in-: indigent,
indigenous
≈ir-: assimilation of in-: irradiate,
irrigate, irritate, irrupt
in-^{2}: **not, negative**
≈in-: inability, inactive,
inadequate, inadmissible,
inadvertent, inanimate, inapt,
inarticulate, inaudible,
inauspicious
≈incalculable, incapable,
incapacitate, incessant, incest,
incivility, inclement, incognito,
incognizant, incoherent,
incommensurable,
incommodious, incomparable,
incondite, incongruous,
inconsiderate, inconsistent,
inconsolable, inconspicuous,

inconstant, incontinent,
inconvenient, incorporeal,
incorrigible, increate,
incredible, incredulity,
incredulous, incurious
≈indecent, indeciduous,
indecorous, indecorum,
indefatigable, indefinite,
indehiscent, indelible,
indelicate, indemnify,
independent, indeterminate,
indignity, indict, indiscreet,
indiscrete, individual, indocile,
indolent, indomitable,
indubitable
≈inedible, ineffable, inelastic,
inelegant, ineluctable, inept,
inerrable, inert, inertia,
inexorable, inexpugnable,
inextirpable, inextricable
≈infallible, infamous, infamy,
infant, infecund, infelicity,
infertile, infidel, infinite,
infirm, inflexible, informal,
infrangible
≈ingratitude, inharmony,
inhospitable, inhumane,
inimical, inimitable, iniquity,
injudicious, injure, injustice
≈innocent, innocuous,
innumerable, inofficious,
inoperable, inopportune,
inordinate, inorganic
≈insalubrious, insanity,
insatiable, inscrutable,
insecure, insensate, insensitive,
insentient, inseparable,
insignificant, insipid, insolent,
insoluble, insolvent, insomnia,
insouciant, insusceptible
≈intact, intangible, integer,
integrate, integrity, intemerate,
intemperate, intestate,
intolerable, intolerance,

intractable, intransigent,
intransitive, intrepid
≈inutile, invalid, invaluable,
invariable, invertebrate,
·   invincible, inviolable, inviscid,
invisible, involuntary,
invulnerable
≈ig-: variant of *in-*: ignoble,
ignominy
≈il-: assimilation of *in-*: illegal,
illegible, illegitimate, illiberal,
illicit, illimitable, illiterate,
illogical
≈im-: variant of *in-*: imbecile
≈im-: assimilation of *in-*:
immaculate, immane,
immaterial, immature,
immeasurable, immediate,
immedicable, immemorial,
immense, immiscible,
immitigable, immobile,
immoderate, immodest,
immoral, immortal,
immovable, immune,
immunity, immutable
≈impalpable, impartial,
impassable, impasse,
impassive, impatience,
impeccable, impecunious,
impenetrable, impenitent,
imperfect, imperforate,
imperishable, impermanent,
impermeable, impersonal,
impertinent, imperturbable
≈impervious, impiety, impious,
implacable, implausible,
impolicy, impolite, impolitic,
importune, impossible,
impotent, impracticable,
impractical, impregnable,
improbable, improper,
impropriety, improvident,
improvise, imprudent,
impudent, impuissance,
impunity, impure

115

≈ir-: assimilation of *in-*: irrational,
irrecusable, irredentist,
irrefragable, irrefrangible,
irrefutable, irregular,
irrelevant, irremediable,
irreparable, irresolute,
irrespirable, irretrievable,
irreverence

in-[3]: intensive
incalescent, incantation,
inebriate, infatuate, intenerate

≈im-: variant of *in-*: impair,
imparadise, impetrate, implore

inan-i: empty, senseless
inane, inanition, inanity

INCARCERATE: to imprison; the noun
is *incarceration*

indig: to be in need; from *ind-*, old
prefix for *in-*, in + *egere*, to need
indigence, indigent

INDIGO: from Spanish *indicum*; lit.,
Indian (dye); a deep violet blue,
designated by Newton as one of
the prismatic or primary colors

-**ine: similar to**; from *eidos*, form,
shape
anserine, aquiline, asinine,
bovine, canine, caprine,
colubrine, columbine, corvine,
equine, feline, hirsine, iodine,
leonine, lupine, ovine,
pavonine, phocine, piscine,
porcine, quercine, serpentine,
taurine, ursine, vespine,
viperine, vulpine

infer-o: low, below, down
≈infer: inferior, infernal, inferno
≈infero-: inferoanterior
≈infra-: infrabranchial,
infrabulge, infracardiac,
infracortical, infracostal,
infradian, infralapsarian,
infrapubic, infrared, infrasonic,
infrastructure

INGUINAL: of or near the groin

insulate: see isl

inter: between
≈inter: interim, interior
≈intern: intern, internal,
internalize
≈inter-: interact, interactive,
intercalary, intercede,
intercept, intercession,
intercessor, interchange,
interclavicle, intercoastal,
intercostal, intercourse,
intercurrent
≈interdental, interdict,
interdependence, interdigitate,
interdisciplinary
≈interface, interfere, interfluve,
interfuse
≈intergalactic, intergrade,
interject
≈interlard, interlinear,
interlocution, interloper,
interlude, interlunar
≈intermediate, intermission,
intermittent, international,
internecine, internode,
interosculate
≈interpellate, interpenetrate,
interplead, interpolate,
interpose, interpret
≈interregnum, interrogate,
interrupt, intersection,
intersexual, intersperse,
interstadial, interstate,
interstellar, interstice
≈intertestamental, intertextual,
intertexture, intertidal, interval,
intervene, interview,
intervocalic, intervolve
[variant forms: entrails,
intelligent]
[phrases: ad interium, inter nos]
interest: see esse

interpret: negotiator, explainer
interpret, interpretation,
interpreter, interpretive,
interpretor

intim: **within**; from *intus*, within
intima, intimacy, intimate,
intimation, intimist

intra-: **within, inside**
Intracoastal Waterway,
intracranial, intradermal,
intrados, intragalactic,
intramural, intraocular,
intrastate, intratelluric,
intrauterine, intravascular,
intravenous, intrazonal
[variant forms: enter, entrée,
entry]

intro-: **inside, within, into**
introduce, introgression,
introit, introject, intromit,
introspection, introversion,
introvert

intus: **within**
intussuscept, intussusception
[variant forms: intestinal,
intestine; labyrinth, denizen,
dedans]
[phrase: intestinal fortitude]
inure: see ergo

iod-o: **violet** [from *ion*, violet +
eidos, form]
≈iod: iodate, iodic, iodide,
iodinate, iodine
≈iodo-: iodoform, iodometry,
iodotherapy

ion-to: **to go**
≈ion: ion, ionic, ionium, ionize
≈iono-: ionogen, ionophore,
ionosonde, ionosphere
≈ionto-: iontophoresis
- ion: anion
- ionization: photoionization
[Saturn model: Ion]

ipsi: **self**
ipsilateral; solipsism
[phrases: ipse dixit, ipsissima
verba, ipso facto, ipso jure,
res ipsa loquitur]

ir: **to be angry**
ire, irate, irascible

[phrase: dies irae]

iren: **Irene**, Greek goddess of peace
irenic, irenics

irid: **iris** the flower; part of the eye;
from "rainbow"
irid, iridescent, iridium;
iridectomy
[variant form: iris]

IRONY: Greek *eiron*, dissembler of
speech; from *eirein*, to speak

ISCHEMIA: a lack of blood supply in
an organ or tissue; from *ischein*, to
hold + -*emia*, blood condition

ischi: **the hip, hip joint**
ischium; ischialgia; ischiocele

ISINGLASS: Dutch *huizenblas*, lit.,
sturgeon's bladder; a form of
mica; also, a form of gelatin
prepared from the membranes of
fish bladders, used as a clarifying
agent

isl: **island**
≈isl: island, isle, islet
≈isolat-e: isolate, isolated,
isolation, isolationist
≈isolo-: isolophobia
≈insul: insular, insulate,
insulation, insulator, insulin
- insula: peninsula
[medical term: islets or,
islands of Langerhans]
{word note: peninsula: lit., almost an
island; that is, surrounded on three
sides by water}

iso-: **same**
≈iso: isobar, isobath, isocheim,
isochromatic, isochrone,
isoclinal, isocracy, isocyclic
≈isodiametric, isodimorphism,
isodose, isodynamic
≈isogamete, isogamy, isogenous,
isogeotherm, isogloss,
isogonic, isogony, isogram,
isohel, isohyet
≈isologous, isomer, isometrics,
isometropia, isometry,
isomorph

≈isonomy, isopiestic, isopleth,
  isopod, isosceles, isoseismal,
  isostasy
≈isothere, isotherm, isotone,
  isotonic, isotope, isotropic,
  isozyme
- iso-: anisogamete, stereoisomer
ist: see s-ist for exist

isthm: narrow passage
  isthmian, isthmus, e.g., the
  Isthmus of Panama, a land bridge
  between Central and South
  America; also, a narrow passage
  between two larger cavities, as the
  isthmus of the fallopian tubes

it: to go
≈itiner: itinerancy, itinerant,
  itinerary, itinerate, itineration
- it: adit, circuit, exit, introit, obit,
  post-obit, preterit, transit
- it-: coitus, comitia, obituary,
  subito, transitory
- itial-: initial, initialism,
  initialize, initially
- itiat-e: initiate, initiation,
  initiative, initiatory
- ition: ambition, coition,
  preterition, sedition, transition
- itious: ambitious, seditious
- itive: transitive, intransitive
  [variant forms: ambience, andante,
   arrant, circumambient;
   commence, entrance, errant,
   exeunt, exeunt omnes, perish,
   perishable, praetor, praetorian,
   sudden, trance, transient,
   count—a nobleman]
  [phrases: ab initio, coitus
   interruptus, obiter dictum]
ITALICS: this style of printing letters
  was devised by an Italian, Aldo
  Manuzio, about 1500

-ite: from *lithos*, stone
  anthracite, arenite, argentite,
  chondrite, nephrite, psammite,
  rhodochrosite, rhodonite,
  siderite, steatite, turbidite

item: so, thus, likewise
  item, itemization, itemize
iterat-e: to repeat
  iterate, iteration, iterative;
  reiterate
ithy: straight, go directly toward
  ithyphallic— of or relating to the
  phallus carried in procession in
  ancient festivals of Bacchus;
  having an erect penis—usually
  used of figures in an art
  representation
itis: inflammation of
≈adenitis, appendicitis, arthritis,
  bronchitis, bursitis, colitis,
  cystitis, diverticulitis,
  encephalitis, enteritis,
  enterocolitis, gastritis,
  gingivitis
≈hepatitis, laminitis, laryngitis,
  mastitis, mastoiditis,
  meningitis, metritis, myelitis,
  myocarditis, myositis
≈nephritis, neuritis, oophoritis,
  orchitis, osteitis, otitis
≈pancreatitis, parotitis,
  periarteritis, pericarditis,
  periodontitis, periostitis,
  peritonitis, phlebitis,
  pneumonitis, polyneuritis,
  prostatitis, pyelitis,
  pyelonephritis
≈rachitis, retinitis, rhinitis,
  rhinopharyngitis, salpingitis,
  scleritis, sinusitis, spondylitis,
  stomatitis
≈tendonitis, tenosynovitis,
  tracheitis, tympanitis
≈urethritis, uveitis, vaginitis,
  vulvitis, vulgovaginitis
ivory: see eburn
IZVESTIA: Russian for *news*; name of
  Russian newspaper; see *Pravda*,
  truth. A popular story in Russia is
  that *Izvestia* doesn't print the truth,
  and *Pravda* doesn't print the news.

J-K

jac: to throw
≈jac: jactitate
- jacent: adjacent, circumjacent,
  interjacent, nonadjacent,
  postjacent, sous-jacent,
  subjacent, superjacent
- jacul-at-e: ejaculate, ejaculum,
  ejaculatory
- ject: abject, deject, eject, inject,
  interject, introject, object,
  project, reject, subject, traject
- ject-: dejected, ejectment,
  interjection; objectivism,
  objectivity, objectify
- jecta: abjecta, dejecta, ejecta
- jection: abjection, bijection,
  dejection, ejection, injection,
  interjection, objection,
  projection, rejection, surjection
- jective: abjective, adjective,
  ejective, injective, objective,
  projective, rejective,
  subjective, surjective
- jector-y: injector, interjector,
  trajectory
- jectur-e: conjectural, conjecture
≈jet-ti: jet, jeté, jeton, jetsam,
  jettison, jetty
  [variant forms: agio, ease; enema;
  gist, jitney; parget]
  [phrases: flotsam and jetsam,
  disjecta membra, objet d'art, objet
  trouvé]
JACKRABBIT: so named because its
  long ears resemble that of a
  jackass
JAI ALAI: Basque for merry festival;
  the game of pelota: Spanish for
  "ball"; an extremely fast court
  game using a very hard ball
jamb: see gamb
jan-itor: from **Janus**, Greek god of
  doors and beginnings
  January, janitor

JANIZARY: Turkish *yehi*, new + *cheri*,
  soldiery; a soldier; orig., a slave in
  the Turkish sultan's guard
JAPAN: a shortening of the Chinese
  compound *Jipenkuo*, lit., land of
  the origin of the sun; thus, Japan's
  sobriquet: Land of the Rising Sun
JASMINE: from Persian *yzsamin*; a
  fragrant flower
JAUNDICE: from OF *jaune*, yellow; a
  disease of the liver
jealous: zeal
  jealous, jealousy
  [variant forms: jalousie, zeal]
jejun-e: empty
≈jejun-e: jejunal, jejune, jejunum
≈jejun-: jejunectomy, jejunitis
≈jejuno-: jejunoplasty,
  jejunorrhaphy, jejunostomy
  [variant forms: déjeuner, dine,
  dinner]
JERKY: from Spanish *charqui*; meat,
  esp. beef, that has been sliced into
  strips and dried; in full, "beef
  jerky"
jeu: game
  jeu; jeu de mots,
  jeu d'esprit
  [variant form: jeopardy]
JIPIJAPA: from a place in Ecuador; a
  plant whose leaves yield a
  flexible, durable straw for hats;
  Panama hat
joc: joke, jest
  jocose, jocular, jocund
  [variant forms: jewel, joke,
  joker, giocoso]
JODHPURS: riding breeches; from
  Jodhpur, India, where they were
  first made popular
join: see jug
jour-nal: from *diurnal*, day
≈journ: journal, journalism,
  journey; journeyman
- journ: adjourn, sojourn
- journalism: photojournalism
  [variant form: toujours]
  [phrases: du jour, plique-à-jour]

{word note: journey: orig., the
distance one could travel by
horseback in a day's time}
JOVIAL: lit., under the influence of
Jupiter; in astrology, Jupiter was
the happiest star of one's birth; the
influence was said to give a
cheerful disposition; see
mercurial; saturnine
joy: from *gaudium*, joy
≈joy: joy, joyful, joyless, joyous
- joy: enjoy, enjoyable,
  enjoyment
- joice: rejoice, rejoicing
  [variant forms: juggle,
  gaudeamos igitur]
judic: **to swear**; from *judge* +
dicere, to speak
≈judic: judicable, judicative,
  judicatory, judicature, judicial,
  judiciary, judicious
- judic-e: adjudicate, injudicious,
  prejudice
- judicial: extrajudicial,
  prejudicial, quasijudicial
≈judg-e: judge, judgment,
  judgmental
- judge: adjudge, prejudge
≈jur: jurat, juratory, juried, jurist,
  juror, jury
≈juri-: juridical
≈juris-: jurisdiction, jurisprudence
- jur-: abjuration, adjuration,
  conjuration, objuration;
  injurious, objurgate
- jure: abjure, adjure, conjure,
  injure, perjure
- jured: injured, perjured
- jury: injury, perjury
≈just: just, justly
≈justic-e: justicable, justice,
  justiciary
≈justi-: justifiable, justification,
  justificatory, justify
- just-: injustice; unjust
  [NB: adjust; see jug]

[variant form: hoosegow]
[law terms: de jure, jus civile,
jus gentium, jus naturae,
jus sanguinis, me judice,
res judicata, sub judice; sui juris]
{word note: hoosegow: jail; in
Mexican Spanish, *juzgado*,
meaning "a tribunal or court"; the
letter *j* is pronounced as *h*;
consequently, Americans tried in
Mexican courts often found
themselves in the *hoosegow*}
jug: **to join**
≈jug: jugal, jugate, jugular,
  jugulate, jugum
- jugal: conjugal
- jugate: bijugate, conjugate,
  subjugate, trijugate, unijugate
- jugation: conjugation
≈junct: junction, juncture
- junct: adjunct, conjunct,
  disjunct
- junction: conjunction,
  disjunction, injunction
- junctiva: conjunctiva
- junctive: adjunctive,
  conjunctive, disjunctive,
  subjunctive
- juncture: conjuncture,
  disjuncture
- join: adjoin, conjoin, disjoin,
  enjoin, rejoin, subjoin
- joinder: misjoinder, nonjoinder,
  rejoinder
- joint: conjoint, disjoint
  [variant term: adjust; Spanish:
  junta]
JUGGERNAUT: Hindi *Jagannath*, lord
of the world; further from Sanskrit
jagat, world + *nantha*, lord; a
relentless force
JUMBO: Gullah *jamba*, elephant
jun: **young**
≈junior: junior, juniority
≈juven: juvenescent, juvenile,
  juvenilia, juvenility
- juvenate: rejuvenate

[variant form: jeunesse]

JUNGLE: Hindi *jangal*, desert forest, jungle; further from Sanskrit *jangala*, wasteland, desert

JUSSIVE: a grammar term expressing a command

jut: from *juvare*, **to help, aid**
adjutant, coadjutant, coadjutor
[variant forms: adjuvant, aid]

juvenescent: see jun

juxta: near, beside
juxtacostal, juxtapose, juxtaposition, juxtaspinal
[variant form: joust]

KAISER: from Caesar, family name of first Roman emperors; titles of the rulers of the Holy Roman Empire, 961-1806; the rulers of Austria, 1804-1918; the rulers of Germany, 1871-1917; see czar

kaleidoscope: see calli

KAMIKAZE: Japanese *kami*, god + *kaze*, the wind; divine wind

KARAOKE: Japanese *kara*, empty + *oke*, short for *orchestra*; a type of amateur singing

KARATE: Japanese *kara*, empty + *te*, hand; a form of self-defense

karyo: a nut, fruit stone, kernel
eukaryote, megakaryocyte, prokaryote, synkaryon

KAYAK: Eskimo; lit., a canoe made of skins

KEEN[1]: from Irish *caoinim*, I wail; a custom of wailing for the dead; a dirge; as a verb, to lament

KEEN[2]: from Old English *cene*, wise, learned

kempt: comb
kempt, unkempt

kenosis: see ceno

KEPI: a French military cap; from French *képi*; further from German *kappe*, a cap; originally from Late Latin *cappa*, cap

kerat: horn, hornlike [see cerat]
≈kerat-: keratitis, keratoid, keratoma, keratosis

≈kerato-: keratocele, keratoconus, keratogenous, keratolysis, keratoplasty, keratotomy
- keratosis: hyperkeratosis
- keratology: orthokeratology

KERYGMA: Greek: to proclaim; the preaching of the Gospel

KETCHUP: Chinese *ke-tsiap*; orig., fish sauce

keton: acetate
≈ket: ketone
≈ket-: ketose, ketosis
≈keto-: ketogenesis, ketosteroid
≈keton-: ketonemia, ketonuria

KGB: Russian for *Komitet Gosudarstawenoi Bezopasnosti*: Committee for Government Security; see MVD, gestapo

KHAKI: Hindi *khaki*, dusty; further from Persian *khak*, dust, earth

KIBITZER: Yiddish; from German *kiebitzen*, "to look on" at cards; giver of unwanted advice

kilo-: one thousand [see chili]
kilocycle, kilometer, kilowatt
[variant form: chiliad]

KIMONO: Japanese *kiru*, to wear + *mono*, thing; "a thing for wearing"

KIND: from Old English *cynd*, akin to German *kind*, child

KINDERGARTEN: German: children's garden

kine: movement [see cine]
≈kin-e: kinase; kinematics; kinesics, kinesis
≈kine-: kineplasty, kinescope
≈kinesio-: kinesiology
- kinase: enterokinase, streptokinase, urokinase
- kinesia: akinesia, acrokinesia, bradykinesia, dyskinesia, heterokinesia, homokinesia, parakinesia, synkinesia
- kinesis: with prefixes: diakinesis, dyskinesis, hyperkinesis, hypokinesis, interkinesis, orthokinesis, telekinesis

- kinesis: with combining forms:
  photokinesis, psychokinesis
≈kinetic: kinetic, kinetics
- kinetic: mitokinetic
- kinetics: pharmacokinetics
≈kineto-: kinetoplast
  [variant forms: cine, cinema]
klepto-: to steal
≈klepto-: kleptocracy,
  kleptolagnia, kleptomania,
  kleptophilia, kleptophobia
- klept: biblioklept
KNAPSACK: from Dutch *knapzak*;
  orig., eating sack
know: to comprehend [see gn]
  know, knowledge;
  acknowledge,
  acknowledgment
KOHLRABI: from German; lit.,
  cabbage turnip; a vegetable similar
  to a turnip
KOSHER: Yiddish; from Hebrew; fit,
  proper; to be appropriate
KREMLIN: from Russian *kreml'*, for
  the citadel of a city; *the Kremlin*,
  the citadel of Moscow,
  headquarters of the former Soviet
  Union
KUDZU: Japanese: a prostrate
  leguminous vine used widely for
  hay and forage and for erosion
  control in the South
kym: a wave [see cym]
  kymogram, kymographion,
  kymography, kymophobia,
  kymoscope

L

lab¹: lip
≈lab: labellum, labial, labialize,
  labiate, labium, pl., labia
≈labio-: labiodental,
  labiogingival, labiology,
  labionasal, labiovelar,
  labioversion

- labial: axiolabial, bilabial,
  buccolabial, dentolabial,
  infralabial, rectolabial,
  vaginolabial
- labiate: bilabiate, trilabiate,
  unilabiate
≈labr: labret, labrum
  [medical terms: labia majora,
  labia minora]
lab²: to slip, fall
≈lab: labile
- labile: thermolabile
≈labor: labor, laboratory, laborer,
  laborious: to work, hardship, pain
- labor: antilabor, belabor,
  prolabor
- laborate: collaborate, elaborate
lab-e: to hold [see lemma]
- lab-e: syllabary, syllabism,
  astrolabe
- labic-: syllabic, syllabicate,
  monosyllabic, polysyllabic
- labify: syllabify
- lable: decasyllable, disyllable,
  octosyllable, syllable,
  tetrasyllable, trisyllable
labor: see lab²
LABRADOR: from Portuguese
  lavarador, landholder; from
  Portuguese explorer Joao
  Fernandes, a landholder in the
  Azores; first applied to Greenland;
  constitutes the mainland part of
  Newfoundland
labyrinth: maze, winding passage
≈labyrinth: labyrinth,
  labyrinthine
≈labyrinth-: labyrinthectomy,
  labyrinthitis
lacco: cistern
  laccolith—an irregular body of
  igenous rock intruded between the
  layers of sedimentary rock,
  making them bulge upward
lace: a noose, snare, trap
  lace, enlace

lacer: **lizard** [see saur]
  lacertilian—sauran, pertaining to
  lizards
  [variant forms: lizard, alligator]
lacerat-e: **to tear**
  lacerate, laceration
  [variant forms: lancinate, laniary]
lachrym: **a tear**
  lachrymal, lachrymose;
  lachrymator, lachrymatory
  [variant forms: lacrimal,
  lacrimation, lacrimator]
LACONIC: concise, terse; from the
  manner of the Laconians, a people
  of ancient Greece
LACROSSE: a game first played by
  Canadian Indians; so named by
  Canadian French explorers after
  crosse, a bishop's staff, which
  resembled the stick used to propel
  the ball
lact: **milk** [see galact-o]
≈lact: lactary, lactate, lactation,
  lacteal, lactescent, lactone,
  lactose
≈lacti-: lactiferous, lactifugal,
  lactigenous, lactigerous,
  lactivorous
≈lacto-: lactobacillus, lactogenic,
  lactometer
- lactation: ablactation,
  delactation, mislactation,
  superlactation
- lactin: prolactin
  [variant form: lettuce]
  [phrases: French: au lait;
  Spanish: café con leche]
  {word note: lettuce: so called
  because of its milky juice}
lacu: **space**; from "lake"
  lacuna, lacunar, lacanule,
  lacustrine
  [variant forms: lagoon, lake]
LADRONE: in Spanish-speaking
  regions of the US, a robber,
  bandit; from Latin *latro*, a hired
  servant

LADY: lit., loaf-kneader; see lord
lagn: **lust**
  algolagnia, antholagnia,
  asthenolagnia, coprolagnia,
  graphelagnia, kleptolagnia,
  osmolagnia, parthenolagnia,
  pornolagnia, scopolagnia,
  scoptolagnia, zoolagnia
LAGNIAPPE: Creole French for
  "something extra"; something
  given by way of good measure
LAGOMORPH—any of various plant-
  eating mammals having fully
  furred feet and two pairs of upper
  incisors, and includes the rabbits,
  hares, and pikas
LAHAR: Javanese; a landslide or
  mudflow of volcanic fragments on
  the flanks of a volcano
lai: **the people**; **not priestly**
  [see liturg]
  laic, laicism, laicize, laity
LAIRD: Scottish form of *lord*; a
  landowner, especially a wealthy
  one
lal: **to babble, talk**
≈lall: lallation
≈lalo: lalopathy
- lalia: allolalia, glossolalia,
  idiolalia, rhinolalia, tachylalia
LAMBENT: to lick, lap; flickering:
  said of a flame, or, of ocean waves
lamell: **layer**; from "thin metal
  sheet"
≈lamell: lamella, lamellate,
  lamellose
≈lameli-: lamellibranch,
  lamellicorn, lamelliform
≈lamin-ate: lamina, laminable,
  laminar, laminaria, laminate,
  laminated, lamination, laminin
≈lamin-: laminitis
≈lamini-: laminiferous
≈lamino-: laminogram
- laminate: bilaminate,
  delaminate, interlaminate
  [variant forms: lamé, omelet]

lament-a: a mourning, wailing
lament, lamentable,
lamentation, Lamentations,
lamented
lamp: to shine
lamp; eclampsia
[Spanish: lampa—lamp]
{word note: eclampsia: lit., a shining
forth; an attack of convulsions}
lance: lance
lance, lancet, lanceted,
lanceolate; lanciform;
oblanceolate
[variant form: launch: lit., to wield
a lance]
langu: to be weary [see lax]
languid, languish, languishing;
languor, languorous
language: see ling
lan-i: wool
≈lan: lanate, lanose
≈lan-: lanolin
≈lani-: laniferous
≈lanug-o: lanugo, lanuginous
lapar: the flank; from *laparos*,
weak, thin
laparocele, laparomyitis,
laparorrhaphy, laparoscope,
laparotomy
[variant form: leper}
lap-id: rock
≈lapid: lapidarian, lapidary,
lapidescent, lapillus
≈lapidi-: lapidific, lapidify
- lapid-: dilapidate, dilapidated,
dilapidation
[variant forms: lapis, lapis lazuli]
laps-e: to fall
≈laps-e: lapse, lapsus
- lapse: collapse, elapse, illapse,
interlapse, prolapse, relapse
- lapsarian: infralapsarian,
prelapsarian, sublapsarian,
supralapsarian
[terms: lapsus calami, lapsus
linguae, lapsus memoriae]

large: large
large, enlarge, enlargement
[variant form: lard]
laryng-o: larynx
≈laryng: laryngeal
≈laryng-: laryngectomy,
laryngitis
≈laryngo-: laryngology,
laryngoscope
- laryngology: otolaryngology,
otorhinolaryngology,
rhinolaryngology
[variant form: larynx]
LASCIVIOUS: wanton, lustful
LASAGNA: Italian; lit., cooking pot; a
kind of noodle dish
LASER: acronym for light
amplification by stimulated
emission of radiation; see *maser*
LASSITUDE: from Latin *lassus*, weary;
alas is from the same root
lat-e: to bear, carry [from Latin
ferre; see fer-e]
- lat-: relational, relativity
- late: with prefixes: collate, elate,
correlate, interrelate, oblate,
prelate, prolate, relate, sublate,
translate
- late: with combining forms:
legislate, ventilate
- lation: correlation, illation,
interrelation, oblation, relation,
translation
- lative: correlative, illative,
relative, irrelative, superlative
- lator-y: legislator, relator,
dilatory
LATENT: from *latere*, to lie hidden;
present but invisible or inactive
later: side, wide; from "to spread
out"
≈later: laterad, laterite
≈lateral: lateral, lateralization
≈latero-: laterotorsion
≈lati: latitude, latitudinarian
≈lati-: laticostate, latifundium

- lat: dilatant, dilatation
- late: ablate, dilate, oblate—one meaning
- lateral: with prefixes: bilateral, collateral, equilateral, multilateral, quadrilateral, septilateral, trilateral, unilateral
- lateral: with combining forms: ipsilateral, ventrolateral
- lation: collation
- latitude: colatitude

lat-r: slave; worship of, to serve
≈latr: latria
- latry: astrolatry, autolatry, bibliolatry, cynolatry, demonolatry, ecclesiolatry, hagiolatry, heliolatry, hygeiolatry, iconolatry, idiolatry, idolatry, litholatry, mechanolatry, monolatry, necrolatry, ophiolatry, parthenolatry, verbolatry, zoolatry
  [variant form: burglar]

laud: to praise
≈laud: laud, laudable, laudation, laudatory
- low: allow, allowance, disallow, disallowance
  [German: lied—song—esp. one whose words and music are of a lyrical, often popular, character]
  [phrases: cum laude, magna cum laude, summa cum laude]

laur: laurel (an evergreen shrub) laureate, laurel, laurel wreath; baccalaureate (academic degree)

lav-a: to wash, flood
≈lav: lava, lavabo, lavage, lavation, lavatory
≈lav-e: lave, lavender, laver; lavish
≈laund: launder, laundry
- luent: abluent, diluent, eluent
- luge: deluge
- lut-: pollutant; polluted

- lute: dilute, elute, pollute
- lution: ablution, dilution
- lutriate: elutriate
- luvial: alluvial, antediluvial, diluvial, eluvial, illuvial
- luvian: antediluvian, postdiluvian
- luviation: illuviation
- luvion: alluvion, diluvion
- luvium: colluvium, diluvium, eluvium, illuvium
  [variant forms: latrine, lotic, lotion]

lax: loose
≈lax: lax, laxative, laxity
- lax: relax, relaxant, relaxation, relaxer
  [variant forms: laches, languid (see separate entry), lease, leash, release, sublease; relish, disrelish; slack, slacks, delay, relay]
  [phrase: laissez faire]

LB.: symbol for pound; abbreviation of Latin *libra ponda*, lit., pound of weight

LEBENSRAUM: German: lit., living room; the space, room, or territory needed, or deemed necessary, to satisify economic necessities

lecith: egg yolk
≈lecit: lecithal, lecithid, lecithin; lecithinase
- lecithal: ectolecithal, heterolecithal, homolecithal, isolecithal, macrolecithal, microlecithal, polylecithal

lectic: to leave off, cease
catalectic, acatalectic

lect: to entice, ensnare
- lect: delectable
- lic-: delicatessen; delicious
- licacy: delicacy, indelicacy
- licate: delicate, indelicate
- licit: elicit
  [variant forms: delight, dildo, dilettante; possibly, luscious]

LEDGER: from Old English *leggen*, to lie flat; originally, a ledger lay flat in one place and was open to public inspection

leg[1]: to send, to appoint as deputy
≈leg: legate
- leg-e: college, collegium
- legate: delegate, relegate; delegation
- league: colleague

leg[2]: to read
≈leg: legend, legendary, legible
- legible: illegible
≈lect: lectern, lectionary, lecture, lecturer
[variant form: lesson]
[phrase: varia lectio]

leg[3]: to choose, gather
≈leg: legion, legionary
- lect: with prefixes: collect, dialect, elect, intellect, neglect, prelect, recollect, select
- lect: with combining form: idiolect
- lect-: analects, dialectic, eclectic, intellectual, selector; collectible
- lection: collection, intellection, predilection, selection
- lective: collective, elective, selective
- lectivity: collectivity, selectivity
- legan-t: elegance, elegant, inelegant
- lege: sacrilege, sortilege
- legit: elegit
- legious: sacrilegious
- lig-ible: negligee; eligible, ineligible, intelligible
- ligence: diligence, intelligence, negligence
- ligent: diligent, intelligent, negligent
- logue: eclogue
≈legum-e: legume, leguminous: anything that can be gathered

[variant forms: elite, coil, cull]
leg[4]: law
≈leg-al: legacy, legal, legate, legation, legist, legitimate
≈legis-: legislate, legislator, legislature
- legal: extralegal, illegal, nonlegal, paralegal, preterlegal
- lege-d: privilege, privileged
- legit-: delegitimize, illegitimate
≈litig: litigable, litigant, litigate, litigation, litigious
[variant forms: leal, loyal, disloyal, disloyalty]
[law terms: lex loci, lex non scripta, lex scripta, lex talionis]

leip: to leave
- leip: paraleipsis
- lips-e: eclipse, ellipse; ellipsis
- liptic-al: ecliptic, elliptical
[variant form: lipogram]
{word note: lipogram: a writing composed of words not having a certain letter or letters, as in the Odyssey of Tryphiodorus there was no A in the first book, no B in the second, and so on}

leit: German: to lead
leitmotif, or leitmotiv

lemma[1]: to seize, assume
[see lab-e]
≈lemma: lemma—one meaning
- lemma: analemma, dilemma
- lepsis: prolepsis, syllepsis
- lepsy: catalepsy, epilepsy, narcolepsy
- leptic: analeptic, epileptic, narcoleptic, neuroleptic, organoleptic

lemma[2]: husk, rind
≈lemma: lemma—one meaning
≈lemmo-: lemmoblast, lemmocyte
- lemma: neurilemma, sarcolemma, tetralemma
LEMON: Persian *limun*

LEMUR: from *lemures*, ghosts; in Roman mythology, walking spirits of the dead; applied to the animal because of its nocturnal habits; lemurs are found only in Madagascar and the Comoro Islands

leni: soft, mild

≈leni-s: leniency, or lenience; lenient, lenis

≈lenit-y: lenitive, lenity

- lent: relent, relentless

LENT: from Old English *lengten*, meaning "the *lengthening* of daylight hours"; the 40 days from Ash Wednesday to Easter

lenti: lentil, lens

≈lenti-l: lenticel, lenticular, lenticulate; lentil

≈lenti-: lenticonus, lentiform, lentiglobus

- lental: retrolental

≈lentig: lentiginous, lentigo
    [variant form: lens—resembles a split lentil]

LEOTARD: a one-piece, tight-fitting garment worn by dancers, acrobats; from Jacques Léotard, 19th-century French aerial performer, who advocated its use

lep-ido: rough, scaly

≈lep-id: leper, lepidote

≈lepido-: lepidolite, lepidopteran

≈lepr-ose: leproma, leprosarium, leprose, leprosy, leprous

lepor: hare

leporid, leporine; leveret

-leptic, -lepsy: see lemma

lepto-n: thin

≈lepton: lepton—a small, thin coin of ancient Greece

≈lept-: leptodontous, leptoid, leptoma

≈lepto-: leptocardia, leptocephalous, leptochromatic, leptocyte, leptodactylous, leptodermous, leptologia, leptophonia, leptopodia, leptotrichia

LESION: an injury; hurt; damage; related term: lèse-majesté

leth: forgetful

≈leth: lethargic, lethargy

- livi-: oblivion, oblivious
    [variant forms: oubliette; Spanish: olvidar—to forget]

leth-al: death

≈lethal: lethal, lethality

≈lethi-: lethiferous

- lethal: hyperlethal, hypolethal, semilethal, superlethal, sublethal

leuk-o: white

≈leuk: leukemia, leukodontia, leukoma, leukapheresis

≈leuko-: leukoblast, leukocyte, leukocytosis, leukodermia, leukopenia, leukoplakia, leukoplasia, leukorrhea

≈leuc-: leucite

≈leuco-: leucoplast, leucopoiesis

LEVIGATE: to make smooth, as by grinding; see act

levo: to the left

levogyrate, levorotation, levorotatory, levoversion
    [variant forms: laeotropic, levulose]

lev-y: to raise; light in weight

≈lev-y: levant, levator, levee, levy

≈lever: lever, leverage

≈levi: leviable, levitate, levitation, levity

- levat-e: elevate, elevation, elevator

- leviate: alleviate

- levant: relevant, irrelevant

- lever: cantilever
    [variant forms: allay; leaven; carnival, relief, relieve, irrelievable]
    [phrase: levy en masse]

lex: **word**; from "to speak"
≈lex: lexeme, lexical, lexicon,
  lexis
≈lexico-: lexicographer,
  lexicography, lexicology
- lexia: alexia, bradylexia,
  dyslexia, hyperlexia, paralexia
LHASA APSO: from *Lhasa*, capital of
  Tibet + *apso*, sentinel; a small dog
libat: **a pouring**; from *libare*, to
  taste, to pour
  libation, prelibation
libel-l: **book**; from "inner bark of a
  tree"
≈libel-l: libel, libellant, libellee,
  libeller
≈libr: librarian, library, libretto
≈libri-: libriform
  [variant forms: liber, ex libris]
liber-al: **to free**
≈liber-al: liberal, liberalism,
  liberality, Liberia
≈liberat-e: liberate, liberation,
  liberator
- liberal: antiliberal, archliberal,
  illiberal, paleoliberal
≈libert-y: libertarian, libertine,
  liberty
≈liberti-: liberticide
  [variant forms: livery, deliver,
  deliverance]
  [phrases: liberal arts,
  mare liberum]
{word note: Liberia: country on west
  coast of Africa; founded in 1821
  by the American Colonization
  Society as settlement for freed US
  slaves; James Monroe was the
  U.S. president; thus, the capital:
  Monrovia}
libid: **pleasure, wantonness**
  [see licen-se]
  libidinal, libidinize, libidinous,
  libido
library: see libel-l
libra: **to weigh, scales**
≈libra: libra, librate

- librate: equilibrate,
  disequilibrate
- librist: equilibrist
- librium: equilibrium,
  disequilibrium
  [variant forms: deliberate, level]
{word note: pound: from *libra
  pondo*, a pound in weight; thus lb.,
  the symbol for pound}
licen-se: **to be permitted** [see libid]
≈licens-e: license, licensure
≈licent: licentiate, licentious
≈licit: licit
- licit: illicit
  [variant forms: leisure; scilicet,
  videlicet]
lid-e: **to strike, injure**
- lide-r: collide, collider, elide
- lision: collision, elision
lig-e: **to bind**
≈liga: ligament, ligate, ligature
≈ligul-e: ligula, ligule
- liance: alliance, reliance
- lig-e: colligate, oblige, obligee,
  obliging, obligor; disoblige
- ligat-e: obligate, obligation,
  obligatory, obbligato
- ligio-n: religion, religionism,
  religiosity, religious
- ly: ally (allied), rally, rely
  (reliant)
  [variant forms: alloy, league,
  legato, liability, liable, reliable;
  liaison, lictor, liege, lien]
lign-i: **wood**
≈lign: ligneous, lignescent,
  lignin, lignite
≈ligni-: lignify, lignivorous
- ligneous: pyroligneous
LILAC: Persian *lilak*, blue
limit: **border, frontier**
≈limit: limit, limitary, limitation,
  limitative, limited, limiting
- limit-: delimit, delimiter,
  illimitable
- limate: sublimate

- lime: sublime
- limin-: postliminium,
  preliminary
- liminal: subliminal,
  supraliminal
- liminate: eliminate
  [variant forms: limbo, limen,
  lintel]

limn-o: marshy lake
≈limn: limnetic
≈limno-: limnobiology,
  limnology, limnophile
- limnion: epilimnion,
  hypolimnion, mesolimnion

line¹: long-fiber flax
line — one meaning, linen;
  linoleum; linseed
  [variant form: linnet — a bird
  that feeds on flax seeds]

line²: a line, row, furrow
≈line: line — one meaning, lineage,
  lineal, lineament, linear,
  linearity, lineate, lineation
- line: aline, interline
- lineal: brachilineal,
  centrolineal, curvilineal,
  interlineal, longilineal,
  matrilineal, mixtilineal,
  multilineal, nonlineal,
  patrilineal, rectilineal,
  unilineal, unlineal
- linear: collinear, interlinear,
  rectilinear, trilinear
- lineate: bilineate, delineate,
  interlineate
  [variant forms: align, alignment;
  collimate, collimator; delete,
  deletion; delirious, delirium;
  delirium tremens]

ling: tongue, language
≈ling-u: lingua, lingual, linguine,
  or, linguini, linguist, linguistics,
  lingulate
≈lingui-: linguidental, linguiform
- lingual: with prefixes: bilingual,
  collingual, monolingual,

multilingual, quadrilingual,
  prelingual, retrolingual,
  sublingual, unilingual
- lingual: with combining form:
  buccolingual, dentolingual,
  distolingual, labiolingual,
  orolingual
- linguistics: metalinguistics,
  paralinguistics, sociolinguistics
≈langu-age: language, languet, or
  languette
- language: metalanguage,
  paralanguage
  [variant forms: ingot; lingo]
  [phrase: lapsus linguae]
{word note: linguine: lit., little
  tongue; pasta in thin, flat, narrow
  strips, often served with seafood
  sauces}

linqu: to leave
- linqu-ent: delinquency,
  delinquent, relinquish
- lic-t-: derelict, dereliction, relic,
  relict
- liqu: reliquary, reliquiae
  [variant form: shrine]

lip-o: fat
≈lip: lipid
≈lip-: lipoid, lipoma
≈lipo-: lipocardiac, lipofuscin,
  lipogenetic, lipolysis,
  lipophilic, liposome,
  liposuction, lipotropic
- lipid-: hyperlipidemia
  [variant form: synalepha]
lipse: see leip for eclipse, ellipse

liqu-e¹: to melt, to be liquid
≈liqu: liquate, liquescent, liquor
≈liquid: liquid, liquidate,
  liquidity
≈lique-: liquefacient,
  liquefaction, liquefy
- liquesce: deliquesce
  [variant forms: prolix, prolixity]

liqu-e²: awry; slanted
  oblique, obliquity

LISLE: after Lisle, France, earlier spelling of *Lille*, where originally made; a strong thread

LISSOME, or lissom; from *lithe*, *lithesome*: bending easily, flexible

LINIMENT: from *linere*, to smear; a medicated liquid to be rubbed on the skin for something sore, sprained, or inflamed

liter: letter

≈liter: literacy, literary, literim

≈literal: literal, literalism, literality, literalize, literally

≈literat-e: literate, literati, literature

- literate: aliterate, alliterate, antiliterate, biliterate, illiterate, obliterate, postliterate, preliterate, semiliterate, subliterate, transliterate

- literal: alliteral, biliteral, heteroliteral, monoliteral, triliteral, uniliteral

- literation: alliteration, obliteration, transliteration [variant forms: ad litteram, litterateur]

lith-o: rock, stone

≈lith: lithia, lithiasis, lithium

≈lith-: lithagogue, litharge, lithoid

≈lithi-: lithify

≈litho-: lithograph, lithology, lithophyte, lithopone, lithosphere, lithotomy, lithotripsy, lithotrity

- lith: with prefixes: acrolith, megalith, microlith, monolith

- lith: with combining forms: albolith, angiolith, arteriolith, broncholith, bursolith, coccolith, coprolith, cystolith, dacryolith, eolith, gastrolith, granolith, hemolith, hepatolith, laccolith, lipolith, oolith, otolith, paleolith, phytolith,

regolith, statolith, urolith, uterolith, xenolith

- lithiasis: urolithiasis

- lithic: antilithic, Eolithic, Mesolithic, monolithic, Neolithic, Paleolithic, protolithic

- litho-: photolithograph

- lite: coprolite, crystallite, granulite, ichthyolite, lepidolite, oolite, ophiolite, phonolite, pisolite, rhodolite, saprolite, spherulite, staurolite, stylolite, variolite

LITTER: from Latin *lectus*, a couch, rough bed; thus, the litter used to transport the injured, as well as the rough bed an animal makes for its young; the young born at one time

LITTORAL: along the shore

liturg: the people; from *laic* + *ergon*, work; thus "work of the people"

liturgical, liturgy

LIVID: from Latin *lividus*, originally, described that which is discolored by a bruise; now, lead-colored, as *to be livid with rage*

lixiv: ashes, lie

lixiviate, lixivium

loath: hate

loath, loathe, loathful, loathing, loathly, loathsome

lob-e: to hang down; an anatomical division of the heart, lungs, ear

≈lob-e: lobate, lobation, lobe, lobule, lobulus

≈lob-: lobectomy

≈lobo-: lobotomize, lobotomy

- lobate: bilobate, quadrilobate, quinquelobate, trilobate

loca-l: a place; in science, cavity, chamber

≈local: local, locale, localism, localite, locality, localization, localize, localizer, locally

≈locat-e: locate, location,
  locative
≈loco-: locofoco, locomobile,
  locomotor
- local: interlocal, matrilocal,
  multilocal, patrilocal, unilocal,
  uxorilocal, virilocal
- locate: allocate, collocate,
  dislocate, translocate
≈locu-l: locus—pl., loci, locular,
  loculate, loculus—pl., loculi
≈loculi-: loculicidal
- locular: bilocular, trilocular,
  unilocular
  [variant forms: couch, lieu,
  lieutenant, milieu; in lieu of;
  lodge, lodger; loge, loggia,
  logistics, louver]
  [phrases: in loco parentis,
  loco citato, locum tenens,
  locus classicus, locus in quo]
  {word note: lieutenant: lit., one who
  "holds the place of" one higher;
  e.g., a first lieutenant is first to
  hold the captain's place; a second
  lieutenant (the rank below first
  lieutenant) is the second}
LOCHIA: of childbirth
**locu: to say, to speak; reasoning,
thought** [see loqu]
≈locu: locution
- locution: allocution, elocution,
  interlocution; illocutionary
- locutor: interlocutor, prolocutor
≈log: logia, logic, logical,
  logistic
≈log-: logarithm
- log-e: homologate; horologe;
  apologetics; eulogia
- logical: mythological,
  nomological, pathological,
  technological, zoological
- logism: amphilogism,
  epilogism, neologism,
  paralogism, syllogism
- logize: neologize, syllogize

≈logo-: logography, logogriph,
  logomachy, logorrhea,
  logotype
- logous: analogous, antilogous,
  autologous, heterologous,
  homologous, tautologous
- logue: catalogue, collogue,
  Decalogue, dialogue, eclogue,
  epilogue, homologue,
  monologue, prologue
- logy: analogy, antilogy,
  apology, etiology, eulogy,
  tautology, tetralogy
  [variant forms: prolegomenon,
  pl., prolegomena, prolegomenous;
  logo]
logy: scientific study of; from
  "word"
≈adenology, aerology,
  agriology, agrology,
  agrostology, algology,
  allergology, anthropology,
  audiology, balneology,
  biology, coprology, cryptology
≈dermatology, dendrology,
  embryology, endocrinology,
  ethnology
≈gemology, geology, glaciology,
  graphology, gynecology
≈hierology, helminthology,
  hematology, herpetology,
  histology, homology,
  hypnology
≈ichnology, ichthyology,
  iconology, ideology,
  kinesiology
≈laryngology, lexicology,
  limnology, lithology
≈malacology, mammalogy,
  menology, meteorology,
  methodology, mineralogy,
  misology, myology, mycology,
  myrmecology, mythology
≈narratology, nematology,
  necrology, neonatology,

nephrology, neurology,
nosology, numerology
≈oceanology, odontology,
oenology, oncology, ontology,
oology, ophiology,
ophthalmology, orchidology,
organology, ornithology,
orology, osteology,
otorhinolaryngology, otology
≈paleethnology,
paleoanthropology,
palynology, parasitology,
pathology, pedology,
penology, periodontology,
petrology, pharmacology,
pharyngology, phenology,
phenomenology, philology,
phlebology, phonology,
photobiology, photogeology,
phraseology, phrenology,
piscatology, psychology,
phycology, phytology,
phytopathology,
phytosociology, planetology,
pneumatology, pomology,
posology, primatology,
proctology, protozoology,
psephology, pteridology
≈radiobiology, radiology,
rheology, rheumatology,
rhinolaryngology, rhinology
≈sarcology, scatology,
sedimentology, seismology,
selenology, semasiology,
seminology, serology,
sociology, somatology,
soteriology, speleology,
splanchnology, stomatology,
symbology
≈technology, tropology
teleology, teratology,
thanatology, thaumatology,
tocology, topology, toxicology,
tribology, trichology, typology

≈uranology, urology,
venereology, vexillology,
virology, volcanology,
zoology, zymology
[Note: Substitute –*logist* for –*logy*
for the word designating who
performs the study, e.g.,
zymologist, one who studies
fermentation.]
LOLLYGAG: an informal usage: to
waste time in trifling or aimless
activity
long: long
≈long-e: longe, longeron, longeur
≈longitud-e: longitude,
longitudinal
≈long-: longanimity, longevity,
longevous, longshoreman
≈longi-: longicorn, longilateral,
longimanous
- long: furlong, oblong, prolong
- longate: elongate
[variant forms: eloign, long, lunge,
purloin, sirloin]
[phrase: chaise longue]
{word notes: longshore: an aphesis
of "along the shore"; furlong:
originally, the length of furrow; a
unit of linear measure equal to one
half mile or 220 yards}
LOOT: Hindi; *lut*; from Sanskrit *lunt*,
to rob; as a noun, loot, plunder; as
a verb, to loot, plunder
lop-er: to leap
elope, interloper, gallop, orlop
lopho: crest, tuff
lophobranch, lophophore
loqu: to speak [see locu]
≈loqua: loquacious, loquacity
- loquence: altiloquence,
blandiloquence, breviloquence,
eloquence, grandiloquence,
ineloquence, longiloquence,
magniloquence, melliloquence,
multiloquence, somniloquence,
stultiloquence

- loquent: eloquent, ineloquent,
  grandiloquent, magniloquent
- loquial: colloquial, ventriloquial
- loquialism: colloquialism
- loquism: ventriloquism
- loquist: ventriloquist
- loquium: colloquium
- loquy: colloquy, obloquy,
  soliloquy, somniloquy
  [phrases: res ipsa loquitur;
  usus loquendi]
LORD: from Old English *hlafweard*;
  lit., loafward; see lady
LORDLY: from Old English *hlafordic*,
  like a lord; noble, grand; also,
  haughty
LORDOSIS: bent backward
LOS ANGELES, CA: founded in 1781
  on a Spanish grant; originally
  named *Nuestra Señora Reina de
  los Angeles*, Our Queen Lady of
  the Angels
LOUCHE: lit., squinting, one-eyed;
  questionable, shady, oblique, odd
low: see laud for allow
LOX: Yiddish; from German *lachs*,
  salmon; a variety of salty smoked
  salmon
loxo: slanted
  loxodont; loxodrome,
  loxosceles, loxotomy
**lubric: to make smooth or
  slippery**
  lubricant, lubricate, lubricator,
  lubricious, lubricity, lubricous
luc: light
≈luc: lucarne, lucent, lucern,
  lucid, lucite, luculent
≈luci-: Lucifer, luciferous
- luca: noctiluca
- lucent: with prefixes:
  hyperlucent, interlucent,
  relucent, translucent, or
  tralucent
- lucent: with combining forms:
  noctilucent, radiolucent
- lucid-: elucidate, pellucid

≈lucubra: lucubration,
  elucubrate: to work by
  candlelight
≈lumin: luminaire, luminance,
  luminaria, luminary,
  luminescence, luminosity,
  luminous
≈lumini-: luminiferous
- lume: illume, relume
- lumin-e: illuminati, illumine,
  illuminism
- luminate: illuminate,
  transilluminate
- luminescence:
  photoluminescence,
  thermoluminescence,
  triboluminescence
≈lust-r: luster, lackluster; lustral,
  lustrate, lustrous, lustrum
- lustr-: illustrate, illustrious
  [variant form: limn—orig., to
  illuminate medieval manuscripts
  with gold, silver, or other brilliant
  colors]
lucr-e: gain, riches
  lucre, lucrative; lucrific
luct: to struggle
  eluctation, ineluctable,
  reluctance, reluctant
  [variant form: lock]
lud-e: to play
≈ludic: ludic, ludicrous
- lude: allude, collude, delude,
  elude, interlude, prelude,
  postlude
- ludible: eludible, ineludible
- lusion: allusion, collusion,
  delusion, disillusion, elusion,
  illusion
- lusive: allusive, collusive,
  delusive, elusive, illusive
LUGUBRIOUS: from *lugere*, to mourn;
  thus, mournful
lumb-o: loin
≈lumb: lumbago, lumbar
≈lumbo-: lumbovertebral

- lumbar: dorsolumbar
  [variant form: loin]

lumbric: **earthworm**
  lumbricalis*, lumbricoid
  *designating certain muscles in the
  palm of the hand and the sole of the
  foot in the fancied shape of
  earthworms
lumin: see luc

lun-e: **moon**
≈lun-e: lunacy, lunar, lunate,
  lunatic, lunation, lune, lunette
≈lunul: lunula, lunulate
≈luni-: lunisolar, lunitidal
- lunar: circumlunar, cislunar,
  interlunar, semilunar, sublunar
- lunary: sublunary, superlunary,
  translunary
- lune: perilune

lure: **to lure, entice**
  lure, allure
LURID: orig., pale yellow; ghastly;
  startling, sensational
LUXATE: to dislocate

lux-e: **extravagance, luxury**
  luxe, luxuriant, luxuriate,
  luxurious, luxury; deluxe

lyc: **wolf**
  lycanthrope, lycanthropy
  [variant form: lupine: pertaining to
  wolves; wolflike; ravenous; also,
  a flower, but the relationship to
  wolf is uncertain

lymph-o: **body fluid**; orig., spring
  water
≈lymph: lymph, lymphatic
≈lymph-: lymphadenitis,
  lymphangial, lymphoid,
  lymphoma
≈lympho-: lymphoblast,
  lymphocyte, lymphopoiesis
- lymph: with prefixes:
  endolymph, perilymph
- lymph: with combining forms:
  cytolymph, hemolymph,
  hydrolymph, karyolymph,
  neurolymph, nucleolymph

[variant form: limpid—perfectly
  clear; transparent]

-lysis: **a loosening**
- lysis: with prefixes: analysis,
  autolysis, catalysis, dialysis,
  heterolysis, paralysis
- lysis: with combining forms:
  acantholysis, acidolysis,
  arthrolysis, glycolysis,
  hemolysis, histolysis,
  hydrolysis, lipolysis,
  neurolysis, photolysis,
  plasmolysis, pneumatolysis,
  proteinolysis, pyrolysis,
  steatolysis, thermolysis,
  zymolysis
- lyst: analyst, catalyst
- lyt-e: tachylyte; analytic,
  catalytic, paralytic
- lyze: analyze, catalyze,
  paralyze, plasmolyze

M

MACHETE: from Spanish *macho*,
  hammer, ax; further frrom Latin
  marcus, hammer; a large heavy-
  bladed knife used for cutting down
  sugar cane, underbrush, etc.,
  especially in Central and South
  America

machi: **to crush**
  machicolate, machicolation
  [second root is *col*, neck]

maciat: **thin**
  macilent; emaciate, emaciated
  [variant form: meager]
MACHIAVELLIAN: expedient; crafty;
  after Nicolò di Bernardo
  Machiavelli (1469-1527),
  Florentine statesman and writer,
  author of *The Prince*

machin-e: **contrivance, machine**
≈machin-e: machinate,
  machination, machine,
  machinery, machinist

≈mechan: mechanic, mechanical,
  mechanician, mechanics,
  mechanism, mechanistic
- mechanic-: aeromechanics,
  photomechanical
  [drama term: deus ex machina, lit.,
  god from a machine]
machy: **a battle**
  gigantomachy, logomachy,
  monomachy, naumachy,
  scimachy, tauromachy,
  theomachy
macro-: **large**
≈macr: macron
≈macr-: macrodont, macruran
≈macro-: macroalgae,
  macrobenthos, macrobiotics,
  macroblast, macrocardia,
  macrocephaly, macroclimate,
  macrocosm, macrocylic,
  macrocyst
≈macroeconomics,
  macroevolution
≈macrogamete, macromolecule,
  macronucleus, macronutrient
≈macrophage, macropterous,
  macroscopic,
  macrosporangium
  [variant forms: amphimacer,
  meager]
macul: **spot, blemish**
≈macula-te: macular, maculate,
  maculation
- maculate: bimaculate,
  emaculate, immaculate
  [variant forms: mackle, maquette,
  trammel
MAELSTROM: swirling tidal current;
  also, agitated state of mind; from a
  violent whirling stream off the
  west coast of Norway
MAGAZINE: Arabic: storehouse
MAGI: plural of *magus*; Persian;
  Magi were members of a priestly
  caste of ancient Persia; commonly
  refers to the wise men who visited

the infant Jesus and who were
  guided by the Star of Bethlehem
magist: **master**
≈magis: magisterial,
  magisterium, magistracy,
  magistral, magistrate
≈master: master, mastery,
  masterful
  [variant forms: German: meister;
  Spanish: maestro; mister, mistral]
magn: **great**
≈magn: magnate, magnitude
≈magn-: magnanimity,
  magnanimous
≈magni-: magnicaudate,
  Magnificat, magnification,
  magnificence, magnificent,
  magnific, magnifico, magnify,
  magniloquence, magniloquent
  [Sanskrit: mahatma]
  [phrases: Magna Charta; magna
  cum laude, magnum opus]
magne: **Magnesia** (in Thessaly)
≈magne-t: magnesia, magnesite,
  magnesium, magnet, magnetic,
  magnetics, magnetism,
  magnetize
≈magneto-: magnetoelasticity,
  magnetochemistry,
  magnetogram, magnetology,
  magnetosome, magnetosphere,
  magnetostriction
  [variant form: manganese]
MAGNOLIA: after Pierre Magnol
  (1638-1715), French botanist; a
  sweet-smelling flower; the tree
maha: **great** (Hindi)
  maharaja, mahatma, maharani,
  mahout
  {word note: mahout: from Sanskrit
  mahamatra, great in measure;
  elephant driver or keeper}
MAIM: to seriously injure; to cripple;
  to mutilate; from the same base
  are *mayhem* and *mangle*
MAI TAI: Tahitian: good; a cocktail of
  rum and fruit juices

maj: greater
  majestic, majesty, major,
  major-domo, majority,
  majoritarian, majuscule
  [variant forms: lèse-majesté,
    maestoso; mayor, mayoralty;
    Spanish: mayor—older, major]
  [phrase: force majeure]
malaco: soft, mollusks
  ≈malac-: malacoma,
    malacostracan
  ≈malaco-: malacoderm,
    malacology, malacophyllous,
    malacophonous
  - malacia: osteomalacia
  ≈moll: mollescent, mollusk
  ≈molli-: mollify
  - mollient: emollient
    [variant forms: moil;
      possibly, amalgam]
  MALAR: of the cheek or cheekbone
mal-e: bad, wrong
  ≈mal: malady, malice, malicious,
    malign, malignancy,
    malignant, malignity, malinger
  ≈mal-: malaise, malaria,
    malformation
  ≈male-: malediction,
    malefaction, malefactor,
    malefic, maleficent,
    malevolence, malevolent
  ≈mal+a: maladroit
  ≈mal+ad: maladaptation,
    maladjusted, maladminister
  ≈mal+ap: malapportion,
    malapropos
  ≈mal+as: malassimilation
  ≈mal+c: malcontent
  ≈mal+d: maldevelopment,
    maldistribution
  ≈mal+e: malentendu
  ≈mal+f: malfeasance,
    malformation, malfunction
  ≈mal+n: malnourished
  ≈mal+o: malocclusion, malodor,
    malodorous

  ≈mal+p: malposition,
    malpractice
  ≈mal+t: maltreat
  ≈mal+v: malversation
  - mal: dismal
    [term: mal de mer]
  {word note: dismal: orig., evil days
    (of the medieval calendar);
    causing gloom and misery}
malle: hammer
  malleable, malleolus, mallet,
  malleus
  [variant forms: maul, mangle,
    mangonel]
mamma-l: breast
  ≈mamm: mamma, mammal,
    mammary
  ≈mamma-: mammalogy,
    mammaplasty
  ≈mammi-: mammiferous,
    mammiform
  ≈mammo-: mammogen,
    mammogram, mammography
  ≈mast-: mastectomy, mastitis,
    mastodon, mastodont, mastoid
  - mast-ia: neuromast;
    gynecomastia
  ≈mammilla: mammilla,
    mammillate: nipple
  MAMMOTH: Russian; *mamont*;
    probably from *mama*, earth; from
    the notion that the animal had
    burrowed in the ground; a genus
    of extinct elephants
man[1]: to glide, flow, pass
  - man-: emanate, emanation
  - mea-: permeability, permeance,
    permeant, permeate
  - meable: permeable,
    impermeable
man[2]: to remain, stay
  ≈man-se: manor, manse, mansion
  - man-: immanentism, Immanuel;
    permanency
  - manence: permanence,
    remanence

- manent: immanent, permanent, impermanent, remanent
- main-: remain, remainder, remains
  [variant forms: demesne, maisonette, menial, remnant; French: ménage, menagerie; messuage]
  [phrase: ménage à trois]

man[3]: **gas**

≈mano-: monograph, manometer, manometry
- mano-: syphgmomanometer

mancy: **divination**
  chartomancy, chiromancy, geomancy, necromancy, oneiromancy, pyromancy, rhabdomancy

mand: **hand**

≈man-age: manacle, manage, management, manager, manege, manicotti, manqué
≈manner: manner, mannered, mannerism
≈manu: manual, manubrium, manus
≈man-: manciple, mandamus, mandate, mandatory, mansuetude; maneuver, manure [second root in latter two words is from *ergon*, work]
- mancipate: emancipate
≈mani: manicure, manifest, manifestation, manifesto, maniple (manipular, manipulate, manipulation)
- manous: amanous, bimanous, longimanous, pedimanous, quadrumanous
≈manu: manufacture, manumission, manuscript
- manuensis: amanuensis
≈main: maintain, maintenance
- main: legerdemain, mortmain
- mand: command, countermand, demand, remand

- mand-: commandant, commandment, commando
- manual: bimanual, nonmanual
- mend: commend, discommend, recommend
- mend-ation: commendam, commendation, recommendation
  [variant forms: commodore, Spanish: mano; maquiladora—manufacturing plant]
  [phrases: Maundy Thursday; Manifest Destiny; mano a mano]
  {word note: manicotti: Italian: muff (from hand); pasta, in the form of long, broad tubes, usually boiled, stuffed with cheese, and baked with a tomato sauce}

mandib: **jaw**
  mandible, mandibulate; mandibuliform
  [variant forms: manger, masseter]
mangle: see maim
MANIFOLD: having many and various forms, features, parts, etc., as *manifold wisdom*; other applications

mani-a: **madness, frenzy**; a craving for

≈mani-a: mania, maniac, maniacal, manic
- mania: anthomania, bibliomania, dipsomania, dromomania, egomania, eleutheromania, ergomania, erotomania, graphomania, gynecomania, hypomania, iconomania, kleptomania, logomania, macromania, megalomania, micromania, monomania, mythomania, narcomania, nostomania, nudomania, nymphomania, pyromania
- maniac: bibliomaniac, dipsomaniac, egomaniac, eleutheromaniac, erotomaniac,

hypomaniac, kleptomaniac, megalomaniac, monomaniac, mythomaniac, nostomaniac, nymphomaniac, pyromaniac

mant: to cover; cloak

≈mant: manta, manteau, mantua

≈mantel: mantel, or mantle, mantelet, manteletta

≈mantel-: mantelpiece, manteltree

- manteau: portmanteau

- mantle: dismantle

manti: prophet, seer

mantic, mantilla, mantis

MARABOUT: French; from Portuguese *marabuto*; orig. from Arabic *murabit*, hermit; a Muslin hermit or holy man, esp. among the Berbers and the Moors; a tomb or shrine for such a man

MARATHON: from the legend of the Greek runner who ran from Marathon to Athens to tell of the victory over the Persians; a race of 26 miles, 385 yards, the distance from Marathon to Athens

MARAUD: lit., tomcat; to rove in search of plunder; make raids

marc: mark

≈marc-h: marc, march, marchioness

- marcate: demarcate

≈margin: margin, marginal, marginalia, marginalize, marginate

- margin-: emarginate, submarginal
  [variant forms: demarche, mark, remark, remarkable, marquess, marquis, marquise, remarque, mush, as in "mushing dog," for French *Marchons!* Let's march on!]

marce: to wither

marcescent—in botany, withering but not falling off, as leaves
[variant form: marasmus]

MARIGOLD: lit., Mary's gold; a flower with a pungent smell

mar-in: sea

≈mar-in-e: maremma, marina, marinara, marinate, marine, mariner, maritime

≈mari-: mariculture

- marine: submarine, transmarine, ultramarine
  [variant forms: mermaid, merman; Maritime Provinces, marish, marsh; rosemary—dew of the sea]
  [phrases: mal de mer, mare clausum, mare liberum]

mar-it: marriage

≈marit: marital

≈mariti-: mariticide

- marital: premarital, extramarital

≈marr: marriage, married, marry
  [Spanish: mariachi—from providing music for marriage celebrations]

MARMOREAL: of, or like, marble

MARSHAL: lit., horse-servant

marsup: pouch, bag

marsupial, marsupium

mart: war; from Mars, god of war martial; martial art, martial law (distinguished from military law); court-martial

martyr-o: witness

≈martyr: martyr, martyrdom, martyrize

≈martyro-: martyrolatry, martyrology

- martyr: protomartyr

marvel: see mir-e

mascul: man

masculine, masculinize; emasculate
[variant forms: macho, male, mallard]

MASER: acronym for microwave amplification by stimulated emission of radiation; see *laser*

masque: a mask

masque, masquerade

[variant forms: mascara, mask;
mum—one meaning, also,
mumm, mummer, mummery]

mass¹: to touch; from French
masser; from Arabic *massa*
massage, masseur, masseuse

mass²: lump, mass
mass, massif, massive; amass
Mass: see miss
mastectomy: see mamma-1

mastic: to chew
masticate, masticatory
[variant form: papier-mâché]

matad: to kill, checkmate
matador—a bullfighter whose
specialty is killing the bull with a
sword thrust at the end of a
bullfight
[variant form: checkmate]

MATELASSÉ: either describes or is a
fabric with a raised design; related
to *mattress*, which see

mathemat: to learn
≈mathemat: mathematical,
mathematician, mathematics
- math-: metamathematics;
polymath
- mathy: chrestomathy,
opsimathy, pharcomathy,
philomathy, polymathy

matr-i: mother
≈matri: matriculant, matriculate,
matrimony, matrix
≈matron: matron, matronize
≈matr-: matronymic
≈matri-: matriarch, matriarchate,
matricentric, matricide,
matriclinous, matrifocal,
matriherital, matrilateral,
matrilineal
≈mater: maternal, maternity
≈mater-: materfamilias
≈material: material, materialism,
materialize, materially
- material: immaterial,
immaterialism

[phrase: alma mater—lit.,
nourishing mother]

MATTRESS: lit., pad; from Arabic, for
"something thrown," as on the
floor (to sleep on)

MATUTINAL: early; of the morning;
after *Matuta*, goddess of dawn

matur-e: ripe, mature
≈matur-e: maturate, maturation,
mature
- mature: immature, premature
[variant forms: maduro, matin,
matinee, demure]

MAUDLIN: foolishly sentimental; after
a variant name for the penitent
Mary Magdalene

maxill-a: the upper jaw
≈maxilla: maxilla, maxillary
≈maxilli-: maxilliped
≈maxillo-: maxillodental,
maxillofacial, maxillojugal,
maxillolabial, maxillotomy
- maxilla-ry: premaxilla,
submaxilla; submaxillary

maxim: greatest
maxim, maximal, maximalist,
maximize, maximum
{word note: maxim: orig. *maxima
propsositio*, greatest premise}

may: power
dismay—to make afraid or
discouraged at the prospect of
trouble or danger

MAYDAY: short for French *venez
m'aider*, come, help me
mayhem: see maim
mayor: see maj

MAZEL TOV: Hebrew: *mazal*, luck +
tov, good; an expression of
congratulation

MAZER: from *maple*; a large drinking
bowl or goblet, orig. of a hard
wood, probably maple, later of
metal

mazo: breast [see mamma-l]
≈maz-: mazodynia
≈mazo-: mazolysis, mazopathy,
mazopexy, mazoplasis

- mazon: amazon—lit., no breasts
MAZUMA: Yiddish; slang for money
MAZURKA: Polish; orig., woman from
  Mazovia, region of central Poland;
  a lively Polish folk dance; the
  music for the dance
mea: see man¹ for permeate
MEANDER: from Meander River,
  from its winding course; to
  wander aimlessly
MEASLY: lit., infected with measles;
  extended to mean "meager,
  worthless"
measure: see mensur
mechanic: see machin-e
meco: **length**
  mecocephalic, mecopteran;
  paramecium
med: **middle**
≈medal: medal, medalist,
  medallion
≈medi-um: mediad, medial,
  median, mediant, mediastinum,
  medium, pl., media
≈mediat-e: mediate, mediation,
  mediatize
≈medi-: medieval, mediocre,
  mediocrity, Mediterranean
- media: multimedia
- mediant: submediant
- mediary: cybermediary,
  intermediary
- mediate-ly: immediate,
  immediately, intermediate
- meditat-e: premeditate,
  premeditation
≈mid-d: middle, middling,
  midland
≈mid-: midriff—second root is Old
  English *hrif*, belly
≈mezz-o-: mezzanine, mezzo;
  mezzo-relievo, mezzo-soprano
- mezzo: intermezzo
≈mizzen-: mizzen, mizzenmast
  [variant forms: mean—one
  meaning; dimidiate; milieu,
  moiety, mullion]

[phrase: in media res]
{word note: mediocre: lit., middle of
  the peak; neither very good nor
  very bad; also, not good enough}
medi-c: **physician**, **counselor**; **to
  attend to**; from "to measure;
  medicine"
≈medic: medic, medicable,
  medical, medicament,
  medicate, medication,
  medicine
≈medit: meditate, meditation
- med-y: remedial, remediate,
  remediation, remedy,
  irremediable
- medic-: aeromedicine;
  immedicable, paramedic
MEERSCHAUM: German; lit., sea
  foam; used for tobacco pipes
mega-: **great**, **large**
≈meg-: megohm
≈mega-: megabase, megabyte,
  megacalorie, megacephalic,
  megacoccus, megacosm,
  megacurie, megacycle,
  megadose, megafauna,
  megahertz, megakaryocyte,
  megalith, megaphone,
  megapode, megascopic,
  megasporangium, megaspore,
  megatherium
- mega: omega
≈megal-: megalodont, megalops,
  megalonyx
≈megalo-: megaloblast,
  megalocardia, megalocyte,
  megalodactyly, megaloglossia,
  megalography, megalomania,
  megalopolis, megalosaur
- megaly: acromegaly,
  adrenomegaly, angiomegaly,
  cephalomegaly,
  dactylomegaly, splenomegaly
MEGO: acronym for My Eyes Glaze
  Over: a reaction, as to a dull news
  story

mei: small, less
  meiosis, meiotic
  [variant forms: mignon,
  mignonette]
  MEIN KAMPF: German for "my
  struggle"; title of Adolph Hitler's
  autobiography
mel[1]: **apple**
  melon, marmalade, chamomile
mel[2]: **limb** (of the body)
  ≈mel-: melagra
- melia: with prefixes: acromelia,
  anisomelia, dysmelia,
  hemimelia, hypomelia,
  mesomelia, micromelia,
  polymelia
- melia: with combining forms:
  arachnomelia, phocomelia,
  rhizomelia
melan-o-: **black**
  ≈melan: melanic, melanism,
  melanite, melanize, melanous
  ≈mela-: Melanesia, melastome
  ≈melan-: melancholy, melanoid,
  melanoma, melanonychia,
  melanosis
  ≈melano-: melanoblast,
  melanochrysum, melanocyte,
  melanoderma, melanogen,
  melanoglossia, melanopathy,
  melanophore, melanorrhea,
  melanosome, melanosperm,
  melanotroph, melanotype
- mel: calomel
melli: **honey**
  ≈melli-: melliferous, mellifluous,
  mellivorous
- mel: caramel, oenomel
  [variant forms: marmalade,
  mildew, molasses, mousse]
melior: **better**
  meliorate, melioration,
  meliorism; ameliorate
mel-o: **song**
  ≈mel: melic, melisma

≈mel-: melodic, melodious,
  melody
≈melo-: melodrama
  [variant form: dulcimer]
member: **part of a body**
  member, membership;
  dismember
membran-e: **fine skin, membrane**
  [see mening]
≈membran-e: membrane,
  membranous
- membrane: biomembrane,
  cytomembrane,
  pseudomembrane,
  transmembrane
memor: **to remember**
≈memor-y: memorabilia,
  memorable, memorandum,
  memorial, memorize, memory
- memor-: commemorate,
  immemorial
- member: remember,
  disremember
- membrance-r: remembrance,
  remembrancer
  [variant forms: memento, memoir]
  [phrases: in memoriam;
  lapsus memoriae]
  MEMPHIS, TN: after the capital of
  ancient Egypt, just south of
  modern-day Cairo; the Tennessee
  city is on the Mississippi
men: **to lead, threaten, project**
≈men: menace
- men-: amenable, promenade
≈min: minacious, minatory
- mination: commination
- minence: eminence,
  imminence, prominence
- minent: eminent, imminent,
  preeminent, prominent,
  supereminent
  [variant forms: demean—one
  meaning, demeanor; promontory]
  {word notes: menace: a threat or the
  act of threatening; amenable: lit.,

able to be driven, that is,
controlled or influenced}

men-o: **moon**, **month**;
  menstruation
≈men: meniscus, mensal—one
  meaning, menses, mensual
≈men-: menarche
≈meno-: menology, menopause,
  menorrhagia, menorrhea,
  menostasis
- menia: catamenia,
  cephalomenia, emmenia
- men-o-: dysmenorrhea,
  emmenagogue
≈menstru: menstrual, menstruate,
  menstruation, menstruum
- menstrual: premenstrual
- mester: bimester, semester,
  trimester
- mestral: semestral, trimestral
- mestrial: bimestrial, trimestrial
  [phrase: per mensem]
mence: see **it**

mend: **flaw**
≈mend: mend, mendacious,
  mendacity, mendicant
- mend-: amend, emend; amends,
  amendment, emendate,
  emendation
MENHADEN: American Indian:
  fertilizer, but actually a small fish
  used for fertilizer

mening: **membrane**
  [see membran-e]
  meninges; meningitis;
  meningioma; meningococcus
MENORAH: Hebrew; from Aramaic
  nur, fire; lampstand; a candelabrum with seven branches, a
  traditional symbol of Judaism;
  also, one with nine branches, used
  during the festival of Hanuka; akin
  to minaret, which see]

mensa: **table**
≈mensa: Mensa, Mensa Society,
  mensal—one meaning

- mensal: amensal, commensal,
  ectocommensal,
  endocommensal
  [Spanish: mesa—tableland;
  Mesa, AZ; mesito—male
  waiter; mesita—female waiter]

mensur: **to measure**
≈mensur: mensurability,
  mensurable, mensural,
  mensurate, mensuration,
  mensurative
- mens-e: dimension,
  dimensional, immense
- mensurable: commensurable,
  immensurable,
  incommensurable
- mensurate: commensurate
≈measur-e: measure, measured
- measurable: immeasurable
- measure: admeasure,
  commeasure

ment[1]: **mind**
≈ment: mental, mentality,
  mentation, mention
- ment-: ament, amentia,
  comment, commentary,
  commentator, demented
≈mind: mind, minded, mindful
- mind-: remind, reminder,
  remindful
- minisc-e: reminisce,
  reminiscence, reminiscent
  [terms: amentia, dementia]
  [phrase: non compos mentis]

ment[2]: **chin**
  mentigerous; mentolabial,
  mentoposterior

meph: **bad-smelling vapor**
  mephitic, mephitis

mer: **thigh**
≈mer-: meralgia
≈mero-: merocele, merosthenic

merc-e: **to trade**, **buy**, **earn**
≈merc: mercantile, mercantilism;
  mercenary

- merc-e: commerce,
  commercial, grammercy
≈merchand: merchandise,
  merchandising
≈merchant: merchant
≈merit: merit, meritorious
≈merito-: meritocracy
- merit-: demerit, emeritus
  [variant forms: market, mart,
  mercy, mora; meretricious: of
  a prostitute]
MERCURIAL: describes one born
  under the influence of the planet
  Mercury; therefore, sprightly and
  fickle like the Roman god; see
  jovial; saturnine
mer-o: part
≈mer: meristem, meristic
≈mero-: meroblastic, merocrine,
  meromorphic, meroplankton,
  merozoite
- mer: enantiomer,
  homopolymer, isomer,
  metamer, monomer, polymer,
  stereoisomer
- mere: with prefixes: antimere,
  ectomere, epimere, micromere,
  telomere
- mere: with combining forms:
  arthromere, centromere,
  chromomere, sarcomere
- meric: centromeric, poromeric
- merism: allomerism,
  tautomerism
- meristic: ameristic
- merous: decamerous, dimerous,
  heptamerous, heteromerous,
  monomerous, octamerous,
  pentamerous, polymerous,
  tetramerous, trimerous
merg-e: to dip, plunge, sink
≈merg: merge, merger
≈merg-: merganser
- merg-e: emerge, emergence,
  emergency, emergent,
  submerge

- mers-: demersal, submersible
- merse: immerse, submerse
- mersed: emersed, immersed,
  submersed
- mersion: emersion, immersion,
  submersion
meri: mid
  meridian, meridional;
  antemeridian, postmeridian
mes-o-: middle
≈mes: mesial, mesic, mesne
≈mes-: mesarch, mesencephalon,
  mesenchyme, mesenteron,
  mesentery
≈meso-: mesobenthos, mesoblast,
  mesobronchia
≈mesocarp, mesocephalic,
  mesocranial, mesocratic
≈mesoderm, mesogastrium,
  mesoglea, mesolimnion,
  Mesolithic, mesomorphic
≈mesonephros, mesopause,
  mesophyll, Mesopotamia,
  mesosphere
≈mesothelioma, mesothelium,
  mesothorax, mesotrophic,
  mesozoan, Mesozoic
  [variant form: moiety]
{word note: Mesopotomia: from
  mesopotomia chora, land between
  the rivers—the Tigis and
  Euphrates}
mester: see men-o for semester
**met-a-: after, along with, among,
  back of, between, beyond,
  change, other, over**
≈met-: metempsychosis,
  metencephalon, meteor,
  method, methodic, Methodist,
  methodize, methodology,
  metonym, metonymy, metope,
  metopic
≈meta-: metabasis, metabolic,
  metabolism, metabolize
≈metacarpal, metacenter,
  metachromatic,

metachromatism,
metacriticism, metafiction
≈metagalaxy, metagenesis,
metagnathous, metalanguage,
metalinguistics
≈metamathematics, metamer,
metamere, metameric,
metamerism, metamorphosis
≈metanephros, metaphase,
metaphor, metaphrase,
metaphysical, metaphysics,
metaplasia, metaprotein,
metapsychology
≈metasomatism, metastable,
metastasis, metatarsus,
metathesis, metathorax,
metaxylem, metazoan
metal: metal, mine, quarry
≈metal: metal, metalist, metalize
≈metali-: metaliferous
- metalism: monometalism
≈metall: metallic, metalline
≈metall-: metalloid, metallurgy
≈metallo-: metallography
- metallic: bimetallic, dimetallic,
monometallic, multimetallic,
oligometallic, organometallic,
submetallic, trimetallic,
unmetallic
[variant form: mettle]
meteor: things in the air [see eor]
≈meteor: meteor, meteoric,
meteorite
≈meteor-: meteoroid
≈meteorio: meteoriological
≈meteoro-: meteorograph,
meteorology
meter: measurement, meter
- meter: measurement of distance:
diameter, parameter, perimeter
- meter: a measuring device:
≈aerometer, anemometer,
barometer, brontometer,
calorimeter, chronometer,
dioptometer

≈extensometer, hygrometer,
hypsometer, inclinometer,
lactometer, manometer,
micrometer, micropyrometer
≈nephelometer, nitrometer,
odometer, olfactometer,
optometer, osmometer
≈pedometer, penetrometer,
phonometer, photometer,
piezometer, planimeter,
pluviometer, pneumatometer,
polarimeter, psychrometer,
pulsimeter, pycnometer,
pyrheliometer, pyrometer
≈radiometer, refractometer,
rheometer
≈sacchrometer, salimeter,
salinometer, scintillometer,
seismometer, sensitometer,
spherometer,
sphygmomanometer,
sphygmometer, spirometer
≈tachometer, tachymeter,
taximeter, thermometer,
telemeter, tensimeter,
tensiometer, tonometer,
turbidimeter
≈ voltmeter, voltameter,
volumeter—volume + meter,
zymometer
- meter: line of verse specifying
number of metrical feet:
≈dimeter, heptameter,
hexameter, octameter,
pentameter, tetrameter
≈metri: metric, metrical,
metricate, metrist
≈metri-: metrify
- metric: with prefixes:
anisometric, dimetric,
diametric, isodiametric,
perimetric, trimetric
- metric: with combining forms:
geometric, hypsometric,
volumetric

- metrical: diametrical,
  geometrical
≈metro-: metronome
- metr-: anisometropia,
  emmetropia, isometropia
- metro-: trimetrogon
- metry: with prefixes: allometry,
  altimetry, asymmetry,
  dissymmetry, isometry,
  perimetry, symmetry
- metry: with combining forms:
  aerometry, anemometry,
  anthropometry, arthrometry,
  astrometry, geometry,
  optometry, photogrammetry,
  photometry, psychometry,
  sociometry, stereometry,
  stichometry, stoichiometry,
  tachometry, trigonometry,
  uranometry, zoometry
**methan-e: a particular flammable
gas**; from "wine"
≈methan-e: methane, methanol
≈metho-: methomania
≈methano-: methanogen
≈meth-yl: methyl, methylate
- methyst: amethyst
{word note: amethyst: lit., not
  drunken; the Greeks believed that
  the amethyst prevented
  intoxication; a purple or violet
  variety of quartz}
METICULOUS: extremely or
  excessively careful about details;
  from "fear"
metr-o: mother, uterus
≈metr-: metralgia, metritis,
  metronymic
≈metro-: metropolitan,
  metropolis, metrorrhagia
- metriosis: endometriosis
- metrium: endometrium,
  myometrium
mezzo: see med
MIAMI, FL: Chippewa: *omaugeg*,
  peninsula people

MIASMA: pollution
MICHIGAN: Chippewa: big lake
mic-a: crumb, grain
  mica, micelle
micr-o: small
≈micron: micron
≈micr-: microdont
≈micro-: microbacterium,
  microbe, microcephaly,
  microcline, micrococcus,
  microcosm, microcyte
≈microencapsulation,
  microfauna, microfiber,
  microflora, microform,
  microfossil
≈microgamete, micrograph,
  microgravity, microhabitat,
  microlith
≈micromere, micrometer,
  Micronesia, microphone,
  microphyte, micropyle,
  micropyrometer
≈microscope, microseism,
  microsome, microsphere,
  microsporangium, microspore,
  microstomatous,
  microstructure, microsurgery
≈microtome, microtomy,
  microtubule, microvillus
- micro-: photomicrograph,
  omicron
mictur-i: to urinate
  micturate, micturition
midge: see musca
MIDRASH: Hebrew: explanation
MIEN: French; a way of carrying
  oneself; a way of looking; bearing
migraine: see cran-i-o and hemi
**migra-te: to move from one place
  to another**
≈migr: migrant, migrate,
  migratory
- migrant: emigrant, immigrant,
  transmigrant
- migrate: emigrate, immigrate,
  in-migrate, transmigrate

- migration: emigration,
  immigration
  [variant form: émigré]
mili: millet, milletlike
  miliaria, miliary, milium
  [variant form: millet]
milit: soldier
≈milit-ia: militant, militate,
  militia
≈militar-y: militarism, militarist,
  militarize, military
- military: paramilitary
mil-l: one thousand
≈mil: mil, millage, millesimal,
  milliary, million, millionaire
≈mil-: milfoil
≈mill-: millenarian, millenary,
  millennium
≈mille-: millefiori, millefleur,
  millepore
≈milli-: millimeter, millipede
- mill-: postmillennial,
  premillennial
  [variant forms: mile, mileage,
  milestone; mille-feuille]
{word note: mile: from *milia
  passum*, one thousand paces; in
  building roads, the Romans placed
  a marker every 1,000 paces; now,
  5,280 feet}
MILLINER: orig., an inhabitant of
  Milan; now, one who designs,
  makes, trims, or sells women's
  hats
MILWAUKEE, WI: Algonquian for
  "good land"; meant "a good place
  to meet"
mim-e: imitator, actor
≈mim-e: mimic, mimosa, mime,
  mimesis, mimetic
≈mimeo-: mimeograph
≈mimi-: mimicry
- mime: pantomime
- mimetic: biomimetic,
  radiomimetic
MINARET: from Arabic *nar*, fire, for
  lighthouse; a high, slender tower
attached to a mosque, with one or
more projecting balconies from
which a muezzin, or crier, calls the
people to prayer; akin to Hebrew
menorah, which see
mine-r-a: metal, ore
  mine, miner; mineral,
  mineralize; mineralogy
  —mineral + -logy
mini: red lead
  minium, miniature
min-im: small, less, minimum
≈minim-al: minim, minimal,
  minimalism, minimalize,
  minimize, minimum
- minish: diminish
≈minor: minor, minority
≈minu: minuend, minuet
≈minus: minus, minuscule
≈minut-e: minute, minutiae
- minu-te: diminuendo;
  comminute; diminutive
- minution: comminution,
  diminution
  [variant forms: menu, mince,
  mincing, minaudière, miniver,
  Miocene, muscovado]
**minister: to serve; from *minor*,
  small**
≈minist: minister; ministrant,
  ministration, ministry
≈minstrel: minstrel, minstrelsy
- minister: administer,
  maladminister
  [variant form: métier—a trade,
  profession, or occupation, esp.,
  the work that one is particularly
  suited for]
minster: see mono
mir-e: to wonder
≈mir-r: miracle, miraculous,
  mirador, mirage, mirror
- mir-e: admirable, admiration,
  admire
  [variant form: marvel]
  [phrase: mirabile dictu—
  wonderful to tell]

mis-: wrong, wrongly; bad, badly
≈misadventure, mischief,
mischievous, misconceive,
misconduct, misconstrue,
miscreant
≈misdemeanant, misdemeanor,
misfeasance, misfire,
misfortune
≈misgovern, misinform,
misjoinder, misnomer,
misprision, misprize,
mispronounce, missent
[variant form: mésalliance]
misc-e: to mix
≈misc: miscellaneous,
miscellany, miscible
≈misce: miscegenation
- misc-: immiscible, promiscuity,
promiscuous
≈mix: mix, mixed, mixer,
mixture
≈mixo-: mixogamous,
mixohaline, mixolimnion,
mixologist, mixotrophic
- mix: commix, intermix, remix
- mixia: apomixia, panmixia
- mixis: amphimixis, apomixis,
automixis, endomixis,
meromixis, panmixis
- mixure: admixure, commixure,
intermixure
[variant forms: apomict, meddle,
intermeddle, medley, mélange,
mélée, mestiza, mestizo, métis,
mingle, commingle, immingle,
intermingle, mustang; mule,
mulatto, mulish]
miser-i: to pity; wretched
≈miser: miser, miserable,
Miserere, miserly, misery
≈miseri-: misericord
- miser-: commiserable,
commiserate
MISHNA, or Mishnah: Hebrew: lit.,
oral instruction: the first part of
the Talmud, containing oral

interpretations of scriptural
ordinances
mis-o: hate
≈mis-: misandry, misanthrope
≈miso-: misogamy, misogyny,
misology, misoneism,
misosophy, misotheism
miss: to send
≈miss: missal, missile, missive
≈mission: mission, missionary
- mise: compromise, demise,
premise, promise, remise,
surmise
- missary: commissary, emissary
- miss: dismiss, remiss
- miss-: commissure, promissory
- missible: admissible,
permissible, impermissible,
inadmissible, irremissible,
omissible, remissible,
transmissible
- missive: emissive, permissive,
submissive
- mission: with prefixes:
commission, decommission,
demission, emission,
intermission, omission,
permission, pretermission,
remission, submission,
transmission
- mission: with combining forms:
manumission, photoemission
- mit: admit, commit, demit,
emit, intermit, intromit, omit,
permit, pretermit, remit,
recommit, submit, transmit
≈mitt: mittimus
- mitt-: committee, permittivity,
remittal, remittance,
transmitter
- mitted: committed,
uncommitted
- mittent: intermittent, remittent
[variant forms: Mass; mess,
entremets; message, messenger]

[phrase: Nunc Dimittis]
MISSISSIPPI: French; from Illinois
missisipioui, lit., big river

mit: **soft**
mitigate, immitigable,
unmitigated

mit-o: **thread**
≈mit-: mitosis
≈mito-: mitochondrian, mitogen,
mitokinetic, mitomycin,
mitoplasm
- mit-: dimity, samite
- mitosis: amitosis, endomitosis,
haplomitosis, karyomitosis,
teleomitosis
mix: see misc-e

mne-m: **memory**
≈mnem: mnemonic, mnemonics,
Mnemosyne
- mnes: amnesty, anamnesis
- mnesia: amnesia, dysmnesia,
ecmnesia, hypermnesia,
hypomnesia, logamnesia,
neomnesia, paramnesia
[variant form: automatic]

mod-e: **measure**
≈mod-e: modal, modality, mode,
model, modem
≈moder-n: moderate, moderation,
moderator, modern
≈modest-y: modest, modesty
≈modicum: modicum
- modal: amodal, bimodal,
hypermodal, hypomodal,
intermodal, trimodal, unimodal
- mode: commode, démodé,
discommode, incommode
- moderate: immoderate
- modern: postmodern
- modest: immodest
- modate: accommodate
- modious: commodious,
discommodious,
incommodious
≈modi-: modify

- modify: commodify,
premodify, remodify
- modity: commodity,
discommodity, incommodity
≈modul-e: modulate, module,
modulus
- modulate: demodulate
[variant form: mold—one
meaning]
[phrases: modus operandi,
modus vivendi}
{word note: modem— mo̱dulator +
demo̱dulator}
MODESTO, CA: so named because its
founder was too "modest" to allow
the city to be named after him; in
Spanish, *modest* is *modesto*

mogri: **to change**
transmogrify—to change
completely, especially in a
grostesque or strange manner
MOGUL: Persian *Mughul*; from
Mongolian; a powerful or
important person, especially one
with autocratic power
MOJO: probably of Creole origin; a
charm or amulet thought to have
magic powers

mol: **to grind**
≈mol-e: molar—one meaning,
mole—one meaning
- mol-: emolument, immolate,
ormolu
- molar: distomolar, equimolar,
paramolar, premolar,
retromolar
{word note: emolument: with
ex-, out, lit., to grind out; gain
from employment or position;
salary; wages; fees}

mold: **to form**, **mold**
mold—one meaning
[variant form: moulage]

mol-e: **mass**
≈mol-e: molal, molar—one
meaning, mole—one meaning,
molecular, molecule

- molar: equimolar
- molecular: bimolecular, biomolecular, equimolecular, intermolecular, intramolecular, macromolecular, micromolecular, monomolecular, multimolecular, orthomolecular, trimolecular

MOLEST: from *moles*, a burden; to annoy, interfere with, or meddle with so as to trouble or harm; to make improper sexual advances, esp. to a minor; in Spanish, *molestar* means "to annoy, to inconvenience," with no implications of sexual impropriety

moli: to build
demolish, demolition
mollify, mollusk: see malac

molybd: iron
molybdenite, molybdenum, molybdic, molybdous

MOMA: Museum of Modern Art, in New York City

MONDAY: lit., moon's day

mone-t: of a mint
monetarism, monetarist, monetary, monetize, money; demonetize

MONGOOSE: from Marathi *mangus*; a carnivore, sometimes trained to kill poisonous snakes, rodents, etc.; plural is mongooses. Marathi is a language of India.

mon-it: to warn, to point out, show
≈monit: monition, monitor, monitorial, monitory
- mon: summon
- monish: admonish, premonish
- monition: admonition, premonition
≈monument: monument, monumental, monumentalize
≈monstr: monstrance, monstrosity, monstrous

- monstrable: demonstrable, indemonstrable
- monstrance: remonstrance
- monstrant: remonstrant
- monstrate: demonstrate, remonstrate
- monstration: demonstration, remonstration
- monstrative: demonstrative, undemonstrative, remonstrative
- monstrator: demonstrator
  [variant forms: praemunire; monster]
  [phrases: monstre sacré; quad erat demonstratum]

monili: necklace
moniliform—shaped something like a string of beads, as some plants' stems and some insect antennae

mon-o: one, alone
≈mon: monachal, monad, monadism, monastery, monastic, moneran, monism
≈monk: monk, monkery, monkish
≈mon-: monadelphous, monandrous, monarch, monatomic, monaural, monaxial, monocle, monocular, monoecious. monody, monomial—mono + nomos, monopsony
- monad: chloromonad, cryptomonad, diplomonad, pseudomonad, trichomonad, xanthomonad
≈mono-: monoacid, monoacidic, monoamine, monobasic, monoblast
≈monocarpellary, Monoceros, monocarpous, monochasium, monochlamydeous, monochord, monochromatic, monochrome, monoclinal,

monocline, monoclinous,
monoclonal, monocoque,
monocotyledon, monocracy,
monoculture, monocyclic,
monocyte
≈monodrama, monofilament
≈monogamy, monogenesis,
monogenic, monogenism,
monoglot, monogram,
monograph, monogynous
≈monohydrate, monolingual,
monolith, monologue
≈monomania, monomer,
monomerous, monometallic,
monometalism,
monomolecular,
mononucleosis
≈monophagous, monophobia,
monophonic, monophthong,
monophyletic, monophyllous,
Monophysite, monoplane,
monoplegia, monoploid,
monopode, monopodium,
monopole, monopoly
≈monosome, monospermous,
monostich, monostome,
monostrophe, monostylous,
monosyllabic
≈monotheism, monotone,
monotonous, monotreme,
monotrichous, monotype,
monovalent, monozygotic
[variant form: minster—the
church or cathedral of a
monastery, e.g., Westminster]
MONSOON: Arabic: a time, season; a
seasonal wind of the Indian Ocean

mont: hill, mountain
≈mont: montage, montane,
monticule
- montage: photomontage
≈mount: mount, mountain,
mountaineer, mountainous,
mounted, mounting
≈mounte-: mountebank

- montane: intermontane,
submontane, tramontane,
transmontane, ultramontane
- mount: with prefixes: amount,
demount, dismount,
paramount, remount,
surmount, tantamount
- mount: with combining form:
seamount
- mountable: insurmountable
[variant forms: mont-de-piété;
Spanish: monte, montero;
Montevideo, Uruguay;
Montreal—King's Mountain,
Canada; piedmont]
[NB: promontory; see men]
{word note: Montevideo, Uruguay;
situated on a mountain and may
have received its name from a
Portuguese sailors's cry, *Monte
vide eu*, I see a mountain}

mony: a resulting condition
matrimony, patrimony
[NB: alimony]
MOO GOO GAI PAN: Chinese:
mushroom chicken slice
MOOSE: Abenaki: *mos*; lit., eats off
the bark; the largest deer; elk

mora : to delay
≈mora-t: mora, moratorium,
moratory
- mora: remora
- mur-r-: demur, demure,
demurrage, demurral, demurrer

moral: manners, customs
≈moral: moral, morale,
moralism, moralist, moralistic,
morality, moralize
- moral-: demoralize, immoral,
immorality
[variant forms: mood, mores,
morose]

mor-bid: disease, to wear away
morbid, morbidity; morbific

mord: to bite
≈mord: mordacious, mordant,
mordent

- morse-: premorse, remorse,
  remorseful, remorseless
  [variant form: morsel]
mor-e: foolish
  moron; morology; sophomore;
  oxymoron
  [NB: sycamore]
morph-o: shape, form
≈morph: morpheme,
  morphemics, morphing
≈morph-: morphallaxis,
  morphosis
≈morpho-: morphogenesis,
  morphology
- morph-: bimorphemic;
  geomorphology;
  gynandromorphy
- morph: with prefixes: amorph,
  allomorph, anamorph,
  dimorph, ectomorph,
  endomorph, holomorph,
  homeomorph, isomorph,
  mesomorph, paramorph,
  perimorph, polymorph,
  pseudomorph, trimorph
- morph: with combining forms:
  biomorph, lagomorph,
  myomorph, xeromorph,
  zygomorph
- morphic: with prefixes:
  ectomorphic, hemimorphic,
  heteromorphic, isomorphic,
  mesomorphic
- morphic: with combining forms:
  actinomorphic,
  anthropomorphic,
  dolichomorphic, geomorphic,
  hystricomorphic, idiomorphic,
  meromorphic, theomorphic,
  theriomorphic, zoomorphic,
  zygomorphic
- morphism: with prefixes:
  amorphism, allomorphism,
  anamorphism, bimorphism,
  dimorphism, dysmorphism,

endomorphism, epimorphism,
  homeomorphism,
  homomorphism, isomorphism,
  isodimorphism,
  isotrimorphism,
  mesomorphism,
  metamorphism,
  monomorphism,
  paramorphism, pleomorphism,
  polymorphism, rheomorphism,
  trimorphism
- morphism: with combining forms:
  geromorphism,
  pathomorphism,
  pedomorphism, zoomorphism
- morphosis: with prefixes:
  anamorphosis,
  heteromorphosis,
  homomorphosis,
  metamorphosis, neomorphosis
- morphosis: with combining
  forms: anthropomorphosis,
  chemomorphosis,
  cytomorphosis,
  gerontomorphosis,
  phyllomorphosis
- morphous: with prefixes:
  amorphous, polymorphous
- morphous: with combining forms:
  rhizomorphous, zygomorphous
mort: death
≈mort: mortal, mortality,
  mortician, mortuary
≈mort-: mortgage, mortmain
≈morti-: mortification, mortify
- mortem: antemortem,
  postmortem
- mort-: amortize, immortal,
  immortalize
  [variant forms: immortelle,
  moribund, murder, murderous,
  smorzando]
  [phrases: in articulo mortis;
  post mortem]
MORTAR: from Latin *mortarium*,
  orig., the vessel in which things

151

were pounded; also the substance
pounded [not related to *mortise*]

MORTISE: from Arabic *murtazza*,
joined, fixed in; a hole or recess
cut, as in a piece of wood, to
receive a projecting part (tenon)
shaped to fit into it; thus, the term
mortise and tenon [not related to
mortar, which see]

mot[1]: **word**; from "grunt"
mot, bon mot, mot juste, motto

mot[2]: **to move**

≈mot: motif, motile, motion

≈motiv-e: motivate, motivation,
motive, motivic, motivity

≈motor: motor, motorial,
motorize

≈motor-: motorcade, motorcycle,
motorpathy

- mot-: emotional, leitmotif

- mote: demote, emote, promote,
remote

- motion: commotion, demotion,
emotion, promotion

- motive: automotive, emotive,
locomotive, pedomotive,
promotive, thermomotive

- motor: arteriomotor,
calorimotor, ideomotor,
oculomotor

≈mob-ile: mob, mobile, mobility,
mobilize

≈mobo-: mobocracy

- mobile: automobile, immobile

- mobilize: demobilize,
immobilize

≈mov-e: movable, move,
movement

- movable: immovable,
removable, irremovable

- move: commove, remove
[variant forms: émeute; moment,
momentarily, momentary,
momentum; mutinous, mutiny]

{word note: mob: from *mobile
vulgus*, the changeable crowd}

MOUE: French: a pouting grimace

mourn: **to sorrow**
mourn, mourner, mournful,
mourning

MOUSSE: French; lit., foam; a dessert;
may be related to honey

MOUTON: French; sheep; in English,
"sheepskin processed to resemble
seal or beaver"

muc: **mucus** [see myx-o]

≈muc: mucin, mucous, mucus

≈muc-: mucoid

≈muci-: muciferous

≈mucino-: mucinogen

muci-l: **to be moldy**
mucid, mucilage, mucilaginous

mucro: **sharp point**
mucro, mucronate

mulc: **to stroke, soothe**
demulcent—lit., stroking down;
as an adjective, soothing; as a
noun, a medication that soothes

MULCT: a punishment; extracting
money by fraud or deceit

MULIEBRITY: woman, womanhood

muls: **to milk**
emulsion; emulsify

multi: **many**

≈multi: multitude, multitudinous

≈multi-: multiatom, multiaxial,
multicausal, multicellular,
multicenter, multicultural,
multiethnic, multifaceted,
multifarious, multifid,
multifold, multiform

≈multilateral, multilingual,
multimedia, multinational,
multinucleate

≈multipara, multipartite,
multiphasic, multiple,
multiplex, multiplication,
multiply

≈multistage, multivalent,
multivariate

- multiplier: photomultiplier
[phrase: multum in parvo]

mum: see masque

mun: **common, public, general**

- mun-: communal,
  communalism, communicate,
  communion, communism,
  excommunicate;
  incommunicable,
  incommunicative;
  incommunicado; immunize
- mune: commune, immune
- munity: community, immunity
- mon-: common, commonable,
  commonality
  [variant forms: mean, one
  meaning]

munc: **to blow, expel**

emunction, emunctory

mund: **world**

≈mundan-e: mundane,
  mundanity
- mundane: antemundane,
  extramundane, inframundane,
  intermundane, intramundane,
  postmundane, premundane,
  supermundane, supramundane,
  transmundane, ultramundane
  [variant forms: demimonde,
  demimondaine]

muni: **a town, gift, work**
  performed [see related mun]

≈muni-: municipal, municipality,
  municipalize, munificence,
  munificent
- muner-: remunerate,
  remuneration, remunerative

muni-t: **fortification**

≈muni: muniment, munition
  (verb), munitions (noun)
- munition: ammunition,
  premunition
[Note: munitions: a plural noun;
  often used with singular verb]

mur-al: **wall**

≈mural: mural
- mural: antemural, extramural,
  intermural, intramural,

panmural, transmural;
photomural
- mure: circummure, immure
{word note: intramural: within the
  limits of a city, college, etc.;
  between or among members of the
  same school, college, etc., as
  intramural sports; in anatomy,
  within the walls of an organ}

mus: **music**; from "Muse," which
  see

≈mus: musette, music, musical
- musia: amusia
  [NB: amuse, bemuse]

musc: **a fly**

muscarine, muscid
  [variant forms: midge, midget,
  musket—orig., a fledged arrow;
  Spanish: mosquito]
  [phrase: muscae volitantes—lit.,
  flying flies; specks, or floaters,
  that appear to float before the
  eyes]

muscle: see my-o

muse: **a place for the Muses or for**
  study [the Muses: the nine
  goddesses who presided over
  literature and the arts and
  sciences]

≈muse: muse, Muse, museum
≈museo: museology
- muse: amuse, bemuse

MUSHROOM: from French *moisseron*,
  moss, fungus

MUSKEG: lit., swamp; a kind of bog
  or marsh containing thick layers of
  decaying vegetable matter, found
  especially in Canada and Alaska

MUSLIN: a fabric first made in Mosul,
  Iraq

MUSTACHE: Greek: *mystax*, upper lip

mut-ual: **change, exchange**

≈muta: mutable, mutant, mutate,
  mutation, mutative
≈mutual: mutual, mutualism,
  mutualize
≈muta-: mutafacient, mutagen,
  mutagenesis, mutamycin

- mutable: commutable, hypermutable, immutable, permutable, transmutable
- mutation: permutation, transmutation
- mutative: commutative, transmutative
- mute: commute, permute, transmute
  [variant forms: miss, molt, also, moult; parimutuel, remuda]
  [phrase: mutatis mutandis]

muti: **blunt**, **maim**
  muticous, mutilate

MVB: from the initials of *Ministerstro Vnutrennikh Deyl*: Ministry of Internal Affairs; the secret police of the former Soviet Union; see Gestapo; KGB

my: **to close**
≈my-: myope, myopia
≈mi-: miosis

myc-o: **fungus**
≈myc: mycelian, mycelium, pl., mycelia
≈myc-: mycosis
≈mycet-: mycetoid, mycetoma
≈myceto-: mycetophagous, mycetozoan
≈myco-: mycobacterium, mycology, mycophile, mycoplasma, mycorrhiza, mycotoxin
- mycelium: promycelium, pseudomycelium
- myces: streptomyces
- mycete: actinomycete, ascomycete, basidiomycete, blastomycete, deuteromycete, discomycete, gasteromycete, gastromycete, hymenomycete, myxomycete, oomycete, plectomycete, zygomycete
- mycin: neomycin, streptomycin

myel-o: **marrow**
≈myel: myelic, myelin

≈myel-: myelalgia, myelencephalon, myelitis, myeloid, myeloma
≈myelo-: myeloblast, myelocyte, myelogenic, myelogram
- myelinate: demyelinate
- myelitis: osteomyelitis, poliomyelitis
  [variant forms: medulla, medullated]

my-o-: **muscle**; from "mouse"
mouse
≈myo-: myomancy
muscle
≈my-: myalgia, myatonia, myodynia, myoma
≈myo-: myocarditis, myocardium, myoclonus, myocolpitis, myodermal, myofibril, myogenic, myoglia, myoglobin, myograph, myology, myoneural, myopathy, myotome, myotonia
≈myos: myosin—a protein in muscles, myosotis
- myosin: actomyosin—a complex of actin and myosin, two proteins, in muscle tissue
- myo-: amyotonia
- mysium: endomysium, epimysium, exomysium, perimysium
≈musc: muscle—lit., little mouse; muscly, muscular, musculature
- muscular: with prefixes: bimuscular, intermuscular, intramuscular, minimuscular, submuscular, unimuscular
- muscular: with combining forms: algiomuscular, cardiomuscular, fibromuscular, idiomuscular, neuromuscular, radiomuscular, striomuscular
  [variant forms: mouse, mussel, French: moule—edible mussel]

{word note: myosotis: lit., mouse's
ear; forget-me-not, a flower; from
myo + *otos*, genitive of *ous*, ear}

myria-d: one thousand

≈myriad: myriad

≈myri-: myriarch

≈myria-: myriagon, myrialiter,
myriapod

myring: eardrum

≈myringa: myringa, myringo

≈myring-: myringectomy,
myringitis

≈myringo-: myringodermatitis,
myringomycosis,
myringoplasty,
myringosclerosis,
myringoscope, myringotome,
myringotomy

myrmeco: ant
myrmecology,
myrmecophagous,
myrmecophile,
myrmecophobia, myrmecophte

myso: pollution
mysophilia, mysophobia

myst-er: a secret

≈myster-y: mysterioso, or,
misterioso, mysterious, mystery

≈mysti: mystique; mystic,
mystical, mysticism

≈myst-: mystagogue

≈mysti-: mystify

≈myth: myth, mythic, mythical,
mythos

≈mytho-: mythography,
mythological, mythology,
mythomania, mythopoeia

- mystify: demystify

myx-o: mucus [see muc]

≈myx-: myxedema, myxoma,
myxomatosis

≈myxo-: myxobacterium,
myxoblastoma, myxocephalus,
myxocyte, myxomycete,
myxomyoma, myxovirus

- myxin: bacillomyxin,
cuprimyxin, polymyxin

N

NABOB: Urdu; *nawwab*; a very rich
or important man

NADIR: Arabic *nazir assamt*: lit.,
opposite the zenith; the lowest
point

NAINSOOK: from Hindi *nain*, the eye
+ *sukh*, pleasure; a lightweight
fabric

nano: dwarf; one billionth part of a
specified unit; the factor 10^{-9}

dwarf

≈nan-: nanoid

≈nano-: nanocephalic,
nanocormia, nanofossil,
nanomelus, nanosoma

billionth

nanoampere, nanocurie,
nanogram, nanosecond

nap: cloth
napery, napkin
[variant forms: apron, map]

narc-o: stupor
narceine, narcissism,
naracissus, narcosis, narcotic;
narcolepsy

{word note: narcissism: Greek
mythology; extreme self-love or
self-admiration; from Narcissus, a
beautiful youth whom Echo loved;
spurning her love, he was
condemned to pine away for love
of his own reflection in a spring;
he changes into the narcissus, a
plant with narcotic effects}

narrat-e: to tell
narrate, narration, narrative,
narrator; narratology

NARTHEX: vestibule of a church;
from "giant fennel," because of
the fancied resemblance

nasc: see nat-e for renascent

nas-o: nose

≈nas: nasion, nasal, nasalize

≈naso-: nasofrontal, nasogastric, nasopharynx

- nasal: endonasal, internasal, orinasal, postnasal
  [variant forms: nares, nasturtium, pince-nez]
  {word note: nasturtium: lit., twisted nose, from its acrid smell}

nast: plant growth condition

nastic; epinasty, hyponasty, thermonasty

nata: to swim

natant, natatorial; natatorium; supernatant
[variant forms: naiad, nekton; Spanish: nadar—to swim]

nat-e: to be born, birth, origin

≈natal: natal, Natal, natality

≈nation: nation, national, nationalism, nationality, nationalize

≈nativ-e: native, nativism, nativity

≈natur-e: natural, naturalism, naturalist, naturalistic, naturalize, nature

≈naturo-: naturology, naturopathic, naturopathy

- natal: antenatal, neonatal, perinatal, postnatal, prenatal
- nate: agnate, enate, cognate, connate, innate, neonate
- nato-: neonatology
- national: binational, international, multinational, supranational, transnational
- natural: antinatural, supernatural, unnatural
- nature: denature
  [variant forms: renaissance, naïve, naiveté, nascent; renascence, renascent, noel, noël, puisne, puny]
  [phrase: au naturel]

{word note: Natal: the smallest province in South Africa; so named by the Portuguese navigator, Vasco da Gama, who sighted the land on Christmas Day, or the Day of Nativity, 1497}

nau: sea; sailor

≈nau: nausea, nauseate, nauseous

≈naut: nautical, nautilus

≈nautil-: nautiloid

≈nau-: naumachy, nauplius

- naut-: astronaut, cosmonaut; aeronautical
  [variant form: noise]
  [phrase: ad nauseum]

nav-e: ship

≈nav-e: naval, nave, navel, navicular, navy

≈nav-: navigable, navigate, navigation, navigator

- navigate: circumnavigate

{word notes: nave: the interior of a cathedral reminded people of a ship with its wooden beams; navel: the small scar, usually a depression in the middle of the abdomen; umbilicus}

NAZI: clipped from German *Nationalsozialist*, National Socialist Workers' Party

ne-: not, negative [see negat-e]

necessary, nefarious, nepenthe, nescience, nescient

neal: to burn

anneal—to heat glass, metals, etc., and then cool to prevent brittleness; also, to strengthen and temper the mind, will, character

nebul-a: vapor, fog, mist

nebula, nebulize, nebulosity, nebulous
[variant forms: nimbus, nimbostratus]

necr-o: death

≈necr-: necrosis, necropsy

≈necro-: necrobiosis, necrolatry, necrology, necromancy,

necrophagia, necrophilia,
necrophobia, necropolis,
necrotomy
- necine: internecine
- nicious: pernicious
[variant forms: nectar, nectarine,
nectary, noyade]
nect: see nex for connect
negat-e: negative [see ne-]
≈neg: negate, negation, negative,
negativism
≈neg-: neglect, negligee,
negligence, negligent,
negligible, negotiate
- neg-: renege, renegade
- negate: abnegate
- negation: abnegation,
denegation, self-abnegation
- negative: abnegative,
binegative, photonegative,
seronegative, trinegative
[variant forms: deny; undeniable,
undeniably; nimiety]
NEIGHBOR: from Old English
neahgebur, nearby peasant
nemat-o: thread
≈nemat: nematic
≈nemat-: nemathelminth,
nematode, nematodont,
nematoid
≈nemato-: nematoblast,
nematocide, nematocyst,
nematocyte, nematology,
nematosome, nematospermia
- nema: chromonema,
chloronema, diplonema,
micronema, pachynema,
protonema, treponema
NEMESIS: from Nemesis, the Greek
goddess of retributive justice, or
vengeance; an agent of
destruction; pl., nemeses
nemo: a wooded pasture
nemophilia—a plant of the
waterleaf family, cultivated for
garden ornaments

neo-n: young, new
≈neo: neoteric, neon
≈neo-: neoanthropic, neoclassic,
Neogene, neogenesis,
neologism, neonate,
neonatology, neopathy,
neophyte, neoplasia, neoplasm,
neoplastic, neoplasty, neoteny
- neism: misoneism
nepho-: cloud, cloudy, moisture
≈nepho: nephogram, nephology,
nephoscope
≈nephelo-: nephelometer
≈nubil: nubilous
- nubilate: enubilate, obnubilate
[variant forms: nuance, nuanced]
[phrase: in nubibus: in the clouds
—merely under consideration]
NEPOTISM: from nephew, niece,
grandson; favoritism shown to
relatives, esp. in appointment to
desirable positions
nephr-o: kidney
≈nephr: nephridium, nephrite,
nephritic, nephron
≈nephr-: nephralgia,
nephrectomy, nephritis,
nephrosis
≈nephro-: nephrogenic,
nephrolith, nephrology,
nephrotomy
- nephrine: epinephrine
- nephritis: pyelonephritis
- nephridium: perinephridium,
protonephridium
- nephros: epinephros,
mesonephros, metanephros,
paranephros, pronephros,
protonephros
ner: sea, sea nymph, liquid
≈ner: Nereid, nereis, neritic
- ner-: aneroid
nerv-e: nerve, vein [see neur-o]
≈nerv-e: nervation, nerve,
nerveless, nervous, nervure

- nervate: binervate,
  curvinervate, denervate,
  enervate, innervate, trinervate,
  uninervate
- nerve: innerve, trinerve,
  unnerve
- nervous: enervous, overnervous

nesia: island
  Indonesia, Melanesia,
  Micronesia, Polynesia

NETHERLANDS: lit., underlands; a
  small kingdom on the North Sea;
  it is aptly named because two-
  fifths of the country's land was
  once claimed by the sea, or by
  lakes and swamps; the Dutch have
  reclaimed much of this land with
  an elaborate system of dikes,
  windmills, and pumps

NEUFCHÂTEL: a cheese first made in
  Neufchâtel, a town in France

neur-o: nerve, vein [see nerv-e]
≈neur: neural, neurility, neuron
≈neur-: neuralgia, neurasthenia,
  neurectomy, neuriatry,
  neurism, neuritis, neuroma,
  neurosis, neurotic
≈neuri-: neurilemma, neurimotor
≈neuro-: neuroblast,
  neuroblastoma, neurocoele,
  neurofibril, neurogenic,
  neuroglia, neurohormone,
  neurohypophysis, neuroleptic,
  neurology, neurolysis,
  neuromast, neuromuscular,
  neuropathology, neuropathy,
  neuropsychology, neurotomy,
  neurotoxin, neurotropic
- neur-: myoneural; polyneuritis
- neurium: endoneurium,
  epineurium, perineurium
- neuron: brachyneuron
- neurosis: acroneurosis,
  aeroneurosis, angioneurosis,
  aponeurosis, cardioneurosis,
  trophoneurosis, vasoneurosis

neutr-o: neutral; lit., not either
≈neutr: neutrino, neutron
≈neutral: neutral, neutralism,
  neutrality, neutralize
≈neutro-: neutropenia,
  neutrophil, neutrosphere,
  neutrotaxis
- neutron: photoneutron
  [variant form: neuter]

nev: birthmark [see gen-e]
  nevus, nevoid

nex: to tie, bind [see nod-e]
≈nex: nexus
- nex-: adnexa, annex, annexation
- nect-: connect, connection,
  disconnect, interconnect

NICOTINE: Nicot's plant, after Jean
  Nicot (1530-1600), who first
  introduced tobacco into France
  (1560); an alkaloid found in
  tobacco leaves

nict: to wink
≈nict: nictate, nictitate
- niv-e: connive, connivent

nid-i: nest
≈nid: nidus, pl., nidi
≈nidi-: nidicolous, nidificate,
  nidifugous, nidify
  [variant forms: niche, nide]
  {word note: nidifugous: describes
  those birds that flee the nest
  shortly after hatching, such as
  chickens, turkeys, grouse,
  pheasants; those that remain in the
  nest until fledged and ready to fly
  are described as *nidicolous*, from
  colere, to dwell}

NIGGARD: from Norwegian dialect;
  as an adjective, afraid, stingy; as a
  noun, a stingy person

NIGGLE: Norwegian *nigla*: to spend
  excessive time on inconsequential
  details

NIGHTMARE: originally, an evil spirit
  believed to haunt and suffocate
  sleeping persons; a frightening
  dream

nigr-i: black
≈nigr: nigrescence, nigrescent,
  negritude
≈nigr-: nigrosine
≈nigri-: nigrify
- nigrate: denigrate
  [variant form: Niger—a country
  in Africa]

nihil: nothing
≈nihil: nihilism, nihility
- nihilate: annihilate
≈null: null, nullity
≈nulli-: nullification, nullifidian,
  nullify, nullipara, nullipore
- nul-: annul, annulment
  [phrases: ex nihilo, nihil obstat;
  nil, nil desperandum, nil nisi
  bonum, de mortuis nil; nisi
  bonum]
{word note: nihil: lit., not (even) a
  little thing; nothing}
NIMBLE: from Old English *niman*, to
  steal; thus, quick, quick-witted,
  alert; agile
NIMIETY: from *ne-*, negative + IE
  miis, little; thus, not little; excess;
  redundancy
NINJA: any of a class of feudal
  Japanese warriors highly trained in
  stealth and employed as spies and
  assassins

nis, nit: to strive, struggle
  nisus; renitent

nitr-o-: native soda, natron
≈nitr-ate: nitrous; nitrate,
  nitration
≈nitri: nitric, nitride, nitrile,
  nitrite
≈nitro-: nitroaniline, nitroaniline,
  nitrobacteria, nitrocellulose,
  nitroform, nitrogen, nitrometer,
  nitromethane
NITWIT: probably from German *niht*,
  nothing + Middle English *wit*,
  intelligence; a person regarded as
  stupid or silly
niv: see nict for connive

niv: snow
  nival, niveous
  [variant forms: Nevada; Sierra
  Nevada—mountain range in
  California; highest peak: Mt.
  Whitney; Spanish: nieve]
nive: see nict-i for connive

nob-le: lit., well-known [see not-e]
≈nob-le: nobility, nobly, noble
- noble: ennoble, ignoble,
  unnoble
  [phrase: noblesse oblige]

noc: to harm
≈noc: nocent, nocuous
- noc-: innocence, innocent;
  innocuous
≈noxious: noxious
- noxious: innoxious, obnoxious,
  unobnoxious; psychobnoxious
  [variant form: nuisance]

noct: night [see nyct]
≈noct: noctuid, noctule, nocturn,
  nocturnal, nocturne
≈noct-: noctambulate, nocturia
≈nocti-: noctiluca, noctilucent
- noctial: equinoctial,
  interequinoctial, trinoctial
- nox: equinox
  [variant form: acronical]
{word note: nocturne: painting of a
  night scene; a musical composition, esp. for the piano, of a
  romantic or dreamy character
  thought appropriate for the night}

nod-e: knot [see nex]
≈nod-e: node, nodal, nodical,
  nodose, nodule, nodus
≈nodi-: nodiflora, nodiflorum,
  nodiflorus
- node: acnode, antinode,
  internode, pseudonode
  [variant forms: denouement, net]
{word note: denouement: from
  French *dénouer*, to untie; the
  outcome, solution, unraveling, or
  clarification, of a plot in a drama,
  story, etc.}

noma: **to distribute; pasture**
  noma, nomad
nom-en: **name**
≈nomen: nomen
≈nomen-: nomenclator,
  nomenclature
- nomen: agnomen, cognomen,
  praenomen
≈nominal: nominal, nominalism
≈nominat-e: nominate,
  nomination, nominative
≈nominee: nominee
- nomer: misnomer
- nominal: pronominal
- nomin-y: ignominy,
  ignominious
- nominate: agnominate,
  annominate, denominate,
  innominate, prenominate,
  renominate
- nominat-: denomination,
  denominative, denominator,
  interdenominational
  [variant forms: name, surname,
  noun, pronoun; nuncupative;
  renown, renowned]
  [phrases: nom de guerre,
  nom de plume]
nom-o: **law**
≈nomo: nomogram, nomography,
  nomological, nomothetic
- nom-e: anomie, antinomian;
  metronome
- nomial: binomial, monomial—
  mono + nomos, polynomial,
  trinomial
- nomical: astronomical
- nomous: with prefixes:
  allonomous, autonomous,
  heteronomous, homonomous
- nomous: with combining form:
  theonomous
- nomy: with prefixes: anomy,
  antinomy, autonomy,
  Deuteronomy, isonomy

- nomy: with combining forms:
  aeronomy, agronomy,
  astronomy, economy,
  gastronomy, taphonomy,
  taxonomy
  [variant forms: numism;
  numismatic, numismatics;
  nummular: from a coin; lit., what
  is permitted by law; exonumia]
non-: **negative**
≈nonage, nonaligned,
  nonchalant, noncombatant,
  noncommittal, noncompliance,
  nonconductor, nonconformist,
  nonconformity, noncustodial,
  nondenominational,
  nondescript, nondisjunction,
  nondurable
≈nonego, nonentity, nonessential,
  nonexistence, nonfeasance,
  nonfeeding, nonferrous,
  noninvasive, nonissue,
  nonjoinder, nonjudgmental,
  nonjuror, nonmoral,
  nonproductive
  [phrases: non compos mentis,
  non obstante, nonpareil,
  non placet, nonplus,
  non prosequitur, non sequitur,
  non suit]
non: **nine, ninety**
≈nona-: nonagon, nonagenarian;
  nonillion—nine million
≈nov: November, novena,
  novenary
{word note: novena: in the Roman
  Catholic Church, the recitation of
  prayers and the practicing of
  devotions on nine days, usually to
  seek some special favor}
norm: **the rule**
≈norm: norm, normal, normalize,
  normally
- normal: abnormal, paranormal,
  subnormal, supernormal
- normity: abnormity, enormity

- normous: enormous
NOSH: Yiddish; from German
naschen, to nibble, taste
nos-o: disease
≈noso: nosocomial, nosography,
nosology, nosophobia
- nose: anthracnose
- nosis: zoonosis
nost-o: a return
nostalgia, nostalgist;
nostomania
[phrase: nostalgie de la boue]
nost-r: our, ours
nostrum; paternoster
NOSTRIL: from Old English nosthyrl;
lit., nose hole
not-e: to note, mark
[see nob-le]
≈notar-y: notarial, notarize,
notary
≈notat-e: notate, notation,
notabilia, notability, notable
≈note: note, noteworthy
≈notice: notice, noticeable
≈notion: notion, notional
- note: connote, denote
≈noti-: notifiable, notification,
notify
- notate: annotate, connotate,
denotate
- notation: annotation,
connotation, denotation
- notary: prothonotary, or
protonotary
≈notor: notoriety, notorious
[phrase: nota bene—NB]
noto-: the back
notochord, notoungulate
NOTRE DAME: lit., Our Lady (mother
of Jesus); famous early Gothic
cathedral in Paris, built 1163-
1257; a Catholic university in
Indiana
no-u: to perceive; mind
noetic; noumenon, nous;
paranoia, paranoid

nounce: see nunci for *announce*
nourish: to feed, nourish
[see nutri]
nourish, nourishing,
nourishment; malnourished
nov: see non for *November*
nov: new
≈nova: nova, novation
≈novel: novel, novelette,
novelize, novelty
≈novi: novice, novitiate
- nova: hypernova, supernova
- novate: innovate, renovate
- novation: innovation,
renovation
[variant forms: new, renew,
renewal; nouveau; nouvelle,
Nova Scotia; Spanish: nuevo]
[phrases: nouveau riche, nouvelle
cuisine; de novo, novus homo]
nox: see noc for obnoxious
nox: see noct for equinox
NOYADE: drowning
nub: to marry
≈nub: nubile
- nubial: connubial, pronubial
≈nupt: nuptial
- nuptial: postnuptial, prenuptial
nubilous: see neph-o
NUCHA: the nape of the neck
nuc-le-o: nut, kernel
≈nucle: nuclear, nucleate,
nucleolus, nucleon, nucleus
≈nucle-: nucleoid, nucleonics
≈nucleo-: nucleocapside,
nucleophile, nucleoplasm,
nucleoprotein, nucleoside,
nucleosome, nucleosynthesis,
nucleotide
- nucleate: anucleate, binucleate,
enucleate, macronucleate,
mononucleate, multinucleate,
paranucleate, trinucleate,
uninucleate
- nucleosis: mononucleosis,
multinucleosis, polynucleosis

- nucleus: macronucleus,
  maritonucleus, meganucleus,
  metanucleus, pronucleus
- nuclear: with prefixes:
  extranuclear, internuclear,
  macronuclear, polynuclear,
  subnuclear
- nuclear: with combining form:
  thermonuclear
  [variant forms: nucellus, nut,
  nuthatch, nutlet, nutmeg; nougat]
  [phrase: nux vomica]

nud-e: nude, bare, naked
≈nud-e: nude, nudism, nudity
≈nudi-: nudibrachiate,
  nudibranch, nudicaudate,
  nudification, nudiflorus
- nud-e: denudate, denude
NUGATORY: trifling, worthless
nuisance: see noy
null: see nihil

num: deity
numen, numinous

numer: to count, number
≈numer: numerable, numeral,
  numerate, numeration,
  numerator, numeric,
  numerical, numerous
≈numero-: numerology
- numer-: enumerate,
  supernumerary
- numerable: denumerable,
  innumerable
  [variant form: number]
  [Spanish: numero, numero uno]

nunci: to report
≈nunci: nunciature, nuncio
- nunci-: pronunciamento
- nunciate: annunciate, enunciate
- nunciation: denunciation,
  enunciation, pronunciation,
  renunciation
- nuncio: internuncio
- nounce: announce, denounce,
  enounce, pronounce, renounce
nupt: see nub for nuptial

nut: to nod
nutant, nutation;
circumnutation
[variant forms: nudge, innuendo]

nutri: to nourish [see nourish]
≈nutri-t: nutrician, nutrient,
  nutriment, nutrition, nutritive
- nutrient: macronutrient
- nutrition: innutrition,
  malnutrition
  [variant forms: nurse, nursery,
  nursing, nursling; nurture]
NUTRIA: water animal; from "water";
  see otter

nyct-: night [see noct]
≈nyct-: nyctalgia, nyctalopia,
  nycturia
≈nycti-: nyctitropism
≈nycto-: nyctohemeral,
  nyctophilia, nyctophobia
- nycal: acronycal

nymph-o: young wife
≈nymph: nymph, nymphalid,
  nymphet
≈nympho-: nympholepsy,
  nymphomania
- nymph: deutonymph,
  paranymph, protonymph,
  seminymph, trichonymph

O

OASIS: Coptic (Egyptian) for "a
  fertile place in the desert";
  pl., oases

**ob-: after, against, at, in front of,
  near, toward**
≈ob-: obconic, obcordate,
  obdurate, obese, obfuscate,
  obit, obituary, object,
  objurgate
≈oblate, obligate, oblige, oblique,
  obliterate, oblivious, oblivion,
  oblong, obloquy
≈obnoxious, obnubilate, obovate

≈obscene, obscure, obsecrate,
obsequies, obsequious,
observe, obsess, obsolete,
obstacle, obstetric, obstinate,
obstipation, obstreperous,
obstruct

≈obtain, obtect, obtest, obtrude,
obtund, obturate, obtuse,
obverse, obviate, obvious

≈o-: truncation of *ob*-: omission,
omit

≈oc-: assimilation of *ob*-: occasion,
occident, occipital, occiput,
occlude, occult, occupant,
occupation, occupy, occur

≈of-: assimilation of *ob*-: offend,
offense, offer, offering,
offertory, office, officer,
official, officiate, officinal,
officious

≈op-: assimilation of *ob*-: oppilate,
opponent, opportune,
opportunity, oppose, opposite,
oppress, opprobrium, oppugn

≈os-: variant of *ob*-: ostensible,
ostensive, ostentation
[phrase: obiter dictum]
obey: see aud

obel: a spit, needle, obelus, obolus
obelisk, obelize, obelus,
obolus
[Note: The Washington Monument,
in Washington, DC, is an obelisk.]
oblivion: see leth
oboe: see alt-i
OBTURATE: to stop up; obstruct
ocarina: see avi
occident: pertaining to the west
occiput: the back of the head
ocean-o: lit., the outer sea
≈ocean: ocean, oceanic
≈ocean-: oceanarium
≈oceano-: oceanography,
oceanology
och: pale, pale-yellow
≈och: ocher, or ochre

≈ochr-: ochroid
- ochroid: xanthochroid
ochlo-: mob
ochlocracy, ochlocrat,
ochlophobia
oct-o: eight
≈oct: octad, octal, octan, octane,
octant, octave, octavo, octet
≈octo: October, octonary
≈octo-: octoroon (*roon* from
quadroon), octillion (octo +
million)
≈oct-: octennial
≈octa-: octachord, octagon,
octahedron, octamerous,
octameter
≈octo-: octodecimo,
octogenarian, octopod,
octopus, octosyllabic,
octosyllable
≈octu-: octuple
- octo-: trisoctohedron
octroi: see auth
ocul-o: eye, sight
≈ocul: ocular, oculist
≈oculo-: oculomotor
≈ocell: ocellate, ocellation,
ocellus
- ocle: binocle, monocle
- ocul-: intraocular; inoculate
- ocular: binocular, binoculars
[variant forms: antler, inveigle,
oeil-de-boeuf, oeillade, ullage]
{word note: antler: from *anteocular*,
before the eyes}
ODALISQUE, or, odalisk: chamber
od-e: to sing [see ed[1]]
≈ode: ode, odium
- ode: epode, palinode
- ody: hymnody, melody,
monody, parody, rhapsody,
prosody
[variant forms: comedy, tragedy—
lit., song of the goat]
odi: to hate
odious, odium

[variant forms: annoy, ennui,
   noisome]
odometer: see h-od-e
odont-o: tooth
≈odont: odontalgia, odontoid
≈odonto-: odontoblast,
   odontoglossum, odontology,
   odontophore
- odon: mastodon
- odont: with prefixes: anisodont,
   diphyodont, haplodont,
   heterodont, homodont,
   microdont, monodont,
   pleurodont
- odont: with combining forms:
   arthrodont, brachyodont,
   conodont, cynodont,
   glyptodont, gymnodont,
   hypsodont, loxodont,
   mastodont
- odont-: periodontal,
   periodontitis, periodontology
- odontics: with prefixes:
   endodontics, exodontics,
   periodontics
- odontics: with combining forms:
   aerodontics, geriodontics,
   hypnodontics, orthodontics,
   pedodontics, prosthodontics
- ondontist: endodontist,
   exodontist, geriodontist,
   orthodontist, pedodontist,
   periodontist, prosthodontist,
   radiodontist
- odus: ceratodus
odor-i: odor, smell
≈odor: odor, odorous
≈odori-: odoriferous
- odor-: deodorant, malodor
- odorous: inodorous,
   malodorous
   [variant forms: cacodyl; redolent]
odyn-e: pain
≈odyn-: odynacusis
≈odyne-: odynephobia

≈odyno-: odynometer,
   odynophagia, odynophonia
- odyne: anodyne
- odynia: allodynia, adenodynia,
   dermatodynia, dorsodynia,
   arthrodynia, cephalodynia,
   gastrodynia, gnathodynia,
   hepatodynia, myodynia,
   neurodynia, odonodynia,
   orchiodynia, osteodynia,
   otodynia, phallodynia,
   pododynia, prostatodynia
ODYSSEY: Greek mythology; from
   the wanderings and adventures of
   Odysseus; a long voyage
oeno: wine
   oenology, oenomancy,
   oenomel, oenophile
oeuvre: work; from erg
   oeuvre, hors d'oeuvre
og: part of Gothic arch
   ogee, ogive
OGLE: prob. from Low German and
   Old English words for *eye*: to keep
   looking boldly and with obvious
   desire; make eyes at
oid: similar to; from *eido*, shape
- oid: acanthoid, acaroid,
   adenoid, adipoid, amygdaloid,
   android, angioid, anthropoid,
   arenoid, asteroid, axoid
≈blastoid, butyroid, cancroid,
   carcinoid, castroid, centroid,
   celluloid, chromatoid, colloid,
   cricoid, crinoid, cuproid,
   cycloid, cymoid, cynoid,
   cystoid, cytoid, dendroid,
   dermoid, desmoid, eunuchoid,
   helicoid, hominoid, hyaloid,
   ichthyoid, kertoid, lipoid,
   lithoid, lumbricoid, lymphoid,
   melanoid, metalloid,
   meteoroid, mucoid, myeloid,
   nautiloid
≈ochroid, odontoid, ornithoid,
   ovoid, paraboloid, paranoid,

phylloid, placoid, platinoid,
prismatoid, porphyroid,
proteinoid, rhizoid, rhomboid
≈scaphoid, schizoid, scleroid,
sepaloid, sialoid, sigmoid,
sphenoid, spheroid, spiroid,
steroid, styloid
≈tabloid, teratoid, theroid,
toxoid, trapezoid, trichoid,
trochoid, varioloid, viroid,
viscoid, xyloid, zooid, zygoid
- oidal: sacchroidal
- oidosis: sarcoidosis
   [variant forms: trematode;
   plasmodium]
OKEFENOKEE: American Indian for
   "trembling earth"; name of a
   swamp in Georgia
OKLAHOMA: lit., red people; from
   Choctaw *okla*, people + *homma*,
   red
OKRA: West African name [see
   gumbo]; a kind of hibiscus; related
   to the cotton family; a vegetable
ol: smell
   olfaction, olfactory,
   olfactometer
ol-e: oil; from "olive tree"
≈ole-o: oleaginous, oleaster,
   oleic, olein, oleo
≈oleo-: oleograph,
   oleomargarine, oleoresin
- ol-: lanolin, linoleum,
   petrolatum, petroleum;
   Vaseline®
- ol: cholesterol
   [variant forms: olivaceous,
   olivary, olive, olivenite;
   olive branch, olive drab]
{word notes: cholesterol: *chole*, bile
   + *stereos*, solid; a white,
   crystalline sterol, found esp. in
   animal fats, blood, nerve tissue,
   and bile; Vaseline®: trademark for
   petrolatum; now, in lower caps as
   well; from German *wasser*, water
   + Greek *elaion*, oil + -ine}

OLECRANON: the part of the ulna
   projecting beyond the elbow joint;
   from *olene*, elbow + *kranion*, the
   head
olesc: to grow [see ali]
   adolescence, adolescent,
   obsolescence, obsolescent;
   obsolete
olig-o: small, scarce, few
≈olig-: oliganthous, oligarch,
   oligarchy, oligodontous,
   oliguria
≈oligo-: oligoarthritis, oligoblast,
   Oligocene, oligochaete,
   oligochrome, oligoclase,
   oligodipsia, oligodynamic,
   oligogalactia, oligogenics,
   oligohaline, oligomenorrhea,
   oligomerous, oligopepsia,
   oligophagous, oligophrenia,
   oligopnea, oligopoly,
   oligopsony, oligosaline,
   oligosepalous, oligotrophic
olive: see ol-e
OLYMPIAN: from Mount Olympus;
   grand, imposing; also, majestic,
   aloof, disdainful
om: shoulder
   acromion [acro- + omos]
   [Spanish: hombro]
oma: tumor
- oma: adenoma, angioma,
   atheroma, blastoma,
   carcinoma, celioma,
   chondroma, cystoma,
   dacryoma
≈glaucoma, glioma, granuloma,
   hemangioma, hematoma,
   leukoma, lymphoma
≈melanoma, meningioma,
   mesothelioma, mycetoma,
   myeloma, myoma, myxoma
≈neuroblastoma, neuroma,
   osteoma, osteosarcoma
≈papilloma, retinoblastoma,
   rhabdomyoma

≈sarcoma, scleroma, scotoma,
  seminoma, teratoma, trachoma,
  xanthoma, zygoma
- omavirus: polyomavirus
- omatosis: adenomatois,
  fibromatosis, carcinomatosis,
  lymphomatosis, myxomatosis
omal: see h-omal for anomaly
**omasum: third stomach in
  ruminants**; from "bullock's tripe"
  omasum, abomasum
ombro: rain
  ombrogenous, ombrology,
  ombrometer, ombrophilous,
  ombrophobia
ombudsman: see amb
omelet: see lamell-i
omentum: see uv
om-i: auger
  omen, ominous, abominate
ommat-o: eye
  ommateum, ommatidium,
  ommatophobia, ommatophore
omni-: all
  omnibus, omnidirectional,
  omnifarious, omni-gatherum,
  omnipotence, omnipotent,
  omniscience, omniscient,
  omnivore, omnivorous
  [drama term: exeunt omnes]
OMOPHAGIA: the eating of raw flesh
omphal-os: navel, central point
≈omphal: omphalic, omphalos
≈omphal-: omphalectomy,
  omphaloncus
≈omphalo-: omphaloskepsis,
  omphalotripsis
  [variant form: umbilical]
ONAGER: wild ass [see agr]
onco-: bulk, mass; tumor
≈onc-: oncoma, oncosis
≈onco-: oncocytoma, oncogene,
  oncograph, oncology,
  oncolysis, oncometry,
  oncotherapy, oncotomy,
  oncovirus

- oncus: nephroncus
on-er: load, burden
≈on-er: onerous, onus
- onerat-e: exonerate,
  exoneration, exonerative,
  exonerator
  [phrase: onus probandi]
oneir-o-: dream
≈oneir: oneiric, oneirism
≈oneir-: oneirodynia, oneiroid
≈oneiro-: oneirology,
  oneiromancy, oneirophobia,
  oneiroscopy
onomast: name
≈onomast: onomastic,
  onomastics, onomatous
≈onomato-: onomatology,
  onomatomania, onomatopoeia
- onomasia: antonomasia,
  paronomasia
**ont-o: being, cell, existence,
  organism**
≈onto-: ontogeny, ontology
- ont: diplont, haplont, schizont,
  sporont
- onto-: paleontography
  [variant forms: Parousia;
  homoiousian, homoousian]
onych-o: nail (fingernail, toenail)
  onychauxis; onychogenic;
  perionychium
  [variant form: onyx]
onym: name
- onym: with prefixes: acronym,
  allonym, anonym, antonym,
  autonym, eponym, heteronym,
  homonym, hyponym,
  metonym, paronym,
  polyonym, pseudonym,
  synonym, tautonym
- onym: with combining forms:
  anthroponym, toponym,
  troponym
- onymic: with prefixes:
  metonymic, synonymic

- onymic: with combining forms:
  matronymic, metronymic,
  synonymic, toponymic
- onymous: anonymous,
  eponymous, heteronymous,
  pseudonymous, synonymous
- onymus: euonymus
- onymy: eponymy, metonymy,
  synonymy, toponymy

{word note: metonymy: with *meta-*,
other, a figure of speech in which
the name of one thing is used in
place of that of another associated
with or suggested by it, e.g., "the
White House" for "the President"}

oo: egg, ovum

≈oo: ootid

≈oo-: oocyst, oocyte, oogamous,
oogenesis, oogonium, oolite,
oolith, oology, oophyte,
oosperm, oosphere, oospore,
ootheca

≈oophor-: bearing eggs, or ova
oophoralgia, oophorectomy,
oophoritis

≈oophoro-: oophoropexy,
oophorotomy

OOLONG: Chinese dialectal form of
wulung, lit., black dragon; a dark
tea from China and Taiwan

opa-c: shady

opacity, opaque
[device: opaque projector]

operate: see opu-s

opercul: to close, shut

operculate, operculum,
inoperculate
[variant forms: aperture; April]

ophi-o: snake

≈ophi: ophidian, ophitic

≈ophi-: ophicleide

≈ophio-: ophiolatry, ophiolite,
ophiology

≈ophidio-: ophidiophobia

{word note: ophitic: from *ophites
lithos*, snake stone; designating a

texture of rock, in which long, flat,
narrow crystals of pagioclase
feldspar are embedded in augite}

ophthalm-o: eye

≈ophthalm: ophthalmia,
ophthalmic

≈ophthalmo-: ophthalmologist,
ophthalmology,
ophthalmoscope

- ophthalmia: xerophthalmia
- ophthalmos: exophthalmos

opin-e: to think; akin to *optare*, to
choose

opine, opinion, opinionated,
opinionative

opistho: behind, back

≈opisth: opisthotic

≈opisth-: opisthodont

≈opistho-: opisthognathous,
opisthograph

OPPIDAN: of a town; urban; as a
noun, person living in a town

panoply: see h-opl

opsi: late

opsigamy, opsimathy, opsiuria

opson-i: to buy victuals

≈opson: opsonin, opsonize

≈opsoni-: opsonify

- opsony: duopsony, monopsony,
  oligopsony

opt: to choose [see opin-e]

≈opt: opt, optative, option,
optional

- opt: adopt, adoptive, co-opt

opto: eye

≈opto-: optoacoustic, optometer,
optometrist, optometry

≈optic: optical, optician

- opter: diopter
- optic: hyperoptic, microptic,
  orthoptic, panoptic, preoptic,
  synoptic
- opticon: stereopticon
- opto-: dioptometer
- optric: catadioptric, catoptric,
  dioptric

- ope: metope, myope
- opean: cyclopean
- opia: condition of the eye
  ametropia, asthenopia,
  deuteranopia, hemeralopia,
  hyperopia, emmetropia,
  isometropia, myopia,
  nyctalopia, photopia,
  presbyopia, protanopia,
  scotopia
- opic: metopic, myopic
- ops: Cyclops, triceratops
- opsis: amblyopsis, stereopsis,
  synopsis, xanthopsis
- opsy: autopsy, biopsy,
  necropsy, thanatopsy

optim: the best [related to opus]
  optimal, optimism, optimist,
  optimize, optimum

opu-s: work, riches
≈oper: opera, operable, operand,
  operant; operetta, operose
≈operat-e: operate, operation,
  operational, operationalism,
  operative, operator
- operable: inoperable
- operat-e: cooperate,
  disoperation
- operative: inoperative,
  postoperative
≈opu-s: opulent, opus, opuscule
  [variant forms: maneuver,
  manure—both referred to that
  which was worked by hand]
  [phrases: magnum opus, a
  person's greatest work;
  masterpiece; modus operandi]

or: gold; from auri
  orange, oriole, ormolu, oroide,
  orphrey—second root is *frieze*;
  orpiment, orpine—second root
  is from *pigment*
  [Note: *orange* itself originally
  from Persian *narang*; Spanish:
  naranja, the fruit; *naranjo*, the
  tree]

**or-al: an opening, mouth; to
  speak, pray**
≈orac: oracle, oracular
≈orad: orad
≈oral: oral, oralism, orality
≈orat-e: orate, oration
≈orator-: orator, oratorical,
  oratorio, oratory, orotund—oral
  + rotund
- orat-e: perorate, peroration
- orable: adorable, exorable,
  inexorable
- or-e: peroral; adore
≈ori-: orifice, orinasal, orison
  [variant form: orle]

orama: a view
  cinerama, cosmorama,
  cyclorama, diorama, georama,
  marinorama, neorama,
  panorama, polyorama
ORANGUTAN: Malay: *oran*, man +
  utan, forest; orig., term for savage
  tribes: first applied to the ape by
  Europeans; an arboreal anthropoid
  ape of Borneo and Sumatra

orb-it: a track, orbit
≈orb: orb, orbicular
≈orbit: orbit, orbiter
- orbit-: exorbitance; exorbitant
- orbital: antorbital, amteorbital,
  biorbital, circumorbital,
  contraorbital, infraorbital,
  interorbital, postorbital,
  preorbital, suborbital,
  supraorbital

orc : to make one swear; from
  horkos, an oath
  exorcise, or exorcize, exorcism,
  exorcist
orchard: see horti

orchestr-a: orig., designated a flat
  surface used for threshing grain;
  then, to dance; related: proselyte
  orchestra, orchestral,
  orchestrate, orchestration,
  orchestrion [see halo]

orchi-d: testicle-s; **orchid**, from the shape of its roots
orchid:
  orchid, orchis; orchidology
testicle-s:
≈orchid: orchidic
≈orchi-: orchialgia, orchichorea, orchitis
≈orchid-: orchidectomy, orchiditis
≈orchido-: orchidotomy
- orchid: anorchid, monorchid
- orchidism: cryptorchidism
ord: to arrange, begin, order
≈ord: ordain, ordnance
≈order: order, orderly
≈ordin: ordinal, ordinance, ordinand, ordinate, ordination; ordinarily, ordinary
≈ordo: ordo, ordonnance
- ordain: foreordain, preordain
- order: disorder, superorder; disorderly
- ordial: primordial
- ordinary: extraordinary
- ordinate: coordinate, incoordinate, inordinate, subordinate, insubordinate, superordinate
- ordium: exordium, primordium
  [variant forms: extraordinaire, ornery]
ORDEAL: from German *uzdailjan*, to deal out; orig., an ancient form of punishment
orex: to reach
  orexis; anorexia, hyperorexia, paraorexia
organ: organ, tool
≈organ: organ, organelle, organic, organicism, organism, organist, organon, organum
≈organ-: organoid, organoma
≈organiz-e: organization, organize, organizer

≈organo: organogel, organogenic, organography, organoleptic, organology, organotherapy, organotropic, organotropism
- organic: inorganic, superorganic
- organism: ectorganism, entorganism, epiorganism, macrorganism, microorganism, superorganism
- organized: disorganized
ORGASM: climax of sexual excitement
ORIEL: bay window
orient: to arise
≈orient: orient, oriental, orientate, orientation, orienteering
- orient: disorient
≈origin: origin, original, originality, originally, originate
- origin-e: aboriginal, aborigine, Aborigene, aborigines—the native animals or plants of a certain region
- ort-: abort, abortion, abortive [theology term: original sin]
orium: a place where
  auditorium, sanitorium; planetarium; factory, lavatory
orn: to fit out
≈orna-ment: ornate, ornament, ornamental, ornamentation
- orn-: adorn, suborn, subornation [phrase: subornation of jury]
ornery: see ord
ornith-o: bird
≈ornith: ornithic, ornithischian
≈ornith-: ornithoid, ornithosis
≈ornitho-: ornithocephalus, ornithology, ornithophilous, ornithopod, ornithopter, ornithorhynchus
≈ornis: ornis

≈orni-: orniscopist, orniscopy
- ornis: amaurornis, epiornis,
  ichthyornis
or-o-: **mountain** [from orient]
  oread; orogeny, orography,
  orology; anticlinorium
orphan: orig., **bereft, work**;
  therefore, needed "work"
  orphan, orphanage
  [variant form: robot]
ortho: **straight, regular, upright**
≈orth-: orthicon, orthodontist,
  orthoptic, orthotics
≈ortho-: orthobiosis, orthocenter,
  orthocephalic, orthochorea,
  orthochromatic, orthoclase,
  orthoclastic
≈orthodox, orthodoxy, orthoepy
≈orthogenic, orthogenesis,
  orthognathous, orthogonal,
  orthograde, orthographic,
  orthography
≈orthokeratology, orthokeratosis,
  orthokinetics, orthology,
  orthomelic, orthometry,
  orthomolecular, orthopedics,
  orthopteran, orthorhombic
≈orthoscope, orthoscopic,
  orthostatic, orthostichy
≈orthotropic, orthotropism,
  orthotropous
- orth-o-: anorthite, anorthosite
oscill: **to swing**
≈oscill: oscillate, oscillation,
  oscillator
≈oscillo-: oscillogram,
  oscillograph, oscillometer,
  oscilloscope
osc-u: **kiss, touching**; from "mouth"
≈oscul: osculant, oscular,
  osculate, osculum
- osculate: inosculate,
  interosculate
  [related forms: oscitancy,
  oscitant: drowsiness]

-**osis**: **condition**; often, a diseased
  condition
- osis: acanthocytosis,
  aeroneurosis, anadiplosis,
  aponeurosis, atherosclerosis,
  diplosis, diverticulosis,
  ecchymosis, endostosis
≈haplosis, heterosis, hidrosis,
  hypnosis, ichthyosis, keratosis
≈melanosis, metempsychosis,
  miosis, mononucleosis,
  mycosis, narcosis, necrobiosis,
  necrosis, nephrosis, neurosis
≈ornithosis, osteosis,
  otosclerosis, parabiosis,
  pediculosis, phimosis,
  pollinosis, pyosis, pycnosis
≈sarcoidosis, scoliosis, siderosis,
  silicosis, spirochetosis,
  stenosis, sycosis, synarthrosis
≈thrombosis, toxicosis,
  toxoplasmosis, trichinosis,
  trichosis, tuberculosis
≈varicosis, virosis, xerosis,
  zymosis
- otic-s: narcotic, orthotics,
  psychotic
osm: **to smell**
≈osm: osmics, osmium
≈osm-: osmesthesia
- osmia: anosmia, cacosmia
osm-o: **impulse, to push**
≈osmos-e: osmose, osmosis;
  osmotic
≈osmo-: osmometer
- osmosis: endosmosis,
  exosmosis
osprey: see oss-i; fract
oss-i: **bone**
≈oss: ossein, osseous, ossicle,
  ossuary
≈ossi-: ossiferous, ossific,
  ossification, ossified, ossiform,
  ossifrage, ossify, ossivorous
- osal: petrosal

[variant forms: osprey, osso buco, oyster]

ost-e: bone
≈oste: osteal
≈oste-: ostealgia, ostearthritis, osteitis, osteoma, osteosis
≈osteo-: osteoacusis, osteoarthritis, osteoblast, osteoclasis, osteoclast, osteocyte
≈osteogenesis, osteology, osteomalacia, osteomyelitis
≈osteopathy, osteophyte, osteoporosis, osteosarcoma, osteotome, osteotomy
- ost-: teleost
- osteo-: acidosteophyte
- osteum: endosteum, mucoperiosteum, periosteum
- ostititis: endostitis, panostitis, or panosteitis, parostitis, periostitis
- ostosis: dysostosis, endostosis, exostosis, hyperostosis

ost-i: mouth, opening
ostiary, ostiole, ostium, ostomy
[variant form: usher]

ostrac: shell
≈ostrac: ostracism, ostracize, ostracod
- ostracan: entomostracan, malacostracan
- ostracum: periostracum
ostrich: see avi

oti: ease
otiose; negotiable, negotiate, nonnegotiable

ot-o: ear
≈ot-: otitis, otodynia
≈oto-: otocyst, otolaryngology, otolith, otology, otorhinolaryngology, otosclerosis, otoscope
- otic: parotic, periotic
- otid: parotid
- otitis: parotitis

OTTER: water animal; from "water"; see nutria
oust, ouster: see s-ist
OUTLAW: from Scandinavian *utlager*, lit., beyond the law
outrage: see ultra

ov-a: egg, ovum
≈ov: oval, ovary, ovate, ovum
≈ov-: ovoid
≈ovari-: ovariectomy
- ovate: obovate, subovate
≈ovi-: oviferous, oviform, oviparous, oviposit, ovisac
≈ovo-: ovotestis
- ovoid: obovoid
≈ovul-e: ovulate, ovulation, ovule
- ovulation: anovulation, superovulation
- ovia: synovia, asynovia
[phrase: ab ovo]
OVATION: celebration of a victory; compare *triumph*
overture: see aper
OVINE: pertaining to sheep; *ewe* is the only other known word pertaining to *ovine*

ox-y: oxygen, sharp
≈oxy-: oxycephaly, oxygen, oxygenize, oxyhemoglobin, oxyhydrogen, oxymoron, oxyphil, oxytocic, oxytone
- oxemia: anoxemia, hyperoxemia, hypoxemia
- oxia: anoxia, gastroxia, hyperoxia, hypoxia, normoxia
- oxy-: anoxyemia, epoxy, paroxytone
- oxysm: paroxysm
≈oxid-e: oxide, oxidize
- oxidant: antioxidant
- oxide: dioxide, dinoxide, hyseoxide, pentoxide, peroxide, phenoxide, protoxide, quadroxide, sesquioxide, suboxide,

sulphoxide, tetroxide, trioxide,
tritoxide
- oxidation: photooxidation
    [variant form: oxazine]
oyere and terminer; oyez: see aud-i-o
oyster: see ossi
OZ.: symbol for and abbreviation of
    Italian *onza*, ounce
ozo-n-e: to smell; a pale-blue gas
    with a penetrating odor
≈ozo-ne: ozonate, ozonation,
    ozone, ozonic, ozonide,
    ozonize, ozonous
≈ozo-: ozocerite, or ozokerite
≈ozoni-: ozoniferous,
    ozonification
≈ozono-: ozonolysis,
    ozonometer, ozonophore,
    ozonoscope, ozonosphere

P

paci: to fix, fasten, strike; from
    "peace"
≈paci-: pacific, pacificate,
    pacifier, pacifist; Pacific
    Ocean
- pact-ed: compact, impact,
    impacted, incompact
≈pag-e: page—of book, pageant,
    pageantry; paginal, paginate,
    pagination
- pag-: propagate; propaganda,
    propagule
≈pay: pay, payable, payee
- pay: repay, repayment
≈peace: peace, peaceable,
    peaceful
- pinge: impinge, impinger,
    impingement
    [variant forms: anapest, appease,
    pact, bibliopegy, pegmatite,
    prune, fang, pact, pail; pax, Pax]
    [phrases: requiescat in pace; in
    pace, Pax Romana; pax tecum]

pace: see pass[1]
pachy: thick
    pachycarpous, pachycephalic,
    pachycheilia, pachychromatic,
    pachychymia, pachydactyly,
    pachyderm, pachydermia,
    pachydermatous, pachyhemia,
    pachynema
PADDY: Malay *padi*, rice in the husk;
    a rice field
pag: peasant, rustic; from *pais*,
    country
    pagan, paganize; peasant
    [Spanish: pais]
pain: see pen-it
pair: see patri
PAISLEY: an intricate multicolored
    pattern; made in Paisley, England;
    design originated in India
PAJAMAS: Hindi for "leg garment";
    from Persian *pai*, a leg + *jama*,
    garment
pala: from Palatium, home of
    Augustus
    palace, palatial, palatine
palat-e: roof of mouth
    palatable, palatal, palatalize,
    palate
palaver: see parable
pal-e: a stake
    pale—one meaning, palisade;
    impale
    [variant forms: peel; travail, travel,
    travois]
pale-o: ancient, old
≈pale-: paleethnology,
    paleoceanology,
    paleontography
≈paleo-: paleoanthropology,
    paleoarctic, paleobiological,
    paleobotanist, Paleocene,
    paleoenvironment,
    paleoethnology, paleography,
    Paleolithic, paleologist,
    paleomammalogy,
    paleopathology, Paleozoic,
    paleozoology

PALESTRA: a place for wrestling in Greece

PALETOT: a man's overcoat

PALETTE: lit., small spade; used by artists

palin: back, backward

palindrome, palingenesis, palingraphia, palinode, palinphrasia

{word note: palindrome, a word or phrase that reads the same backward and forward, e.g., dad, madam, mom, pop; Madam, I'm Adam; A man, a plan, a canal, Panama}

pal-l: to grow pale

≈pal-e: pale— one meaning, palish

≈pall: pall, pallid, pallor

- pall: appall, appalling

palli-at-e: to ease; from "to cloak, conceal"

palliate, palliation, palliative, pallium

palm: palm of the hand; also, the palm tree because its leaves resemble the palm of the hand

≈palm: palm, palmar, palmary, palmate, palmation, palmer, palmette, palmetto, palmistry, palmy, palmyra

≈palmati-: palmatifid, palmatilobed, palmatisected

- palmate: totipalmate

[variant form: pelmet]

PALOMINO: Spanish: dove-colored; a golden-tan or cream-colored horse

palp: to touch; to pat

≈palp: palpable, palpate, palpitate, palpus

- palp: pedipalp

- palpable: impalpable

PALPEBRAL: pertaining to the eyelids

PALTER: orig., rag, piece of cloth; then, haggling over cloth prices; now, to talk or act insincerely

PALUDAL: pertaining to a marsh

PALYNOLOGY: the study of living or fossil plant spores and pollen

pamp-a: plain, field

pampa, pampean, pampero—a strong, cold wind that blows from the Andes across the SA pampas

[variant form: paramo]

PAMPER: orig., to feed too much

PAMPHLET: short for "Pamphilus, or on Love," title of 12th-c. amatory poem

pan-: all

≈pan-: panacea, Pan-American, panchromatic, pancosmism, pancratium, pancreas [see separate entry]

≈pandect, pandemic, pandemonium, Pandora

≈panegyric, pangenesis, pangram

≈panmixia, panmnesia, panoply, panoptic, panorama

≈pantheist, pantheon, panurgic

≈panto-: pantograph, pantomime, pantophagist

[variant form: diapason]

[NB: panther]

pancrea-s: lit., all flesh; pancreas

≈pancrea-s: pancreas, pancreatic, pancreatin

≈pancrea-: pancreatomy

≈pancreo-: pancreolith, pancreolysis

≈pancreat-: pancreatalgia, pancreatectomy

≈pancreato-: pancreatoblastoma, pancreatogenic, pancreatolysis, pancreatopathy

pand: to spread, extend

≈pand: pand

- pand: expand, expanded, repand

- pans-e: expanse, expansible, expansile, expansion, expansionism, expansive

[variant form: sponson]

PANDURATE: shaped somewhat like a violin, as some leaves

pane-l: a piece of cloth

pane, panel, paneling; impanel
[variant form: pawn—one
meaning]

panic[1]: ear of millet, a swelling

panic— one meaning, panicle

PANIC[2]: after Pan, a god of wild
animals

pan-n: bread

≈pan-n: panada, panatela,
panettone, panino, panocha,
pantry; pannier

- panage: appanage
- panation: impanation
- paniment: accompaniment
- panion: companion
- pany: company, accompany

{word notes: pantry: orig., a place
near the kitchen where bread was
stored; companion: lit., bread
fellow, messmate; a calque of
Gothic *gahlaiba*, one who eats of
the same bread—*ga*, with + *hlaifs*,
loaf (of bread)—see lady, lord}

PANZER: German for armor; a tank
used in WWII; orig. from Latin
pantex, belly, paunch

papil-l: butterfly

papilionaceous, papillon,
papillote
[variant form: pavilion—a tent;
so called from its shape]

{word notes: papillon: a breed of toy
spaniel; so named from the
fancied similarity of the shape of
the ears to the butterfly}

pap-ill-a: pimple, nipplelike

papule, papilla, papillary,
papillectomy, papilloma
[variant form: pimple]

**papyr-o: papyrus; a tall water
plant** [used to make the first
writing paper]

papyraceous, papyrus;
papyrograph, papyrology,
papyrophobia—fear of paper
[variant forms: paper, paparazzo,

pl., paparazzi, papier collé,
papier-mâche; taper, from use of
papyrus as a wick]

{word note: paparazzo: orig., a
scribbler; the plural *paparazzi* now
designates free lance
photographers who take candid
shots, often in an obtrusive
manner of celebrities for
newspapers and magazines}

par: to be visible

- par-: apparent, apparition,
apparitor, transparency,
transparent
- pear: appear, disappear
- pearance: appearance,
disappearance
[variant form: peer—one
meaning]

par-a-[1]: alongside

≈par-: paragon, parallax, parallel,
parallelepiped, parallelism,
parallelogram, paramount,
paramour

≈paregoric, parenchyma,
parenteral, parenthesis,
parenthetical, parergon,
paresis, paresthesia

≈parhelion

≈parody, paronomasia, parotic,
parotid, parotitis, Parousia,
paroxysm, paroxytone

≈para-: parabiosis, parablast,
parable, parabola, parabolic,
parabolize, paraboloid,
paraclete, paradigm, paradox,
paradoxical

≈paragenesis, paragraph,
paragraphia, paralanguage,
paralegal, paraleipsis,
paralinguistics, paralogism,
paralysis, paralyze

≈paramecium, paramedic,
parameter, paramilitary,
paramnesia, paramorph,
paramorphism, paranoia,

paranoid, paranormal,
paranymph

≈paraphernalia, paraphilia,
paraphrase, paraphrastic,
paraphysis, paraplegia,
parapraxis

≈paraselene, parasexual, parasite,
parasympathetic, parasynapsis,
parasynthesis

≈paratactic, parataxis,
parathyroid, paratyphoid,
paravane, parazoan
[variant forms: palsy, parish]

**para-²: to arrange, prepare,
protect**
parachute, parapet, parasol
[variant form: rampart]

para-³: little
paraffin—lit., too little affinity,
from its chemical inertness

PARADISE: lit., around a wall; any
place or condition of great beauty,
or great satisfaction, happiness, or
delight; capitalized, heaven

parapet: see pector

parasit-e: from *para-* alongside +
sitos, food, grain; orig., one who
ate at the table of another

≈parasit-s: parasite, parasitic,
parasitism

≈parasito-: parasitology

- parasite: antiparasite,
cleptoparasite, ectoparasite,
endoparasite, hemiparasite,
hemoparasite, hyperparasite,
macroparasite, microparasite,
mycoparasite, necroparasite,
nosoparasite, phytoparasite,
superparasite, xenoparasite,
zooparasite

**par-e¹: to set in order, to bring
forth**

≈par-e: pare, parade

≈parent: parent, parentage,
parental, parenting

≈pari: parity—one meaning

≈parr: parrel, parry

≈parure: parure

- para: nullipara, primipara

- parable: inseparable, irreparable

- par-ate: apparatus; separate,
separatism, separatist,
separator

- paration: preparation,
reparation, separation

- parative: reparative, separative

- par-e: apparel, prepare

- parous: with prefixes:
ambiparous, biparous,
equiparous, multiparous,
primiparous, uniparous

- parous: with combining forms:
aquiparous, dentiparous,
dorsiparous, fetiparous,
fissiparous, gemmiparous,
oviparous, pupiparous,
ramiparous, sebiparous,
sporiparous, viviparous

≈parri-: parricide

≈parturi: parturient, parturition

≈parturi-: parturifacient

- partum: antepartum,
intrapartum, peripartum,
postpartum

- per-: puerperal, puerperium;
viper, viperine, viperous;
vituperate

- pertoir-e: repertoire, repertory
[variant forms: comprador,
emperor; repair— one meaning,
disrepair; sever]

{word note: parade: from Spanish
parar, to stop; first meant "a
stopping"; French interpreted
parade as a halting on horseback
for stately display}

par-e²: equal

≈par: par, parity—one meaning,
parlay

≈pari-: parimutuel, paripinnate

- parable: comparable,
equiparable, incomparable

- par-e: compare, comparison,
  disparage, disparate, disparity,
  nonpareil
  [variant forms: pair, peer—one
  meaning, peerage, peeress,
  peerless; compeer; price, pricey;
  prix fixe; prize—one meaning,
  misprize; umpire]
  [phrases: au pair, pari passu;
  ceteris paribus; peer group]
  {word note: apparel: orig., to put like
  with like; clothing}
PAREVE: Yiddish *parev*; without
  meat or milk products; hence,
  permissible to be eaten with either
  meat or dairy dishes, in accordance with the laws of kashrut, the
  dietary laws of Judaism
PARIAH: Tamil; a member of one of
  the lowest castes in India; orig., a
  drummer; Tamil is a language of
  India

parie-t: **wall**
  paries, parietal, parietitis;
  biparietal, frontoparietal,
  squamoparietal
  [pellitory; Spanish: pared—wall]
PARKA: Russian for a skin shirt; fur
  coat; see Eskimo anorak

par-l: **to talk**
≈parl: parlance, parlando, parley,
  parlor
≈parliament: parliament,
  parliamentarian, parliamentary
≈parol: parol, parole, parolee
  [variant form: pour-parler]
parochial: see ec-o

pars: **to spare**
  parsimonious, parsimony
parson: see person

partheno: **virgin**
≈parthen: Parthenon, Parthenos
≈partheno-: parthenocarpy,
  parthenogenesis,
  parthenolagnia, parthenolatry,
  parthenology, parthenophilia,
  parthenophobia, parthenospore

part-i: **a part, to divide, side**
≈part: part—one meaning, partake
  (part + take), partner,
  partnership; party; partway
≈parti: partible, particle, partisan,
  partite, partition, partitive;
  partial, partiality
≈parti-: participant, participate,
  participatory, participle; parti-
  colored
≈particular: particular,
  particularism, particularity,
  particularize, particularly
≈particulate: particulate
- part-: apart, apartheid, departed,
  departure, impartial,
  impartible, quasiparticle,
  repartee
- partite: bipartite, hexapartite,
  multipartite, pinnatipartite,
  pluripartite, quadripartite,
  tripartite
- partition: tripartition
- part: apart, compart,
  counterpart, depart, impart
- partment: apartment,
  compartment, department
- portion: apportion,
  disproportion, proportion,
  malapportion
- portional: proportional
- portionate: proportionate,
  disproportionate
≈parc: parcel, parcenary,
  parcener
- parecenary: coparcenary
  [variant forms: parse, portion,
  jeopardy]
  [phrases: ex parte, particeps
  criminis, parti pris]
PASCAL: after Blaise Pascal
  (1623-62), the French philosopher
  and mathematician who built the
  first desk calculator-type adding
  machine; a multiuse computer
  program

pass[1]**: a step**
≈pass: pass, passable, passably,
   passade, passado, passage,
   passing
≈passe: passé, passementerie,
   passenger
- pass: compass, encompass,
   surpass, trespass
- passable: impassable [see
   impassible, next family]
   [variant forms: pace, impasse, pas,
   paseo, pasodoble, passepied,
   passacaglia, passim]
   [phrases: pas de deux, passe-
   partout, en passant, laissez-
   passer, pari passu, pas de chat,
   pas seul]
pass[2]**: to suffer, to feel**
≈pass: passible, passive,
   passivism, passivity
≈passion: passion, passional,
   passionate, Passionist,
   passionless
- passion: compassion,
   impassion, impassioned
- passible: impassible [see
   impassable, previous family]
- passionate: compassionate,
   dispassionate, impassionate,
   incompassionate
- passive: impassive
≈pati: patience, patient
- patien-ce: impatience, impatient
- patible: compatible,
   incompatible
past: to feed
≈past-or: pastille, pastor,
   pastoral, pastorale, pastorate,
   pastorium
≈pastur-e: pasturable, pasturage,
   pasture
- past-o: repast, antipasto
   [variant forms: pabulum, pester]
   {word note: pastor: regarded as one
   who "feeds" the flock; a spiritual
   shepherd}

past-e: to sprinkle, paste
≈past-e: pasta, paste, pastel,
   pasticcio, pastiche, pastina,
   pastry
- past-e: impaste; impasto
   [variant forms: pâte, pâtisserie,
   pâtissier]
   [phrase: pâté de foie gras]
PATAGIUM: lit., border; a fold of skin
   between the fore and hind limbs of
   bats, flying squirrels, etc.,
   enabling them to fly or glide
   through the air
pate: to walk
   peripatetic—lit., walking around;
   as a noun—and capitalized—a
   follower of Aristotle
pate-ll-a: pan, kneecap; from "to
   spread out"
   patella, patellar; patelliform
   [variant form: paten: metal disk or
   plate]
pat-ent: open; from "to spread out"
≈pat-ent: patent, patently
≈patin: patin, patina, patinate
≈patul: patulent, patulous
≈pate-: patefaction
   [variant form: patio]
pater-n: father
≈pater-n: pater, paternal,
   paternalism, paternity
≈pater-: paterfamilias,
   paternoster
≈padr-e: padre, padrone
- padre: compadre
≈patr: patriate, patrician,
   patriciate, patristic
≈patr- patronymic
≈patri-: patricide, patrilineal,
   patrilocal, patrimony
- patriate: expatriate, repatriate
- patriation: expatriation,
   repatriation
- patric: allopatric, sympatric
- patrid: eupatrid
≈patriot: patriot, patriotism

- patriot: compatriot, superpatriot
≈patr-on: patron, patronage,
    patronal, patroness, patronize,
    patroon
    [variant forms: compère; pattern,
    paterfamilias; perpetrate]
    [phrases: pater patriae; Gloria
    Patri, glory to the Father;
    repair—one meaning]
patience, patient: see pass[2]
patio: see patent; also, spac-e
path-os: to suffer; feeling, disease;
    see pass[2]
≈path: pathetic, pathos
≈patho-: pathogen, pathogenesis,
    pathognomonic, pathology
- path: sociopath
- pathetic: sympathetic,
    parasympathetic
- pathic: with prefixes: allopathic,
    amphipathic, antipathic,
    autopathic, deuteropathic,
    exopathic, monopathic,
    protopathic
- pathic: with combining forms:
    angiopathic, arthropathic,
    cardiopathic, cytopathic,
    dermatopathic,
    encephalopathic, erotopathic,
    etiopathic, gynopathic,
    idiopathic, sociopathic,
    theopathic, toxipathic
- pathize: empathize, sympathize
- pathology: histopathology,
    neuropathology,
    phytopathology
- pathy: with prefixes: apathy,
    allopathy, antipathy, empathy,
    sympathy, telepathy
- pathy: with combining forms:
    anthropopathy homeopathy,
    hydropathy, myopathy,
    naturopathy, neuropathy,
    osteopathy, retinopathy
    [Spanish and Italian: simpatico]
PATOIS: lit., uncultivated speech

pauro: few, scarce
    paurometabolous
    [variant forms: paucity;
    pauciloquy]
pause: a stopping; from "to bring
    to an end"
≈pause: pause
- pause: with prefixes: diapause,
    interpause, mesopause
- pause: with combining forms:
    aeropause, heliopause,
    menopause, stratopause,
    tropopause
    [variant form: posada]
pav: peacock
    pavane, pavonine
    [Spanish: pava: turkey]
pav-e: to ram, beat
    pave, pavé, pavement, paver,
    pavid, paving, pavior
PAVIS: a large shield; from Pavia,
    Italy, where first made
pavilion: see papil
pawn[1]: see pane-l
pawn[2]: see ped-i
pax: see paci
pay: see paci
peace: see paci
PEACH: from *Persian* apple
pearl: see sphere+
peasant: see pag
peat: see piece
PECAN: from Illinois *pakani*
pecc-a: to sin
≈pecca: peccable, peccancy,
    peccant, peccadillo, peccavi
- peccable: impeccable
- peccant: impeccant
    [NB: peccary: a piglike animal]
    {word note: peccadillo: lit., a minor
    or petty sin, as in "an innocent
    peccadillo"; a slight fault}
PECK[1]: from Middle English *picken*,
    to pick; to strike with a pointed
    object
PECK[2]: ultimately from Greek *bikos*,
    wine jar; a unit of dry measure
    equal to one-fourth bushel, or

eight quarts; figuratively, a large
amount, as a peck of trouble; from
the same root is *beaker*
pect: see s-spec-t for expect
pect[1]: **to congeal**
pectic, pectic acid, pectin
pect[2]: **comb, toothlike**
pecten, pectinate; pectiniform
[variant form: peignor]
pector: chest
≈pector: pectoral, pectorial
≈pectori-: pectoriloquial,
pectoriloquy
- pector-: expectorant,
expectorate: to expel from the
chest
[variant forms: parapet, petronel]
pecun: money, private property;
from "cattle"
pecuniary; impecuniosity,
impecunious
[variant forms: peculiar,
peculiarity; peculate: to steal
property; peculation]
ped: foot [see pod]
≈ped: pedal, pedate, pedestal,
pedestrian, peduncle,
pedunculate
≈pedic: pedicel, pedicle,
pediculate, pedicule
≈pedim: pediment, pedimented
≈ped-: pedorthics
≈pedi-: pedicure, pedigree,
pedipalp
≈pedo-: pedomancy, pedometer,
pedopathy
- ped: aliped, biped, fissiped,
parallelepiped, quadruped
- pedance: impedance
- pedal-: sesquipedalian;
bipedalism
- pede: centipede, impede,
millepede, multipede,
octopede, velocipede
- pedient-: expedient, inexpedient
- pediential: expediential

- pediment: impediment,
impedimenta
- pedit-e: expedite, expediter,
expedition, expeditious
[variant forms: cap-a-pie,
charpoy, dispatch, fetlock,
fetter; impeach, impeachable,
unimpeachable; pawn—one
meaning, peon, pied-à-terre,
piedmont, pioneer, pyramid;
trapeze, tranpezium, trapezius,
trapezoid; trivet, diapedesis: lit.,
a leaping through]
[phrase: vampex pede Herculem]
{word note: pioneer: orig., *peoneer*,
a foot soldier who preceded the
army to clear the way}
peddl: a basket
peddle, peddler; pedlar
pedicul: lice
pedicular; pediculicide;
pediculosis; pediculophobia
ped-o[1]: **child**
≈ped: pedant, pedantry
≈ped-: pedagogue, pedagogic,
pederasty, pediatrician,
pediatrics, pedodontics
≈pedo-: pedobaptism, pedology,
pedomorphism, pedophile,
pedophilia, pedophobia
- ped-: encyclopedia; orthopedics
- paed-: propaedeutic
[variant form: page—an
attendant]
ped-o[2]: **earth**
≈ped-: pedalfer—al (alum) +
ferrum (iron), pedocal
≈pedo-: pedogenesis, pedograph,
pedologic, pedology
PEEVE, PEEVED, PEEVISH: hard to
please
pegmatite: see paci
pegy: see paci for bibliopegy
pejor: to make worse; from "foot"
pejoration, pejorative
[variant forms: impair; Spanish:
peor; French: pisaller]

pel: **mud, slime**

sapropel—black, decaying,
organic bottom deposits in some
lakes, rivers, etc. that lack oxygen
and are rich in hydrogen sulfide

pel: see puls-e for repel

pelag: **sea**

≈pelag: pelagic

- pelagic: abyssopelagic,
allopelagic, archipelagic,
bathypelagic, epipelagic,
mesopelagic

- pelago: archipelago

PELARGONIUM: from *pelargos*, stork;
a flower resembling a stork's bill;
related to *geranium*, both
etymologically and semantically
[see ger³]

pel-l: **skin** [see pil-e¹]

≈pel-t: pelage, pelisse, pellicle;
pelt—one meaning, peltry

≈pell-: pellagra, pellagrin,
pellagrous

≈pellagro-: pellagrophobia

- pelas: erysipelas
[variant forms: fell, film, pillion,
surplice]

pell: see puls-e for *repellant*

pellitory: see parie-t

pelmet: see palm

PELORIA: abnormal flower shape

PELORUS: from Pelorus, pilot of
Hannibal's ship; a device for
taking bearings that fits over a
compass card

PELOTA: Spanish for "ball";
Spanish name for "jai alai"

pelt: **shield**

peltast—in ancient Greece, a
soldier carrying a light shield;
peltate—shield-shaped, as certain
leaves

pelv: **basin**; in the shape of a basin
pelvic, pelvis; pelviform

PEMMICAN: Cree for dried lean meat;
from *pimihkeew*, makes grease

PEMPHIGUS: watery blisters on skin

pen¹: **almost**

≈pen-: peninsula, penult,
penultimate, penumbra

≈pene-: peneplain

- penult: antepenult,
antepenultimate

pen²: **penalty, fine, punishment**
[see pen-it]
penal, penalize, penalty;
penology
[variant forms: penal code, penal
servitude, penalty box;
pine—one meaning, repine,
sub poena, lit., under penalty]

PENDRAGON—Welsh; the dragon
symbol, or war standard, implied
head or leader; hence, supreme
chief or leader: a title used in
ancient Britain; see penguin

pend: **weight; to hang, to weigh**

≈pend: pendant, pendency,
pendent, pendentive, pending,
pendulous, pendulum

- pend: with prefixes: append,
compend—a noun; same as
compendium, depend, expend,
impend, perpend, propend,
suspend

- pend: with combining forms:
stipend, vilipend

- pend-: appendicitis, appendix,
compendious, expenditure,
independence, perpendicular,
stipendiary, suspenders

- pendable: dependable,
expendable, undependable,
unexpendable

- pendent: dependent, impendent,
independent

- pendium: antependium,
compendium

≈pens: pensile, pension,
pensionary, pensioner, pensive

- pens-: dispensary, dispensator,
dispensatory, propensity,
suspensor

- pensable: dispensable,
  indispensable
- pensate: compensate,
  overcompensate
- pensation: compensation,
  decompensation, dispensation,
  recompensation
- pense: dispense, expense,
  prepense, propense, suspense
- pension: suspension
- pensive: expensive,
  inexpensive, recompensive,
  superexpensive, suspensive,
  unexpensive
≈pond: ponder, ponderable,
  ponderous, ponderosa
- ponderable: imponderable
- pondersant: equiponderant,
  preponderant
- ponderate: equiponderate,
  preponderate
  [variant forms: penchant; pensée,
  pensionne, peso; poise, poised,
  counterpoise, equipoise; pansy,
  pound—one meaning; spend;
  speiss]
penetr-o: **to enter** [from *penates*,
  inner house + *intrare*, enter (from
  in- + *trans-*, across]
≈penetr: penetrable, penetralia,
  penetrance, penetrant,
  penetrate, penetrating,
  penetration
≈penetro-: penetrometer
- penetrable: impenetrable,
  unpenetrable
- penetrate: interpenetrate
  [variant form: penates]
PENGUIN: Welsh: white head; see
  pendragon
pen-i: **tail**, **penis**
  pencil, penis; penicillate,
  penicillin, penicillium
  [variant forms: pintle;
  Spanish: pene—penis]
  {word note: pintle: a pin or bolt}

pen-it: **to feel sorry for a wrong
done** [see pen[2]]
≈pen-it: penance, penitence,
  penitent, penitential,
  penitentiary
- penitent: impenitent
- pent-: repent, repentance,
  repentant
  [variant forms: pain, pine—
  one meaning, repine]
pen-n: **feather**; **leaflet**
≈pen-n: pen—the writing
  instrument, penna, pennant,
  pennate, pennon
≈penni-: penniform
- pennate: bipennate,
  brevipennate, impennate,
  latipennate, longipennate,
  planipennate, quadripennate,
  semipennate, tripennate,
  unipennate
- pennage: empennage
≈pinna: pinna, pinnacle, pinnate
≈pinnati-: pinnatifid, pinnatiped,
  pinnatisect
≈pinni-: pinniform, pinnigrade,
  pinniped
- pinnate: bipinnate,
  digitipinnate, even-pinnate,
  odd-pinnate, paripinnate,
  pseudopinnate, quadripinnate,
  tripinnate
  [variant forms: panache, panne,
  pinion, pinnule]
pense: see pend for dispense
PENSACOLA, FL: Choctaw: lit., hairy
  people
pent-a: **five**
≈pent: pentacle, pentad
≈pent-: pentangular, pentarchy,
  pentathlete, pentathlon,
  pentode, pentoxide
≈penta-: pentacapsular,
  pentachloride, pentadactyl,
  pentagon, pentachord,
  pentacoccus, pentacrostic,

pentadactyl, pentagram,
pentamerous, pentameter,
pentaploid, pentastich,
Pentateuch, pentatonic,
pentavalent
≈pente: Pentecost, Pentecostal:
fiftieth
[variant form: penstemon]
penthe: **sorrow, grief**
nepenthe—a drug supposed by
the ancient Greeks to cause
forgetfulness of sorrow
penur: **want, lack of**
≈penur: penurious, penury
- penia: basopenia, calcipenia,
chloropenia, cytopenia,
ductopenia, eosinopenia,
erythropenia, glucopenia,
glycopenia, granulopenia,
leukopenia, neutropenia,
glucopenia, glycopenia,
hematopenia, leukopenia,
lipopenia, neuropenia,
osteopenia, sarcopenia,
sideropenia, thrombopenia
peon, peonage: see ped-i
PEONY: from Apollo, physician of the
gods; a flower once known for its
medicinal properties
peps: **to digest**
≈peps: pepsin, pepsinate
- pepsia: anapepsia, autopepsia,
bradypepsia, dyspepsia,
eupepsia, hyperpepsia,
hypopepsia, oligopepsia
≈pept: peptic, peptize, peptone,
peptonize
- peptic: dyspeptic, eupeptic
- peptide: polypeptide
per-: **by, by means of, through;
completely, thoroughly, very;
each**
by
≈peradventure, per curiam
completely
≈perdition, perdu, or perdue

each
≈per capita, percent, percentage,
percentile, per diem, per
mensem
intensive
≈perdition, perdure, peremptory,
perfervid, perfidious, perfidy,
perform, perfume, perfunctory,
permutation, permute,
perpendicular, perquisite,
persevere, persuade, pertain,
pertinacious, perturb, pertussis,
peruse, perverse, pervert
thoroughly
≈pernicious, perpetrate
through
≈perambulate, perceive,
perception, percipient,
percolate, percutaneous,
peregrinate, perennate,
perennial, perfect, perfoliate,
perforate, perfuse, perish—root
is *it*, perjure, permeable,
permanent, permeate,
permission, permit, peroral,
peroration, perpend, perpetual,
perplex, persecute, persiflage,
persist, perspective,
perspicacious, perspicuous,
perspire, persulfate, pervade,
pervious
≈par-: variant of *per*-: parboil,
pardon, pardoner, parfait,
parget, parterre, parvenu
≈pel: assimilation of *per*-, through:
pellucid
≈pol-: assimilation of *per*-,
intensive: pollute
≈por-: variant of *per*-, through:
portend, portent, portentous
≈pur-: variant of *per*-, for: purloin
per: **to set in order**
imperative, imperator;
imperial, imperious, imperium
[variant forms: empire, emperor]

PERCALE, PERCALINE: Persian:
fragment, scrap; a closely woven
cloth, used for sheets, etc.
peregrinate: see egr
PERINEUM: from *peri-*, around +
inein, to defecate; the region of the
body between the thighs at the
outlet of the pelvis
PERGOLA: an arbor with climbing
vines

per-i-: around
≈per-: perineum
≈peri- perianth, periapsis,
periapt, periblem
≈pericarditis, pericardium,
pericarp, perichondrium,
periclinal, pericline, pericope,
pericranium, pericycle,
pericynthian, periderm
≈perigee, perigynous, perihelion,
perilune, perilymph
≈perimeter, perimorph,
perimysium, perinatal,
perinephrium, perineurium
≈period, periodic, periodical,
periodontics, perionychium,
periosteum, periostracum,
periotic
≈peripatetic, peripeteia,
peripheral, periphrasis,
periphrastic, periphyton
≈perisarc, periscope, peristalsis,
peristome, peristyle,
perithecium, peritoneum,
peritrichous
[variant form: paradise]

peril: to try
≈peril: peril, perilous
- perience-d: experience,
experienced, inexperienced
- periment-: experiment,
experimental,
experimentalism,
experimentation
- pert-: expert, inexpertly;
expertise; expertize

[variant forms: empirical, fear;
parlous, peritus, pl., periti]
PERIDIUM: lit., small leather sack; the
outer coat of the spore-bearing
organ in certain fungi
PERIDOT: a yellowish-green gem;
peridotite
PERIPETEIA: a sudden change of
fortune or reversal of circum-
stances, as in a drama; see per-i
perish: see it
PERISSODACTYL: having an uneven
number of toes on each foot; see
dactyl
PERIWIG: a peruke, a wig
PERONEAL: near the fibula
PERSIMMON: from Virginia
Algonquian *pessemins*

person: actor, person
≈person: person, persona,
personable, personage,
personal, personalia,
personalism, personality,
personalize, personally,
personate, personnel
≈personi-: personification,
personify
- personal: impersonal,
interpersonal, intrapersonal,
monopersonal, nonpersonal,
superpersonal, transpersonal,
tripersonal, unipersonal
- personate: impersonate
[variant forms: parson,
parsonage]
[phrases: in persona, persona
grata, persona non grata,
in propria persona]

pessim: worse
pessimal, pessimism,
pessimist, pessimistic
pest: see paci for *anapest*

pest-i: plague
≈pest: pest, pestilence, pestilent,
pestilential
≈pesti-: pesticide, pestiferous,
pestivirus

pestle: to pound, grind
   pestilation, pestle; pestle and
   mortar
   [variant forms: pesto, pistil,
   pistillate, piston]

petal: leaf; from "to spread out"
≈petal: petal, petalous
≈petal-: petalody, petaloid
- petal: acropetal, axipetal,
   basipetal, cellipetal, centripetal
- petalous: with prefixes:
   apetalous, antipetalous,
   apopetalous, bipetalous,
   catapetalous, dipetalous,
   enneapetalous, epipetalous,
   hexapetalous, oligopetalous,
   polypetalous, sympetalous,
   tetrapetalous, unipetalous
- petalous: with combining forms:
   andropetalous, basipetalous,
   choripetalous, gamopetalous,
   stenopetalous

pet-e: to seek, rush at, desire
≈pet: petition, petulance, petulant
- petal: cellipetal, centripetal,
   cerebripetal, corticipetal,
   spinipetal
- pet-e: compete; inappetence;
   appetency; repetend; impetigo,
   impetus; competitor,
   repetitious
- petent: competent, incompetent
- petite: appetite
- petition: competition, repetition
- petitive: competitive, repetitive
- petu-: impetuosity, impetus,
   perpetual, perpetuate,
   perpetuity
- piti-: propitiate, propitious
   [variant forms: fathom, petasos,
   repeat]
   [phrases: petitio principii—
   begging of the question; a logical
   fallacy; in perpetuum—forever]
PETECHIA: a small hemorrhage spot
   in the skin; from "a writing tablet"

petiol-: leafstalk; from *ped*, foot
   petiolar, petiolate, petiole,
   patiolule

petr-i: rock
≈petr-: petrosal, petrolatum,
   petroleum
≈petri-: petrifaction, petrifactive,
   petrified, petrify
≈petro-: petroform, petrogenesis,
   petroglyph, petrology
   [variant forms: parsley, perron,
   Peter]
   {word note: Petrified Forest National
   Park, in the Painted Desert of
   northern Arizona, contains the
   greatest and most colorful
   concentration of petrified wood in
   the world}

pet-t: small
   petite, petty
   [variant forms: petticoat,
   pettifogger, pettitoes]
   [phrases: petit four, petit jury, petit
   larceny, petit mal, petit point]
PETUNIA: from Tupi (a South
   American Indian language) for
   tobacco; reason unknown; a
   flower

phac, phak: lentil, lens
≈phac-: phacoid, phacoma
≈phaco-: phacocele, phacocyst,
   phacoerysis [last root means
   "pulling, drawing off"],
   phacolite, phacometer,
   phacoscope, phacosclerosis
- phacos: pseudophacos,
   prosthetophacos

phag-o: to eat
≈phago: phagocyte, phagolysis,
   phagomania, phagophobia,
   phagoplasm, phagosome,
   phagotrophic, phagotype
- phage: with prefixes:
   macrophage, microphage,
   polyphage
- phage: with combining forms:
   bacteriophage, biophage,

coprophage, entomophage,
glucophage, gonophage,
hematophage, melanophage,
osteophage, phytophage
- phagia: with prefixes: aphagia,
dysphagia, hyperphagia,
polyphagia
- phagia: with combining forms:
aerophagia, bradyphagia,
chthonophagia, geophagia,
gliophagia, hemophagia,
lignophagia, lipophagia,
necrophagia, omophagia,
onychophagia, xerophagia
- phagous: with prefixes:
euryphagous, monophagous
- phagous: with combining forms:
anthropophagous,
carpophagous, coprophagous,
dendrophagous,
entomophagous,
hematophagous, hylophagous,
ichthyophagous,
myrmecophagous,
oligophagous, phyllophagous,
phytophagous, rhizophagous,
saprophagous, stenophagous,
xylophagous, zoophagous
- phagus: esophagus,
anthropophagus, sarcophagus
- phagy: anthropophagy,
aerophagy, autophagy,
cytophagy, entomophagy,
geophagy, omophagy,
xerophagy

phalan-ge: line of battle; also,
bones between two joints of the
fingers or toes
≈phalan-ge: phalanstery,
phalange, phalangeal,
phalanger, phalanges
≈phalang-: phalangitis
- phalangeal: interphalangeal
[variant forms: plank; phalanx,
planchet, planchette]

{word note: phalanstery: orig., a
socialist community; any
communal association}

phall-o: penis
≈phall: phallic, phallicism,
phallus
≈phall-: phallectomy
≈phallo-: phallocentric,
phallophilia, phallophobia,
phalloplasty
- phallia: diphallia
- phallic: ithyphallic,
macrophallic, teratophallic
[variant form: baleen]

phaner-o: to show, appear
≈phanero-: phanerogam,
phanerophyte, Phanerozoic
≈phant: phantom, phantasm,
phantasy, or fantasy (see variant
forms)
≈phantasm-: phantasmagoria
- phan-e: allophane, cellophane
- phanite: aphanite
- phanous: autophanous,
diaphanous, epiphanous,
monophanous
- phant: hierophant, sycophant,
tonophant
- phany: epiphany, theophany
≈phas-e: phase, phasis, pl., phases
- phas-is: emphasis, emphasize,
multiphasic
- phase: anaphase, diphase,
interphase, metaphase,
polyphase, prophase, telophase
- phatic: emphatic
- phenics: euphenics
≈pheno-: phenocryst, phenology,
phenotype
≈phenom: phenom, phenomenal,
phenomenon, pl., phenomena
≈phenomeno-: phenomenology
- phenom-: epiphenomenon
[variant forms: fancy, fantasy,
fantasia, fantasist, fantasize,
fantast, fantastic]

185

pharmac: a poison; **medicine**;
  orig., to practice witchcraft; to
  practice medicine
≈**pharmac-y**: pharmaceutical,
  pharmaceutics, pharmacist,
  pharmacy
≈**pharmaco-**: pharmacodynamics,
  pharmacogenetics,
  pharmacognosy,
  pharmacokinetics,
  pharmacology, pharmacopeia,
  pharmacotherapy
pharyngo: **throat**, **pharynx**
≈**pharyng**: pharyngeal
≈**pharyng-**: pharyngitis
≈**pharyngo**: pharyngology,
  pharyngoscope
- pharyng-: rhinopharyngitis
  [variant form: pharynx]
phasia: **speech**
  aphasia, bradyphasia,
  cataphasia, dysphasia,
  endophasia, exophasia,
  heterophasia, monophasia,
  paraphasia
  [variant forms: phatic;
  blasphemous, blasphemy,
  euphemism, prophecy, prophesy,
  prophet]
PHEASANT: after Phasis, a river of
  Colchis, now Georgia; it is said
  that the birds gathered there in
  great numbers
phell-o: **cork**
  phellem; phelloderm,
  phellogen
pher-o: **to bear**, **carry** [see phor-e]
≈**phero-**: pheromone (phero +
  hormone)
- pher-: paraphernalia, peripheral,
  periphery, telpher
- pheresis: leukapheresis,
  plasmapheresis
PHETA: feta: a slice of cheese
phil: **love of**
≈**phil**: philter, philately

≈phil-: Philadelphia,
  philadelphus, philander,
  philanthropy, philharmonic
≈philo-: philodendron,
  philogyny, philology,
  philoprogenitive, philosopher,
  philosophic, philosophy
- phil-e: with prefixes: heterophil,
  homophile
- phil-e: with combining forms:
  acidophile, bibliophile,
  chromophil, cryophile,
  eosinophil, halophile,
  hebephile, hemophile,
  neutrophil, nucleophile,
  oenophile, oxyphil, pedophile,
  rheophile, spermophile,
  technophile, thermophile,
  xenophile, xerophile, zoophile
- philia: coprophilia, hemophilia,
  necrophilia, nemophilia,
  paraphilia, pedophilia,
  pictophilia, zoophilia
- philic: hydrophilic, lyophilic,
  psychrophilic
- philite: chrysophilite,
  lithiophilite, toxophilite
- philous: photophilous,
  tropophilous, xerophilous
PHILIPPIC: from the verbal attacks of
  Demosthenes against King Philip
  II of Macedonia, an ancient
  kingdom in the Balkan Peninsula;
  a bitter verbal attack
PHILTRUM: vertical indentation
  between the upper lip and the nose
PHIMOSIS: a muzzle
phleb-o: **vein**, **veins**
≈**phleb-**: phlebalgia,
  phlebangioma, phlebectasia,
  phlebectomy, phlebitis,
  phlebosis
≈**phlebo-**: phlebogram,
  phlebograph, phlebology,
  phleborrhagia, phlebosclerosis,
  phlebotomy

phlegm: clammy humor of the body, suggesting "sluggishness"

≈phlegm: phlegm, phlegmatic

≈phlegm-: phlegmagogue

PHLOEM: vascular tissue in vascular plants

phlog: fever, inflammation

≈phlog: phlogistic, phlogiston

≈phlogo-: phlogocyte, phlogogen

- phlogistic: aphlogistic, antiphlogistic, prophlogistic [variant form: phlox]

phlycten: to blister, bubble up

≈phlycten: phlycten, phlyctena, phlyctenule

≈phlycten-: phlyctenoid, phlyctenosis

phob-ia: abnormal fear of

≈phob: phobic, phobia

- phobia: acrophobia, aerophobia, autophobia, brontophobia, gynephobia, homophobia, isolophobia, kleptophobia, kymophobia, monophobia, necrophobia, pediculophobia, photophobia, pyrophobia, rhabdophobia, scotophobia, technophobia, thanatophobia, zoophobia [hundreds of others; see authors' *A Thesaurus of Medical Roots*; also, *onelook.com*] [Note: To indicate the person who has a particular fear, or to describe such a person, substitute –*ic* for –*ia*, e.g., *kymophobic* is one who has an abnormal fear of ocean waves]

phoc-o: a seal—the animal phoca, phocal, phocine; phocomelia

PHOENIX: a symbol of immortality; from the legend of a beautiful bird that lived in the Arabian desert for 500 or 600 years and then consumed itself in a fire, rising renewed from the ashes to start

another long life; Phoenix, AZ, is said to be named after the legend

phon-e: sound

≈phon-e: phon, phonate, phone, phoneme, phonemics, phonic, phonics, phonon

≈phonet: phonetic, phonetics, phonetist

≈phono-: phonogram, phonograph, phonolite, phonology, phonometer, phonoscope, phonotype

- phon: antiphon—anthem

- phone: with prefixes: allophone, baryphone, diphone, diaphone, homophone, isophone, megaphone, megalophone, microphone, polyphone, telephone

- phone: with combining forms: actinophone, aerophone, audiphone, chordophone, dictaphone, geophone, hydrophone, ideophone, idiophone, saxophone, xylophone

- phonia: aphonia, dysphonia, euphonia, hyperphonia, hypophonia, leptophonia, microphonia, odynophonia, olophonia

- phonic: with prefixes: aphonic, allophonic, antiphonic, cataphonic, diaphonic, dodecaphonic, dysphonic, euphonic, homophonic, microphonic, monophonic, polyphonic, quadraphonic, symphonic

- phonic: with combining forms: actinophonic, baryphonic, electrophonic, hydrophonic, leptophonic, melophonic, photophonic, radiophonic, stereophonic, telephonic

- phonious: cacophonious,
  euphonious, symphonious
- phonium: euphonium
- phonous: aphonous,
  cacaphonous, euphonous,
  homophonous,
  malacophonous,
  megalophonous,
  microphonous, monophonous,
  polyphonous, uniphonous
- phony: acrophony, allophony,
  antiphony, apophony,
  baryphony, cacophony,
  echophony, dysphony,
  euphony, heterophony,
  homophony, monophony,
  stereophony, symphony,
  telephony
  [variant form: anthem—from
  antiphon]

phor-e: to carry, bear
- phor-a: metaphor; amphora,
  anaphora
- phor-: rhynchophoran;
  phosphorescence; diaphoresis;
  pyrophoric; canephoros
- phore: androphore, aerophore,
  anthophore, blastophore,
  carpophore, chromatophore,
  chromophore, conidiophore,
  ctenophore, embryophore,
  gametophore, gonophore,
  gynophore, ionophore,
  lophophore, melanophore,
  odontophore, ommatophore,
  photophore, pneumatophore,
  semaphore, siphonophore,
  spermatophore, sporophore,
  trocophore
- phoria: adiaphoria, anaphoria,
  anisophoria, anophoria,
  cataphoria, cyclophoria,
  dysphoria, euphoria,
  exophoria, heterophoria,
  hyperphoria, hypophoria,

isophoria, katophoria,
orthophoria
- phorous: adiaphorous,
  galactophrous, odontophorous,
  theophorous
- pher: Christopher, telpher
  [variant forms: ampul, ampulla]

phot-o: light
≈phot: photic, photon
≈phot-: photodynia, photopia
≈photo-: photoactinic,
  photoautotrophic
≈photobiology, photobiotic,
  photocathode, photochromic,
  photochronograph,
  photocoagulation,
  photocomposition,
  photoconductive, photocurrent
≈photodegradable, photodetector,
  photodiode,
  photodisintegration,
  photodissociation,
  photodynamic
≈photoelasticity, photoelectric,
  photoemission,
  photoengraving
≈photofission,
  photofluorography,
  photogenic, photogeology,
  photogrammetry, photograph,
  photographer, photographic,
  photography, photogravure
≈photoionization,
  photojournalism, photokinesis
≈photolithograph,
  photoluminescence, photolysis
≈photomechanical, photometer,
  photomicrograph,
  photomontage,
  photomultiplier, photomural
≈photonegative, photoneutron,
  photooxidation, photoperiod,
  photoperiodism, photophilous,
  photophobia, photophore,
  photopositive

≈photoreceptor, photoresist,
 photosensitive, photosphere,
 photosynthesis
≈phototaxis, phototelegraphy,
 phototherapy, photothermic,
 phototonus, phototransistor,
 phototropism, phototube
- photic: aphotic, euphotic
- photo-: telephotograph
≈phos-: phosphene,
 phosphorescence, phosphorus
phragm, phrax: to enclose
 phragmoplast, diaphragm;
 phrenic—one meaning
phras-eo: to speak
≈phras-e: phrasal, phrase,
 phrasing
≈phaseo-: phraseogram,
 phraseologist, phraseology
- phrase: metaphrase, paraphrase
- phrasis: antiphrasis, periphrasis
- phrastic: paraphrastic,
 periphrastic
phreat-o: a well, groundwater
 phreatic, phreatophyte
phren-o: mind
≈phren: phrenetic, phrenic—one
 meaning
≈phreno-: phrenology
- phrenia: bradyphrenia,
 cardiophrenia, cyclophrenia,
 hebephrenia, hyperphrenia,
 hypophrenia, oligophrenia,
 oneirophrenia, orthophrenia,
 paraphrenia, schizophrenia,
 somatophrenia
 [variant form: frantic]
PHTHIRIASIS: infestation with lice,
 esp. the crab louse
PHTHISIS: wasting away; a wasting
 disease
phthong: voice, sound
≈phthongo-: phthongometer
- phthong: diphthong,
 monophthong, triphthong

- phthongia: aphthongia
phu: to grow
 euphuism, euphuistic
PHYCOLOGY: the branch of botany
 that deals with algae; same as
 algology; see algo[3]
phyl-o: phylum, genealogy, from
 "tribe"
≈phyl: phyletic, phylum
≈phylo-: phylogeny,
 phylogeography
- phyletic: cytophyletic,
 diphyletic, holophyletic,
 interpyletic, paraphyletic,
 monophyletic, polyphyletic
phylact: to guard, protect
≈phlact: phylactery
- phylactic: prophylactic
≈phylax: phylaxis
- phylaxis: with prefixes:
 aphylaxis, anaphylaxis,
 apophylaxis, cataphylaxis,
 epiphylaxis, prophylaxis,
 tachyphylaxis,
 ultraprophylaxis
- phylaxis: with combining forms:
 biophylaxis, calciphylaxis,
 cytophylaxis, radiophylaxis
phyll-o: leaf
≈phyllo: phyllo, or filo
≈phyll-: phylloid, phyllome
≈phyllo-: phyllophagous,
 phyllotaxis, phylloxera
- phyll: cataphyll, chlorophyll,
 cladophyll, mesophyll,
 sporophyll, xanthophyll
- phyllite: apophyllite
- phyllous: with prefixes:
 aphyllous, decaphyllous,
 diphyllous, endophyllous,
 epiphyllous, exophyllous,
 heterophyllous, homophyllous,
 isophyllous, microphyllous,
 monophyllous, polyphyllous,
 quadriphyllous, triphyllous

- phyllous: with combining forms:
  acanthophyllous,
  gamophyllous, leptophyllous,
  leucophyllous,
  malacophyllous,
  sclerophyllous, stenophyllous,
  xanthophyllous, xipophyllous
  [variant forms: chervil, filo]

**phys-i: to grow, to bring forth;
nature, natural science**

≈physi: physic, physical,
  physicalism, physician,
  physicist, physics, physique

≈phys-: physiatrics

≈physio-: physiocracy,
  physiocrat, physiogenesis,
  physiognomy, physiognosis,
  physiography, physiology,
  physiotherapy

- physical: antiphysical,
  biophysical, cataphysical,
  extraphysical, geophysical,
  hyperphysical, metaphysical,
  superphysical, ultraphysical

- physics: astrophysics,
  biophysics, cytophysics,
  economphysics, geophysics,
  iastrophysics, plasmaphysics,
  radiophysics

- physiology: biophysiology,
  histophysiology,
  neurophysiology,
  psychophysiology

- physis: with prefixes: apophysis,
  diaphysis, diapophysis,
  epiphysis, hypophysis,
  paraphysis, symphysis

- physis: with combining forms:
  neurohypophysis,
  zygapophysis

- physite: Monophysite

phys-o-: bellows, bladder; to blow

≈physo-: physocele,
  physostigmine, physostomous

- physema: emphysema

phyto-: plant, flora, vegetation

≈phyto: phytoalexin,
  phytochemistry, phytochrome,
  phytoflagellate, phytogenesis,
  phytogenic, phytogeography,
  phytohemagglutinin,
  phytohormone, phytolith,
  phytology, phytopathology,
  phytophagous, phytoplankton,
  phytosociology, phytosterol,
  phytotoxic

- phyt-: epiphytology; periphyton

- phyte: with prefixes: autophyte,
  endophyte, entophyte,
  epiphyte, heterophyte,
  microphyte, neophyte

- phyte: with combining forms:
  aulophyte, cryophyte,
  embryophyte, gametophyte,
  geophyte, halophyte,
  hydrophyte, lithophyte,
  oophyte, osteophyte,
  phanerophyte, phreatophyte,
  psilophyte, pteridophyte,
  saprophyte, schizophyte,
  spermatophyte, sporophyte,
  thallophyte, tracheophyte,
  tropophyte, xerophyte,
  zoophyte, zygophyte

- phytic: with prefixes: autophytic,
  endophytic, epiphytic,
  entophytic, exophytic,
  heterophytic, holophytic,
  macrophytic, mesophytic,
  microphytic, periphytic

- phytic: with combining forms:
  bryophytic, dermatophytic,
  entomophytic, eophytic,
  gametophytic, geophytic,
  halophytic, hydrophytic,
  hygrophytic, lithophytic,
  oophytic, osteophytic,
  photophytic, psilophytic,
  spermatophytic, thallophytic,
  tropophytic, xerophytic

- phytotic: enphytotic,
  epiphytotic

pi: to atone, appease
≈piacular: piacular
≈piet-y: Pietà, pietism, piety
≈pio: piosity, pious
≈pit: piteous, pitiable, pitiful,
  pity
≈pitt: pittance
- pi-: expiable, inexpiable;
  expiate, expiation, expiatory;
  impiety; impious
{word note: pittance: orig., portion
  of food allowed a monk; a small
  or barely sufficient amount of
  money; any small amount or
  share}

pia-no: soft; from *planus*, smooth
  pia mater; pianism, pianissimo,
  pianist, piano, pianoforte

pica: to prick
  picadillo, picador, picayune
  [variant forms: pickle, pincers,
  pinch; piquant, pique, piqué;
  Spanish: picante, pince-nez]

picar: rascal; from "knavish,
  roguish, vile"
  picaresque, picaro, picaroon
{word note: picaroon: a picaro; also,
  a pirate or pirateship}

PICCOLO: Italian; small; a musical
  instrument considerably smaller
  than a flute, and pitched an octave
  higher than the ordinary flute

PICHICIEGO: lit., small-blind; a South
  American armadillo

picr-o: bitter, picric acid
  picrol, picrolite, picromel

pict-o: to paint
≈pictorial: pictorial
≈pictur-e: picture, picturesque,
  picturize
≈picto-: pictogram, pictograph,
  pictography, pictophilia
- pict-: depict, depiction, depictor
≈pigment: pigment, pigmentation
- pigmentation: depigmentation

[variant forms: orpiment, paint,
  pentimento, pimiento, pint,
  pintado, pinto, file—one meaning,
  pinxit]
{word note: pint: orig., probably a
  spot marking the level of
  measure}

PIDGIN: supposed Chinese
  pronunciation of *business*;
  a mixed language, or jargon

piece: part
  piece, piecemeal
  [variant forms: peat;
  Spanish: pieza—piece]
  [phrase: pièce de résistance]

pierce: see tund

PIERRE, SD: capital of South Dakota;
  named after Pierre Chouteau, an
  early fur trader

piezo: pressure
  piezochemistry,
  piezoelectricity, piezogenic,
  piezometer, piezoresistance
  [variant form: isopiestic]

PIGGY BANK: orig., an earthernware
  jar; from Scottish *pygg*, the clay
  from which the jar was first made;
  jars were later made in the form of
  a pig

pigm: see pict-o for pigment

pil-e[1]: hair [see pel-l]
≈pil-e: pile—one meaning, pileate,
  pileous, piles, pileum, pileus
≈pilos-e: pilose, pilosity, pilous
≈pili-: piliferous, piliform,
  piligerous
- pil-l: depilate, epilation,
  horripilation, caterpillar
  [variant forms: peel; pluck, plush,
  poilu]

**pil-e[2]: to compress, ram down; a
  column**
  pile—one meaning, pillar,
  pillory; compilation, oppilate;
  compile

pilfer: to steal
  pilfer, pilferage; pillage
pilgrim, pilgrimage: see egr

pilot: orig., **oar blade**; akin to *ped*, *pod*, foot
  pilot, pilotage, piloting
PILSNER, or Pilsener: a light Bohemian beer; originated in Pilsen, Bohemia

pin-a: **pine tree, pineapple**
≈pina: pinaceous, pinaster, piñata, piña cloth, piña colada—lit., strained pineapple
≈pine: pine—one meaning, pineal, pinery, pinetum, piney
  [variant forms: pinnace, pennon, pinot, pinyon]
pinge: see paci for *impinge*
PINGUID: fat, greasy, oily
pinni: see pen-n

pip-er: **pipe**
  pipage, pipe, piper, piping, pipette, or, pipet
  [variant form: pibroch]

pir: **a trial, experiment**
≈pir: piracy, pirate
- pir-: empiric, empirical, empiricism
pire: see -s-pire for *expire*
PIROGI: Russian; pie; a small pastry turnover with a filling
PIROGUE: Carib, or Arawak; a dugout canoe
PIROUETTE: whirling around on one foot or toe—in ballet

pis: **pea**
  pisiform, pisolite

pisc: **fish**
≈pisc: piscary, piscation, piscator, piscatorial, piscatory, Pisces, piscine
≈piscato-: piscatology
≈pisci-: piscicide, pisciculture, pisciform, piscivorous
  [variant forms: porpoise; Spanish: pescado; piscina— swimming pool]
PITHECANTHROPUS: in full: *Pithecanthropus erectus*; orig. name for Java man; from Greek,

pithekos, ape + *anthropos*, man; lit., ape man
PITUITARY: from *pituita*: phlegm, rheum
pity: see pi
PITYRIASIS: skin disease; from "bran, scale"
PIXILATED: lit., led away by pixies; mentally confused; daft; whimsical

plac: **to please**
≈plac: placable, placate, placet, placid
- placable: implacable, unplacable
- placency: complacency
- placent: complacent
- plaisance: complaisance
- plaisant: complaisant
≈plea-d: plea, plead, pleadings
- plead: counterplead, implead, interplead, misplead, replead
- pleader: impleader, interpleader, repleader
≈pleas-e: pleasance, pleasant, pleasantry, please, pleasing
≈pleasur-e: pleasurable, pleasure
- pleas-e: displease; displeasure
  [variant form: placebo—a one-word Latin sentence, "I shall be pleasing"]
  [phrases: non placet
  French: sil vous plait]

plac-e: **flat, broad**
≈plac: place, placer
≈plac-: placoid
≈placo-: placoderm, placophobia
- place: displace, emplace, replace
- placement: displacement, emplacement, replacement
≈placent-: placentoid
≈placenta-te: placenta, placentate
- placental: aplacental, displacental, ectoplaental, extraplacental, implacental, preplacental, retroplacental

≈platitud-e: platitude,
  platitudinize
  [variant forms: piazza, plaza;
  Spanish: playa: beach]
plagio: slanting
  plagal; plagiocephalic,
  plagioclase, plagiograph,
  plagiostome, plagiotropic
  [French: plage]
plagiar: kidnapping, literary thief
  plagiarism, plagiary
plain-t: to cry out; to beat one's
  chest [see plor-e]
≈plain-t: plaint, plaintiff,
  plaintive
- plain-t: complain, complainant,
  complaint
  [variant form: plangent]
plan-e: flat, level; from "to spread
  out"
≈plan-e: planar, planarian,
  planation, plane, planer
≈plani-: planimeter, planisphere
≈plano-: plano-concave,
  plano-convex, planography,
  planosol
- plana-: explanation;
  explanatory; aplanatic,
  esplanade
- planar: complanar, uniplanar
- plane: aeroplane, biplane,
  deplane, monoplane
- plain-: explain, inexplainable,
  peneplain
≈planet: planet, planetary,
  planetesimal
≈planet-: planetarium
≈planeto-: planetology
≈plano-: planoblast,
  planogamete, planogram
- planet-: interplanetary,
  protoplanet
≈plankton: plankton
- plankton: meroplankton,
  phytoplankton, zooplankton

≈plat-e: platan, platane, plate,
  plateau, plated, platelet, platen,
  plater, plating, platter,
  platy—one meaning
  [variant forms: flake—one
  meaning, piano, plain, plantain,
  plankter, plane tree; platform;
  Spanish: llano—level plain]
  [phrases: plat du jour, plate
  tectonics]
plan-t: sprout, twig; orig., sole of
  the foot
≈plan-t: plan, plant, planta,
  plantain, plantar, plantation,
  planter
≈planti-: plantigrade,
  plantivorous
- plant: explant, implant,
  supplant, transplant
  {word note: plantain: so named from
  the shape of the leaves; listed in
  previous family as well}
plaque: patch, plaque, spot
  plaque; erythroplakia,
  leukoplakia
  [variant form: placard;
  Spanish: placa: license plate]
plasm-a: to mold, form
≈plasm: plasma, plasmid,
  plasmin
≈plasm-: plasmodium
≈plasma-: plasmagel, plasmagene,
  plasmapheresis, plasmasol
≈plasmino-: plasminogen
≈plasmo-: plasmolysis,
  plasmolyze
- plasia: aplasia, alloplasia,
  anaplasia, cataplasia, displasia,
  dysplasia, hyperplasia,
  hypoplasia, metaplasia,
  neoplasia
- plasm: with prefixes: alloplasm,
  cataplasm, deuteroplasm,
  ectoplasm, endoplasm,
  metaplasm, neoplasm,
  protoplasm

- plasm: with combining forms:
  hyaloplasm, idioplasm,
  nucleoplasm, somatoplasm,
  trophoplasm
- plasma: mycoplasma
- plasmosis: histoplasmosis,
  toxoplasmosis
≈plast: plaster, plastid, plastique,
  plastron
≈plasti-: plastisol
≈plastic: plastic, plasticize,
  plasticizer
≈plasto-: plastogene
- plast: with prefixes: alloplast,
  apoplast, autoplast, ectoplast,
  endoplast, mesoplast,
  metaplast, monoplast,
  orthoplast, proplast, protoplast
- plast: with combining forms:
  aeroplast, aminoplast,
  chiroplast, chloroplast,
  chondroplast, chromoplast,
  gymnoplast, kinetoplast,
  leucoplast, myeloplast,
  osteoplast, rhizoplast,
  rhodoplast, spheroplast,
  trophoplast
- plastic- anaplastic, esemplastic,
  euplastic, homoplastic,
  neoplastic; superplasticity
- plasty: with prefixes: alloplasty,
  anaplasty, anoplasty,
  autoplasty, heteroplasty,
  neoplasty
- plasty: with combining forms:
  alveoplasty, angioplasty,
  anoplasty, arterioplasty,
  arthroplasty, ceroplasty,
  colpoplasty, coreoplasty,
  cystoplast, keratoplasty,
  mammaplasty, rhinoplasty
- plasy: homoplasy
platin: silver
  platinic, platinoid, platinous,
  platinum

platitude: see plac-e
platy-: flat
  platycephalic, platyglossa,
  platyglossal, platyhelminth,
  platymeter, platypnea,
  platypod, platypus, platyrrhine
  [variant forms: plafond, plaice]
plaud: to clap, applaud
≈plaud: plaudit
- plaud: applaud
≈plaus: plausible, plausive
- plaus-e: applause, implausible
- plode: explode, implode
≈plos: plosion, plosive
- plosion: explosion, implosion
- plosive: explosive, implosive
play: to be active
  play, player, playlet; foreplay,
  interplay
pleb-e: common people
  plebe, plebeian, plebs;
  plebiscite
  {word note: plebiscite: with *scire*, to
  know, an expression of the
  people's will by direct ballot on a
  political issue}
plect-o: to twist, weave, braid
≈plecto-: plectognath,
  plectomycetes
≈plex: plexor, plexus
≈plexi-: plexiform, Plexiglas®,
  pleximeter
- plex: complex, multiplex,
  perplex, quadruplex
- plex-: complexion, perplexed;
  amplexicaul
- plexity: complexity, perplexity
  [variant form: plique-à-jour]
pledg-e: warranty, pledge
≈pledg-e: pledge, pledgee,
  pledger, pledgor
- plev: replevin, replevy,
  irrepleviable
plegia: stroke, paralysis
- plegia: blepharoplegia,
  bronchoplegia, cardioplegia,

cephaloplegia, colicoplegia,
cycloplegia, cystoplegia,
diplegia, enteroplegia,
hemiplegia, laloplegia,
monoplegia, paraplegia,
quadriplegia
- plectic: apoplectic
- plexy: apoplexy
 [variant forms: plectrum,
 plessograph]
pleio-: more
≈pleo: pleonasm
≈pleio-: pleiotaxy, pleiotropy
≈pleo-: pleochroism, pleocytosis,
 pleomorphism, pleopod
≈plio-: Pliocene
≈pleisto-: Pleistocene: most
plen: full, to fill
≈plen: plenary, plenitude,
 plenitudinous, plenum
≈plent: plenteous, plenty
≈pleni-: plenipotentiary
- ple: maniple
- plement-: complement,
 implement, supplement
- plementary: complementary,
 supplementary
- plenish: replenish
- plete: complete, deplete,
 incomplete, replete
- pletion: completion, depletion,
 impletion, suppletion
- pletive: completive, depletive,
 expletive, repletive, suppletive
- pliment-: compliment,
 complimentary
- plish-: accomplish,
 accomplishment
- ply: comply, supply
 [variant forms: manipulate,
 terreplein]
 [Note: See pli- for imply and
 reply.]
plesio: near
 plesiochronous, plesiosaur

pleth-ora: number, quantity,
 suggesting "fullness"
≈plethor: plethora, plethoric
- pleth: isopleth
≈plethysmo: plethysmograph
pleur-e: rib, side
≈pleur: pleura, pleural, pleurisy,
 pleuron
≈pleur-: pleurodont, pleurodont,
 pleurodynia
≈pleura-: pleuracentesis
≈pleuro-: pleurobrachia,
 pleurobranchia, pleurocentrum,
 pleurolysis, pleuropneumonia,
 pleurotomy
- pleure: somatopleure
plev: see pledg-e for replevin
pli: to fold, bend [see simpl-e]
≈pli: pliable, pliant, plié, pliers,
 plight, plissé
- pla: hexapla, octapla
- play: display
- ple: decuple, multiple, octuple,
 quadruple, quintuple, simple,
 supple
- plet: quadruplet, quintuplet,
 sextuplet, septuplet
- plex: duplex, simplex
- pliance: appliance, compliance
- pliant: compliant, incompliant,
 suppliant
≈plica: plica, plicate, plication,
 plicature
- plica: replica
- plicable: applicable, explicable,
 inexplicable, inapplicable
- plicate: complicate, duplicate,
 explicate, implicate,
 induplicate, quadruplicate,
 replicate, supplicate, triplicate
- plication: application,
 complication, duplication,
 explication, implication,
 multiplication, replication,
 supplication, triplication

- plic-e: accomplice, applicant,
  complicated, multiplicand;
  explicative; explicatory
- plicit: explicit, implicit,
  inexplicit
- plicitous: complicitous,
  duplicitous
- plicity: biplicity, complicity,
  duplicity, implicity,
  multiplicity, simplicity,
  triplicity
- plied: implied
- ploid: euploid, haploid,
  heteroploid, hyperploid,
  hypoploid, monoploid,
  pentaploid, polyploid,
  tetraploid, triploid: number or
  type of chromosomes
- ploit-: exploit, exploitable,
  exploitation, exploitative
- ploy: counterploy, deploy,
  employ, disemploy
- ploy-: employable, employee,
  employer
≈ply: ply, plywood
- ply: apply, imply, multiply,
  reply
  [Note: See plen for comply,
  supply.]
  [variant forms: appliqué, plait,
  pleat, ploidy, ploy, splay]
PLINTH: the square block at the base
  of an architectural column
plius: to sail
  nauplius—a kind of shellfish that
  sails in its shell as in a ship; the
  first larval stage in the development of certain crustaceans
  [variant form: pleuston]
plode: see plaud for *explode*
plor-e: to cry out, wail [see plain-t]
- plore: deplore, explore, implore
- plor-: exploration, exploratory,
  explorer
- plorable: deplorable,
  explorable, inexplorable

plosion: see plaud for explosion
plot: a ball
≈plot: plot, plotline, platoon
≈plott: plottage, plotter
- plot: applot, complot,
  counterplot, subplot, underplot
plum-e: feather
≈plum-e: plumage, plumate,
  plume, plumose, plumule
≈plumi-: plumicorn,
  plumigerous, plumiped
- plume: deplume; nom de plume
  [Spanish: pluma: ink pen, from
  early use of quills of feathers as
  writing instruments]
plum-b: lead, lead weight
≈plumb: plumb, plumbago,
  plumbeous, plumber,
  plumbing, plumbous,
  plumbum
≈plumbi-: plumbiferous
  [variant forms: plummet, plunge,
  plunger, aplomb]
plunder: trash, baggage
  plunder, plunderage
plural: many
≈plural: plural, pluralism,
  plurality
≈pluri-: pluriaxial, plurifarious,
  plurilocular, pluripara,
  pluripotent, plurisignation
≈plu-s: pluperfect; plus
- plus: nonplus, surplus
  [motto: e pluribus unum;
  term: ne plus ultra]
pluto: wealth
  Pluto, plutocracy, plutocrat,
  plutology
pluvi: rain
  pluvial, pluviose, pluvious;
  pluviometer
  [variant forms: plover;
  Spanish: lluvia—rain]
pneum-at: air, breath, lung, spirit
≈pneum-at: pneuma, pneumatic,
  pneumatics, pneumonia

- pnea: anapnea, apnea,
  bathypnea, bradypnea,
  dyspnea, eupnea, hyperpnea,
  hypopnea, oligopnea,
  orthopnea, platypnea,
  polypnea,tachypnea, trepopnea
≈pneum-: pneumectomy
≈pneumato-: pneumatology,
  pneumatolysis,
  pneumatometer,
  pneumatophore
≈pneumo-: pneumobacillus,
  pneumococcus,
  pneumoconiosis,
  pneumogastric, pneumograph
≈pneumon-: pneumonitis
≈pneumono-: pneumonothorax
- pnoan: dipnoan
po: to make
≈po-et: poem, poet, poetaster,
  poetic, poetical, poetics, poetry
- pee: epopee
- peia: pharmacopeia, or
  pharmacopoeia
- poeia: mythopoeia,
  onomatopoeia, pharmacopoeia,
  or, pharmacopeia, prosopopoeia
- poiesis: angiopoiesis,
  hematopoiesis, leucopoiesis,
  lymphopoiesis, uropoiesis
- poietic: galactopoietic,
  hematopoietic, sarcopoietic
- poietin: erythropoietin
  [phrase: poète maudit]
poco: a little
  poco, poco a poco,
  pococurante—as an adjective,
  caring little; indifferent;
  as a noun, an indifferent person
pod: foot [see ped]
≈pod: podium
≈pod-: podagra, podarthritis
  podiatrist, podiatry
≈podo-: podobranch, podocarp,
  podocarpus, podometer

- pod: with prefixes: apod,
  amphipod, autopod, bipod,
  decapod, hexapod, isopod,
  megapod, octopod, pleopod,
  polyp, tetrapod, tripod
- pod: with combining forms:
  arthropod, brachiopod,
  cephalopod, chilopod,
  copepod, gastropod, myriapod,
  ornithopod, phyllopod,
  pteropod, rhizopod, sauropod,
  scaphopod, schizopod,
  stomatopod, theropod
- pode: apode, antipode,
  hemipode, megapode,
  monopode, pseudopode
- podium: filopodium,
  monopodium, pseudopodium,
  stylopodium, sympodium
- podous: apodous, amphipodous,
  gastropodous, isopodous,
  pachypodous, polypodous
- pody: chiropody, dipody,
  polypody
- poggiatura: appoggiatura
- pos: tripos
- pus: octopus, platypus, rhizopus
  [variant form: galosh]
poikilo: varying
  poikilothermal—coldblooded
  [variant form: platy]
{word note: platy—clipped from
  Platypoecilus (a genus of flat fish)
  + *poikilos*, many-colored; a
  brightly colored livebearer fish,
  often found in tropical aquariums}
POINSETTIA: after Joel Roberts
  Poinsett (d. December 12, 1851),
  U.S. ambassador to Mexico,
  where he found the plant growing
  wild; Poinsettia Day is celebrated
  December 12, the anniversary of
  Poinsett's death
pol: to polish, dress up
≈polish: polish, polished
≈polit-e: polite, politesse

- polite: impolite
- polate: extrapolate, interpolate
pol-e[1]: axis of the heavens
≈pole: pole, polestar, Pole Star
≈polar: polar, polarity,
   polarization, polarize, polaron
≈polari-: polarimeter, polariscope
≈polaro: polarography
- polar: ambipolar, bipolar,
   circumpolar, dipolar,
   interpolar, isopolar,
   monopolar, multipolar,
   peripolar, pluripolar, subpolar,
   unipolar
- polarize: depolarize
- pole: dipole, monopole
pol-e[2]: to sell
- pol-e: bibliopole, monopolize
- poly: duopoly, monopoly,
   oligopoly
polemic: war
   polemic, polemicist,
   polemicize, polemics
polio: gray
≈poli-: poliosis
≈polio-: poliocidal, polioclastic,
   poliodystrophy,
   polioencephalitis,
   poliomyelitis, polioneuromere,
   poliovirus
poli-s: city
≈poli: police; policy
≈poli-: policlinic
≈polis: polis
- polis: acropolis, amphipolis,
   cosmopolis, ideopolis,
   megalopolis, metropolis,
   necropolis, propolis; part of the
   names of many Greek places [see
   word notes] and American cities:
American cities
   Annapolis, MD
   Caraopolis, PA
   Copperopolis, CA
   Cosmopolis, WA
   Demopolis, AL

Galliopolis, OH
Illiopolis, IL
Indianapolis, IN
Kannapolis, NC
Kanopolis, KS
Lithopolis, OH
Mediapolis, IA
Minneapolis, MN
Perryopolis, PA
Pinopolis, SC
Thermopolis, WY
Uniopolis, OH
- policy: impolicy
- politan: acropolitan,
   cosmopolitan, megalopolitan,
   metropolitan, micropolitan,
   neopolitan, tripolitan
≈polit-ic: politic, political,
   politician, politicize, politics,
   polity
- politic-al: impolitic; apolitical,
   geopolitical
   [variant forms: police action,
   police officer; French: policier;
   Spanish: policía]
{word notes: acropolis: the fortified
   upper part of an ancient Greek
   city; capitalized, that of Athens,
   where the Parthenon was built;
   Decapolis: ancient region in
   Palestine; Heliopolis: ancient city
   in the Nile delta, just south of
   where Cairo now stands: center
   for the worship of the sun god Ra;
   Helios—in Greek mythology, the
   sun god; Hieropolis: an ancient
   city of northwest Asia Minor in
   present-day Turkey. The Roman
   city was known for its baths fed
   by hot springs. Hierapolis was also
   an early center of Christianity;
   Neapolis: a town in Thrace at
   which Paul first landed in Europe
   (Acts 16:11)}
POLL: prob. akin to Middle Dutch
   pol, where it referred to "the top of
   the head," or "the head" itself;
   thus, a counting, listing, or register
   of persons, esp. of voters

poll: **to be strong**
equipollent—equal in force,
weight, or validity; equivalent in
meaning or result; as a noun,
something *equipollent*
pollen: see pulver
POLO: from a Tibetan dialectal
variant of *pulu*, the name of the
ball used in the game of polo, a
game played on horseback
POLONAISE: a stately Polish dance in
triple time, almost processional in
character; music for this dance
poly-: **many**
≈poly-: polyacid, polyacoustic,
polyadelphous, polyalphabetic,
polyandrous, polyandry,
polyanthus, polyatomic,
polybasic
≈polycarpellary, polycarpic,
polycentrism, polychaete,
polychromatic, polychrome,
polyclinic, polycotyledon,
polycyclic, polycystic,
polycythemia, polydactyl
≈polyembryony, polyester
≈polygamous, polygamy,
polygenesis, polygenism,
polyglot, polygon, polygonum,
polygyny
≈polyhedron, polyhydric
≈polymath, polymer, polymorph,
polymorphism, polymorphous,
polymyxin
≈Polynesia, polyneuritis,
polynomial, polynuclear
≈polyp [second root is pod],
polypary, polypeptide,
polypetalous, polyphagia,
polyphase, polyphone,
polyphonic, polyphony,
polyphyletic, polyploid,
polypody, polyptych
≈polyrhythm, polysaccharide,
polysemy, polysome,
polysyllabic, polysyndeton

≈polytechnic, polytheism,
polytocous, polytonality,
polytrophic, polytypic
≈polyuria, polyvalent,
polyzoarium
pom-e: **apple, pome**
≈pom-e: pomace, pomaceous,
pomade, pome, pommel;
Pomona; Pomana, CA
≈pom-: pomander
≈pome-: pomegranate
≈pomi-: pomiculture,
pomiferous, pomiform
≈pomo-: pomology
[variant form: pommel; an
interesting history from meaning
"a small apple" to the knob on a
sword, and finally to use as a verb
"to beat"]
pomp: **solemn procession**
pomp, pompon, pomposity,
pompous
ponder: see pend
pone: **work, product of work**
lithopone; lit., product of work; a
white pigment made by mixing
barium sulfate with zinc sulfide;
used in paints, lineoleums, etc.
pone: see pos-e for postpone
poor: see pover
pons: **bridge**
≈pons: pons
≈pont: pontiff, pontoon
≈ponti-: pontifical, pontificate
- pontine: intrapontine,
transpontine
[variant form: punt—one
meaning]
[phrase: pons asinorum]
POPLITEAL: behind the knee
PONCHO: Araucanian; orig., a woolen
cloth used for covering against the
elements; see anorak, parka
popul: **people**
≈popul: populace, popular,
popularity, popularize,
populate, population, populous

- populate: depopulate,
  outpopulate, overpopulate,
  repopulate
≈public: public, publican,
  publication, publicist, publicity
- public: republic
≈publish: publish, publisher
  [variant forms: people, repeople;
  Spanish: pueblo]
  [phrases: pro bono publico;
  vox populi; res publica]

porc: pig
  porcelain, porcine, porcupine
  [variant forms: pork, porpoise]

por-e: pore, passage, way
≈por-e: pore—one meaning,
  porism, porosity, porous
≈pori-: poriferan, poriferous
≈poro-: poromeric
- por-: aporia, emporium
- pore: blastopore, gonopore,
  millepore, neuropore,
  nullipore, oligopore
- porosis: osteoporosis

porn: prostitute
  pornography, pornolagnia

porphyry: purple
≈porphyr: porphyry, porphyrytin,
  porphyria, porphyrin,
  porphyrytic
≈porphyr-: porphyroid,
  porphyropsin
- phyre: granophyre,
  lamprophyre, melaphyre

port[1]: door, gate, opening, port
≈port: port, portal, porter—one
  meaning, porterage, portico
≈port-: portcullis
- portun-: importunate,
  opportunism, opportunistic
- portune: importune,
  inopportune, opportune
- porunity: importunity,
  opportunity
  [variant forms: porch, porte-
  cochere, porte-monnaie,

Spanish: puerta—door;
Puerto Rico]

port[2]: to carry
≈port: port—one of four meanings,
  portable, portage, portamento,
  portative, porter—one meaning
≈port-: port arms, portfolio,
  portmanteau
- port: comport, deport—two
  meanings, disport, export,
  import—two meanings, purport,
  rapport, report, support,
  transport
- port-: importance, important,
  importantly, reportedly
- portable: deportable,
  exportable, importable,
  insupportable, reportable,
  supportable, transportable
- portation: exportation,
  importation, teleportation,
  transportation
- porter: importer, exporter,
  reporter, supporter
- porteur: colporteur
- portment: comportment,
  deportment
  [variant forms: rapporteur, fare,
  ferry, sport, sportif]
  [phrase: en rapport]
pos: see pot for symposium

pos-e: to place, put
≈pos-e: pose, poser, poseur
- pos-: apropos, imposing,
  malaprop, malapropos,
  malapropism
- posable: disposable,
  indecomposable, opposable
- posal: disposal, proposal,
  supposal
- pose: appose, compose,
  decompose, depose,
  discompose, dispose, expose,
  exposé, impose, interpose,
  juxtapose, oppose, predispose,

presuppose, propose, purpose,
repose, superpose, suppose,
transpose
- posed: composed, disposed,
indisposed, superposed
- posive: purposive,
nonpurposive
≈posit: posit, position, positive,
positivism, positivity
- posit-: deposit, depositary,
oviposit, reposit
- posite: apposite, composite,
inapposite, opposite
- position: with prefixes:
apposition, composition,
contraposition, deposition,
disposition, exposition,
imposition, indisposition,
interposition, juxtaposition,
malposition, opposition,
postposition, preposition,
proposition, reposition,
supposition, transposition
- position: with combining form:
photocomposition
- posititious: supposititious
- positive: with prefixes:
appositive, diapositive,
dispositive, postpositive,
prepositive, suppositive
- positive: with combining form:
photopositive
- positor: depositor, expositor
- pository: depository,
expository, repository,
suppository
≈post: post—one meaning,
postiche
- post-: compost, impost;
impostor; imposture
- posure: composure,
discomposure, exposure,
opposure, overexposure,
preexposure, reposure,
supposure

- pone: postpone, repone
- ponent: component, deponent,
exponent, opponent, proponent
- ponential: exponential
- ponentiation: exponentiation
- pot-e: compote, depot, entrepôt
- pound: compound, expound,
propound
[variant form: provost]
[phrases: compos mentis,
non compos mentis]
POSOLOGY: the scientific study of
drug dosages

poss: power

≈poss: posse, possibility,
possible, possibly
≈pos-: possess, possessed,
possession, possessive,
possessor, possessory
- pos- dispossess, prepossess,
repossess
- possib-le: impossibility;
impossible
≈poten-t: potency, potent,
potentate, potential, potentiate
- pot-: despot, despotic,
despotism
- potence: armipotence,
impotence, omnipotence,
totipotence
- potency: impotency, prepotency
- potent: with prefixes: equipotent,
impotent, multipotent,
omnipotent, overpotent,
pluripotent, prepotent,
subpotent, totipotent, unipotent
- potent: with combining forms:
armipotent, idempotent,
ignipotent, nilpotent
- potent-: equipotential;
plenipotentiary
[variant forms: podesta, power;
puissant, impuissant,
impuissance]
[phrases: in posse,
in posse comitatus]

post[1]: to stand
  post, postage, postal
  {word note: post: originally referred
  to the series of mounted men
  stationed at intervals, or posts, for
  the rapid carrying of message}

post[2]: after, behind
  ≈post: postil, posthumous
  ≈poster-n: posterior, posterity,
  postern
  ≈post-: postaxial, postbellum,
  postcardinal, postcava,
  postcentral, postdated,
  postdiluvian, postencephalon,
  postganglionic, postglacial,
  posthypnotic, postliminium,
  postlude
  ≈postmeridian, postmeridiem,
  postmillennial, postmodern,
  postmortem
  ≈postnasal, postnatal,
  postnuptial, post-obit,
  postoperative, postorbital
  ≈postpartum, postpone,
  postposition, postprandial,
  postscript
  - post-: apostil, preposterous
  [phrases: a posteriori, post hoc
  ergo propter hoc; ex post facto]
  {word note: preposterous: orig., with
  first last, and the last first;
  inverted; so contrary to nature,
  reason, or common sense as to be
  laughable; absurd; ridiculous}

postul: to demand
  postulant, postulate;
  expostulate

pot: to drink
  ≈pot: pot, potable, potation,
  potion, potiche
  ≈pot-: potash [see separate
  entry—potas]
  ≈pott: pottage, pottery, pottle
  - posi-: symposiac, symposiast,
  symposium; symposiarch
  [variant form: poison]

{word note: symposium: orig., a
  drinking together; in ancient
  Greece, a drinking party at which
  there was intellectual
  conversation}

potam: river
  ≈potamo-: potamography,
  potamology
  - potamia: Mesopotamia
  - potamic: autopotamic
  - potamus: hippopotamus

potas: potash, potasssium
  ≈potash: potash
  ≈potass: potassamide, potassium
  ≈potass-: potassemia, potassoxyl
  - potassemia: hyperpotassemia,
  hypopotassemia
  POTATO: Spanish patata

poul-t: chicken, poultry
  poulard, poult, poulterer,
  poultry
  [variant forms: poltroon, pullet,
  polecat, pullorum disease,
  pullulate; French: poulet;
  Spanish: pollo, as in *arroz con
  pollo*: rich with chicken]

pover: to be poor
  poverty, impoverish
  [variant forms: poor; pauper]
  POWWOW: from Narragansett and
  Massachusett *powwaw*, priest;
  orig., a North American medicine
  man or priest; a conference

practic-e: to do
  ≈practic-e: practicable, practical,
  practically, practice,
  practicum; practitioner
  - practice: chiropractic, eupractic,
  orthopractic
  - practic-e: impractical;
  malpractice
  ≈pragmat: pragmatic, pragmatics,
  pragmatism
  - prax-: apraxia, parapraxis
  [variant forms: pratique, praxis]
  PRAIRIE: from Old French *pré*,
  meadow

prandial: dinner
prandial; postprandial,
preprandial
PRAVDA: Russian: truth; one of the
official newspapers of the former
Soviet Union; see *Izvestia*, news
[Note: Some wit has said that *Pravda*
doesn't print the "news," and
Izvestia doesn't print the "truth."]
prav-e: crooked
depravation, deprave,
depraved, depravity,
indepravit, undepraved
pre-: before [in time or place]
≈pre-: preadaption, preamble,
prearrange, preaxial
≈prebend, prebendary, prebiotic
≈precancerous, precaution,
precava, precede, precensor,
precentor, precept, precess,
precinct, precipice, precipitant,
precipitate, precipitation,
precipitous, précis, precise,
precisian, precision,
preclinical, preclude, precocial,
precocious, precognition,
preconceive, preconception,
preconcert, precondition,
preconize, preconscious,
precritical, precursor,
precursory
≈predate, predecease,
predecessor, predesignate,
predestinarian, predestinate,
predetermine, predicable,
predicament, predicant,
predicate, predicatory, predict,
prediction, predigest,
predilection, predispose,
predominant, predominate
≈preeminent, preempt,
preestablish, preexilic, preexist
≈prefabricate, preface, prefatory,
prefect, prefecture, prefer,
prefigure, prefix, preformation,

prefrontal, preganglionic,
prehensile [see separate entry]
≈preignition, prejudge, prejudice
≈prelacy, prelapsarian, prelate,
prelect, prelibation,
preliminary, preliterate,
prelude
≈premarital, premature,
premaxilla, premeditate,
premenstrual, premise,
premolar, premonish,
premonition, premunition
≈prenatal, prenuptial
≈preoccupation, preordain
≈prepare, prepense,
preponderant, preposition,
prepositive, prepossess,
preposterous, prepotency,
preprandial, prepuce
≈prequel—patterned after *sequel*
≈prerequisite, prerogative
≈presage, prescience, prescind,
prescribe, prescript,
prescription, presence, present,
presentable, presentiment,
preservative, preserve, preside,
presidium, presignify,
presume, presumption,
presuppose
≈pretend, pretense, pretest,
pretrial
≈prevail, prevailing, prevalent,
prevaricate, prevenient,
prevent, preview, previous,
previse, prevision, prevocalic
prec: to pray
≈prec: precarious, precation,
precatory
- precate: deprecate, imprecate
- precation: apprecation,
comprecation, deprecation,
imprecation, self-deprecation
- precat-: deprecative; deprecator,
deprecatory
[variant forms: prayer, prie-dieu]

preci: price, dear
≈preci: preciosity, precious
- preciable: appreciable,
  depreciable, inappreciable
- preciate: appreciate, depreciate
- preciation: appreciation,
  depreciation
- preciative: appreciative,
  depreciative, inappreciative
  [variant forms: praise; appraisal,
  dispraise; prize—one meaning;
  disprize]

pred: to plunder, to prey
≈preda: predacious, predation,
  predator, predatory
- predat-e: depredate, depredation
  [variant form: prey]

prehen-s: to seize, from *pre-*,
  before + IE base *ghend-*, to grasp
  [see pris; pred]
≈prehens: prehensible,
  prehensile, prehension
- prehensible: apprehensible,
  comprehensible,
  inapprehensible,
  incomprehensible,
  reprehensible
- prehension: apprehension,
  comprehension, reprehension
- prehensive: apprehensive,
  comprehensive,
  inapprehensive, reprehensive
- prehend: apprehend,
  comprehend, reprehend
≈pregn: pregnable, pregnant
- pregn-: impregnable;
  impregnate
- pren: apprentice, entrepreneur
  [variant forms: impresario, prey,
  prison, prize—one meaning;
  enterprise]

presby: old
≈presby: presbytia
≈presbyter: presbyter,
  presbyterate, prysbyterial,
  Presbyterian, presbytery

≈presby-: presbyacousia,
  presbyatrics, presbycardia,
  presbycusis, presbyopia
≈presbyo-: presbyophrenia
  [variant form: priest]

presence: from *pre-*, before + *esse*,
  being
≈presence: presence
- presence: omnipresence,
  telepresence
≈present: present, presentable,
  presentation,
  presentationalism,
  presentative, presentee,
  presentism, presentment,
  presently
- present: multipresent,
  omnipresent, represent,
  misrepresent
- present-: representation,
  representative

pres-s: to press; from IE *per-*, to
  strike
≈press: press, pressing, pressor,
  pressure, pressurize
- press: compress, depress,
  express, impress, oppress,
  repress, suppress
- pres-s-: cypress; also, cy pres,
  espresso, impressionable,
  impressments
- pressage: expressage
- pressed: appressed,
  compressed, oppressed,
  repressed, suppressed
- pressible: impressible,
  incompressible, inexpressible,
  insuppressible, irrepressible
- pressly: expressly
- pressionism: expressionism,
  impressionism
- pression: compression,
  depression, expression,
  impression, oppression,
  repression, suppression

- pressive: compressive, depressive, expressive, impressive, inexpressive, oppressive, repressive
- pressivity: expressivity
- pressor: with prefixes: compressor, depressor, oppressor
- pressor: with combining form: vasopressor
- pressured: geopressured
  [variant forms: reprimand; print, printable; imprint, reprint; fingerpint, footprint]

prest: **to lend**; from *pre-*, before + *stare*, to stand
  prest, imprest
  [variant forms: French: prêter; Spanish: prestar: to lend]
  {word note: imprest: a loan or advance of money; in accounting, designating a fund, as of petty cash, that is replenished in exactly the amount expended from it}

preter-: **beyond, past**
  preterhuman, preterit, preterition, pretermission, pretermit

prick: **point**
  prick, pricker, pricking, prickle, prickling, prickly

prim-e: **first, before**
≈prim-al: prim, primacy, primal
≈primar-y: primarily, primary
≈primate: primate
≈prime-r: prime, primer, primero
≈priming: priming
≈primitiv-e: primitive, primitivism
≈prim-: primeval, primordial, primordium, primrose
≈primato-: primatology
≈primi-: primipara
≈primo-: primo, primogenitor, primogeniture
- primario: comprimario

- primis: imprimis—in the first place
≈prin-: principal, principality, principium, principle, principled
≈prior-: prior, prioress, priory; prioritize, priority
- priority: apriority
  [variant forms: premier, premiere, pristine; prince, princely, princess]
  [phrases: a priori; prima ballerina, prima donna, prima facie, editio princeps, primum mobile, primus inter pares]

pris: **to seize, take** [see prehen-s]
≈prison: prison, prisoner
- prisal: appraisal, comprisal, reprisal, surprisal
- prise: apprise, comprise, emprise, enterprise, reprise, surprise
- prision: misprision
- prison: imprison
  [variant forms: prize—one meaning, disprize, en prise]

prism-at: **something sawed**
  prism, prismatic, prismatoid

priv-e: **separate, peculiar**
≈priv: privacy, private, privateer, privation, privatism, privative, privatize, privity, privy
≈privi-: privilege
- privation: deprivation
- priv-e-: deprival, deprive, deprived
- privilege-d: disprivilege, underprivileged
  [German: privatdocent]

pro-: **before** [in place or time]; moving forward, forth, substituting for, according to
≈pro-: proactive, problem, problematic, proboscis
≈procambium, procarp, procathedral, procedure,

proceed, procephalic, process,
proclaim, proclamation,
proclitic, proclivity, proconsul,
procrastinate, procreant,
procreate, procumbent,
procure, procurator

≈prodrome, produce, product,
proencephalon, proenchyma,
proestrus, profane, profess,
professor, proficient, profile,
profit, profligate, profluent,
profound, profundity, profuse,
profusion

≈progenitive, progenitor,
progeny, progeria,
progestational, progesterone,
proglottid, prognathous,
prognosis, prognostic,
prognosticate, program,
progress

≈prohibit, project, prolactin,
prolapse, prolate,
prolegomenon, prolepsis,
prolific, prolix, prolocutor,
prolong

≈promenade, promiscuous,
promise, promontory, promote,
promulgate, promycelium

≈pronephros, pronominal,
pronoun, pronounce,
pronucleus, pronunciamento,
pronunciation

≈propaedeutic, propagate,
propagule, propel, propend,
propensity, prophase,
prophecy, prophesy, prophet,
prophylactic, prophylaxis,
propitiate, propolis, proponent,
proportion, proposal, propose,
propraetor, proptosis,
propulsion

≈prorate, prorogue, proscenium,
proscribe, proscription,
prosector, prosecute, prospect,
prospectus, prosper, prostate,

prostitute, prostomium,
prostrate

≈protasis, protect, protest,
prothalamion, prothallium,
prothesis, protract, protrude,
protuberant

≈provenance, provenience,
proventriculus, proverb,
provide, providence, provident,
provirus, provision,
provitamin, provocation,
provoke, provost

- pro-: reciprocal, reciprocate,
reciprocity

≈por-: variant of *pro-*: portrait,
portraiture, portray

≈prod-: variant of *pro-*: prodigal,
prodigy

≈pron-e: pronate, pronator, prone

≈prono-: pronograde

≈pur-: variant of *pro-*: purchase
[terms: pro bono, pro bono
publico, procès-verbal, pro forma,
pro patria, pro rata, pro tempore]

prob-e: good, proper

≈prob-e: probablism, probability,
probable, probably, proband,
probate, probation, probative,
probe, probity

- prob-: improbable, improbity

- probate: approbate, reprobate

- probation: approbation,
reprobation

≈proof: proof, proofed, proofer

- proof: disproof, reproof

≈prove: prove, proven

- prov-: approval, improvident

- prove: approve, disprove,
disapprove, reprove
[variant form: reprieve]
[phrase: onus probandi]
[see improve]

probr: to bear

opprobrious, opprobrium

PROCRUSTEAN: lit., to stretch out;
drastic; ruthless; from Procrustes,

a mythological giant innkeeper of
Attica, who stretched or cut off the
legs of his guests to fit the bed
proct-o: **anus**
≈proct-: proctalgia, proctodaeum,
proctodynia
≈procto-: proctocele, proctology,
proctorrhea, proctoscope,
proctostomy
- proct: cytoproct, ectoproct,
endoproct, entoproct, epipoct,
paraproct, periproct
- procta: aprocta, cryptoprocta,
ectoprocta, endoprocta
PROFITEROLE: French; a small cream
puff; reason unknown
prol-e: **offspring**; from *pro-*, before
+ *alere*, to nourish
≈prole: proletarian, proletariat,
proletary
≈proli-: proliferate, proliferous,
prolific, prolificacy,
proligerous
prop: **near, close**
≈prop: propinquity
- proach-: approach, reproach,
reproachful; inapproachable,
irreproachable
≈proxim-: proximics, proximal,
proximity, proximo
- proximat-e: approximate,
approximation
[French: rapprochement]
prop-ri: **one's own**
≈proper: proper, property
≈propriet: proprietary, proprietor,
propriety
≈proprio-: proprioceptive,
proprioceptor
- proper: improper
- propriate: appropriate,
expropriate, impropriate,
inappropriate, misappropriate,
reappropriate
- propriety: impropriety
[Spanish: proprio—one's own]

pros: **to, toward, at**
≈pros-: proselyte, prosenchyma,
prosodic, prosody, prosthesis,
prosthetic, prosthetics;
prosthodontics—prosthetic +
odontics
≈proso-: prosopyle
prose: see vers, diprosopus
prosop-o: **face**; from *pros*, near +
ops, eye
≈prosop: prosopagnosia,
prosopalgia
≈prosopo-: prosopography,
prosopopoeia
prostat-e: **prostate gland**; from
pro-, before + *stare*, to stand
≈prostat-e: prostate, prostatism
≈prostat-: prostatectomy,
prostatitis
PROTEAN: variable in form; assuming
various forms or characters; from
Proteus, the mythical god who
could change his shape at will
prot-: **first**
≈prot: protein [see separate entry],
protist, protium, proton
≈prot-: protagonist, protanopia
≈proto-: protocol, protogalaxy,
protolithic, protomartyr,
protonema, protonephridium,
protonymph, protopathic,
protoplanet, protoplasm,
protoplast, protostele,
prototrophic, prototype,
protoxylem, protozoan
≈protero-: Proterozoic
≈protho-: prothonotary
prote-in: **protein**; from *proto*, first,
primary
≈prot-ein: proteose, protein,
proteinaceous
≈protein-: proteinoid, proteinuria
≈proteino-: proteinoclastic,
proteinolysis
- protein: metaprotein,
nucleoprotein, scleroprotein

PROTREPTIC: intended as instructional
proud: see esse
provinc-e: outside territory
  [uncertain background]
  province, provincial,
  provincialism
  [variant form: prow]
provost: see pon
prox: see prop for approximate
prud: sound judgment; from "to
  provide for"
≈pruden: prudence, prudent,
  prudential
- prudence: jurisprudence
- prudent: imprudent
PRUDE: from French *prudefemme*,
  proud woman; one who is overly
  modest
prur: to itch, be wanton
  prurience, prurient, prurigo,
  pruritus
psalm: psalm, song; from *psalmos*,
  a twanging with the fingers
≈psalm: psalm, psalmist,
  psalmody
≈psalter: psalterium*, Psalter,
  psaltery: **song sung to the harp**
  *unusual connection to omasum
psamm: sand, pebble
  psammite, psammon
  [variant form: psephology]
pseud-o: false
≈pseudo: pseudo
≈pseud-: pseudepigrapha,
  pseudonym, pseudonymous
≈pseudo-: pseudocarp,
  pseudoclassic, pseudocyesis,
  pseudogene, pseudomorph,
  pseudopodium, pseudoscience
psilo-: bare
  psilocin, psilocybin,
  psilophyte, psilosopher
PSORIASIS: a chronic skin disease
psych-e: the mind
≈psych-e: psychal, psychalia,
  psyche, psychic, psychical

≈psych-: psychagogic,
  psychalgia, psychasthenia,
  psychosis, psychedelic,
  psychiatry, psychosis,
  psychotic
≈psycho-: psychodrama,
  psychokinesis, psychology,
  psychometry, psychomotor,
  psychosomatic
- psychic: allopsychic,
  autopsychic, biopsychic,
  cenopsychic, extrapsychic,
  infrapsychic, interpsychic,
  intrapsychic, physiopsychic,
  polypsychic, somatopsychic
- psychotic: antipsychotic
- psychosis: metempsychosis
- psychology: metapsychology
psychro-: cold
  psychroalgia, psychrometer,
  psychrophilic, psychrophore
pterido-: fern; from *pteron*, feather
≈pterid-: pteridoid
≈pterido-: pteridograph,
  pteridology, pteridophyte,
  pteridosperm
pter-o: wing, feather
≈pter-: pteryla [second root is hylo]
≈ptero-: pterodactyl, pteropod,
  pterosaur
- pter: calypter, chiropter,
  helicopter, ornithopter
- pteral: apteral, dipteral,
  hemipteral, monopteral
- pteran: anisopteran,
  coleopteran, dipteran,
  homopteran, lepidopteran,
  mecopteran, orthopteran,
  trichopteran
- pterid: eurypterid
- pterium: apterium
- pterous: apterous, dipterous,
  hemipterous, heteropterous,
  hymenopterous, macropterous,
  orthopterous, tetrapterous

[variant forms: accipiter, feather,
ptarmigan; peripeteia; pterygium,
pterygoid; apteryx, coleoptile]

pto-m: to fall

≈ptom: ptomaine

- ptom-: symptom, symptomatic,
symptomatology

≈ptosis: ptosis

- ptosis: with prefixes: antiptosis,
apoptosis, proptosis

- ptosis: with combining forms:
blepharoptosis, cardioptosis,
carpoptosis, colpoptosis,
glossoptosis, hysteroptosis,
mastoptosis, odontoptosis,
onychoptosis

- ptote: asymptote

pty-al: spitting

≈ptyal: ptyalin, ptyalism

≈ptyalo-: ptyalocele

- ptysis: hemoptysis

ptych: to fold

diptych, polyptych, triptych;
anaptyxis—epenthesis of a
vowel, or the insertion of an
unhistoric sound or letter in a
word, as in athalete for athlete

puber: adult, of ripe age; may be
from *puer*, boy

≈puber: puberty, puberulent

≈pubo-: pubofemoral, puborectal

≈pub-es: pubic, pubis, pubes,
pubescence, pubescent: pubic
hair

public: see popul

puce: penis

prepuce—the fold of skin
covering the end (glans) of the
penis; foreskin; a similar fold over
the end of the clitoris

pud: to be ashamed

≈puden: pudency, pudendum, pl.,
pudenda

- pud-: impudent, impudicity,
repudiate
[French: pudeur]

puer-ile: boy [see puber]

≈pueril-e: puerile, puerilism,
puerility

≈puer-: puerperal, puerperium
[variant form: pusillanimous]

pug-n: to fight

≈pug-n: pugilism, pugilist;
pugnacious

- pugn: expugn, impugn, oppugn,
repugn

- pugnable: expugnable,
inexpugnable, impugnable

- pugnance: repugnance

- pugnant: oppugnant, repugnant

- pugnation: impugnation

- pugner: impugner, oppugner
[variant form: poniard]

puissant: see pot

PUKKA: Hindi; genuine, real

PULCHRITUDE: physical beauty; from
pulcher, beautiful

PULLMAN (sleeping car): developed
by George M. Pullman (1831-97);
the first car was used to bear
President Lincoln's body from
Washington, DC, to Springfield,
IL, for burial

pul-mon: lung, lungs

≈pulmon: pulmonary, pulmonate,
pulmonic

≈pul-: pulmotor—pulmo + motor

≈pulmo-: pulmogastric,
pulmograde, pulmolith,
pulmometer

PULPIT: stage, scaffold [see falque]

puls-e: to push, drive, strike

≈puls-e: pulsant, pulsate,
pulsatile, pulsation, pulsative,
pulsator, pulse—one meaning

≈pulsi-: pulsimeter

- pulse: impulse, repulse

- pulsion: compulsion, expulsion,
propulsion, repulsion

- pulsive: compulsive, expulsive,
impulsive, propulsive,
repulsive

- pulsory: compulsory, propulsory, repulsory
- pel: appel, compel, dispel, expel, impel, propel, repel
- pellant: appellant, expell*a*nt, or, expell*e*nt; propell*a*nt, or, propell*e*nt; repellant, or, repell*e*nt
- pellate: appellate, interpellate
- pellat-: appellation, appellative
- pellee: appellee
- peller: impeller, propeller
  [variant forms: peal, appeal, repeal, irrepealable; catapult, rappel, repoussé]

pulver: **dust**, **pollen**
≈pulver: pulverize, pulverulent
≈pollin: pollinate, pollinium, pollinization, pollinize
≈pollin-: pollinosis
≈pollini-: polliniferous, pollinigerous, pollinivore
  [variant forms: polenta, pollen, pulse—one meaning, poultice, powder, pozzuolana]
pulvi-n: **pillow**, **cushion**
  pulvillus, pulvinate, pulvinus
  [variant form: pillow]
PUMICE: foam; a spongy, light, porous volcanic rock used in solid or powdered form for scouring, smoothing, and polishing; see pounce[1]
pun-i: **to punish**, **penalty**
  punish, punishment; punitive; impunity
  [variant form: subpoena—lit., under penalty, the first words in a Roman writ requiring that a person appear in court]
punct: **point**
≈punct: punctate, punctilio, punctilious, punctual, punctuate, punctuation, punctulate, puncture
- punction: compunction, expunction, interpunction
- punctious: compunctious
- puncture: acupuncture, aquapuncture, ignipuncture, micropuncture, sonopuncture, vasopuncture, venipuncture
- puntal: contrapuntal
- pane: counterpane
≈point: point, pointed, pointelle, pointer, pointillism
- point: appoint, counterpoint, disappoint, pourpoint
  [variant forms: expunge, trapunto, poignant, pink, pinking shears, pizza, pounce—one meaning, pun, puncheon, punt—one meaning; punch, pungent, punty, spontoon; point]
  [phrase: point d'appui]
PUNDIT: from Hindi *pandit*; further from Sanskrit *pandita*, learned person
puny: see nat
pup-il: orig., **orphan**, **ward**; from a girl, doll
≈pup: pupa, pupate; pupil, pupilage, pupillary—two meanings
≈pupi-: pupiparous
≈pupp: puppet, puppy
PURDAH: orig., Persian; Urdu and Hindi *pardah*, veil; the practice among some Muslims and Hindus of secluding or hiding women from strangers; a curtain or partition used for this; the section of a house reserved primarily for women
pur-e: **pure**, **clean**
≈pur-e: pure, purée, or puree, pureness, purine, purism, purist, Puritan, puritanical, purity
≈pure: purebred
≈puri-: puification, purificator, purify
- purate: depurate

- pure: impure
- purity: impurity
≈purg-e: purgation, purgative,
    purgatorial, purgatory, purge
- purgate: expurgate,
    unexpurgated
- purgation: compurgation,
    expurgation
{word note: Puritan: a member of a
    Protestant group, either in England
    or the American colonies, that
    desired to purify the Church of
    England}

purpur-e: purple
    purpura, purpure, purpurin
purse: see burs-a

pur-ul: pus
    purulence, purulent; suppurate;
    seropurulent
    [variant form: pus]
pusillanimous: see puer-ile

pustul-e: blister, pimple
    pustulant, pustular, pustulate,
    pustule

**put-a: to reckon, cut, cleanse,
    prune**
≈put: putamen, putative
- putant: disputant
- putate: amputate
- putable: disputable,
    disreputable, incomputable,
    indisputable, reputable
- putatious: disputatious
- putation: amputation,
    computation, deputation,
    disputation, reputation;
    miscomputation
- pute: compute, depute, dispute,
    disrepute, impute, repute,
    reputed
- puty: deputy
    [variant forms: count—one
    meaning, account; berate]

putr-: rotten
≈putresc-e: putresce, putrescent,
    putrescible

≈putre-: putrefacient,
    putrefaction, putrefied, putrefy
- putrescible: imputrescible
≈putrid: putrid
    [variant forms: olla-podrida,
    potpourri]
{word note: potpourri: French; lit.,
    rotten pot; orig., the same as
    Spanish *olla-podrida*, a stew; a
    mixture of dried flower petals with
    spices, kept in a jar for fragrance;
    a medley, miscellany, or
    anthology}

pycn-o: thick, dense
≈pycn-: pycnodont, pycnosis
≈pycno-: pycnocline,
    pycnogonid, pycnometer
    [variant form: pyknosis]

pyel: basin
≈pyel: pyelitis
≈pyelo-: pyelogram,
    pyelography, pyelonephritis
- pyelitis: nephropyelitis

pyg: buttocks
    pygidium; callipygian,
    steatopygian, uropygian

**pyl-e: gate, opening from the
    stomach**
    pylon, pylorus; pylorectomy;
    micropyle

py-o: pus
≈py-: pyemia, pyosis
≈pyo-: pyoderma, pyogenesis,
    pyorrhea
- pyema: empyema

pyren-e: grain of wheat
    pyrene, pyrenoid

pyr-o: fire, fever, light
≈pyr-e: pyralid, pyre, pyretic,
    Pyrex®, pyrexia, pyridine,
    pyrite
≈pyr-: pyrheliometer, pyrosis,
    pyroxene
≈pyro-: Pyroceram®, pyroclastic,
    pyrogen, pyrogenic,
    pyrography, pyroligneous,

pyrolysis, pyromancy,
pyromania, pyromaniac,
pyrometer, pyrophobia,
pyrophoric, pyrostat,
pyrotechnics
- pyrea-n: empyreal, empyrean
≈pyreto-: pyretogenesis
- pyretic: apyretic, antipyretic
- pyrexia: apyrexia, eupyrexia,
  hyperpyrexia, physiopyrexia
- pyrite: chalcopyrite
- pyro-: micropyrometer

Q

quadr: four, forty, square
≈quadr: quadrant, quadrat,
  quadrate, quadratic, quadratics,
  quadrature, quadric, quadrille,
  quadrillion
≈quadr-: quadrangle,
  quadrennial, quadrennium,
  quadrumvirate: quadra +
  tri<u>umvirate</u>
≈quadra-: quadragesimal,
  quadraphonic
≈quadri-: quadricentennial,
  quadriceps, quadrifid,
  quadriga—ga from jug,
  quadrilateral, quadrilingual,
  quadripartite, quadriplegia,
  quadrisect, quadrivalent,
  quadrivium
≈quadru-: quadrumanous,
  quadruped, quadruple,
  quadruplet, quadruplex,
  quadruplicate
≈quar-t: quarantine, quart,
  quartan, quarter, quarterage,
  quartered, quartering,
  quarterly, quartern, quartet,
  quartic, quarto
≈quater: quaternary, quaternion
≈quatre-: quatrefoil

≈quattro-: quattrocentism,
  quattrocentist, quattrocento
  [variant forms: cadre, carrefour,
  casern, escadrille, quarrel—one
  meaning, quarrier, quarry—one
  meaning, quatrain, quire; square,
  squadron, trocar]
  {word note: quarantine: a period of
  40 days, whether of the Lenten
  season, of indulgence, or of
  holding a trading ship coming
  from an infected port; a cordon}
quaint: see gn
quale: what kind
≈quale: quale
≈qualit-y: qualitative, quality
≈quali-: qualification, qualified,
  qualify
- qualify: disqualify, prequalify,
  requalify
QUALM: Old English cwealm, death,
  disaster; now usually means "a
  twinge of conscience"
quant-i: how much
≈quant: quantic, quantile,
  quantitative, quantity,
  quantize, quantum
≈quanti-: quantifier, quantify
  [variant form: quandary]
quash: to shake, break
  quash—to quell or suppress an
  uprising
  [variant forms: cashier, one
  meaning; cask, rescue, squash—
  one meaning]
quasi-: as if
  quasicrystal, quasijudicial,
  quasiparticle; Quasimodo
QUELL: from Old English cwellan, to
  kill; to crush, subdue, put an end
  to, as to quell a riot
QUEER: possibly from German quer,
  crosswise, crooked; odd, strange
QUENCH: from Old English cwencan,
  to extinguish; to put out (a fire), to
  satisfy
querc: oak, oak forest
  quercetin, quercine, quercitron

quer: to complain
    querulous—inclined to find fault;
    complaining; full of complaint;
    peevish
    [variant form: quarrel—one
    meaning]

quest-ion: to seek, ask
≈quest: quest, question,
    questionable, questionless,
    questionnaire
- quest: acquest, conquest,
    inquest, request
- quire: acquire, inquire, require
- quiry: inquiry
- quis-: conquistador, inquisitive,
    inquisitor, inquisitorial
- quisite: exquisite, perquisite,
    prerequisite, requisite
- quisition: acquisition,
    disquisition, inquisition,
    requisition
    [variant forms: quaere, quaestor;
    query; conquer]
    [Note: bequest, from *bequeath*, is
    not in this family.]
queue: see caud
QUIBBLE: from *qui*, which, who;
    orig., a legal word
QUIDDITY: the essential quality of a
    thing; from *quid*, what? who?
QUIDNUNC: an inquisitive, gossipy
    person; Latin for "what now?"
QUID PRO QUO: lit., something for
    something; an equivalent or
    substitution

qui-es: quiet
≈quies: quiescent
- quiesce-: acquiesce, acquiescent
≈quiet: quiet, quieten, quietism,
    quietude, quietus
- quiet-: disquiet, disquietude,
    inquietude
- quil-: tranquil, tranquilize,
    tranquilizer, tranquility
≈quit-e: quit, quite, quits
≈quit-: quitclaim
≈quitt: quittance, quitter

- quit-e: acquit, requital, requite;
    unrequited
- quitt-: acquittal, acquittance
    [variant forms: coy; Requiem]
    [phrase: requiescat in pace]

quil: to dwell, from *colere*, to dwell
    inquiline—an animal, usually an
    insect, that commensally lives in
    the nest, burrow, or dwelling of
    another, usually without harm to
    the host, usually an animal of a
    different species

quin-t: five
≈quin: quinary, quinate
≈quint: quintain, quintan, quinte,
    quintet, quintile, quintillio
≈quin-: quincentenary, quincunx,
    quindecagon, quindecennial,
    quindecemvir
≈quinqu-: quinquennial
≈quinque-: quinquefoliolate,
    quinquevalent
≈quint-: quintessence
≈quintu-: quintuple, quintuplet
QUIP: indeed, forsooth; from *quid*,
    what

quip: ship, gear
    equip, equipage, equipment
quire: see quest-ion for inquire,
    require
quis: see quest-ion for requisite
QUISLING: from Vidkun Quisling
    (1887-1945), a Norwegian
    politician who betrayed his
    country to the Nazis during
    WWII; a traitor
QUIXOTIC: impratical, impulsive;
    from name of visionary hero of
    Don Quixote by Cervantes
QUIZ: from *quid*, what

quo-d: who
    quorum; quodlibet
QUONDAM: once, at one time, as *a
    quondam friend*
QUONSET HUT: a prefabricated metal
    structure once common on
    military installations; made in
    Quonset Point, RI

quot-e: how many, how much
≈quot-e: quota, quotable,
   quotation, quote, quotient
≈quoti-: quotidian
- quot: aliquot
QUO WARRANTO: lit., by what
   warrant; orig., a writ ordering a
   person to show by what right he
   exercises a right, franchise, or
   privilege

R

rab: to rage, madness
≈rab: rabid, rabidity, rabidness,
   rabies, rabietic, rabious
≈rabi-: rabiform
≈rag-e: rage, raging
- rage: enrage, enraged
racem-e: cluster of grapes
   raceme, racemic, racemism,
   racemization, racemose
   [variant form: raisin]
RACCOON: from Virginia Algonquian
   aroughcun, the scratcher
rach: spine, stalk
≈rach: rachial, rachilla, rachis
≈rach-: rachitis
≈rachi-: rachiocentesis,
   rachiodont, rachitome
   [variant form: rickets]
ract: to strike
   cataract—orig., floodgate of
   heaven; floodgate of the eye
rad: root
≈radic: radicand, radicle
≈radical: radical, radicalism,
   radicalize, radically
≈radish: radish
- radicate: eradicate
   [variant form: deracinate]
rad-e: to scrape
≈rad: radula
- rade: abrade, corrade
- radicable: ineradicable

≈ras: rascal, rasher, rasorial,
   raster
- ras-e: erase, erasure, inerasable
- rasion: abrasion, erasion
- rasive: abrasive
   [variant forms: raclette, ramentum,
   rapier, raze, razee, razor]
   [phrase: tabula rasa]
radi-o: ray, rod, spoke of a wheel
≈radi: radial, radiance, radiate,
   radiation, radiator, radium,
   radius
≈radio: radio, radiolarian
≈radio-: radioactive,
   radiobiology, radiocalcium,
   radiogenic, radiograph,
   radiology, radiolucent,
   radiometer, radiomimetic,
   radioscopy, radiotherapy,
   radiothermy
- rad-: interradial, irradiance,
   irradiation
- radiate: biradiate, corradiate,
   eradiate, irradiate, reradiate,
   sexradiate—having six rays:
   said of certain sponge spicules,
   triradiate
   [variant forms: ray; Spanish:
   rayo: lightning; also, ray of
   light]
ragout: see gust
RAJAH: Hindi: prince or chief
   [see rani]
ram: branch
≈ram: ramet, ramulose, ramus
≈rami-: ramification, ramiform,
   ramiflorous, ramify,
   ramigerous, ramiparous
- ramous: biramous, uniramous
RAMADAN: Arabic; lit., the hot
   month; the ninth month in the
   Muslim year; a period of fasting
   from sunrise to sunset
ranc: to be rank
   rancid, rancidity, rancor,
   rancorous; rank—one meaning

range: **to arrange, set in a row**

≈rang-e: range, ranger, rangy

- range-: arrange, arrangement, derange, disarrange, prearrange
[variant forms: ranch, rank — one meaning]

RANI: Hindi for the wife of a rajah, or a woman who is a queen or princess in her own right [see rajah]

RANKLE: orig., to fester; become or make inflamed; to cause or cause to have long-lasting anger, rancor, resentment; diminutive of Latin *draco*, dragon

RANSACK: Old Norse *rann*, house + *soekja*, to seek; to search through for plunder; thus, pillage, rob

rap-t: **to seize**

≈rap-e: rapacious, rapacity, rape

≈rapi-d: rapid, rapidity, rapine, rapist

≈rapt: rapt, rapture

≈raptor: raptor, raptorial

- rapt-: enrapt, enrapture

≈rav: ravage, raven — one meaning, ravin, ravine, ravish

- rept-: subreption, surreptitious
[variant form: erepsin]

rar-e: **rare, loose, thin**

rare, rarity; rarefy; rarify
[phrase: rara avis — lit., rare bird; an unusual or extraordinary person or thing]

rat-e: **to reason**

≈rat-e: ratable, rate

≈ratio: ratio, ratiocinate, ratiocination

≈ration: ration, rational, rationale, rationalism, rationality, rationalize

≈rati-: ratify

- rate: disrate, prorate

- rational: antirational, irrational

≈reason: reason, reasonable, reasoning, reasonless

[variant forms: arraign, raisonneur]
[phrases: raison d'état, raison d'être, pro rata]
[NB: berate; see put-a]

RATHSKELLER: German *rath*, town hall + *keller*, cellar; a restaurant usually below street level

rave: **to roam, to dream**

rave, raver, raving
[variant form: reverie]

ray of light: see radi-o

ray: **to put in order**

array, disarray

re-: **again, back, backward**

≈re-: react, reanimate

≈rebarbative, rebate, rebel, rebuke, rebut

≈recalcitrant, recalescence, recant, recapitulate, recapture, recede, receipt, receive, recent, receptacle, reception, recess, recession

≈recidivist, recipe, reciprocate, recision, recite, reclaim, reclamation, recline, recluse

≈recognition, recognize, recoil, recollect, recombinant, recommend, recommit, reconcile, recondite, reconnaissance, reconnoiter, record, recount, recoup, recourse, recover

≈recreant, re-create, recreate, recreation, recrement, recriminate, recrudesce, recruit, recumbent, recuperate, recur, recurrence, recursion, recurvate, recusant, recycle

≈redress, redouble, redoubt [root is *ducere*, to lead], redoubtable [root is *dubitare*, to doubt], reduce, reduplicate

≈refection, refer, referendum, reflect, refluent, reform, refract, refractory, refrain,

refrangible, refrigerant, refuge,
refulgent, refund, refuse, refute

≈regard, regelation, regenerate,
register, regorge, regress,
regret, regurgitate

≈rehabilitate, rehearsal,
reimburse, reincarnate,
reiterate, reject, rejuvenate

≈relapse, relate, relax, release,
relegate, relent, relevant,
reliable, relic, relict, relief,
relieve, religion, relinquish,
reliquary, relish, relucent,
reluctant, relume, rely

≈remain, remand, remark,
remedial, remedy, remember,
remind, reminisce, remise,
remiss, remit, remix,
remonstrance, remora,
remorse, remote, remount,
remunerate

≈renaissance, renascence,
renegade, renitent, renounce,
renovate, renown

≈repair—two meanings, repand,
reparation, repast, repatriate,
repeal, repeat, repel, repellant,
repent, repeople, repercussion,
repertory, repetend, repetition,
repine, replace, repleader,
replevin, replica, reply, report,
repose, repossess, reprehend,
represent, repress, reprieve,
reprimand, reprint, reprise,
reproach, reprobate, reproduce,
reproof, reprove, repudiate,
repugnant, repulse, reputation,
repute

≈request, require, requisite,
requite

≈rescind, rescission, rescript,
rescue [root is *quatere*, to shake],
research, resect, resemble,
resent, reserve, reside, resign,
resilient, resist, resolve,

resonant, resorb, resound,
resource

≈respect, respiration,
resplendent, respond, response,
restaurant, restitution, restive
restore, restrain, restrict,
restructure, result, resupinate,
resurge, resurrect

≈retail, retain, retaliate, retard,
retentive, reticent, retire, retort,
retrace, retract, retread, retreat,
retrench, retribution, retrieve,
retroussé, return, retuse,
reunify, reunion.

≈revaluate, revanchism, reveille,
revenant, revenge, reverberate,
revere, reverse, revert, revest,
review, revile, revise, revive,
revoke, revolt, revolute,
revolve, revue, revulsion,
reward

≈red-: variant of *re-*: redact,
redeem, redemption, redolent,
redound, redundant

≈redi-: variant of *re-*: redivivus

≈ren-: variant of *re-*: rencounter,
render, rendition

real: **real**; from *res*, thing

≈real: real, realia, realistic,
realism, realist, reality, realize,
Realtor®

- real-: irreal, surreal, surrealism
[variant forms: rebus, reify,
republic]
[phrases: res adjudicata, res
gestae, res ipsa loquitur, res
judicata, res publica; in rem]
{word note: rebus: from French
rébus; further from Latin *res*,
thing; a kind of puzzle consisting
of pictures or drawings of
"things"—objects, letters, etc.}

reason: see rat-e

REBUKE: from *re-*, back + *buchier*, to
beat; lit., to beat back; to criticize
or reprove sharply; reprimand

reconnaissance, reconnoiter: from
gn, to know [see gnom-e]
rect-i: straight, right, rule
≈rect: rectitude, rectrix
≈rect-: rectitis—same as proctitis
≈recto: recto, rector, rectory
≈rectu: rectum, rectus
≈rect-: rectangle
≈recti-: rectify, rectilinear
≈recto-: rectocele, rectoscope
- rect-: directed, directorate,
   directory, directrix, erectile
- rect: correct, direct, erect,
   incorrect, indirect, misdirect,
   porrect, resurrect
- rection: correction, direction,
   erection, insurrection,
   resurrection
- rectional: directional,
   omnidirectional
- rectitude: correctitude
- rective: corrective, directive
- rector: director, erector
≈reg: regal, regalia, regality,
   regency, regent, reglet
≈regi: regimen, regiment, reginal,
   regius
≈regi-: regicide
≈region: region, regional,
   regionalism, regionalize
≈regna-: regnal, regnant
- regnum: interregnum
≈regula-r: regular, regulate,
   regulation, regulator, Regulus
- regul-: deregulate, irregular
≈rex: rex; interrex: king
- rigendum: corrigendum
- rigible: corrigible, dirigible,
   incorrigible
- droit: adroit, maladroit
   [variant forms: alert, dirge, dress,
   dressage, dresser; address,
   redress; droit, escort, rake—the
   implement; rank—one meaning,
   realm; reckon, reckoning, rex,
   reign, right, royal, rule, ruler]

[phrases: droit du seigneur,
   en règle]
REGATTA: a boat race; original
   meaning: striving for mastery
reg-o: to dye
regolith, regosol
REGRET: from Gothic *gretan*, to
   weep; orig., to mourn the dead; to
   feel sorry about or mourn for a
   person or thing gone, lost, etc.
   [There are no other known English
   words from *gretan*.]
rem-e: oar
≈remi-: remiform
- reme: bireme, quinquereme,
   trireme
   [variant forms: trierarch,
   trierarchy—from *trireme*]
ren-i: kidney
≈ren: renal
≈reni-: reniform, renipelvic,
   reniportal
- renal: adrenal, suprarenal
   [variant form: reins—one
   meaning]
rept: to crawl
reptant, reptile, reptilian
ret-ic: net
≈reti-c: retiarius, reticle
≈reticul-e: reticulate, reticulation,
   reticule, reticulose, reticulum
≈reti-: retiform
≈reticul-: reticuloid
≈reticulo-: reticulocyte,
   reticulotomy
≈retin: retina, retinal, retinene
≈retin-: retinitis, retinoid,
   retinoma, retinosis
≈retino-: retinoblastoma,
   retinocytoma, retinography,
   retinomalacia, retinopathy,
   retinopexy, retinoscope,
   retinochisis, retinoscopy,
   retinotomy, retinotopic,
   retinotoxic
   [variant form: reseau]

retro-: back, backwards
retroact, retroaction,
retroactive, retrocede, retrofit,
retroflex, retroflection, also,
retroflexion, retrograde,
retrogress, retrogression,
retrolental, retrorse— second
root is from *verse*, retrospect,
retroversion, retrovirus
[variant forms: rear, arrears,
derrière, reredos]
revel: see belli
RH FACTOR: a group of antigens first
discovered in the blood of rhesus
monkeys
rhabdo-: rod
≈rhabd-: rhabdoid, rhabdome
≈rhabdo-: rhabdocoele,
rhabdocyte, rhabdolith,
rhabdology, rhabdomancy,
rhabdomyoma, rhabdophilia,
rhabdophobia, rhabdopleura,
rhabdosphere, rhabdovirus
rhaps: to sew together
≈rhaps-: rhapsode, rhapsodic,
rhapsodist, rhapsodize,
rhapsody
≈raph: raphe, raphide
- rrhapy: staphylorrhapy,
tenorrhaphy
rheo-: to flow
≈rheo-: rheobase, rheology,
rheometer, rheophile, rheostat,
rheotaxis, rheotropism
- rrh-ea: catarrh, blennorrhea,
bronchorrhea, diarrhea,
dysmenorrhea, gonorrhea,
hemorrhage, leukorrhea,
logorrhea, menorrhea,
pyorrhea, rhinorrhea,
seborrhea, steatorrhea: to
overflow
- rrhoid: hemorrhoid, lymphoroid
≈rheum-a: rheum, rheumatic,
rheumatism
≈rheumato-: rheumatology

[variant forms: rennet, rennin,
rhyton—an ancient drinking
vessel]
rhetor: to speak, declaim
rhetor, rhetoric, rhetorical,
rhetorician
rhin-e: nose
≈rhin: rhinal, rhinism
≈rhin-: rhinalgia, rhinitis
≈rhino-: rhinoceros, rhinocele,
rhinolaryngology, rhinology
≈rhinometer, rhinopathy,
rhinopharyngitis, rhinoplasty,
rhinorrhea, rhinoscope,
rhinostenosis, rhinovirus
- rhino-: otorhinolaryngology
- rrhine: catarrhine, platyrrhine
{word note: rhinoceros: with Greek
keras, horn, lit., nose-horned; a
pachyderm with one or two
upright horns on the snout}
RHINESTONE: translates French
caillou du Rhin: so called because
originally made at Strasbourg on
the Rhine
rhiz-o: root
≈rhiz-: rhizoid, rhizome
≈rhizo-: rhizobium, rhizocarpous,
rhizocephalan, rhizoctonia,
rhizogenic
≈rhizomorphous, rhizophagous,
rhizopod, rhizosphere,
rhizotomy
- rrhiza: glycyrrhiza,
hymenorrhiza, leptorrhiza,
megalorrhiza, monorrhiza,
mycorrhiza
rhod: rose, red
≈rhod: rhodium
≈rhod-: rhodamine, rhodopsin
≈rhodo-: rhodochrosite,
rhododendron, rhodolite,
rhodoplast
≈rhodon-: rhodonite
RHODESIA: now parts of Zimbabwe
and Zambia; a former region in

South Africa; named after Cecil
Rhodes (1853-1902), the founder
of Rhodes scholarships

rhomb-o: **to turn**
≈rhom: rhombic, rhombus
≈rhomb-: rhombencephalon,
rhomboid, rhomboideus
. ≈rhombo-: rhombogen,
rhombohedral, rhombohedron,
rhombomere
- rhombic: clinorhombic,
orthorhombic

rhynch-o: **bill, snout**
≈rhyncho-: rhynchocephalian,
rhynchophoran
- rhynchus: ornithorhynchus,
phyllorhynchus

rhyt: **wrinkle**
rhytidectomy; rhytidoplasty

rhythm: **measure**
≈rhythm: rhythm, rhythmics,
rhythmicity, rhythmist
≈rhythmo-: rhythmometer
- rhythm: polyrhythm
- rhythmia: allorhythmia,
arrhythmia, bradyrhythmia,
dysrhythmia
[variant form: rhyme]

ribald: **to be wanton**; from Old
High German *riban*, to copulate
ribald, ribaldry
{word note: ribald: characterized by
coarse or vulgar joking or mock-
ing, esp. dealing with sex in a
humorously earthy or direct way}

RICE: from Sanskrit *vrihih*

ri-d: **to laugh**
≈ri-d: riant, ridicule, ridiculous
- ride: deride
≈risi: risibility, risible
- ris-: derision, derisive
[Spanish: una risa—a laugh]

rig[1]: **to be stiff**
rigid, rigor, rigorous; rigidify
[phrases: de rigueur,
rigor mortis]

rig[2]: **to water**
irrigate, irrigation, irrigative,
irrigator
risible: see ri-d

rit: **excite, agitate**
irritable, irritant, irritate,
irritation, irritative

riv-al: **shore, riverbank**
≈riv: river, rival, rivalrous,
rivalry, rivulet
- rival: arrival, co-rival, corrival
- rivation: derivation
- rive: arrive, derive
[variant forms: riparian; arriviste]

rob: **strong, hard**; from "oak tree"
robust, robustious;
corroborant; corroborate
[variant form: rambunctious]

rob-e: **to steal**; orig., spoils, booty
rob, robe; disrobe, enrobe
[phrase: robe de chambre]

robot: see orphan

ROCOCO: from French *rocaille*, rock
work; a style of art that developed
from the Baroque period; profuse,
overdone, florid

rod-e: **to gnaw, to peck**
≈rod: rodent
- rode: corrode, erode
- rose: erose
- rosion: corrosion, erosion
- rosive: corrosive, erosive
[variant form: rostrum)

rog: **to ask**
≈rog: rogation
- rog-: surrogacy, arrogance,
arrogant
- rogate: abrogate, arrogate,
interrogate, subrogate,
supererogate, surrogate
- rogation: derogation,
subrogation, supererogation
- rogative: derogative,
interrogative, prerogative
- rogatory: derogatory,
interrogatory, supererogatory

- rogue: prorogue
  [variant forms: corvée; possibly, rogue]

ros: rose

≈ros-e: rosary, rosarian, rose, roseate, roseola, rosily

≈ros-: rosanaline

≈rosi-: Rosicrucian

{word note: rosary: orig., a garland of roses}

rota: wheel

≈rota: rota, rotary

≈rotat-e: rotate, rotation, rotative, rotator

≈rota-: rotameter

≈roti-: rotifer, rotiferous, rotiform

≈roto-: rotogravure

- rotation: controrotation, cyclorotation, dextrorotation, levorotation, sinistrorotation

- rotatory: circumrotatory, dextrarotatory, levorotatory

≈rotund-a: rotund, rotunda; orotund—oral + rotund

- rol-l-: control, controller; comptroller, enroll

- rollable: incontrollable, uncontrollable

≈rond: rondeau, rondel, rondo, rondure

≈round: round, roundelay

- round: around
  [variant forms: barouche, rodeo, role, roll, rotor, roué, roulade, rouleau, roulette, rundle, rundlet, tondo]
  {word notes: roué: lit., broken at the wheel; a dissipated man; rake, debauchee; rôle: orig., a register of actors}

ROTISSERIE: from French *rostir*, to roast; orig., one who roasts meats for sale

RSVP: initials for French *répondez s'il vous plait*; lit., respond if you please; please reply

rub-e: red

≈rube: rubella, rubeola, rubescent

≈rubi: rubicund, rubiginous, rubious

≈rube-: rubefacient, rubefaction

≈rubr: rubric, rubrical, rubrician

- rubin: bilirubin
  [variant forms: rouge, ruby, ruddy, rufous; rutilant, rutile]
  [phrase: rouge et noir, lit., red and black; a card game]

ruct: to belch

eruct, eructate, eructation, eructative

rud-e: roughness

rude, rudiment, rudimentary; erudite, erudition
  [variant form: rough]

rug: to wrinkle

rugose, rugulose
corrugate, corrugation

RUGBY: a type of football game first played at Rugby school, in central England

rum: throat, gullet

rumen, ruminant, ruminate

RUMOR: directly from Latin: noise, hearsay; general talk not based on definite knowledge; mere gossip

RUNCINATE: to plane off

rupt: to break

≈rup-t: rupestrine, rupture

- rupt: abrupt, corrupt, disrupt, erupt, incorrupt, interrupt, irrupt, bankrupt

- ruptible: corruptible, incorruptible

- ruption: abruption, corruption, disruption, eruption, incorruption, interruption, irruption, supereruption

- ruptive: corruptive, disruptive, eruptive, interruptive, irruptive

- rupter-: corrupter, or, corruptor; disrupter, or, disruptor

- rumpent: erumpent

[variant forms: rout—one
meaning; route, routine]
{word note: route: from *rupta via*,
lit., path broken through; as a
verb, to send, forward by a
specific route}
rust: the country
rustic, rusticate
[variant form: rural]

S

SABAOTH: Hebrew: armies, hosts, as
in "the Lord God of Sabaoth"
SABBATH: Hebrew *shavat*: to rest
SABER: orig. Hungarian *szablya*; a
heavy cavalry sword
sabot: wooden shoe
sabot, sabotage
[variant form: savate]
{word note: sabotage: orig., damage
done to machinery by wooden
shoes; intentional destruction
often in labor disputes}
SABULOUS: sandy
sac-c: sack, bag, sac
sac, saccade, saccadic, saccate,
saccular, sacculate, saccule,
sacculus
[variant forms: cul de sac, sack,
sacque, satchel]
sacchar-o: sugar
≈sacchar: saccharase, saccharate,
saccharic, saccharide,
saccharin, saccharine,
saccharinic
≈sacchar-: saccharoidal,
saccharose
≈sacchari-: sacchariferous,
saccharify
≈saccharo-: saccharometer
- saccharide: holosaccharide,
polysaccharide
SACHEM: from New England
Algonquian: leader of a tribe; any
of the leaders of the Tammany

Society, a powerful Democratic
political organization in Boston
SACK: orig., *wyneseck*; from French
vin sec, dry wine; sec from Latin
siccus, dry
sacr-al: holy, sacred
[see sanc-ti]
≈sacr: sacrarium, sacred,
sacristan, sacristy, sacrum
≈sacral: sacral, sacralize
≈sacrament: sacrament,
sacramental, sacramentalism,
sacramentarian, sacramentary,
Sacramento, KY, CA
≈sacri-: sacrifice, sacrificial,
sacrilege, sacrilegious
≈sacro-: sacroiliac, sacrosanct
- sacralize: desacralize
≈sacer-: sacerdotal
- s-ecrable: execrable
- s-ecrate: consecrate, desecrate,
execrate, obsecrate
[variant forms: saint, sexton]
SADIST: one who enjoys cruelty or
infliction of pain; from *Marquis
de Sade*, who incurred infamy by
torturing the women he loved
SAFARI: Arabic *safar*: to journey
SAFFRON: from Arabic *za faran*; a
plant used for coloring and
flavoring food
sag-e: to perceive
sagacious, sagacity; sage—one
meaning; presage
{word note: presage: as a noun, a
sign or warning of a future event;
as a verb, to have a foreboding;
also, to predict}
sagitt: arrow
Sagitta, sagittal, Sagittarius,
sagittate
SAHARA: from Arabic *sahra*, desert;
thus, redundant to say Sahara
Desert; simply, the Sahara
SAHIB: Hindi; from Arabic; master;
sir; a title used in colonial India
when speaking to or of a
European, and later extended to

any male as a sign of respect or
formality
SAIGA: Russian: a small, stocky
antelope, native to the steppes of
Russia and Siberia
SALAAM: Farsi (the modern language
of Iran): peace, a greeting [see
shalom]
sal: **salt**
≈sal: salad, salami
≈salar-y: salariat, salaried, salary
≈salin-e: salina, salinize, saline
≈salt: salt, salter, saltern, saltine,
salty
≈sali-: saliferous, salify,
salimeter
≈salino-: salinometer
- salination: desalination
[variant forms: sauce, sausage,
silt, souse]
[phrases: sal volatile, cum grano
salis—with a grain of salt]
saliva: **saliva**
salivarian, salivary, salivate,
insalivate
[variant form: slime]
salping: **trumpet**; fallopian,
eustachian, or uterine tubes
≈salping: salpingian
≈salping-: salpingectomy,
salpingitis
≈salpingo-: salpingolysis,
salpingoplasty, salpingorrhapy,
salpingoscopy, salpingotomy
[variant form: salpinx]
salt: **to jump, leap**
≈sal: salacious, salient,
salientian, sally, salmon
≈salt: saltant, saltarello, saltier,
saltire
≈saltat: saltation, saltatorial
≈salti-: saltigrade
- sail-: assail, assailant,
assailable, assailer, assailment,
unassailable
- sile: resile

- silience: resilience, transilience
- silient: dissilient, irresilient,
resilient, transilient
- s-ult-: desultory, exult, insult,
result, resultant, exultation
[variant forms: assault,
somersault; saltimbocca, sauté]
[phrase: per saltum]
salv: **safety, health**
≈salv-e: salvable, salvage,
salvation, salve—one meaning,
salver, salvo, salvor
≈salver-: salverform; also, salver-
shaped
≈salvi-: salvific
≈salubr: salubrious, salubrity
- salubrious: insalubrious
≈salut-e: salutary, salutation,
salutatorian, salutatory, salute
[variant forms: safe, safety; save,
saving, savior, Savior]
sam: Russian: **self**
samizdat, samovar, Samoyed
{word notes: samizdat: lit., self-
published; samovar: lit., self-
boiler; a metal urn; Samoyed: lit.,
self-eater; a dog}
SAMOSA: a small pastry turnover,
originally of India, filled with a
spicy meat or vegetable mixture,
as of potatoes or peas
SAMPAN: Chinese *sam*, three + *pan*,
plank; a small sailing boat
SAMSARA: Sanskrit: lit., running
together; in Hinduism, the
continuing cycle in which the
same soul is continually reborn
SAMURAI: Japanese *saburai*, to serve;
in feudal Japan, a member of the
military class
sanc-ti: **holy** [see sacr-al]
≈sanct: sanction, sanctimonious,
sanctimony
≈sanctu: sanctuary, sanctum,
Sanctus
≈sancti-: sanctified, sanctify
- sanct: sacrosanct

[variant forms: corposant;
Sangreal—the Holy Grail]
[phrase: sanctum sanctorum]

san-e: healthy

≈san-e: sanative, sane, sanicle,
sanity

≈sanit-ary: sanitarian, sanitary,
sanitation

≈sanit-: sanitarium, or, sanatorium

- san-e: insane, insanity

- sanitary: insanitary, unsanitary

sang-uin-e: blood

≈sang: sangaree, sangria

≈sanguin-e: sanguinaria,
sanguinary, sanguine,
sanguineous, sanguinolent

- sanguine: consanguine,
ensanguine, exsanguine

- sanguineous: consanguineous
[variant form: sang-froid]

sans: French: **without**
sans-culotte, sans-doute, sans
genre, sans pareil, sans
reproche, sans-serif, sans souci

SANSEI: Japanese: *san*, three + *sei*,
generation; a native American or
Canadian citizen whose
grandparents were Japanese
immigrants

SANSKRIT: lit., made together; well-
arranged; the language of poetry;
so called in distinction to Prakrit,
the common spoken language

SANTA FE, NM: lit., holy faith;
capital of New Mexico

sap: **taste, know** [see savor]

≈sapi-d: sapid, sapient, sapiential

≈sapor: sapor, saporosity,
saporous

≈sapori-: saporific
[variant forms: savant; insipid]
[phrases: savoir faire, savoir vivre;
Homo sapiens]

sapon: **soap**

≈sapon: saponaceous, saponin

≈sapon-: saponite (a soft rock)

≈saponi-: saponify

[variant form: soap]

sapr-o: rotten

≈sapr-: sapremia

≈sapro-: saprobic, saprogenic,
saprolite, sapropel,
saprophagous, saprophyte,
saprozoic

- saprobic: polysaprobic

sarc-o: flesh

≈sarc: sarcasm, sarcastic, sarcous

≈sarc-: sarcoidosis, sarcoma

≈sarco-: sarcocarp, sarcoderm,
sarcoglia, sarcology,
sarcomere, sarcophagus

- sarc-a: anasarca, ectosarc,
coelosarc, perisarc

- sarcoma: angiosarcoma,
liposarcoma, osteosarcoma

- sarcosis: syssarcosis

SARDONIC: from a Sardinian herb,
which when chewed supposedly
distorted the chewer's face;
bitterly ironic, sarcastic

SARI: Hindi; from Sanskrit *sati*; the
principal outer garment of a
woman of India and Pakistan

sartor: **to patch, tailor**
sartor, sartorial, sartorius

SATELLITE: from Etruscan; orig., an
attendant, guard; a moon
revolving around another planet;
other meanings

sat-i: complete, enough, full

≈sat-e: sate; satiable, satiate,
satiety

- satia-: insatiable, insatiate

≈satir-e: satire, satirical, satirist,
satirize

≈satis-: satisfaction, satisfactory,
satisfy

- satis-: dissatisfaction,
dissatisfied, dissatisfy

- satisfactory: dissatisfactory,
unsatisfactory

≈satur: saturable, saturate,
saturation

- saturate: supersaturate
  [variant form: asset]
SATIN: from Arabic *atlas zaituni*,
  satin of Zaitun, medieval name of
  Quanzhou, China, where the fabric
  was first made
SATRAP: Persian *xsathra*: dominion;
  protector of the land; a ruler of the
  land
SATURDAY: from Latin *Saturni dies*,
  Saturn's Day; translates Greek
  hemera Khronu, Cronus' Day
SATURNINE: morose, sluggish,
  taciturn; having lead poisoning;
  see jovial; mercurial
SATYRIASIS: abnormal desire for
  sexual intercourse by a man; from
  satyr, a class of woodland deities
sauer: German: **sour**
  sauerbraten, sauerkraut
sault: see salt for *assault*
SAUNA: Finnish: a very hot bath
saur-o: **lizard**
≈saur: saurian
≈sauro-: saurognathous, sauropod
- saur: dinosaur, hadrosaur,
  elasmosaur, ichthyosaur,
  pterosaur, tyrannosaur
- sauros: brontosauros
- saurus: allosaurus, dinosaurus,
  dipsosaurus, dolichosaurus,
  eosaurus, plesiosaurus,
  stegosaurus
SAVANNAH, GA: may be from
  Spanish *sabana*, earlier Carib
  zavana, a treeless plain, or
  relatively flat, open region
savor: **taste, smell**; akin to *sapor*, to
  taste [see sapor]
  savor, savories, savory
{word note: savories: in Canada and
  England, a small, highly seasoned
  portion of food served at the end
  of a meal or as an appetizer}
sax-i: **rock**
  saxtile; saxicolous, saxifrage,
  saxify, saxigenous, saxitoxin
  [variant form: sassafras]

say: **to do**
  assay, essay, essayist,
  essayistic
SAYONARA: Japanese *sayo*, that way
  + *nara*, if; if it is to be that way;
  goodbye, farewell
scab-r: **scab**
≈scab-r: scab, scabby, scabies,
  scabietic, scabious, scabrous
≈scabi-: scabicide
scal-e^1: **to climb; ladder**
≈scal: scalage, scalar, scale
≈scarlari-: scalariform
≈scan: scan, scandent
≈scandal: scandal, scandalize,
  scandalous
≈scans: scansion, scansorial
- scend: ascend, descend,
  condescend, transcend
- scend-: condescendence,
  condescending, descender,
  descendible, transcendentalism
- scendant: ascendant, descendant
- scendent: ascendent,
  interdescendent, transcendent
- scension: ascension,
  condescension, descension
- scent: ascent, descent
  [variant forms: echelon, escalade,
  escalate, escalation, Escalator®;
  slander, slanderous]
{word note: scandal: lit., cause for
  stumbling; orig., unseemly
  conduct of a religious person that
  discredits religion or causes moral
  lapse of another}
scal-e^2: **shell**
  scale—one meaning, scallop,
  escallop
SCALENE: uneven, as scalene
  muscles, or scalene triangles
SCALLION, SHALLOT: onionlike plants
  from Ascalon, a city in Philistia
scaph-o: **ship, trough**
≈scaph: scaphism, scaphite
≈scaph-: scaphoid

≈scapho-: scaphocephaly,
scaphopod, scaphosepalum

SCAPULA: lit., spade, from use of the
bone as a spade; the shoulder
blade

scari: to scratch, sketch
scarification, scarificator,
scarify

SCATHE: from Old Norse *skatha*,
harm: to denounce fiercely

scato: feces, excrement
scatoma; scatology,
scatophagous, scatophilia,
scatophobia
[variant form: skatole]

scel-o: leg
scelotyrbe; isosceles,
loxosceles
[variant root: triskelion]

scen-e[1]: from *caenum*, filth
obscene, obscenity

scen-e[2]: covered place, tent, stage

≈scen-e: scena, scenario, scene,
scenery, scenic

≈sceno-: scenograph,
scenography

- scenium: parascenium,
postscenium, proscenium

SCEPTER: lit., a staff to lean on; a rod
or staff, highly ornamented, held
by rulers on ceremonial occasions
as a symbol authority; as a verb, to
furnish with a scepter; invest with
royal or imperial authority

SCHADENFREUDE: German: glee at
another's misfortunes

SCHATCHEN: a Jewish marriage
broker or matchmaker

schem-a: form, appearance

≈shema: schema, schematic,
schematism, schematize

≈schem-e: scheme, scheming

≈schemato-: schematograph

scent: see scal-e[1] for ascent, descent

SCHENECTADY, NY: Dutch form of
Mohawk *skahnehati*, "on the other
side of the pines"

scherz-o: jest, lively [music terms]
scherzando, scherzo

schiz-o: to split

≈schiz-: schizoid, schizont

≈schizo-: schizocarp, schizocyte,
schizogamy, schizogenesis,
schizogony, schizophrenia,
schizophyte, schizopod,
schizothymia

≈schis: schism, schismatic, schist

≈schisto-: schistosome,
schistosomiasis
[variant forms: schist, schedule]

SCHLEMIEL: or schlemihl; Yiddish;
from Hebrew (Num. 1:6); an
ineffectual, bungling person

SCHLEP: Yiddish *shlepn*, to drag; as a
noun, an ineffectual person

SCHLIEREN: German: streaks; small
streaks or masses in igneous rocks

SCHMALTZ: Yiddish; from German;
lit., rendered fat; highly
sentimental and banal music,
literature, etc.

schol: school; Greek for *leisure*,
that in which leisure time was
used in ancient Greece

≈scholi: scholiast, scholium

≈scholar: scholar, scholarly

≈scholas: scholastic,
scholasticate, scholasticism
[variant forms: school; Yiddish:
shul; French: école; Spanish:
escuela]

SCHOOL: from Dutch *scole*, a large
group, mass, crowd, as *a school of
fish*; also, shoal

SCHOONER: prob. from Scottish *scun*,
to skip a flat stone across water; a
sailing vessel; also, the sturdy
covered wagon used by pioneers
to cross the American prairies

sci[1]: to know

≈scien: science, sciental,
scientism, scientist;
scilicet—science + license

≈scienti-: scientific

- science: with prefixes:
  conscience, nescience,
  omniscience, prescience,
  protoscience, pseudoscience
- science: with combining forms:
  geoscience, neuroscience
- scient: nescient, omniscient
- scientious: conscientious
- scionable: unconscionable
- scious: conscious,
  subconscious, unconscious
- scititious: adscititious
  [variant form: nice]
  [phrase: scire facias]

sci²: shadow
  scimachy; episcia
  [variant form: squirrel: lit.,
  shadow tail]

sciat: hip
  sciatic, sciatica

SCIMITAR: from Persian *shimshir*: a
  short, curved sword with an edge
  on the convex side, used chiefly
  by Turks and Arabs

scind: see sciss for *rescind*

scinti-: spark
≈scintilla-te: scintilla, scintillant,
  scintillate, scintillated,
  scintillating, scintillation,
  scintillator, scintillous
≈scinti-: scintigram, scintigraphy,
  scintiscanner
≈scintillo-: scintillometer,
  scintilloscope
  [variant forms: stencil, tinsel]

SCION: from Old English *kith*, sprig;
  a shoot or bud of a plant; also, a
  descendant

scirr: see sclera-o

sciss: to cut
≈sciss: scissile, scission, scissor,
  scissors
- scissa: abscissa
- scissile: abscissile,
  circumscissile
- scission: abscission, rescission

- scind: abscind, exscind,
  interscind, prescind, rescind
  [variant forms: scythe, shingle—
  one meaning]

scler-o: hard
≈scler: sclera, sclerite, sclerosed,
  sclerosis, sclerotic, sclerotium,
  sclerous
≈scler-: sclerenchyma, scleritis,
  scleroid, scleroma
≈sclero-: scleroderma,
  sclerodermatous, sclerometer,
  scleroprotein, sclerotomy
- sclerosis: arteriosclerosis,
  atherosclerosis, otosclerosis,
  phlebosclerosis
≈scirrh: scirrhous, scirrhus
≈scirrh-: scirrhoid
- scirrhus: mastoscirrhus

scol-ex: worm
  scolecite, scolex; scoliosis
sconce: see cond

scop-e: to examine, see
≈scope: scope
- scop-: episcopal, episcopacy
- scope: with prefixes:
  dichroscope, endoscope,
  epidiascope, microscope,
  orthoscope, periscope,
  synchroscope, tachistoscope,
  telescope, telespectroscope
- scope: with combining forms:
  aeroscope, anemoscope,
  arthroscope, cystoscope
≈dichroscope, gastroscope,
  gyroscope, horoscope,
  hydroscope, hygroscope,
  kaleidoscope, kinescope,
  laryngoscope, nephoscope,
  oscilloscope, otoscope
≈pharyngoscope, phonoscope,
  polariscope, resectoscope,
  retinoscope, rhinoscope,
  seismoscope, sigmoidoscope,
  statoscope, stereoscope,

stethoscope, stroboscope,
thermoscope, urethroscope,
vaginoscope
- scopic: macroscopic,
megascopic, microscopic,
orthoscopic, periscopic,
stereoscopic, telescopic
- scopy: bioscopy, cryoscopy,
radioscopy, retinoscopy,
stereoscopy, uroscopy
[variant form: bishop]
SCOPULA: in zoology, a brushlike tuft
of hairs
SCORE: from Old Norse *skor*, to cut;
a notch

scot-o: darkness
scotoma, scotopia;
scotophobia, scototherapy
scout: see auscult
SCRAP, SCRAPE: from Old Norse;
orig., to cut

scrib-e: to write
≈scrib-e: scribal, scribble,
scribbler, scribe
- scribable: ascribable,
circumscribable, indescribable
- scribe: ascribe, circumscribe,
describe, inscribe, prescribe,
proscribe, subscribe,
superscribe, transcribe
≈scrip-t: scrip, scripsit, script,
scriptorium, scripture
- script: with prefixes: adscript,
conscript, nondescript,
postscript, prescript, rescript,
superscript
- script: with combining forms:
manuscript
- scriptible: prescriptible,
imprescriptible
- scription: ascription,
conscription, description,
inscription, prescription,
proscription, rescription,
superscription, transcription,
trendscription (a medical term)

- scriptive: ascriptive,
circumscriptive, descriptive,
inscriptive, prescriptive,
rescriptive
[variant forms: escritoire,
scrivener, serif, shrift,
shrive; Spanish: escritorio—
writing desk]
[phrases: sans serif; lex non scripta]
SCRIMMAGE: from *skirmish*; a rough-
and-tumble fight; tussle; in
football, a practice session
SCRIMSHAW: intricate decoration and
carving of bone, ivory, etc., as of
whales and walruses, done esp. by
sailors on long voyages
SCRIMP: Scandinavian: to shrink
SCROBICULATE: in biology, pitted or
furrowed
SCROFULOUS: morally corrupt; *scrofa*
in Latin meant "breeding sow";
scrofula, a diminutive, meant "a
little pig." It is possible that the
uncleanliness of pigs led to the
meaning of scrofulous.
SCROTUM: testicle sac

scrup: small sharp, rough stone
scruple, scrupulous,
unscrupulous

scrut: trash
scrutable, scrutinize, scrutiny;
inscrutable
SCUBA: acronym for <u>s</u>elf-<u>c</u>ontained
<u>u</u>nderwater <u>b</u>reathing <u>a</u>pparatus
SCUD: to run or move swiftly; glide
or skim along easily; a sudden
gust of wind; a particular missile

sculpt: to carve
sculpt, sculptor, sculpture,
sculpturesque; sculpsit
[variant form: scalpel]

scur-e: to cover
- scur-e: obscurant,
obscurantism, obscuration,
obscurity, obscure
- scuro: chiaroscuro

scurril-e: vulgar, coarse
scurrile, scurrility, scurrilous

scu-te: **shield**, **plate**
≈scut-e: scutage, scutate, scute, scutum
≈scutell: scutellate, scutellation, scutellum
≈scuti-: scutibranch, scutiferous, scutiform, scutigerous
[variant forms: écu, escudo, scudo; esquire, squire]

scyph-ist: **cup**
scyphus; scyphistoma; scyphozoan

se-: **apart**
≈se: secede, secern, secession, seclude, seclusion, secret, secretary, secrete, secure, seduce, sedulity, sedulous, segregate, select, separate
≈sed-: variant of *se-*: sedition
search: see circ

seb: **tallow**
≈seb: sebaceous, sebum
≈sebi-: sebiferous, sebiparous
≈sebo-: seborrhea, sebotropic
[variant form: suet]

sect¹: **to follow**
≈sect: sect, sectarian
≈second: second, secondary
≈secund: secund, secundines
- s-ecu-: executant, executer, executor, executory, executrix
- s-ecute: execute, persecute, prosecute
- s-ecution-er: consecution, execution, persecution; executioner
- s-ecutive: consecutive, executive, inconsecutive
≈segu-e: segue, seguidilla
≈sequ: sequacious, sequel, sequela, sequence, sequencer, sequent, sequential, sequester, sequestration
- sequential-: inconsequential
- sequi-: obsequies, obsequious

- sequence: consequence, subsequence
- sequent: consequent, inconsequent, subsequent
- suan: pursuance, pursuant
- sue: ensue, pursue
≈suit: suit, suitable, suite, suitor
- suit: pursuit
[variant forms: exequatur, extrinsic, intrinsic; pursuivant; secundum; sue]
[phrases: en suite; nolle prosequi, non prosequitur, non sequitur]

sect²: **to cut**
≈sec: secant, secateurs
- secant: cosecant
≈sect: section, sector
- sect: bisect, dissect, exsect, insect, intersect, quadrisect, resect, transect, trisect
- sect-: dissected; insectarium, insectile
- secti-: insecticide, insectivore
- section: with prefixes: dissection, exsection, intersection, resection
- section: with combining forms: venesection, vivisection
- sector: dissector, prosector
- sectoscope: resectoscope
≈segment-: segment, segmental, segmentation
[variant forms: sail, sickle]

secul: **age**, **generation**; extended to mean world, worldly
≈secular: secular, secularism, secularity, secularities, secularize
- secular-: supersecular, unsecularize
[variant form: siècle]

sed-ent: **to sit**
≈sed: sedan, sedate, sedative, sedentary, sedilia
≈sediment: sediment, sedimentary, sedimentation

≈sedimento-: sedimentology
- sed-e: supersede, supersedeas
≈sess: sessile, session
- sess: assess, obsess, possess,
  dispossess, repossess
- session: intersession, obsession,
  possession, supersession
- sessive: obsessive, possessive
- sessorial: insessorial
- sid-: insidious, presidio,
  presidium, subsidiary,
  subsidize, subsidy
- side: preside, reside, subside
- siden-: residency, residential,
  residentiary
- sidence: dissidence, residence
- sident: dissident, president,
  resident
- sidu-e: assiduity, assiduous,
  residual, residuary, residue,
  residuum
  [variant forms: assize, excise—
  one meaning; séance, seat, see,
  sejant, or sejeant, settle, sewer—
  one meaning, siege, size; besiege,
  cease: surcease: see supersede]
[NB: obsidian—stone of Obsius;
  finder of the stone in Ethiopia]
SEERSUCKER: Hindi *shirshaker*; from
  Persian *shir u shakr*, milk and
  sugar; a type of fabric
sei: Japanese: **generation**
  sansei, issei, nisei
seism-o: **earthquake, to shake**
≈seism: seism, seismal, seismic,
  seismical, seismicity
≈seismo-: seismogram,
  seismograph, seismology,
  seismometer, seismosaur,
  seismoscope
- seism: bathyseism, bradyseism,
  megaseism, microseism,
  myoseim—medical term,
  teleseism
- seismal: coseismal, isoseismal,
  teleseismal

seleno-: **moon**
≈selen: selenium
≈seleno-: selenocentric,
  selenodesy, selenography,
  selenology
- selene: paraselene, periselene
sema: **sign**
≈sem: semantic, semantics,
  sematic, semiotics
- sematic: aposematic
≈sema-: semaphore
≈semasio-: semasiology
≈semio-: semiology
- semy: monosemy, polysemy
  [variant form: semiotics]
semen: **seed**
≈semen: semen
≈semina-te: seminal, seminar,
  seminarian, seminary,
  seminate, semination
≈semin-: seminoma
≈semini-: seminiferous,
  seminification
- seminate: disseminate,
  inseminate
- seminule: disseminule
  [variant form: semé]
semi-: **half, partly, twice in a**
  specified period, lower
≈semi-: semiannual,
  semicentennial, semicircle,
  semidiameter, semidiurnal,
  semidome, semilunar: half
≈semi-: semiprecious: lower
≈semi-: semiarid,
  semiautonomous,
  semicivilized, semicolon,
  semiconscious: partly
≈sin-: variation of *semi-*: sinciput:
  half
[NB: sincere is not related]
semper: **always**
  semper fidelis, semper paratus,
  sempiternal— semper + eternal
  [variant forms: sempre; Spanish:
  siempre]

sen: old
≈senat-e: senate, senator,
   senatorial
≈senes: senescent, seneschal
≈senil-e: senile, senility
≈senior: senior, seniority
   [variant forms: sir, sire; Spanish:
   señor, señora, señorita; French:
   seigneur, seignior, seigniorage,
   seigniory; Portuguese: senhor,
   senhora, senhorita]
senc-e: to be [see esse]
- sence: absence, essence,
   quintessence
- sent: absent, present
   [variant form: interest]
   [phrase: in absentia]
sens-e: to feel, sense
≈sensat-e: sensate, sensation,
   sensational, sensationalism,
   sensationalize
≈sens-e: sense, senseless,
   sensibility, sensible
≈sensitiv-e: sensitive, sensitivity
≈sensitize: sensitize
≈sensito-: sensitometer
≈sensor-y: sensor, sensorium,
   sensory
≈sensori-: sensorimotor,
   sensorineural, sensorivascular,
   sensorivasomotor
≈sensu-al: sensual, sensuality,
   sensualize, sensuous
- sens-: consensual, desensitize,
   dissension, insensate
- sensible: insensible,
   supersensible, unsensible
- sensical: nonsensical
- sensitive: hypersensitive,
   hyposensitive, insensitive,
   oversensitive
- sensory: chemosensory,
   extrasensory, intersensory
- sensus: consensus, dissensus
≈sent: sentence, sententious;
   sentry

≈senti: sentience, sentient,
   sentinel
≈sentiment: sentiment,
   sentimental, sentimentality
- sent: assent, consent, dissent,
   resent
- sent-: consentaneous, dissenter,
   dissentientious, presentiment,
   resentful, resentment
- sentation: assentation,
   presentation, representation
- sentient: dissentient, insentient
   [variant forms: scent;
   French: ressentiment]
sepal: sepal; from "a covering"
≈sepal: sepal
≈sepal-: sepaloid
- sepalous: with prefixes:
   asepalous, antesepalous,
   antisepalous, aposepalous,
   disepalous, episepalous,
   monosepalous,
   oppositisepalous,
   polysepalous, synsepalous,
   tetrasepalous, trisepalous
- sepalous: with combining forms:
   gamosepalous, oligosepalous
sep-s: putrefaction
≈sep-sis: sepia, sepsis
- sepsis: asepsis, antisepsis
≈septic: septic
≈septi-: septicidal
≈septic-: septicemia
- septic: aseptic, antiseptic
sept[1]: enclosure, divider
≈sept: sept, septarium, septum
≈septi-: septicidal, septifragal
≈septo-: septonasal
- sepiment: dissepiment
sept[2]: seven
≈sept: September, septenary[1],
   septet, septillion, septime
≈sept-: septenary[2], septennial
≈septi-: septifarious, septifluous,
   septilateral

≈septu-: Septuagint, septuple, septuplet
[variant form: settecento]
SEPULCHER: from *sepelire*, to bury; a burial place
SEQUIN: Arabic: a mint, small coin; now, a shiny ornament or spangle
ser: **locked**; Turkish: palace
seraglio, serai, serried
SERAPHIM: Hebrew: heavenly being
SERENDIPITY: unexpected good luck; from a Persian fairy tale: *The Three Princes of Serendip* (Sri Lanka)
seren-e: evening, calm; from *xeros*, dry
serenade, serenata, serene, serenity
seric: silk; from *Seres*, a people of East Asia, probably China
≈seric: sericeous, sericin
≈seri-: sericulture, serigraph
≈seric-: sericite
≈serine: serine
[variant form: serge]
SERMON: a talk; discourse; from IE *swer-*, to speak; which also yields *swear*

serp: **to crawl, creep**
serpent, serpentine, serpigo
serra: **a saw**; thus, notched
≈serr-ate: serranid, serrate, serrated, serration
≈serrulat-e: serrulate, serrulation
- serrate: biserrate, monoserrate
[variant forms: cero, sear—one meaning, sierra; Sierra Leone, Sierra Madre, Sierra Nevada]
s-er-t: **to join, fasten together**
≈ser-e: sere—one meaning, series
≈serial: serial, serialism
≈seriat-e: seriate, seriatim
≈sertularian: sertularian
- sere: subsere, xerosere
-s-ert: assert, desert—one meaning, exert, exsert, insert
- sertation: dissertation

- serted: exserted, inserted
- s-ertion: exertion, exsertion, inexertion, insertion
ser-um: **bodily fluid**
≈ser: serous, serum
≈sero-: seroculture, serocystic, serofluid, serology, serofibrous, seropurulent
- serum: antiserum
[variant form: sérac]
serv-e[1]: **to serve**
≈serv-e: servant, serve, server
≈servi: service, serviette, servile, serving, servitor, servitude
- serve: deserve, disserve, subserve
- serv-: deserving, subservience
- service: disservice, in-service, interservice, reservice
- sert: desert—one meaning, dessert
[variant forms: sergeant, concierge, serf, sirvientes; Italian: ciao—see separate entry]
{word note: dessert: from Old French *desservir*, to clear the table}
serv-e[2]: **to keep watch**
- serv-: observant, observational, observer, preservative, reserved, reservist, reservoir
- servance: observance, inobservance
- servation: observation, preservation, reservation
- servatory: conservatory, observatory
- serve: conserve, observe, preserve, reserve
sesqui-: **more than half, one and a half**
sesquibasic, sesquicarbonate, sesquicentennial, sesquihora, sesquihydrate, sesquilepidous, sesquioxide, sesquipedality,

sesquipedalian, sesquiplicate,
sesquitone

set-ac: bristles

≈seta: seta, setaceous

≈seti-: setiferous, setiform,
setigerous

- setum: equisetum

sever: to separate; see se-, apart +
par-e[1], to set in order

≈sever: sever, severable, several,
severally, severality, severance

- sever-: dissever, disseverance

sever-e: earnest, strict; lit., not
friendly; from se-, apart + IE wer-,
friendly

≈sever-e: severe, severity

- severance: perseverance

- severate: asseverate,
perseverate

- severation: asseveration,
disseveration, perseveration

- severe: persevere

sewer, sewage: see aqu-a

sexton: see sacr-a

sex-t: six, sixth, sixty

≈sex: sext, sextant, sextet,
sextile, sextillion

≈sex-: sexennial

≈sexa-: sexagenarian,
Sexagesima, sexagesimal

≈sexto-: sextodecimo

≈sextu-: sextuple, sextuplet

≈senary: senary

≈sest: sestet, sestina

[variant forms: semester;
Spanish: siesta] [NB: sexton]

{word note: siesta: Spanish; orig.,
siesta hora, sixth hour (from
sunrise); therefore, the hottest part
of the day, a time to rest; compare
calm}

**sex-ual: possibly from secare, to
cut, divide**

≈sex: sex, sexed, sexiness,
sexism, sexless, sexuality,
sexualize, sexy

- sex: intersex, unisex

- sexual: asexual, ambisexual,
amphisexual, antisexual,
bisexual, contrasexual,
heterosexual, homosexual,
hypersexual, intersexual,
nonsexual, pansexual,
parasexual, transsexual,
unisexual

SHADOOF: Arabic; a device for
raising water; used in irrigation

SHALOM: Hebrew: peace, a greeting;
see salaam

SHAMAN: Russian; orig. from
Sanskrit: Buddhist ascetic; a priest
or medicine man

SHAMAS: Hebrew: servant, sexton

SHAMBLES: orig., a bench for
displaying fresh meat; disorder

SHAMPOO: Hindi champo, imperative
of champna, to press, massage the
head

SHAMROCK: Irish: clover

SHANTY: Canadian French:
workshop; lumberers' quarters

SHAWL: Urdu for Indian town of
Shaliat; a shoulder wrap

SHEBOYGAN, WI: Menomini: hearing
distance through the woods

SHED: as a noun, from "shade,
shadow, shady"

SHEIK: Arabic: old man

SHEKEL: Hebrew: to weigh; an
ancient unit of weight used by
Hebrews, Babylonians, etc.; equal
to about half an ounce

SHELTER: Middle English: shield
troops

SHERIF: Arabic: sharif, lit., noble; an
Arab prince or chief

SHERIFF: Middle English: shire,
county + reeve, officer

SHERBET: Arabic: syrup; a frozen
dessert

SHERRY: from Xeres, now Jerez,
Spain; lit., Caesar's town

SHIATSU: Japanese shi, finger + atsu,
pressure + ryoho, treatment; finger
pressure treatment

SHIBBOLETH: Hebrew: stream: a test word

SHIELING: Scottish: pasture; a shepherd's rude hut or cottage

SHIITAKE: Japanese: a particular type of mushroom

SHILLELAGH: from Shillelagh, a village in Ireland; a club or cudgel

SHILLY-SHALLY: acting in a vacillating manner; a reduplication of "Shall I or shall I not?"

SHINDIG: a dance, party, entertainment or other gathering, esp. of an informal kind; prob. from "a kick in the shin," which could likely happen at a square dance with amateur dancers

SHINTO: Japanese *shin*, god + *to*, way; god-way; a principal religion of Japan

SHIVA: from Hebrew for "seven"; in Judaism, the formal mourning period of seven days

SHIVAREE: altered from French *charivari*; orig. Greek *karebaria*, headache; a noisy demonstration or celebration; esp. a mock serenade to a couple on their wedding night

SHOGUN: from Sino-Japanese; further from Chinese *chiang-chun*, military leader

SHOVE, SHOVEL: from Middle English *shoven*, to push

SHRAPNEL: from H. Shrapnel (1761-1842), British general who invented the explosive device

SHUFFLE: see shove, shovel

SIAL: the upper layer of the crust of the earth

sial: saliva

≈sial: sialagogue, sialoid

- sial-: asialism, antisialic

sibil: to hiss, to whistle

sibilant, sibilate; assibilate
[variant form: persiflage]

sicc: to dry

siccative; desiccant; desiccate, exsiccate

[variant form: secco]

sider[1]: star

≈sider: sidereal

≈sidero-: siderostat

- sider-: consider, desideratum, desiderative, reconsider, unconsidered

- siderable: considerable, inconsiderable

- siderate: considerate, desiderate, inconsiderate
[variant forms: desirable, desirous, desire]

sider[2]: iron

≈sider-: siderite, siderosis, siderurgy

≈sidero-: sideroblast, siderocyte, sideroderma, siderophile, siderodromophobia—fear of trains, railroads or train travel, sideromancy, siderophage

sigma: the letter *S*

≈sigma: sigma, sigmate

≈sigm-: sigmodont, sigmoid

≈sigmoido-: sigmoidoscope, sigmoidoscopic, sigmoidoscopy

sign: to mark, sign

≈sign: sign, signage, signation, signature, signet, signory

≈signal: signal, signalize, signalment

≈signi-: significance, significant, signification, signify

- sign-: designate, designing, insignia, resigned

- sign: assign, cosign, consign, countersign, design, ensign, resign

- signment: assignment, consignment

- signate: designate, obsignate

- signation: assignation, designation, obsignation, resignation, subsignation

- signi-: insignificant, presignify
  [variant forms: segno, seal,
  sealant]
  [phrases: dal segno, locus sigilli
  (L.S.)—place of the seal; often
  interpreted as legal signature,
  which, in reality, it is]
  sil: see salt for *resilient*

sil-e: pit for storage
  silage, silo; ensilage, ensile

SILHOUETTE: from Étienne Silhouette
  (1709-67), French minister of
  finance, in derogatory reference to
  his fiscal policies and to such
  amateur portraits by him, both
  regarded as inept; an outline of a
  figure, garment, etc.

sili: pod
  silicle, silicula, silique

silic-a: silica: flint, quartz
  ≈silic-a: silica, silicate, siliceous,
  silicic, silicide, silicium,
  silicon, silicone, siliculose
  ≈silic-: silicosis
  ≈silici-: siliciferous, silicify

silv: trees, forest
  ≈silva: silva, silvical
  ≈silvi-: silivicide, silvicolous,
  silviculture
  ≈sylva: sylvan, sylvan, sylvatic
  [variant form: savage—belonging
  to the woods; wild]
  [state: Pennsylvania—lit., Penn's
  woods; from William Penn,
  founder of the colony; so named
  against his wishes, because of his
  modesty]

simil: same
  ≈similar: similar, similarity
  ≈simil-e: simile, similitude
- simil-e: dissimilarity,
  dissimilulate, verisimilitude;
  facsimile
- similar: dissimilar, verisimilar
- similate: assimilate, dissimilate
- similation: assimilation,
  dissimilation, malassimilation

≈sembl: semblable, semblance
- semble: assemble, disassemble,
  dissemble, ensemble, resemble
≈simul: simulacrum, simulant,
  simulate, simultaneous,
  simulation, simulator
≈simul-: simulcast
- simulate: dissimulate
  [variant forms: seem, seeming,
  seemly, some]

simpl-e: *single,* **one** + *ply,* **to fold**
  [see pli]
≈simple: simple, simpleton,
  simplex, simply
≈simpli: simplicity, simplist,
  simplistic
≈simpli-: simplify
≈single: single, singlet
≈singular: singular, singularity,
  singularize

sine: without
  sinecure, sinecurism
  [variant forms: sunder, sundry]
  [phrases: sine die, sine prole,
  sine qua non]

sin-e: bend, curve
  ≈sin-e: sine, sinuate, sinuated,
  sinuosity, sinuose, sinuous,
  sinus, sinusal
  ≈sinu-: sinupalliate
  ≈sinus-: sinusitis, sinusoid
- sine: cosine, homolosine
- sinuate: insinuate

sinist-ro: left, left-hand
  ≈sinist-r: sinister, sinistral,
  sinistrous
  ≈sinistro-: sinistrodextral,
  sinistrorse—*rse* from *verse*
- sinister: ambisinister

siopesis: to be silent
  aposiopesis—a sudden breaking
  off of a thought in the middle of a
  sentence as if one were unable or
  unwilling to continue, e.g., the
  horrors I saw there—but I dare not
  tell them

sip: to throw
dissipate, dissipated,
dissipation

siphon-o: tube
siphon; siphonophore,
siphonostele

SIROCCO: Arabic for the east, or
toward the rise of the sun; a
steady, hot, oppressive wind

sist: see stan-d for resist, exist

SISYPHEAN: from Sisyphus; endless
and toilsome

sito: food, grain [see parasite]
sitology; parasite

sit-u: to place; compare *position*,
under pose
site, situate, situated, situation
[phrase: in situ]

skel: see sceles for triskelion

skeleton: dried up; originally
skeleton soma, dried-up body
skeleton; endoskeleton,
exoskeleton

skeptic, skeptical: see speci

SKIRMISH: from Old High German
skirmjan, to protect; a brief fight
or encounter between small
groups; see *scrimmage*

SKOAL: Danish: peace, a greeting;
see shalom, salaam

SKUNK: American Indian Abenaki
segogw

SLAINTE: Irish: to your health: a
toast; see skoal

SLALOM: Norwegian: sloping trail;
thus, a downhill ski race over a
zigzag course marked by flag-
topped poles; as a verb, to take
part in a slalom

SLOGAN: Gaelic: battle cry

SLY: *sly, slaughter,* and *slay* are from
an Indo-European root that means
to hit; cognate of Irish *slace*,
sword

SMITH: orig., a metalworker, e.g.,
blacksmith (iron), coppersmith,
goldsmith, locksmith, metalsmith,
tinsmith, silversmith

SMITHEREENS: from Irish *smidirini*,
fragments, little bits

SMITHSONIAN Institution: in
Washington, DC; named after
James Smithson (d. 1829), a
British scientist, and the
institution's first benefactor

SMORGASBORD: Swedish: buttered
goose board

SMORREBROD: Danish: buttered bread

SMUG: probably from Low German
smuk, trim, neat; has come to
mean self-satisfied to an annoying
degree: an example of pejoration

SNICKERSNEE: Dutch: thrust cut: a
large knife used as a weapon

SNOOP: Dutch *snoepen*, to eat snacks
on the sly; to look about in a
sneaking, prying way; as a noun, a
person who snoops

SNORKEL: German: breathing tube;
related to "snore"

sob-r: without drink; from *sed-*,
without + *ebrius*, drunk
sober; sobriety, insobriety

SOBRIQUET: French; orig., chuck
under the chin; nickname

SOCCER: altered from "as<u>soci</u>ation"
football

soci-o: companion
≈soci: sociable, social, socialism,
sociality, socialize; societal,
society
≈socio-: sociobiology,
sociocultural, socioeconomic,
sociogram, sociolinguistics,
sociology, sociometry,
sociopath
- soci-: dissociable, dissocial,
phytosociology
- sociate: associate, consociate,
dissociate, disassociate
- sociation: association,
dissociation; photodissociation

SODALITY: fellowship;
companionship; an association or
brotherhood; IE base *swedh-* also
yields ethical

SOIGNÉ (male), SOIGNÉE (feminine): well-groomed; sophisticated

sol: sun
≈sol: sol, solar, solarium
≈sol-: solstice
- sol: girasol, parasol
- solar: subsolar
- solat-e: insolate insolation
{word notes: sol: the basic monetary unit of Peru; from the radiant sun used as as emblem on one side; parasol: with para-, protection, that which protects against the sun; an umbrella, lit., small shade}

sol-e: to comfort
≈sol: solace
- sol-e: consolation, consolatory, inconsolable, disconsolate; console

SOLECISM: from Soloi, city in Cilicia; speaking incorrectly

solen-o: a channel
≈solen: solenoid, solenonychia
≈soleno-: solenocyte, solenoglyph

sol-i[1]: alone, one
≈sol: solo, solus
≈soli: solitaire, solitary, soliton, solitude
≈sol-: solipcism
≈soli-: soliloquize, soliloquy
- solat-e: desolate, desolation

sol-i[2]: ground, floor, soil
solum; solifluction; entresol
[variant forms: soil, subsoil, sullage, sullen, sully]

sol-i[3]: whole, solid
≈sold: solder, soldier, soldiery
≈soli-: solicit, solicitor, solicitous, solicitude
≈solid: solid, solidago, solidarity, solidity, solidus
≈solidi-: solidify
- solidate: consolidate
[variant forms: insouciant; solemn: orig., yearly festival,

thus stately; solemnity, solemnize, solemnify; see ann]

SOLON: from Solon, Athenian statesman; a wise lawmaker or legislator

solv-e: to loosen
≈solv-e: solvable, solvate, solve, solvent
- solve: absolve, dissolve, resolve; resolved
- solvable: insolvable, irresolvable, resolvable
≈solub-le: solubility, soluble
- soluble: dissoluble, indissoluble, insoluble, irresoluble, resoluble
≈solut-e: solute, solution
- sol: aerosol, plasmasol, plastisol
- solut-: absolutism; absolutive
- solute: absolute, dissolute, irresolute, resolute
- solution: absolution, dissolution, resolution
- solvency: insolvency
- solvent: dissolvent, insolvent, resolvent
[variant form: assoil]

soma-t-o: body
≈som: soma—one meaning, somatic, somite
≈somato-: somatogenic, somatology, somatoplasm, somatopleure, somatostatin, somatotropin, somatotype
- somatic: psychosomatic
- somatism: metasomatism
- some: with prefixes: acrosome, aposome, autosome, episome, heterosome, melanosome, microsome, monosome, polysome
- some: with combining forms: calciosome, chromosome, desmosome, hyalosome, hydrosome, liposome,

nucleosome, schistosome,
tryponosome
- somiasis: schistosomiasis,
trypanosomiasis
- somic: centrosomic,
chromosomic, macrosomic,
microsomic, monosomic,
trisomic
[variant forms: sorites, sorosis,
sorus]
SOMMELIER: from *summer*, pack
horse; wine steward in restaurant
[not related to *summer*, season of
the year, which is from Sanskrit
sama, half year]
somn-i: sleep [see sopor-i]
≈somn: somnolent, Somnus,
Sominex®
≈somn-: somnambulate,
somnambulism
≈somni-: somnifacient,
somniferous, somnific,
somniloquy, somnipathy,
somniphobia
- somnia: hypersomnia,
hyposomnia, insomnia,
parasomnia
son-e: sound
≈son-e: sonance, sonant, sonata,
sonatina, sonde, sone, sonnet
≈sonic: sonic, sonicate
≈sonor: sonorant, sonority,
sonorous
≈soni-: soniferous, sonification
≈sono-: sonobuoy, sonogram
- son: unison
- sonat-e: resonator, resonate
- sonance: assonance,
consonance, dissonance,
resonance
- sonant: assonant, consonant,
dissonant, inconsonant,
resonant
- sonde: ionosonde
- sonic: hypersonic, infrasonic,
Panasonic®, quadrasonic,

subsonic, supersonic,
transonic, ultrasonic
[variant forms: sound—one of
four meanings; resound,
resounding]
[phrase: son et lumière]
SOOTH: from Old English *soth*, truth;
found in archaic *forsooth* and in
phrase *in sooth*, truly; in fact
soph-o: clever, skillful, wise
≈sophis-t: sophism, sophist,
sophistry
≈sophistica-te: sophistical,
sophisticate, sophisticated,
sophistication
≈sopho-: sophomore, sophomoric
- sopher: philosopher
- sophic-al: philosophic,
philosophical
- sophy: anthroposophy,
philosophy, theosophy
sopor-i: deep sleep [see somn-i]
sopor; soporiferous, soporific
sorites, sorosis, sorus: see soma-t-o
sorb: to suck in
≈sorb: sorbent
- sorb: absorb, adsorb, desorb,
resorb
- sorbent: absorbent, adsorbent
≈sorption: sorption
- sorption: absorption,
adsorption, desorption,
resorption
- sorptive: absorptive, resorptive
[Spanish: sorba—straw]
sord: filth
sordid, sordor
sorg: sorghum; orig., Syrian grass
sorghum, sorgo
soror-i: sister
sororal, sororate, sorority;
sororicide
[variant form: cousin]
SORRY: from Old English *sar*, sore
sort-i: lot, chance
≈sort: sort, sortie

≈sorti-: sortilege
- sort: assort, consort, resort
- sortium: consortium
- sortment: assortment
≈sorc: sorcerer, sorcery
- sorcell: ensorcell
sote-rio: to save, preserve
 soteriology; creosote
SOUCHONG: Mandarin; lit., small
 kind; black tea
SOUTACHE: Hungarian: pendant:
 braid for trimming
SOVIET: Russian: council; second
 word of CCCP, English for USSR;
 see soyuz, next entry
SOYUZ: Russian: union; first word of
 CCCP; see soviet, previous entry
SPA: from Spa, Belgium; a health
 resort
spac-e: to walk, roam; space
≈space: space
- space: aerospace, cyberspace,
 hyperspace, interspace,
 subspace
≈spatial: spatial
- s-pate: expatiate
 [variant form: patio]
SPAGHETTI: Italian: small cord; a
 form of pasta
SPANAKOPITA: Greek for a phyllo-
 spinach dish
SPANIEL: lit., Spanish; a medium-
 sized hunting dog with large,
 drooping ears; a servile, fawning
 person
spasm: to draw, pull, wrench;
 spasm
≈spasm: spasm, spasmodic
- spasm: clonospasm,
 colpospasm, cryospasm,
 logospasm, prosopospasm,
 vasospasm
 [variant form: spastic]
spatul: blade; flat blade
 spatula, spatulate
 [variant forms: epaulet, or
 epaulette, epee, or épée, espalier]

{word notes: epaulet: a shoulder
 ornament for certain uniforms,
 especially, military uniforms;
 épée: a thin, pointed sword
 without a cutting edge, like a foil
 but heavier and more rigid;
 espalier: a lattice or trellis}
speci: to see
≈special: special, specialism,
 specialist, speciality
≈speciation: speciation
≈speci-es: specie, species,
 specimen, specious
≈speci-: specific, specification,
 specificity
- special: especial, especially
≈spect: spectacle, spectacular,
 spectate, spectator, specter
- species: subspecies
- specific: conspecific,
 infraspecific, interspecific,
 intraspecific, monospecific
≈spectr: spectral, spectrum
≈spectro-: spectrogram,
 spectrograph, spectroscope,
 spectroscopy
- spectro-: telespectroscope
-s-pec-t-: expectancy, expectant,
 expectation, respectability,
 respectable, respecter,
 respecting, respectively;
 inspectorate
- spect: aspect, expect, inspect,
 introspect, prospect, respect,
 retrospect, suspect
- spectful: respectful,
 disrespectful, self-respectful,
 suspectful
- spection: inspection,
 introspection, retrospection
- spective: circumspective,
 disrespective, irrespective,
 perspective, prospective,
 respective, retrospective
- spector: inspector, prospector

- spectus: conspectus, prospectus
≈specul: specular, speculate,
  speculation, speculative,
  speculator, speculum
- spi-: espial, espionage
- spic-e: auspice, despicable,
  suspicion, perspicacious,
  perspicacity
- spicious: auspicious,
  inauspicious, suspicious
- spicuous: conspicuous,
  inconspicuous, perspicuous,
  transpicuous, unconspicuous
  [variant forms: auspex, despise;
  despite, respite, frontispiece,
  skeptic, skeptical,
  omphaloskepsis; soupçon, spice,
  spy; Spanish: espejo—mirror]
  {word note: soupçon: lit., a
  suspicion; a slight trace, as of a
  flavor; hint; suggestion; a tiny
  amount; bit}

spele-o: cave
≈spel: spelean, spelunker
≈speleo-: speleology, speleothem

sper: to hope
  desperado, desperate,
  desperation, prosper,
  prosperity, prosperous
  [variant form: despair]

sperg: to sprinkle, strew
- sperg: Asperges, aspergillum
- sperse: asperse, disperse,
  intersperse
- spersion: aspersion, dispersion
- spersorium: aspersorium

sperm-ato: seed, germ
≈sperm: sperm, spermary,
  spermatic, spermatid,
  spermatium, spermine
≈sperma-: spermaceti,
  spermagonium, spermatheca
≈spermat-: spermatoid
≈spermato-: spermatocele,
  spermatocyst, spermatocyte,
  spermatogenesis,

spermatology, spermatopathia,
  spermatophore, spermatophyte,
  spermatozoid, spermatozoon
≈spermi-: spermicide, spermiduct
≈spermio-: spermiocyte,
  spermiogenesis,
  spermiogonium, spermiogram
≈spermo-: spermoblast,
  spermogonium, spermology,
  spermophile, spermophyte,
  spermotoxin
- sperm: with prefixes: endosperm,
  episperm, mesosperm,
  monosperm, perisperm,
  polysperm
- sperm: with combining forms:
  angiosperm, chrysosperm,
  gymnosperm, oosperm,
  podosperm, pteridosperm,
  rhodosperm, zygosperm
- spermous: aspermous,
  dispermous, monospermous
sperse: see sperg for disperse
SPHACELATE: gangrenous
SPHAGNUM: kind of peat moss
  growing in bogs
sphalt: to cause to fall, injure
  asphalt—with a-, not; lit., not to
  fall; may be so named because of
  use as protective substance for
  walls

sphen-o: wedge
≈sphene: sphene
≈sphen-: sphenodont, sphenoid,
  sphenorbital
≈spheno-: sphenocephaly,
  sphenogram, sphenomorphus,
  sphenopagus
- sphenoid: bisphenoid,
  disphenoid

spher-o: ball, globe
≈spher-e: spheral, sphere,
  spherical, sphericity, spherics,
  spherule, spherulite, sphery
≈spher-: spheroid
≈sphero-: spherometer

- sphere: with prefixes: ensphere,
  exosphere, hemisphere,
  heterosphere, homosphere,
  mesosphere, microsphere
- sphere: with combining forms:
  asthenosphere, astrosphere,
  atmosphere, bathysphere,
  biosphere, chemosphere,
  chromosphere, heliosphere,
  hydrosphere, ionosphere,
  lithosphere, oosphere,
  ozonosphere, photosphere,
  planisphere, thermosphere,
  troposphere
- spheric: aspheric
  [variant forms: pearl, perlite]

sphincter: to draw close
≈sphincter: sphincter, sphincteral
≈sphincter-: sphincteralgia,
  sphincterectomy, sphincteritis,
  sphincteroid
≈sphinctero-: sphincteroplasty,
  sphincteroscope,
  sphincteroscopy,
  sphincterotomy
  [variant forms: sphinx, spinnaker]
{word notes: <u>sphinx</u>: lit., the
  strangler; <u>spinnaker</u>: a sail; said to
  be after the Sphinx, the name of a
  yacht which carried the sail}

sphygm-o: to throb; the pulse
≈sphygmic: sphygmic
≈sphygmo-: sphygmogram,
  sphygmograph,
  sphygmomanometer,
  sphygmometer
  [variant forms: asphyxia,
  asphyxiate]

spic: point
≈spic: spica, spicate; spiculate,
  spiculum, spicule
≈spin-e: spinal, spine, spinel,
  spineless, spinescent, spinet,
  spinney, spinose, spinosity,
  spinous, spinule, spiny
  [variant forms: porcupine,

  spigot, spike, spikelet,
  spikenard]

spin: to pull, drawn, spin
spin, spindle, spinner,
  spinneret, spinster
  [variant form: spider]
{word note: spinster: lit., one who
  spins; in times past, the accepted
  activity for unmarried women to
  fill their time in doing}
SPINACH: from Persian *aspanakh*
spine: see spic

spire: spike
spire; acrospire

spir-e: breath, courage, the soul
≈spir: spiracle, spiracular, spirant
≈spirit: spirit, spirited, spiritism
≈spiritu: spirituous, spiritual,
  spiritualism, spirituality,
  spiritualize, spirituel
≈spiro-: spirograph, spirometer
- spira-: aspirant, aspirate,
  conspiracy, inspirational,
  respirator
- spirable: irrespirable, respirable
- s-piration: expiration,
  inspiration, perspiration,
  respiration, transpiration
- s-piratory: expiratory,
  inspiratory, perspiratory,
  respiratory
- s-pire: aspire, conspire, expire,
  inspire, perspire, respire,
  suspire, transpire
- spirit: dispirit, dispirited,
  inspirit
  [variant forms: esprit, spiritoso,
  sprite]
  [phrase: esprit de corps: lit., the
  spirit of the body; high morale]
{word note: spirituel: French: having
  a refined nature}

spir-o: to turn, spiral
≈spir: spiral, spirea, spireme,
  spirillum, spirula
≈spir-: spiroid

240

≈spiri-: spiriferous

≈spiro- spirochete, spirochetosis

- spirin: aspirin

  [variant forms: espadrille, esparto]

  {word note: aspirin: with *a*-, without; so named (1899) by H. Dresser, German chemist, because compounded without using spirea, in which the natural acid is found}

spiss: thick, dense, tightly packed

  spissated, spissitude; conspissate, inspissate

splanchn-o: viscera

≈splanchn: splanchnic

≈splanchno-: splanchnoblastic, splanchnocele, splanchnoderm, splanchnolith, splanchnology, splanchnomegalia, splanchnopathy, splanchnopleural, splanchnoptosis, splanchnoscopy, splanchnotomy, splanchnotribe

splen: spleen

≈splen: splenetic, splenetical, splenic, splenius

≈splen-: splenodynia, splenectomy, splenectopia, splenemia, splenoid, splenoma

≈spleno-: splenoblast, splenocele, splenocyte, splenomalacia, splenomegaly

- splenic: asplenic, perisplenic

splend-i: to gleam, shine

≈splend: splendent, splendid, splendor

≈splendi-: splendiferous

- splendent: resplendent

spol: to spoil, rob

  spoliate, spoliation; despoliation

  [variant forms: spoil, spoilage]

spond: to pledge, to promise solemnly

≈spond: spondee

- spond: correspond, despond, respond

- spondence: correspondence, respondence

- spondent: correspondent, despondent, respondent

- sponder: transponder

≈spons: sponsion, sponsor

- spons-e: response, responsibility, responsory

- sponsible: responsible, irresponsible

- sponsive: responsive, irresponsive

  [variant forms: riposte; spousal, spouse; espousal, espouse]

spondyl: vertebra

≈spondyl-e: spondyle, spondylous

≈spondyl-: spondylalgia, spondylarthritis, spondylitis, spondylodynia, spondylosis

≈spondylo-: spondylolysis, spondylomalacia, spondylopathy, spondyloptosis, spondyloschisis, spondylotomy

spong: sponge

≈spong-e: sponge, sponger, spongin, spongy

≈spong-: spongoid

≈spongi-: spongiitis, spongiosis

≈spongio-: spongioblast, spongiocyte, spongioplasm

≈spongo-: spongoblast, spongology

- spongium: neurospongium, trophospongium

spontan: of one's free will

  spontaneity, spontaneous

SPOONERISM: from the Reverend Spooner who unintentionally reversed letters in words; an unintentional interchange of sounds, such as his once saying to a student, "You have tasted two worms," for "You have wasted two terms."

spor-e: to scatter, sow, seed

≈spor-e: sporadic, spore

≈spor-: sporangium

≈spori-: sporiferous

≈sporo-: sporocarp, sporocyst, sporogenesis, sporogonium, sporogony, sporophore, sporophyll, sporophyte, sporozoan, sporozoite

- spora: Diaspora
- spore: with prefixes: diaspore, endospore, exospore, microspore, teliospore
- spore: with combining forms: arthrospore, gymnospore, oospore, teleutospore, uredospore, zoospore, zygospore
- sporangium: with prefixes: macrosporangium, megasporangium, microsporangium, tetrasporangium
- sporangium: with combining form: actinosporangium, androsporangium, zoosporangium
- sporous: with prefixes: acrosporous, anisosporous, aposporous, endosporous, heterosporous, homosporous, isosporous, microsporous, polysporous
- sporous: with combining forms; angiosporous, arthrosporous, carposporous, oosporous, polysporous, zoosporous
- spory: apospory

≈sporul-e: sporulate, sporulation, sporule

SPORRAN: Gaelic: leather pouch or purse, usually covered with fur, worn hanging from the front of the belt in the dress uniform of Scottish Highlanders

spum-e: foam

spume, spumescent, spumoni; despumate

SPURIOUS: not true or genuine

SPUTNIK: Russian: co-traveler

SQUABBLE: Swedish: to quarrel

SQUALID, SQUALOR: foul or unclean; from *squalere*, to be stiff with dirt

squama: a scale, scaly

≈squam-a: squama, squamate, squamation, squamosal, squamous, squamulose

≈squamo-: squamoparietal

- squamate: desquamate, esquamate

[variant form: squarrose]

square: see quadr

staff: rod, pole (used as support)

staff; distaff

stable: see stan-d

stadium: see stan-d

stage: see stan-d

STAGNANT: adj.; without motion or current; not flowing or moving; verb: stagnate; see tank

stal: to send

- stalsis: anastalsis, bradystalsis, catastalsis, diastalsis, peristalsis, retrostalsis
- staltic: anastaltic, catastaltic, centrostaltic, diastaltic, peristaltic, sustaltic, systaltic
- stle: apostle, epistle, epistler
- stolary: epistolary
- stole: anastole, adiastole, diastole, peristole, systole
- systole: antesystole, eusystole, extrasystole, hemisystole, hypersystole, hyposystole, parasystole, hysterosystole, intersystole, parasystole, perisystole
- stolic: apostolic, diastolic, epistolic, peristolic, systolic

STALAG: German: abridgement of *Stammlager*, base camp; in WWII, a German prisoner-of-war camp

STALWART: from Old English *stathol*, foundation + *writhe*, worth; firm, resolute, robust

stamen: see stan-d

stan-d: to stand

≈stan: stance, stanza

≈stand: stand, standard, standing

- stand-ard: understand; misunderstand, substandard

- s-ist-: resistless, irresistible; resistance; resistant; existence; resistivity

- s-ist: with prefixes: assist, consist, desist, exist, insist, persist, resist, subsist

- sist: with combining form: photoresist

- s-istence: existence, insistence, persistence, subsistence

- sistency: consistency, inconsistency

- s-istent-: consistent, existent, inconsistent, inexistent, insistent, persistent; existential, existentialism

- sistible: resistible, irresistible

- s-istor: with prefixes: resistor, transistor (trans- + sist)

- s-istor: with combining forms: phototransistor, thermistor, varistor (<u>vari</u>ous + re<u>sistor</u>)

≈stab-le: stabile, stability, stabilize, stable

- stab-: constabulary, instability

- stable: constable, metastable, unstable

- stablish: establish, establishment, disestablish

≈stad: stadium, pl., stadia

- stadial: interstadial

≈stag-e: stage, stager, staging

- stage: with prefix: multistage

- stage: with combining form: uredostage

≈stall: stall, stallion

- stall-: install, installation, installment

≈stam[1]: stamen, pl., stamina, staminal[1], staminate; orig. thread; orig., warp in an upright loom; a pollen-bearing organ

≈stamini: staminiferous

≈stam[2]: stamina, staminal[2]: endurance

≈stanch: stanch, stanchion

- stance: circumstance, distance, instance, substance

- stancy: constancy, instancy

- s-tant: constant, distant, equidistant, extant, inconstant, instant

- stant-: instantaneous, instanter, instantly, substantive

- stantial: circumstantial, substantial, insubstantial, transsubstantial, uncircumstantial, unsubstantial

- stantiate: distantiate, instantiate, substantiate, transubstantiate

≈stasis: stasis

- stase: diastase

- stasy: apostasy, ecstasy, eustasy, isostasy

- stasis: with prefixes: anastasis, antistasis, apocatastasis, apostasis, catastasis, diastasis, epistasis, hemostasis, homeostasis, hypostasis, metastasis

- stasis: with combining forms: blennostasis, brachystasis, cryostasis, galactostasis, hemostasis, iconostasis, leukostasis, menostasis, morphostasis

≈stat-e: state, stately, statement; static, statics, statism, stative

≈station: station, stationary,
  stationer, stationery
- stat: with prefixes: antistat,
  autostat, barostat, hyperstat
- stat: with combining forms:
  aerostat, barostat, biostat,
  blepharostat, cephalostat,
  chemostat, cryostat, heliostat,
  hemostat, homeostat,
  humidistat, hygrostat,
  laryngostat, pyrostat, rheostat,
  thermostat
- stat-: hypostatize; somatostatin
- state: apostate, estate, instate,
  interstate, intrastate, prostate,
  tristate
- static: with prefixes: astatic,
  distatic, ecstatic, epistatic,
  orthostatic
- static: with combining forms:
  astatic, adrenostatic, aerostatic,
  algistatic, cryostatic,
  hemostatic, hydrostatic
- stationary: geostationary
≈stato-: statoblast, statocyst,
  statocyte, statolith, statometer,
  statoscope, statosphere
≈stator: stator
≈statu-e: statuable, statuary,
  statue, statued, statuesque,
  stature, status, statusy, statute,
  statutory
≈stauro-: staurolite
- staur: instauration, restaurant
  [from store]
≈stead: stead, steady, steadfast
- stead: homestead, instead
≈steer: steer, steerage
- stetric: obstetric, obstetrics,
  obstetrician
- stice: with prefixes: interstice
- stice: with combining forms:
  armistice, solstice
- stin-e: destination, destine,
  destiny, obstinacy, obstinate

- stit-: interstitial, superstition,
  superstitious; unconstitutional
- stitute: constitute, destitute,
  institute, prostitute, substitute
- stituent: constituent, substituent
- stitution: constitution,
  institution, prostitution,
  substitution
- stor-e: restoration, restorative,
  restore
  [variant forms: arrest, cost,
  étagère, etamine, contrast,
  obstacle, ostinato, oust, ouster,
  penstemon; post, praedial;
  staunch, store; Spanish:
  estancia; press—one meaning;
  rest—meaning "the remainder,"
  staid, stay—one meaning, steer,
  sterling, stet, stoa, stud, valet]
  [phrases: in statu quo, raison
  d'état, non obstante, pou sto,
  Stabat Mater; stare decisis; Statue
  of Liberty; status quo, status quo
  ante, status symbol]
  {word note: valet: varlet; vassal:
  orig., a groom, yeoman; one who
  "stood by"; a man's personal
  manservant}

stann: tin
≈stann: stannary, stannate,
  stannic, stannous
≈stanni-: stanniferous
≈stanno-: stannotype
staphylo-: grapelike[1], uvula[2]
  staphylococcus[1],
  staphylorrhapy[2]
STARBOARD: lit., steer board; right
  side of a boat or ship; from the old
  rudder being a large oar used on
  the right side of a ship
stax: to fall in drops
≈staxis: staxis (same as
  hemorrhage)
- staxis: with prefixes: apostaxis,
  epistaxis
- staxis: with combining forms:
  bronchostaxis, cystistaxis,

cystostaxis, enterostaxis,
gastrostaxis, hematostaxis,
menostaxis, metrostaxis,
urethrostaxis

steal: **to steal**
steal, stealth, stealthy

stear-o: **tallow, fat**
≈stear: stearate, stearin
≈stearo-: stearoptene;
steapsin — stearo- + pepsin
≈steat-: steatite, steatoma
≈steato-: steatoblast,
steatogenesis, steatolysis,
steatopygia, steatorrhea

stel-e: **post, slab, stem**
stele; eustele, protostele,
siphonostele

stell-i: **star**
≈stell: stellar, stellate, stellular
≈stelli-: stelliferous, stelliform
- stellat-e: constellate,
constellation
- stellar: circumstellar,
interstellar, substellar,
ultrastellar
[NB: stellionate: Scots and Roman
law: any fraud not distinguished
by a more special name]

stem-o: **to set, stand**
diastem, diastema, epistemic,
system; epistemology

sten-o: **narrow**
≈sten-: stenosed, stenosis
≈steno-: stenobath, stenocardia,
stenocephaly, stenography,
stenohaline, stenohygric,
stenophagous, stenotherm,
stenotopic, stenotype,
stenotypy, stenoxenous
STENTORIAN: from *Stentor*, in Greek
mythology, a Greek herald; very
loud

sterc-or-i: **feces, dung** [after
Sterculius, the deity of manuring]
sterculia, stercoraceous;
stercoricolous

stere-o: **hard, solid**
≈ster-e: stere, steric
≈ster-: steroid
≈stere-: stereome, stereopsis,
stereopticon
≈stereo-: stereobate,
stereochroma, stereogram,
stereograph, stereoisomer,
stereometry, stereophonic,
stereoscope, stereoscopic,
stereoscopy, stereotaxis,
stereotomy, stereotropism,
stereotype, stereotyped,
stereotypical
- steric: allosteric
- sterol: cholesterol, coprosterol,
phytosterol, tachysterol,
zoosterol
- sterone: testosterone

steril-e: **barren**
sterilant, sterilize, sterile;
desterilize

stern: **to terrify**
consternate, consternation

stern-um: **breastbone**
≈stern: sternal, sternum
- sternum: with prefixes: asternum,
entosternum, episternum,
hyposternum, mesosternum,
metasternum
- sternum: with combining forms:
ensisternum, hyosternum,
omosternum, pelvisternum,
xiphosternum
STERNUTATION: a sneeze; sneezing
STERTOR: the act of snoring
stet: see stand

stetho: **chest**
≈steth-: stethacoustic, stethalgia
≈stetho-: stethograph,
stethometer, stethomyitis,
stethophone, stethoscope,
stethoscopy, stethospasm
STEWARD: orig., a keeper of pigs
[sty + ward]

sthen-o: strength

≈sthen: sthenic

- sthene: hypersthene,
  megasthene, microsthene
- sthenia: asthenia; angiosthenia,
  ergasthenia, eusthenia,
  hypersthenia, hyposthenia,
  neurasthenia, psychasthenia
- sthenic: with prefixes: asthenic,
  hypersthenic, hyposthenic,
  megasthenic, metasthenic,
  microsthenic
- sthenic: with combining forms:
  calisthenic, myasthenic,
  myosthenic, neurasthenic,
  psychasthenic, urosthenic
- sthenics: calisthenics
- sthen-: asthenopia
- stheno-: asthenosphere
  [NB: demosthenic: from
  Demosthenes, orator]

stich-o: a row, line of poetry

≈stich: stich, stichous

≈sticho-: stichochrome,
  stichology, stichomancy,
  stichometric, stichometry,
  stichomythia, stichosome

- stic-h: acrostic, distich,
  hemistich, heptastich,
  hexastich, monostich,
  octostich, orthostich,
  pentastich, telestich, tetrastich,
  tristich
- stichous: astichous, distichous,
  monostichous, octostichous,
  orthostichous, pentastichous,
  polystichous, tetrastichous,
  tristichous
- stichy: orthostichy
  [variant form: cadastre]

stifl-e: to smother

  stifle, stifling
  [variant form: étouffée—a
  Cajun stew, the main ingredient
  of which is crayfish, or crawdads]

stigma: to prick

≈stigma: stigma, stigmatic,
  stigmatism, stigmatize

- stig-: instigate; anastigmatic;
  astigmatism; physostigmine

STILE[1]: a step or set of steps used in
  climbing over a fence or wall

STILE[2]: from Dutch *stijl*, doorpost; a
  vertical piece in a panel or frame,
  as of a door or window

still: a drop

≈still: still—one meaning

- still: distill, instill
- still-: distillate, distillation,
  distilled, distiller, distillery

stinct: to prick

- stinct: distinct, contradistinct,
  indistinct, instinct
- stinction: contradistinction,
  distinction
- stinctive: distinctive, instinctive
- sting-: distingué, distinguish,
  distinguished

s-tinct: to quench, extinguish [from
  stinguere, **to extinguish**]

- s-tinct-: extinct, extinction,
  extinctive
- s-tinguish-: extinguish,
  inextinguishable

stip: to cram, pack

  constipate, constipation,
  obstipation
  [variant forms: costive, steeve—
  one meaning, stevedore]

{word note: stevedore: from Spanish
  estivar, to stow, ram tight; lit., one
  who stows; a longshoreman}

stip-ul: orig., a small coin; bargain

  stipend, stipendiary,
  stipulate—one meaning,
  stipulation

s-tip-ul-e: stalk, straw

  stipe, stipel, stipes, stipple;
  stipular, stipulate—one
  meaning, stipule; exstipulate
  [variant form: stubble]

STIRRUP: lit., a mounting rope

s-tirp: **root**; **lower part of a tree**
extirpate, inextirpable
{word note: extirpate: to pull out by the roots; root out, as *to extirpate a bad habit*}

STOCCADO: a stab or thrust with a pointed weapon

STOCHASTIC: arising from chance

STODGY: orig., pertaining to unpalatable food; heavily built

STOIC: from the Stoics, a Greek school of philosophy; from *stoa*, Greek portico from which Zeno taught indifference to pain, joy, suffering, etc.

STOICHIOMETRY: a branch of chemistry dealing with relationships of elements

stole: see stal for diastole

stom-a: **mouth, stomach**

≈stoma: stoma, stomatal, stomatous

≈stomach: stomach, stomacher, stomachic

≈stom-: stomodaeum

≈stomat-: stomatitis

≈stomato-: stomatology, stomatopod

- stoma: scyphistoma

- stomatous: astomatous, microstomatous

- stome: cyclostome, distome, melastome, monostome, peristome

- stomium: prostomium

- stomosis: anastomosis

- stomous: with prefixes: astomous, amphistomous, microstomous, monostomous

- stomous: with combining forms: angiostomous, cyclostomous, gymnostomous, malacostomous, physostomous, saprostomous

- stomy: androstomy, angiostomy, apicostomy,

arthrostomy, bronchostomy, cavernostomy, cecostomy, enterostomy, ileostomy, ureterostomy

STONEHENGE: from Middle English *stone* + *henge*, something hanging; a circular arrangement of prehistoric megaliths on Salisbury Plain, England; see *cromlech*

stop: **to stop**
stop, estop, estoppel
{word note: estop: orig., to stop up; in law, to bar or prevent by estoppel, the barring of a person from making allegations or denials which are contrary to either a previous statement or act by that person or a previous adjudication}

store: see stan-d

STORY (of a building): murals that told a story painted on successive floors or stories of a building

STOVE: Dutch: heated room

strain: see string

strange: see extr-a

strang-le: **halter, twisted; to choke, strangle**
strangle, stranglehold; strangulate, strangury

strat[1]: **to spread, strew, stretch out; a layer** [related to strat[2]]

≈strat: stratum, pl., strata, or stratums, stratus

≈strati-: stratification, stratiform, stratify, stratigraphy

≈strato-: stratocumulus, stratopause, stratosphere

- strat-e: prostrate, prostration

- stratum: substratum, superstratum

- stratus: cirrostratus, nimbostratus

[German: *Strasse*]

[variant forms: stray, street]

{word notes: <u>stray</u>: orig., to wander in the streets; <u>street</u>: from *via strata*, paved way; word entered

Anglo-Saxon during early Roman occupation of ancient Britain}

strat[2]: **generalship; device or act of a general** [related to strat[1]]

≈strat-: stratagem [second root *agere*, to act]

≈strateg: strategic, strategist, strategy

≈strato-: stratocracy, stratocrat, stratography

STRENUOUS: requiring or characterized by great effort or energy

streper: to roar

obstreperous: noisy, boisterous, or unruly, esp. in resisting or opposing; vociferous

strepto-: twisted

streptococcus, streptokinase, streptomyces, streptomycin

stress: see string

stria: narrow groove or channel

stria, striatal, striate, striation

strict: see string

strid-ul: to make a grating noise

strident, stridor, stridulate

string: to bind, to draw together

≈string: string, stringency, stringent; stringendo

- stringent: astringent, subastringent

≈strain: strain, strained

- strain: constrain, distrain, restrain

- strain-: distrainee, restrained, restrainer

- straint: constraint, distraint, restraint

≈stress: stress, stressed-out, stressor

- stress-: distress, distressed, distressful

≈strict: strict, striction, stricture

- strict: abstrict, constrict, district, restrict, restricted

- striction: abstriction, constriction, restriction

- strictive: constrictive, restrictive

- sti-g-e: prestige, prestigious [variant forms: strait, stretto, strong, distraught]

stroph-e: to turn

≈strophe: strophe

- strophe: anastrophe, antistrophe, apostrophe, catastrophe, epistrophe, exstrophe, hypostrophe, monostrophe

- strophic: geostrophic

- strophism: diastrophism

≈strob-e: strobe, strobila, strobile

≈strobil-: strobiloid

≈strobili-: strobiliform

≈strobo-: stroboscope

struct: to build

≈struct: structure; structural, structuralism, structuralist

- struct: construct, instruct, obstruct

- structible: destructible, indestructible

- struction: construction, destruction, instruction, obstruction

- structionist: obstructionist

- structive: constructive, destructive, instructive, obstructive

- structor: instructor

- structure: infrastructure, microstructure, prestructure, restructure, substructure, superstructure

- strum: instrument, instrumental [variant forms; destroy; construe, industrial, industrious, industry, misconstrue]

STUB, STUBBORN: akin to Dutch *stok*, a stick

stud: to apply oneself, study

student, studied, studio, studious, study [variant forms: étude, etui]

stult: firm, slow, stupid
  stultify, stultiloquy; stolid
stup-e: to be stunned
≈stup-id: stupendous, stupid,
  stupidity, stupor
≈stupe-: stupefacient,
  stupefaction, stupefy
  [variant form: stutter]
styl-e[1]: **pillar**; from "to stand"
≈styl: stylite
≈stylo-: stylobate, styloglossus,
  stylograph, stylolite
- stylar: astylar, amphistylar
- style: amphiprostyle, epistyle,
  hypostyle, peristyle, prostyle
- stylous: astylous, distylous,
  heterostylous, homostylous,
  monostylous, tristylous
- styly: heterostyly, homostyly
  [variant forms: still—one
  meaning, stilt, stolid, stolen,
  stultify]
styl-e[2]: **pointed**
≈styl-e: stylar, style, stylet, stylus
≈stylis-t: stylish, stylist, stylistic,
  stylistics, stylize
≈styl-: styloid
≈styli-: styliform
≈stylo-: stylograph, stylography,
  stylopodium
  [variant forms: stiletto; stimulant,
  stimulate, stimulus]
STYMIE: origin unknown; a golfing
  situation in which an opponent's
  ball obstructs the line of play of
  one's own ball; figuratively, an
  impasse; a quandary
suas-: **sweet**
≈suas: suasion
- suasion: dissuasion, persuasion
- suasive: assuasive, dissuasive,
  persuasive
- suad-e: dissuade, persuade,
  persuader
  [variant forms: assuage, suave,
  suavity]

sub-: **under, below**
≈sub-: subacid, subacute
  subaltern, subalternate,
  subaqueous, subaudition
≈subclavian, subconscious,
  subcostal, subculture,
  subcutaneous
≈subdivide, subdominant,
  subduction, subdue, subfamily,
  subfusc
≈subgenus, subglacial, subgrade,
  subito
≈subjacent, subject, subjugate,
  subjunctive
≈sublapsarian, sublate, sublease,
  sublethal
≈submarginal, submarine,
  submaxilla, submediant,
  submerge, submerse,
  submission, submit,
  submontane
≈subnormal, subnuclear
≈suborbital, subordinate, suborn,
  subpoena
≈subreption, subrogate, subrosa
≈subscribe, subscript,
  subscription, subsequence,
  subsequent, subserve,
  subservience, subside,
  subsidiary, subsidize, subsidy,
  subsist, subsoil, subsonic,
  subspace, subspecies,
  substance, substandard,
  substantial, substantiate,
  substantive, substellar,
  substituent, substitute,
  substratum, substructure,
  subsume, subsumption,
  subsurface
≈subtangent, subtend,
  subterranean, subtext, subtitle,
  subtle, subtonic, subtopic,
  subtotal, subtract, subtrahend
≈subumbrella, suburb
≈subvene, subversion, subvert

≈s-: truncated form of *sub*-:
sombrero—lit., under the shade

≈so-: variant of *sub*-: sojourn—lit.,
under a day

≈sof: variant of *sub*-: soffit—lit.,
fixed under; the horizontal
underside of an eave, cornice, etc.;
the intrados of an arch or vault

≈sotta: Italian form of *sub*-: sotto
voce

≈sou-: a French form of *sub*-:
soufflé, souffle, soupçon—see
suspicion, soutane, souvenir

≈sous: a French form of *sub*-: sous-
chef

≈su-: truncation of *sub*-: suspect,
suspicion, suspire

≈subter: variant of *sub*-: subterfuge

≈suc-: assimilation of *sub*-:
succeed, success, succession,
succinct, succor, succubus,
succumb

≈sud-: assimilation of *sub*-:
sudden: see *it*

≈suf-: assimilation of *sub*-: suffer,
sufferable, sufferance,
suffering, suffice, sufficiency,
sufficient, suffix, sufflate,
suffocate, suffragan, suffrage,
suffragist, suffruticose,
suffumigate, suffuse

≈sug-: assimilation of *sub*-:
suggest, suggestion, suggestive

≈sum- assimilation of *sub*-:
summon, summons

≈sup-: assimilation of *sub*-:
supplant, supple, supplement,
suppletion, suppliant,
supplicate, supply, support,
suppose, suppositive,
suppository, suppress,
suppurate

≈sur-: assimilation of *sub*-:
surreptitious, surrogacy,
surrogate

≈sus- variant of *sub*-: susceptance,
susceptible, susceptive,
suspect, suspend, suspenders,
suspense, suspension, sustain,
sustenance, sustentation,
sustention; resuscitate
{word note: sub rosa: lit., under the
rose; an ancient symbol of
secrecy}

suber: cork
suberin, suberize

suet: see seb

SUBULATE: in botany, awl-shaped, as
some plants; slender and tapering
to a point

suc-t: to suck
succulent; suction; liposuction
[variant forms: suck, sucker, sup,
supper, prosciutto]

s-ud-e: to sweat
≈suda: sudarium, sudatorium,
sudatory
≈sudori-: sudorific
- sudorific: antisudorific
- s-ud-e: exudate; transude,
exude
[variant forms: suint, sweat]

sue in court: see sect

sue: to be accustomed
assuetude, consuetude,
desuetude, insuetude,
mansuetude
[variant form: insolent]

SUGAR: from Persian *sakar*; Arabic
sukkar

sui-: self
suicidal, suicide; suicidology
[phrases: sui generis, sui juris;
suo jure, suo loco]

sulc: to furrow, groove
sulcate, sulcus; bisulcate

sul-f: sulfur
sulfate, sulfide, sulfite,
sulfonate, sulfone, sulfonium;
sulfur, sulfureous, sulfuric,
sulfurize, sulfurous

SULKY: showing resentment; also, a
light, two-wheeled, one-horse
carriage, possibly in the sense of
keeping aloof
sully: see sol soil
sult: see salt for result
sul-t: to deliberate, consider [see
concil-e]
consul, consular, consulate,
consult, consultancy,
consultant, consultation,
consultative, consultor;
proconsul
SULTAN: Arabic: Muslim ruler;
sultana, sultanate
sum: highest
≈sum-m: sum, summa,
summation, summit, summitry
≈summar-y: summarize,
summary
- summate: consummate
[phrases: ad summam, summa
cum laude, summum bonum]
{word note: sum: from the Roman
practice of placing the total
amount derived from adding a
column of numbers at the top of
the column}
summon: see mon-it
sump: to take up, claim
≈sumpt: sumptuary, sumptuous
- sumable: inconsumable,
presumable
- sume: assume, consume,
presume, resume, résumé,
subsume
- sumer: assumer, consumer,
presumer, resumer
- suming: unassuming
- sumpsit: assumpsit
- sumption: absumption,
assumption, consumption,
misassumption, presumption,
resumption, subsumption
- sumptive: assumptive,
consumptive, presumptive,
resumptive, subsumptive

- sumptuous: presumptuous
[variant forms: consommé; seize,
seizure, disseize]
SUMMER: Sanskrit; half season
sunder: away from, part, separate
sunder, asunder
super: above, beyond
≈super: super, superable, superb,
superior, superiority, supernal
≈super-: superabound,
superabundant, superacid,
superacute, superadd,
superaltern, superanal,
superannuate, superannuated,
superantigen
≈superciliary, supercilious,
superclass, superconductor,
supercritical
≈supereminent, supererogation
≈superfamily, superfecta,
superfecundation,
superfetation, superficial,
superficies, superfine,
superfluidity, superfluity,
superfluous
≈supergiant, superheat,
superhuman, superimpose
≈superincumbent, superinduce,
superintend, superintendent,
superjacent
≈superlative, superlunary,
superman
≈supernatant, supernatural,
supernormal, supernumerary
≈superorder, superorganism,
superovulation
≈superparasite, superpatriot,
superphysical, superpose
≈supersaturate, superscribe,
superscript, superscription,
supersede, supersedeas,
supersensible, supersession,
supersonic, superstition,
superstratum, superstructure
≈supervene, supervise

- superable: insuperable
≈suprem-e: supremacist,
   supremacy, supreme
≈sir-: variant of super-: sirloin
≈somer-: variant of *super-*:
   somersault
≈supra-: variant of *super-*:
   supralapsarian, supraliminal,
   supranational, supraorbital,
   suprarenal
≈sur: variant of *super-*: surbase,
   surcease, surcharge, surcingle,
   surcoat, surface, surfeit,
   surmise, surmount, surname,
   surpass, surplice, surplus,
   surprise, surreal, surrender,
   surround, surtax, surtout,
   surveil, surveillance, survey,
   survive
   [variant forms: soprano, soubrette,
   sovereign]
SUMO: Japanese: to compete, as in
   sumo wrestling
supin-e: upside down; probably
   from *sub-*, under
≈supin-e: supinate, supinator;
   supine
- supinate: resupinate
SUPPER: from Old French *souper*,
   which itself is from *soupe*, soup;
   in Russian, *soup* is pronounced the
   same as in English, but is spelled
   суп
SURAL: from *sura*, calf of the leg;
   thus, pertaining to the calf of the
   leg
SURCULOSE: in botany, having
   suckers
sur-e: care [see cur-e]
≈sur-e: sure, surely, surety
- surance: assurance, insurance
- sure: assure, ensure, insure
   [variant form: secure]
surd: dull, deaf, insensible
   surd, absurd, absurdist,
   absurdity
   [phrase: reductio ad absurdum]

surg-e: to rise; from *sub-*, from
   under + *regere*, to direct
   surge; resurge, resurgent;
   assurgent, insurgent
   [variant forms: source, resource,
   resourceful]
surg-ery: to work with the hands;
   from *cheiros*, hand + *ergein*, to
   work
≈surg: surgeon, surgery
- surgery: cryosurgery,
   electrosurgery, microsurgery
surplice: see pel-l
SURREY: a light pleasure carriage;
   first built in Surrey, a county in
   southeast England
SUSHI: Japanese: lit., raw seafood
SUSURRANT, SUSURRATE, SUSURRUS:
   pertaining to a whispering,
   murmuring sound
SUTLER: from Dutch *soeteler*, to do
   dirty work; a person following the
   army to sell food, liquor, etc. to its
   soldiers
SUTURE: to sew, to join together
SWAIN: from Old Norse *sveinn*, boy,
   servant; orig., designated a rustic
   youth; a lover, or suitor
SWAHILI: Arabic; lit., belonging to
   the coast; a prominent language of
   East Africa
SWAMI: Hindi: lord, master
SWASTIKA: Sanskrit: well-being;
   party emblem of Nazi Germany
swear: see sermon
SYCAMINE, SYCAMORE: trees bearing
   mulberries; may be related to
   Greek *sykon*, fig
syc-o: fig
   syconium, sycosis;
   sycophancy, sycophant
   [variant form: sycamore]
SYLLABUS: lit., a list, register; an
   academic course outline
sylum: right of seizure
   asylum; hence, no right of
   seizure; a haven, e.g., insane
   asylum, political asylum
   sylva: see silv-a

sym-: with, together

≈sym: symbiont, symbiosis, symbol, symmetry, sympathetic, sympathy, sympetalous, symphony, symphysis, sympodium, symposium, symptom, asymmetry

≈sy-: truncation of *sym-*: systaltic, system, systematic, systematics, systemic, syzygy

≈syl-: assimilation of *sym-*: syllabary, syllabic, syllabicate, syllabify, syllabism, syllable, syllepsis, syllogism, syllogize

≈syn-: variant of *sym-*: synagogue, synalepha, synapse, synapsis, synarthrosis

≈syncarpous, synchronize, synchroscope, synclinal, synclinorium, syncopate, syncopation, syncope, syncretism, syncytium

≈syndactyl, syndesis, syndesmosis, syndetic, syndic, syndicate, syndrome

≈synecdoche, syneresis, synergetic, synergid, synergism, synergy, synesis, synesthesia

≈syngamy, syngeneic, syngenesis

≈synizesis [see h-izeis], synkaryon

≈synod, synodical, synoecious, synonym, synovia

≈syntactic, syntagma, syntax, synthesis, synthetic

≈sys-: variant of *sym-*: syssarcosis

- syn-: geosynchronous, polysyndeton

syring: reed, pipe

≈syring-e: syringa, syringe, syringeal; syrinx

≈syring-: syringadenoma, syringitis, syringoid, syringoma

≈syringo-: syringocele, syringomyelia, syringotome

{word note: syrinx: the vocal organ of birds}

SYRUP: from Arabic *sharab*, lit., a drink

T

TABASCO: from Tabasco, a state of Mexico; an extremely hot pepper sauce

TABBY: Arabic; the quarter of Baghdad where the striped material was first made; also, a striped cat

tabernacle: see trab

TABES, TABESCENT: wasting away, due to disease

TABLA: Arabic: drum

tabl-e: board, table

≈tabl-e: tablature, table, tableau, pl., tableaux, tablet, tabloid

≈tabula: tabular, tabulate, tabulator

- tabl-e: entablature, entablement [phrases: tableau vivant, table d'hôte, tabula rasa—an erased tablet]

TABOO: Polynesian: sacred prohibition

TABOR, TABORET, TABORIN: Persian: a drum

tac-it: to be silent

tacet, tacit, taciturn; reticence, reticent

tach: stake

attach, attaché, detach, detachment, unattached [variant forms: attack; staccato]

tachy: swift

≈tachy: tachyon

≈tachy-: tachycardia, tachygraph, tachygraphy, tachylyte, tachymeter, tachyphylaxis, tachysterol

≈tachisto-: tachistoscope

≈tacho-: tachometer

tact: to touch

≈tact: tact, tactful, tactile,
tactless, tactual

- tact: contact, intact

- tagi-: contagion, contagious

- tain: attain

- taminate: contaminate

≈tang: tangible, tangent,
tangential

- tangent: cotangent, subtangent

- tangible: intangible

≈tast-e: taste, tasteful, tasteless

- taste: distaste, distasteful

- teger: integer

- tegr-: integrable, integral,
integrand, integrant

- tegrate: integrate, disintegrate

- tegration: integration,
disintegration,
photodisintegration

- tegrity: integrity

≈tent: tent—one meaning,
tentacle, tentative

- tiguous: contiguous

- tingent: contingent

- tire-e: entire, entirely, entirety
[phrase: noli me tangere]

taenia: ribbon, tape, tapeworm;
related to "thin," as in tenuous and
extenuating
taenia, taeniasis; taeniacide
[variant form: zygotene]

TAFFETA: Persian: woven; a fabric

TAHINI: Arabic: flour, meal; a food
paste made from sesame seeds

TAI CHI: Mandarin: grand ultimate

TAIGA: Russian for a transitional
plant community between the
arctic tundra and the boreal
coniferous forests

tail-le: to cut

≈tail-le: tailor; taille, tailleur

- tail: curtail, detail, entail,
disentail, retail

[variant forms: fee tail; tallage,
tally, intaglio]

taint: to moisten
taint, attaint; attainture
{word note: attainture: now obsolete,
orig. meant attainder: forfeiture of
property and loss of civil rights of
a person sentenced to death or
outlawed, as in bill of attainder;
also meant dishonor}

TAJ MAHAL: Persian: best of
buildings; located in Agra, India

TALC: Persian; a soft, light-colored
monoclinic mineral

TALENT: orig., a unit of weight

tal: such
tales, talion: legal terms

tali: punishment in kind; akin to
Welsh *tal*, compensation
retaliate, retaliation

TALISMAN: Arabic: magic figure;
related to *tele-*, end

TALLAHASSEE: Creek *talwa*, town +
hasi, old; thus, "old town"; capital
of Florida

TALLY-HO: from French *taïaut*: the
cry of a hunter on sighting the fox

TALMUD: Hebrew: learning,
instruction; the Talmud consists of
two parts: the Mishna (text) and
the Gemara (commentary)

TAMBOUR, TAMBOURIN,
TAMBOURINE: Arabic: drum

TAMBOURA: Persian: a flutelike
instrument

TAMPION, TAMPON: a plug or stopper;
a tampion is put in the muzzle of a
gun not in use; a tampon is put
into a body cavity or wound to
stop bleeding or absorb secretions

TANAGER: from Portuguese *tángara*;
ultimately from Tupi *tangara*

TANDEM: one behind the other; in
single file

TANDOOR, TANDOORI: Hindi: clay
oven

tangent: see tact

TANGERINE: a mandarin orange from
Tangier

TANGRAM: a Chinese puzzle

TANIST: Irish and Gaelic: next heir

TANK: from *stagnant*; orig., a pool, stoppage of flow; as a military term for an armored vehicle, the word was used for the purpose of secrecy during manufacture

TANTALIZE: from Tantalus, doomed in the lower world to stand in water that always receded when he tried to drink it and under branches of fruit that always remained just out of reach

TANTAMOUNT: equal or equivalent to as much, as in "his confession was tantamount to guilt"

TAOISM: from Chinese *tao*, the way: a Chinese religion based on the doctrines of Laotzu and advocates simplicity and selflessness

tap-e: carpet; in scientific usage, a layer

tape, tapestry, tapetum, tapis

tapho: tomb, fossil

taphephobia, taphonomy; cenotaph, epitaph

TAPIOCA: Tupi and Guarini: squeezed-out drugs

TAPIR: Tupi; lit., large animal; a large hoglike animal of tropical America and the Malay Peninsula

tara: to disturb

ataractic, ataraxia

TARANTELLA (a vivacious dance), TARANTISM (a disease), TARANTULA (a spider): from Taranto, Italy

tardi: to make slow

≈tardi-: tardigrade

- tard-: ritardando; retard, retardant, retardate, retardation, retarded, retarder

≈tardy: tardy, tardyon
 [variant form: retine —retard + -ine]

TARGET: Middle French: small shield

TARIFF: Arabic: information, explanation; a tax upon imports

TARMAC: short for tarmacadam: *macadam* from John L. McAdam, Scottish road engineer

TARNISH: from French: to make dim

tars-o: flat of the foot, ankle; edge of eyelid

≈tars: tarsal, tarsier, tarsus, pl., tarsi

≈tarso-: tarsometatarsus

- tars-: metatarsal, metatarsus

TASMANIA: named for Abel Tasman, Dutch navigator who discovered Tasmania and New Zealand

TASS: Russian: *Telegrafroe Agenstvo Sovetskova Soyuz*: Telegraph Agency of the Soviet Union; former Soviet news agency

TATAMI: Japanese: to pile up, fold up: a floor mat for sitting on, as for eating

TATTER: from Old Norse *töturr*: rags

TATTOO[1]: Polynesian: to puncture the skin

TATTOO[2]: Dutch: to shut the tap: a signal for closing barrooms; a signal for summoning military members to their quarters

tass[1]: a cup

tass, demitasse

tass[2]: knob, knot

tassel, detassel

TAUPE: French: mole: both the animal and its color

taur-o: bull

taurine, Taurus; tauromachy; Minotaur
 [Spanish: toreador, torero, toro]

taut-o: the same

≈taut-: tautonym, tautonymous

≈tauto-: tautological, tautologism, tautologous, tautology, tautomerism, tautoousious, tautophony, tautosyllabic, tautozonal

tavern: see trab

TAWDRY: from "St. Audrey laces": cheap and showy; from cheap laces bought at St. Audrey's Fair

tax: to appraise, reckon
  tax, taxation, taxi; taxicab,
  taximeter; surtax
  [variant form: task]
{word note: taxicab: from *taximeter*
  + *cabriolet*, he-goat}
tax-i: to arrange
≈tax: taxeme, taxis
≈taxi-: taxidermy
≈taxo-: taxonomy
- tax: syntax
- taxis: with prefixes: heterotaxis,
  homotaxis, hypotaxis,
  parataxis
- taxis: with combining forms:
  aerotaxis, chemotaxis,
  geotaxis, heliotaxis,
  phototaxis, phyllotaxis,
  rheotaxis, rhizotaxis,
  stereotaxis, thermotaxis,
  thigmotaxis, psychotaxis,
  sitotaxis, stereotaxis,
  trophotaxis
- taxy: anthotaxy, epitaxy,
  eutaxy, heterotaxy, homotaxy,
  phyllotaxy, pleiotaxy,
  stereotaxy
≈tactic: tactic, tactical, tactician,
  tactics
- tactic: paratactic, syntactic,
  syntactics
≈tagm: tagmeme, tagmemic,
  tagmemics
- tagma-: syntagma, syntagmatic
TCHOTCHKE: Yiddish: knickknack
TEA: Mandarin for the tree from
  which the leaves are brewed for a
  drink
TEAPOY: Hindi; from Sanskrit *tri-*,
  three + Persian *pai*, foot; a three-
  legged stand
techn: to weave, build, join
≈techn: technic, technical,
  technicality, technician,
  technique
≈tech-: technomic

≈techno-: technocracy,
  technography, technological,
  technology, technophile,
  technophobia
- technic: polytechnic,
  pyrotechnics
≈tecto-: tectology
- tect: architect
≈tectonic: tectonic, tectonics
- tectonic: architectonic,
  geotectonic
tect: see teg-u for detect, protect
tectic: to melt
  eutectic, hypereutectic,
  hypoeutectic
  [variant form: tektite]
ted: disgust, offensive, weary
  tedious, tedium
  [variant form: fastidious]
  [phrase: taedium vitae]
teg-u: to cover
≈teg-u: tegmen, tegular,
  tegument
- tegument: integument
- tect: detect, obtect, protect
- tectant: protectant
- tectopm: detection, protection
- tective: detective, protective;
  cryoprotective, cytoprotective,
  overprotective
- tector-: with prefixes: detector,
  protector, protectorate,
  protectory
- tector: with combining form:
  photodetector
  [variant forms: protégé, thatch,
  tile, toga, togs, tuille; toga virilis]
tel-e-: afar
≈tel-: telencephalon, telesthesia,
  telpher
≈tele-: telecast, telecommerce,
  teleconference, telecommuting,
  telecomputing, telegenic,
  telegony, telegraph,
  telegraphy, telekinesis,

telemeter, teleost, telepathy,
telephone, telephotograph,
teleportation, telescope,
telescopic, telespectroscope,
television
≈telo-: telodynamic
- tele-: phototelegraphy
tel-eo: the end
≈tel: telial, telic, telium, telos,
  telson
≈tel-: telome, telangiectasis
≈tele-: telestich
≈teleo-: teleology, teleonomy,
  teliospore, or, teleutospore
≈telo-: telomere, telophase
- tele-: atelectasis; entelechy
- telic: atelic, autotelic,
  heterotelic, ureotelic
  [variant form: talisman]
tellur: earth
≈tellur: tellurian, telluric,
  tellurium, tellurize, tellurous
- telluric: intratelluric
tem: strong drink
  abstemious—moderate,
  especially in eating and drinking;
  temperate; also, characterized by
  abstinence
temer: dark, blindly, rashly
≈temer: temerarious, temerity
≈tenebri-: tenebrific
  [variant forms: Tenebrae,
  tenebrous—also, tenebrious]
temn: to scorn
- temn: contemn
- tempt: contempt [see tempt for
  attempt]
temper: to mix in proportion
≈temper: temper, tempera,
  temperament, temperamental,
  temperance, temperate,
  temperature, tempered
- temper-: distemper,
  intemperance, intemperate
  [variant forms: tamper, temple—
  one meaning]

**templ-e: place marked out,
  sanctuary**
  templar, template, temple—one
  meaning; contemplate
temp-or: time
≈temp-o: tempo; tempest,
  tempestuous
≈tempor: temporal, temporality,
  temporary, temporize
- tempor-e: contemporaneous,
  extemporaneous; extempore,
  extemporize
- temporary: contemporary,
  extemporary
  [variant form: tense—one
  meaning]
  [phrases: pro tempore—pro tem,
  tempus fugit, ex tempore]
tempt: to try, test; from "temper"
  tempt, temptation, tempter,
  tempting; attempt [see temn for
  contempt]
  [variant forms: tent—one
  meaning, attentat]
TEMPURA: Portuguese: condiment,
  flavor
tenebrous: see temer
tener: soft, delicate
  intenerate—to make tender or
  soft
  [variant form: tender—one
  meaning]
tens-e: to stretch
≈tens-e: tense—one meaning,
  tensible, tensile, tension,
  tensity, tensive, tensor
≈tensi-o: tensimeter, tensiometer
- tense: intense, pretense
- tensify: intensify; intensifier
- tensible: distensible, extensible,
  inextensible, ostensible
- tensile: thermotensile
- tensin: angiotensin
- tension: extension,
  hypertension, intension,
  pretension

- tensity: extensity, intensity
- tensive: extensive, intensive, ostensive
- tenso-: extensometer
- tensor: extensor
≈ten-d: tend, tendency, tendentious, tender—one meaning, tendinous, tendon, tendril
≈tendin: tendinitis—also, tendonitis
≈teno-: tenorrhaphy, tenosynovitis, tenotomy
- tend: attend, contend, distend, extend, intend, portend, pretend, subtend, superintend
- tend-: intendance, intendant
- tended: extended, intended, pretended, unattended
- tendent: superintendent
- tender: extender
- tendible: extendible
- tendu: malentendu
≈tent: tent—one meaning, tenter, tenterhook
- tent: content, detent, discontent, extent, intent, malcontent, portent
- tentat-: ostentation; ostentatious
- tented: contented
- tentious: abstentious, contentious, pretentious
- tentional: intentional
- tente: détente, entente
- tention: abstention, attention, contention, detention, distention, intention, retention
- tentious: pretentious
- tentive: attentive, inattentive, irretentive, retentive
≈tenu: tenuis, tenuity, tenuous
- tenuat-: attenuate, attenuation, attenuator, extenuate, extenuating, extenuatory
- tenuse: hypotenuse

- teny: neoteny
  [variant forms: anatase; entasis, epitasis, protasis; tenesmus; thin]
  [phrases: in extenso, nolo contendere]
ten-t: to hold
≈ten: tenable, tenaille, tenement, tenet, tennis, tenon, tenor, tenure, tenuto
≈tenac-e: tenace, tenacious, tenacity, tenaculum
≈tenan-t: tenancy, tenant, tenantry
- tenable: untenable
- tenance: countenance, discountenance, maintenance, sustenance, appurtenance
- tenant: lieutenant, setenant
- tentaculum-: sustentaculum
- tentation: sustentation
- tention: sustention
- tain: abstain, appertain, contain, detain, entertain, maintain, obtain, pertain, retain, sustain
- tain-: containment, detainer, sustainable
- tinac-: pertinacious, pertinacity
- tinence: abstinence, continence, incontinence, pertinence
- tinent-: continent, impertinent, incontinent, pertinent; transcontinental
- tinu-: continual, continuous, continuum
- tinuance: continuance, discontinuance
- tinuation: continuation, discontinuation
- tinue: continue, detinue, discontinue, retinue
- tinuity: continuity, discontinuity
- tinuous: discontinuous
  [variant forms: rein, sostenuto]
  [phrase: locum tenens]
TEOCALLI: Nahuatl: *teo*, god + *kalli*, house: temple

TEOSINTE: Nahuatl: *teo*, god + *sinyi*, maize; ancestor of maize

tep-e: to be slightly warm
tepid, tepefy

TEPEE: from Dakota *t'i*, to dwell + *-pi*, a suffix indicating an indefinite, or abstract form; a cone-shaped tent of animal skins or bark

tephr-a: ashes
tephra, tephrite

TEQUILA: region in Mexico; orig., name of tribe; a strong alcoholic liquor of Mexico

ter: third
≈ter: terce, tercet
≈ter-: tercentenary, tervalent
≈tern: ternary, ternate
≈tert: tertial, tertian, tertiary
[variant forms: tierce, tiercel]
[phrases: terza rima, tertium quid]

terat-o: monster, monstrosity; malformed, abnormal
≈terat: teratic, teratism
≈terat-: teratoid, teratoma, teratosis
≈terato-: teratogen, teratology

terg-e: to wipe
absterge, deterge; abstergent, detergent
[variant forms: terse, detersive]

terg-i: the back
tergal, tergum, tergiversate

TERIYAKI: Japanese: *teri*, to shine + *yaki*, to broil, because the sauce makes the meat or fish shiny

TERMAGANT: name of an imaginary Muslim deity; scolding woman

term-in-e: to set bounds, end, limit
≈term: term, termer, termor
≈termin: terminable, terminal, terminate, termination, terminator, terminus
≈termino-: terminology
- term-: conterminous, determine, determiner, exterminate,

exterminative, exterminatory, indetermination
- terminable: determinable, interminable, indeterminable
[phrases: terminus ad quem, terminus a quo]
termite: see trit-e

terpsi: to delight in; dancing
Terpsichore, terpsichorean
{word note: terpsichorean: as a noun, a dancer; as an adjective; related to dancing}

ter-r: earth
≈terra: terra, terrace, terrain, terrane, terrarium, terrazzo
≈terre: terrene, terrestrial
≈terri: terrier, terrine
≈territor-y: territorial, territorialize, territory
≈terr-: terraqueous
≈terre-: terreplein
≈terri-: terricolous, terrigenous
- ter-: inter, disinter; interment, disinterment
- terr-e: extraterrestrial, extraterritorial, parterre
- terranean: Mediterranean, subterranean
[variant forms: trass, turmeric, verditer]
[phrases: tureen, terra alba, terra cotta, terra firma, terra incognito, pied-à-terre, Terre Haute, IN; terre-verte]

TERRAPIN: Virginia Algonquian: tortoise

terr-i: to frighten
≈terr: terrible, terribly
≈terror: terror, terrorism, terrorize, terror-stricken
≈terri-: terrific, terrify
- ter-r: deter, deterrent

test: shell, pot, head
≈test-a: test, testa, testaceous, tester—one meaning, testily, teston, testy

≈testud: testudinal, testudinate,
  testudo
{word note: testudo: lit., tortoise,
  tortoise shell; hence, protective
  covering; a movable shelter, used
  as protection by ancient Roman
  soldiers}
[variant form: tête-à-tête]

test-i: to witness, testicle

witness

≈testa: testacy, testament,
  testamentary; testate, testator,
  testatrix
≈testimon-y: testimonial,
  testimony
≈testi-: testification, testify
- test: attest, contest, detest,
  obtest, pretest, protest
- test-: incontestable, intestate,
  intertestamental, Protestant,
  protestation

testicle:

≈test: testicle, testicular,
  testiculate, testis, pl., testes
≈testo-: testosterone
- testis: ovotestis

tetan: acute infectious disease;
  from *tonos*, stretch
  tetanic, tetanize,
  tetanus, tetany

tetr-a: four

≈tetr: tetracid, tetrad, tetrarch,
  tetrarchy, tetratomic, tetrode,
  tetroxide
≈tetra-: tetrabasic, tetrabrach,
  tetrabranchiate, tetrachloride,
  tetrachord, tetracycline,
  tetragon, tetragram
≈tetrahedral, tetrahedron,
  tetralogy, tetramerous,
  tetrapetalous, tetraploid,
  tetrapod, tetrasporangium
≈tetrastich, tetrastichous,
  tetrasyllable, tetravalent
- tessaron: diatessaron
≈tetarto: tetartohedral: one fourth

[variant forms: tessellate, tessera]
TETRAZZINI: from L. Tetrazzini, an
  Italian soprano (1871-1940); a
  noodle dish named in her honor

teuch: tool, book
  Heptateuch, Hexateuch,
  Pentateuch

text: to weave

≈text: text, textile, textual,
  texture, textured
- text: context, hypertext, subtext
- textual: intertextual
- texture: contexture, intertexture
  [variant forms: tessitura; subtle,
  subtlety, toilet, toils]

thal: valley
  thaler, Neanderthal
  [variant forms: taler, dollar]

thalam: inner chamber, bridal
  chamber

≈thalamus: thalamus
≈thalam-: thalamencephalon
≈thalamo-: thalamotomy
- thal-: epithalamium,
  hypothalamus, prothalamion

thalass: sea

≈thalass: thalassic
≈thalass-: thalassemia,
  thalassoma
≈thalasso-: thalassocracy,
  thalassography, thalassometer,
  thalassophilous,
  thalassophobia, thalassoposia,
  thalasssotherapy

thall-o: young, green shoot

≈thall: thallic, thallium, thallous,
  thallus
≈thall-: thalloid
≈thallo-: thallogen, thallophyte,
  thallospore
- thallic: heterothallic,
  holothallic, homothallic
- thallium: prothallium
{word note: thallium: so named by
  Crookes, its discoverer, because of
  its green spectral line}

thalp: **to heat**

    enthalpy—the measure of the energy content of a system per unit mass

than-ato: **death**; from Thanatos, death personified as a god

    ≈thanat: thanatopis, thantoid, thanatosis

    ≈thanato-: thanatology, thanatophobia

    - than-: euthanasia, euthanize

thauma-to: **miracle**

    thaumatrope; thaumaturge, thaumaturgic; thaumatology

    [variant forms: theater, theatrical; theorem, theory]

thec: see thesis for apothecary

thegm: **to utter**

    apothegm—a short, pithy saying, e.g., easy come, easy go

thelium: **nipple, nipplelike**

≈thel-: thelerethism, thelitis

- thelioma: mesothelioma

- thelium: endothelium, epithelium, mesothelium, perithelium

THENAR: the palm of the hand; sometimes, the sole of the foot; the bulge of the thumb

the-o: **God**

≈the: theism

≈the-: theurgy

≈theo-: theocentric, theocracy, theogony, theology, theomachy, theomania, theomorphic, theonomous, theopathy, theophany, theophobia, theosophy

- theism: atheism, ditheism, henotheism, monotheism, pantheism, polytheism, tritheism

- theist: atheist, antitheist, autotheist, bitheist, ditheist, duotheist, henotheist, hylotheist, monotheist,

nontheist, pantheist, polytheist, tritheist

- theon: pantheon

- theosis: apotheosis

    [variant forms: enthusiasm, enthusiast, enthusiastic; Timothy, Theodore, Dorothy]

    [NB: theodolite—a surveying instrument used to measure vertical and horizontal angles]

THEORBO: a large 17th-century lute

theor-em: **to look at**

    theorem, theoretical, theoretician, theoretics, theorize, theory

therap-y: **treatment**

≈therap-y: therapeutic, therapy

- therapeutics: acrotherapeutics

- therapy: aerotherapy, heliotherapy, hydrotheraphy, organotherapy, pharmacotherapy, phototherapy, physiotherapy, radiotherapy

there: **summer**

    isothere—a line on a map connecting points on the earth's surface that have the same mean summer temperature

ther-io: **beast**

≈ther-: theroid

≈theri-: therianthropic

≈therio-: theriomorphic

≈thero-: therolatry, theropod

- there: dinothere, elasmothere

- therium: megatherium

    [NB: panther]

therm-o: **heat**

≈therm: therm, thermae, thermal, thermel, thermic

≈thermion: thermion, thermionics

≈therm-: thermanesthesia, thermesthesia, thermistor—therm + resistor

≈thermi-: Thermidor

≈thermo-: thermocline,
  thermodynamic,
  thermogenesis, thermograph
≈thermolabile,
  thermoluminescence,
  thermolysis, thermometer,
  thermonuclear
≈thermophile, thermoscope,
  thermosphere, thermostat,
  thermotaxis, thermotensile,
  thermotropism
- therm: with prefixes: allotherm,
  eurytherm, exotherm,
  heterotherm, homotherm,
  isotherm, isogeotherm,
  ultratherm
- therm: with combining forms:
  dermotherm, dynatherm,
  stenotherm
- thermal: with prefixes:
  altithermal, ectothermal,
  endothermal, homeothermal,
  hypothermal
- thermal: with combining forms:
  geothermal, hemathermal,
  poikilothermal
- thermancy: athermancy,
  diathermancy
- thermia: hyperthermia,
  hypothermia
- thermic: with prefixes:
  diathermic, endothermic,
  exothermic
- thermic: with combining forms:
  photothermic, xerothermic
- thermy: diathermy, radiothermy
THESAURUS: Greek: treasure,
  storehouse
thesis: to place, put
≈thesis: thesis
- thesis: with prefixes: antithesis,
  diathesis, epenthesis,
  hypothesis, metathesis,
  parasynthesis, parenthesis,
  prothesis, prosthesis, synthesis

- thesis: with combining forms:
  nucleosynthesis,
  photosynthesis
≈thec-a: theca, thecate
- thec-a: hypothec; bibliotheca,
  odontotheca, ootheca,
  prototheca, spermatheca
- thecary: apothecary
- thecate: hypothecate
- thecium: amphithecium,
  apothecium, endothecium,
  perithecium
≈them-e: thematic, theme
- them-a: apothem, anathema
≈thet: thetic
- thet: antithet, epithet
- thetic-s: with prefixes: antithetic,
  homothetic, metathetic,
  monothetic, parenthetic,
  prosthetic, prosthetics,
  synthetic
- thetic: with combining form:
  nomothetic
- thetical: antithetical,
  hyperthetical, hypothetical,
  epithetical, parenthetical,
  synthetical
  [variant forms: Spanish: bodega,
  biblioteca]
thigm-o: to touch
  thigmotactic, thigmotaxis,
  thigmotropism
thio: sulfur
≈thio: thionic, thionine
≈thio-: thiogenic, thiourea
thorax: chest, breastplate
  thorax; mesothorax,
  metathorax, pneumonothorax
thrall: slave
  thrall, thralldom; enthrall,
  disenthralled
thrill: to pierce
  thrill, thriller; nostril
thromb-o: blood clot
≈thromb: thrombus

≈thromb-: thrombosis
≈thrombo-: thrombocyte
- thrombin: prothrombin
THUG: from Hindi *thag*, swindler;
further from Sanskrit *sthaga*, a
cheat, rogue; a member of a
former group in India that
murdered and robbed in the
service of Kali, a Hindu goddess
viewed as both destroying life and
giving it; in lower case, a rough,
brutal hoodlum, gangster
thryroid: thyroid; from "door"
thyroid; euthyroid,
hyperthyroid, hypothyroid,
parathyroid
thur: incense
≈thurible: thurible
≈thuri-: thurifer, thuriferous,
thurification, thurify
[variant form: thyme]
thym[1]: spirit, mind
≈thym: thymic—one meaning
≈thymo-: thymogenic
- thymeme: enthymeme
- thymia: cyclothymia,
dysthymia—one meaning,
schizothymia
thym[2]: thymus: a gland
≈thym: thymic—one meaning,
thymus
≈thym-: thymectomy, thymitis,
thymoma
- thymia: dysthymia—one
meaning
- thymism: euthymism
thyr: thyroid; lit., door-shaped
shield
≈thyr: thyroid, thyroidism
- thyroid: euthyroid
- thyroidism: hyperthyroidism,
hypothyroidism
tice: to set fire, excite
entice—to attract by offering
hope of reward or pleasure; tempt;
allure

TICKET: etiquette
tier: see tire
tim-id: to fear
≈tim: timid; timorous
- timidate: intimidate—to make
timid, make afraid; daunt
tinct: to dye, tinge, wet
tinctorial, tincture; intinction
[variant forms: distain, taint,
tinge, tint]
tinguish: see sting for distinguish
tinguish: see stinc-t for extinguish
TINTINNABULAR, TINTINNABULARY,
TINTINNABULATION: pertaining to
bells or the ringing of bells
tire: in a row, in order
attire—to dress, esp. in fine
garments; clothe; array
[variant forms: artillery, tier]
tir-e: to draw [for entire: see tact]
retire, retired, retiree,
retirement, retiring
tirp: see s-tirp for extirpate
tit-le: label, title, sign
titer, title, titlist, titular; entitle,
subtitle; entitlement
[Spanish: tilde—˜, as in señor]
toc-o: childbirth
≈toco-: tocology
- tocia: atocia, bradytocia,
deuterotocia, dystocia, eutocia,
oxytocia, thelytocia
- tocous: polytocous
TODDY: Hindi; *tari*; in present use, a
drink of brandy, whiskey, etc. with
hot water, sugar, and often spices
TOKEN: from same base as *teach*, to
point, show; a sign, indication, or
symbol
toler: to bear, sustain, tolerate
≈tolerat-e: tolerable, tolerance,
tolerant, tolerate
- toler: intolerable, intolerance,
intolerate
- tol: extol
[variant forms: telamon, toll—one
meaning]

TOMAHAWK: Virginia Algonquian
tamahaac: a tool for cutting off; a
light ax used as a tool and weapon
TOMATO: from Nahuatl, a tribal
language of Mexico

tomb: burial vault
tomb, entomb
[variant form: catacomb]

tom-e: to cut
≈tome: tome
- tom-: atom, atomism, diatom;
tritoma
- tome: with prefixes: apotome,
epitome, macrotome,
microtome
- tome: with combining forms:
angiotome, arthrotome,
cystotome, enterotome,
myotome, osteotome
- tomic: atomic, diatomic,
tetratomic
- tomize: epitomize, lobotomize
- tomology: entomology
- tomous: zylotomous
- tomy: with prefixes: anatomy,
autotomy, dichotomy,
microtomy, polychotomy
- tomy: with combining forms:
appendectomy, craniotomy,
episiotomy, gastrotomy,
hysterotomy
≈keratotomy, lithotomy,
necrotomy, nephrotomy,
neurotomy, osteotomy
≈phlebotomy, pleurotomy,
rhizotomy, sclerotomy,
stereotomy
≈tenotomy, tracheotomy,
trichotomy, vagotomy,
varicotomy, vasotomy,
zootomy, zylotomy
[variant form: tmesis]

ton: thunder
astonish, detonate
[variant forms: astound;
tornado]

ton-e: to stretch, tension
≈ton-e: tonality, tone
≈tono-: tonogram, tonography,
tonometer, tonoplast
- ton-: atonal, intonate,
monotonous, peritoneum,
phototonus, polytonality;
peritonitis
- tone: with prefixes: intone,
monotone, overtone, tritone
- tone: with combining forms:
baritone, oxytone
- tonia: with prefixes: catatonia,
dystonia, hypertonia, isotonia
- tonia: with combining forms:
amyotonia, myatonia,
normotonia, vagotonia
- tonic: atonic, catatonic,
diatonic, hypertonic, isotonic,
pentatonic, subtonic, syntonic
[variant forms: tune, attune]
TONSORIAL, TONSURE: pertaining to
shaving, shearing
TOOTHSOME: appetizing; sexually
alluring

top-o: place
≈top-ic: topiary, topic, topical,
topos
≈top-: toponym
≈topo-: topography, topology
- tope: epitope, isotope
- topia: dystopia, ectopia,
heterotopia, utopia
- topic: with prefixes: dystopic, or,
allotopic, ectopic, entopic,
eutopic, eurytopic, heterotopic,
homotopic, isotopic, subtopic
- topic: with combining forms:
nomotopic, orthotopic,
retinotopic, somatotopic,
stenotopic, tonotopic
TORII: Japanese *tori*, bird + *iru*, to be;
shrine gateway

torp-or: to be numb, stiff
torpedo, torpid, torpor;
torporific

torr: thirst; parch, roast, boil
torrent, torrential, torrid;
torrefy
[variant forms: thirst, thirsty,
torsk]
tort: to turn, twist
≈tort: tort, torta, torte, tortellini,
tortile, tortilla, tortious,
tortoise, tortoni
≈tortu: tortuosity, tortuous,
torture, torturous
≈tort-i: tortfeasor; torticollis
- torn-: attorney, ritornello
≈torque: torque, torques
≈tors: torsade, torsibility
- torsion: retorsion
- tort: bistort, contort, detort,
distort, extort, retort
- tortion: contortion, distortion,
extortion, retortion
- tortionate: extortionate
≈tour: tour, tourism, tourist,
touristic, touristy
- tour-age: contour, detour;
entourage
≈tourn: tournament, tourney,
tourniquet [see *tunic* for original
meaning of *tourniquet*]
[variant forms: retroussé, terret,
torment, tormentor, tornillo,
truss, trousseau, retroussé,
tournedos; turn, return;
nasturtium]
[phrases: tour de force, tour
d'horizon, tour en l'air, tour jeté]
TORUS: bulge, muscle
TORY: Irish: robber, pursuer
TOSTADA: American Spanish: toast,
roast
tot-al: all, whole
≈total: total, totalistic,
totalitarian, totality, totalize
≈tota-: totaquine
≈toti-: totipalmate, totipotent
- total-: subtotal, teetotal,
teetotalism

- totum: factotum, teetotum
[variant forms: surtout;
Italian: tutti, tutti-frutti]
[French forms: in toto, tout,
tout à fait, tout court, tout de
suite, tout ensemble, tout le
monde]
TOUT: to peep, look out after
TOVARICH, TOVARISH: Russian:
comrade
TOWN: orig., an enclosure for
protection
tox: poison; orig., arrow
≈tox-ic: toxic, toxicant, toxin
≈tox-: toxanemia, toxemia,
toxoid
≈toxic-: toxicosis
≈toxico-: toxicogenic, toxicology
≈toxo-: toxophilite,
toxoplasmosis
- toxic-: detoxicate, intoxicant,
intoxicate; phytotoxic
- toxin: with prefixes: antitoxin,
autotoxin, endotoxin, exotoxin
- toxin: with combining forms:
actinotoxin, hemotoxin,
mycotoxin, neurotoxin,
saxitoxin
trab: a beam
trabeated, trabecula
[variant forms: architrave;
tabernacle, tavern, taverna;
trave]
trach-ea: windpipe; from "rough"
≈trachea: trachea, tracheal,
tracheate, tracheid, tracheole
≈trach-: trachoma
≈trache-: trachealgia, tracheitis
≈tracheo-: tracheobronchial,
tracheopathia, tracheophyte,
tracheorraohy, tracheoscopy,
tracheotomy
- tracheal: bronchotracheal,
endotracheal, extratracheal,
infratracheal
≈trachyt-e: trachyte, trachytic

trachel: neck; **neck of an organ**
≈trachel: trachelate, trachelism
≈trachel-: trachelectomy,
   trachelitis, trachelodynia
≈trachelo-: trachelocele,
   trachelocystitis, trachelology,
   trachelopexy, tracheloplasty,
   tracheloschisis, trachelotomy
tract: to draw, pull; from "trahend"
≈tract: tract, tractable, tractate,
   tractile, traction, tractive,
   tractor
- tract: abstract, attract, contract,
   detract, distract, extract,
   protract, retract, subtract
- tractable: contractable,
   intractable, retractable
- tracted: abstracted, distracted
- tractile: protractile, retractile
- traction: abstraction,
   contraction, detraction,
   distraction, extraction,
   retraction
- tractive: abstractive, attractive,
   contractive, distractive,
   retractive
- tractor: attractor, or, attracter,
   detractor, protractor, retractor
- trahend: subtrahend
≈trait: trait
- trait-: distrait, portrait,
   portraitist, portraiture
- tray-: portray, portrayal
≈treat: treat, treatment
- treat-y: entreat, entreaty,
   estreat, maltreat, retreat
   [variant forms: trace, tracery,
   retrace; train, entrain; treatise,
   treaty, trattoria, tret, distraught]
   {word note: trattoria: Italian; orig.,
   innkeeper; a small, inexpensive
   restaurant in Italy}
tradit-e: a surrender; from *trans-*,
   across + *dare*, to give
≈tradition: tradition, traditional,
   traditionalism, traditionist

- tradit-e: extradite, extradition
   [variant forms: traitor, treason,
   betray]
trahend: see tract for subtrahend
trait: see tract
trance: see **it**, as in transit
TRANCHE: a slice
trans-: **across, through**
≈trans: transom, lit., that which is
   across; a crossbeam
≈trans-: transact, transalpine,
   transaminase, transanimation,
   transaxle
≈transceiver, transconductance,
   transcontinental
≈transduction, transfection,
   transfer, transfigure,
   transfinite, transfix, transform,
   transfuse
≈transgender, transgenic,
   transgress, transhumance,
   transient, transilluminate,
   transit, transitory
≈translate, transliterate,
   translocation, translucent
≈transmarine, transmigrant,
   transmigrate, transmissible,
   transmit, transmogrify,
   transmontane, or, tramontane,
   transmundane, transmute,
   transnational
≈transparent, transpierce,
   transplant, transport, transpose
≈transsexual, transvalue,
   transvestite
≈tra-: truncation of *trans-*:
   tramontane, or, transmontane,
   trapeze, trapezium, trapezoid,
   trapunto, traverse, travesty
≈tran-: truncation of *trans-*:
   tranquil, transcend, transcribe,
   transcription, transect,
   transilient, transistor,
   transonic, transpicuous,
   transpire, transponder,
   transubstantiate, transude

≈tre-: variant of *trans-*: trebuchet
≈tres-: variant of *trans-*: trespass
   [variant form: trestle]
trauma-t: injury, wound
≈trauma: trauma, traumatic,
   traumatism, traumatization,
   traumatize
≈trauma-: traumatherapy
≈traumato-: traumatogenic,
   traumatology, traumatophobia,
   traumatotropism
travail, travel, travois: see pal-e
trave: see trab
tray: see tract for portray
tray: see tradit-e for betray
treason: see dat-e; trans-
trec: a plait, leap
   entrechat—in ballet, a leap
   straight upward during which the
   dancer crosses the legs and beats
   the calves together
TREK: Afrikaans: to travel by ox
   wagon; thus, a treacherous journey
trem: to tremble
≈trem: tremble, tremendous,
   tremolo, tremor, tremulous
≈trep: trepidation
- trepid: intrepid
   [Spanish: temblor—earthquake]
   [phrase: delirium tremens]
tremat: a hole
   trematode; monotreme,
   peritreme
trench: see trunc-h
trepan: to bore (a hole)
   [see trypono]
   trepan, trepanation
trepid: see trem
trestle: see trans
tri-: three
≈tri: triad, Triassic, tribe,
   tribunal, trillium, trinary, trine,
   trinity, trio, triolet, triton
≈tri-: triacid, triangle, triarchy,
   triathlete, triaxial, tribrach
≈tricameral, tricentennial,
   triceps, triceratops, trichroism,

trichromatic, triclinic,
   triclinium, tricolor, tricorn,
   tricostate, tricrotic, tricuspid,
   tricycle
≈trident, tridentate, triennial
≈trifacial, trifecta, trifid, trifocal,
   trifoliate, trifoliolate, triforium,
   triform, trifurcate
≈trigeminal, triglyph, trigon,
   trigonometry, trigonous,
   trigram
≈trihedral, trihydrate, trijugate
≈trilateral, trilineal, triliteral,
   trilobate, trilocular, trilogy
≈trimerous, trimester, trimetric,
   trimetrogon, trimorph,
   trimorphism
≈trinomial, trioecious, trioxide
≈tripartite, tripartition,
   triphthong, tripinnate, triple,
   triplet, triplex, triplicate,
   triplicity, triploid, triply,
   tripod, tripos, triptych
≈triquetrous, triradiate, trireme
≈trisect, triskelion, trisomic,
   tristate, tristich, trisyllable
≈tritheism, tritone, triune, trivial,
   trivalent, trivet, trivium
≈tre-: variant of *tri-*: treble,
   trecento, trefoil, trellis,
   treillage, trephine
≈tricho: variant of *tri-*: trichotomy
≈tripl-: *tri- + ply*: triploid,
   triplopia
≈triplo-: *tri- + ply*: triploblastic
≈tris-: variant of *tri-*:
   triskaidekaphobia,
   trisoctohedron
≈trium-: variant of *tri-*: triumvir,
   triumviral, triumvirate
   [variant forms: drilling (through
   German), trammel, travel, travail,
   trey; trocar—second root is quad;
   Spanish: Trinidad—trinity;
   tribe—see trib-e^2]

trib-e[1]: **to rub** [see trit-e]
≈trib: tribadism, tribulation
≈tribo-: tribology,
   triboluminescence
- tribe: diatribe
   [variant forms: detriment,
   detrimental]
trib-e[2]: **to assign, allot**
≈trib-e: tribe, tributary, tribute,
   distributary
- tribute: attribute, contribute,
   distribute
- tribution: attribution,
   contribution, distribution,
   maldistribution, retribution
- tributive: attributive,
   contributive, distributive,
   retributive
- tributor: contributor, distributor
- tributory: contributory
TRIBECA: triangle below Canal
   Street, in Manhattan: noted as a
   center for artists, art galleries, etc.
tric: **hindrance, perplexity**
- tric: extricate, inextricable,
   intricacy, intricate
- trig-: intrigant, intrigue,
   intriguing
trich: **hair, hairlike, cilia, flagella**
≈trich: trichiasis, trichinous,
   trichina
≈trich-: trichite, trichoid,
   trichome, trichosis
≈trichin-: trichinosis
≈tricho-: trichobaceria,
   trichochrome, trichocyst,
   trichogyne, trichology,
   trichomonad, trichopathy,
   trichopteran
- trich: gastrotrich, heterotrich,
   hypotrich
- trichous: monotrichous,
   peritrichous, ulotrichous
TRIFLE, TRIFLING: of little value
trig: see tric for *intrigue*
trimaran: see catamaran

TRIMURTI: Sanskrit for the trinity of
   Hindu gods: Brahma, Vishnu, and
   Siva: from *tri*, three + *murti*, body,
   shape
trinsic: see secu
trit-e: **to rub, grind** [see trib-e[1]]
≈trite: trite, tritely, triteness
- trite: attrited, contrite
- trition: attrition, contrition,
   detrition
- tritus: detritus
≈tritur: triturate, trituration
- trity: cholelithotrity, lithotrity
   [variant forms: detriment,
   detrimental; lithotripsy;
   teredo, terete, termitarium,
   termite]
TRIUMPH, triumphalism, triumphant:
   hymn to Bacchus; sung in festal
   processions, especially after a
   great military victory; compare
   ovation
triv-e: **to turn**
   contrivance, contrive
troch-ee: **wheel**; from "to run"
≈troch: trochaic, trochal,
   trochanter, troche, trochee,
   trochilus
≈trochl: trochlea, trochlear
≈troch-: trochoid
≈trocho-: trochometer—an
   odometer, trochophore
   [variant forms: truck—one
   meaning, truckle]
trog-lo: **cave**; from "to gnaw"
   trogon; troglobiont, troglodyte,
   troglophile
   [variant form: trout]
trop-e: **to turn, change**
≈trop-e: trope, tropic, tropics,
   tropical, tropism
≈tropo-: tropology, tropopause,
   tropophilous, tropophyte,
   troposphere
- trope: heliotrope, hemitrope,
   thaumatrope
- tropia: esotropia, exotropia

- tropical: intertropical
- tropy: allotropy, apotropy, dystrophy, entropy, pleiotropy
- tropic: with prefixes: anisotropic, dexiotropic, isotropic
- tropic: with combining forms: glycotropic, laeotropic, lipotropic, neurotropic, organotropic, orthotropic, plagiotropic, vagotropic
- tropism: with prefixes: atropism, allotropism, autotropism, diageotropism, diatropism, orthotropism
- tropism: with combining forms: anemotropism, biotropism, chronotropism, geotropism, heliotropism, hydrotropism, lipotropism, meterotropism, neurotropism, nyctitropism, organotropism, phototropism, rheotropism, stereotropism, thermotropism, thigmotropism
- tropous: with prefixes: atropous, allotropous, amphitropous, anatropous, anisotropous, antitropous, hemitropous, heterotropous, homotropous, isotropous, orthotropous, peritropous, pleurotropous
- tropous: with combining form: campylotropous
  [variant forms: trophied, trophy, troubadour]

troph: to nourish, feed
≈troph: trophic
≈troph-: trophallaxis
≈tropho-: trophoblast, trophocyte, trophoderm, trophoedema, trophoneurosis, trophology, trophonucleus, trophopathia, trophoplasm, trophozoite
- trophy: atrophy, autotrophy, dystrophy, hypertrophy

- trophic: with prefixes: autotrophic, auxotrophic, dystrophic, eutrophic, heterotrophic, mesotrophic, oligotrophic, polytrophic, prototrophic
- trophic: with combining forms: mixotrophic, photoautotrophic
- trophin: somatotrophin

trov-e: to find
trove, trover
[variant forms: retrieve, retrievable, retriever, irretrievable]
TRUANT: Celtic: wretched; orig., a lazy, idle person

tru-e: a pledge; from "to stand"
truce, true, trust, trustee, trusty
[variant forms: truth, truthful]
TRUCULENT: cruel, mean, scathing; from *trux*, fierce, savage

trud: to thrust
- trude: detrude, extrude, intrude, obtrude, protrude
- trus-e: abstruse, protrusile
- trusion: detrusion, extrusion, intrusion, obtrusion, protrusion
- trusive: extrusive, intrusive, obtrusive, protrusive

trunc-h: a stem, trunk
≈truncate: truncate, truncated
- truncate: detruncate
≈trench: trench, trenchant, trencher, trencherman
- trench-: entrench, retrench, retrenchment
  [variant forms: trend, trinket, truncheon, trundle, trunk, trunnion]

trust: to stand
trust, distrust, distrustful, entrust
[variant forms: betroth, betrothed; truth]

try: to attempt
try; triage, trial; pretrial

trypano: to wear away, to bore
[see trepan]

≈trypano: trypanosome,
    trypanosomiasis

≈trypsin-o: trypsin, trypsinogen

- trypsin: chymotrypsin

TRYST: orig., a hunting station;
    hunting rendezvous; a secret
    appointment

TSETSE fly: Bantu; lit., fly that kills
    animals

TSORIS: Yiddish; trouble, distress,
    woe, misery

TSUNAMI: Japanese; *tsu*, a harbor +
    nami, a wave; a huge sea wave

TUATARA: Maori for an amphibious,
    lizardlike reptile

tub-e: tube

≈tub-e: tuba, tubal, tube, tubing

≈tubul: tubular, tubulate, tubule,
    tubulin, tubulous, tubulure

≈tubi-: tubifex

≈tubuli-: tubuliflorous

- tubate: extubate, intubate

- tube: phototube

- tubule: desmotubule,
    microtubule, myotubule,
    neurotubule

tuber: bump, bulge

≈tuber: tuber, tubercle, tuberose,
    tuberosity, tuberous

≈tubercul: tubercular,
    tuberculate, tuberculin

≈tubercul-: tuberculosis

- tuber-: extuberance,
    protuberance, protuberant

- tuberate: extuberate,
    protuberate
    [variant form: truffle]

tui: to look at

≈tuit: tuition

≈tute-l: tutee, tutelage, tutelary

≈tutor: tutor, tutorial

- tuit-: intuition, intuitive

TULIP: Turkish: *turban*, from the
    similarity of appearance

tum: to swell [see turg]

≈tum: tumescence, tumescent,
    tumid, tumor

≈tume-: tumefacient,
    tumefaction, tumefy

≈tumul: tumular, tumulose,
    tumulus

≈tumult: tumult, tumultuary,
    tumultuous

- tum-: contumacious, contumacy

- tume-: contumelious, contumely

- tumesce: intumesce

- tumescence: detumescence,
    intumescence

- tumescent: detumescent,
    intumescent
    [variant forms: thigh, thumb]

tune: see tone

tund: to beat, strike

- tund: obtund, retund

- tuse: contuse, obtuse, retuse

- tus-: contusion; obtusity
    [variant forms: pierce, transpierce]

TUNGSTEN: Swedish: heavy stone;
    orig. name for scheelite

tunic: a covering
    tunic, tunica, tunicate, tunicle
    [variant form: tourniquet—
    one meaning]

TUPELO: Creek *ito*, tree + *opilwa*,
    swamp; swamp tree

TURBAN: Turkish: turban, sash; see
    tulip

turb-id: to whirl; to disorder

≈turb: turbellarian, turbid;
    turbidite; turbinado sugar;
    turbinate, turbine

≈turbul: turbulence, turbulent

≈turbidi-: turbidimeter

≈turbo-: turbocharge,
    turbogenerator, turbojet,
    turboprop(eller)

- turb-: disturb, disturbance,
    perturb; perturbable,
    perturbation, imperturbable
    [variant forms: tourbillion,

trouble, troubled, troublesome,
troublous; trowel; turmoil]
{word note: tourbillion: a fireworks
device that rises with a spiral
motion}
turg: to swell [see tum]
turgescent, turgid, turgor
turn: to turn in a lathe
turn, return, returnable,
returnee; turnpike
{word note: turnpike: orig., similar
to a turnstile which allowed one
person to pass at a time; the
turnpike was equipped with a set
of pointed spears, or pikes, that
could be turned aside to let
travelers pass when they paid the
toll}
TURPITUDE: base, vile; from IE base,
meaning "from which one must
turn away"
TURQUOISE: orig., brought to
Western Europe through Turkey; a
semiprecious stone; the color of
turquoise: greenish blue
turr: tower
turret, turreted
[variant forms: tower, towering:
Spanish: torre—tower]
{word note: turreted: shaped like a
turret; also, having whorls forming
a high, conical spiral, as some
shells}
TUSCALOOSA, AL: Choctaw; *taska*,
warrior + *lusa*, black; Black
Warrior, name of Indian chief;
Black Warrior River flows
through Tuscaloosa
tuse: see tund for contuse, obtuse
tuss: to cough
tussive; antitussive,
Hypertussis®, pertussis—
whooping cough, Robitussin®
TWEED: orig. so called because the
fabric was made with a double
thread, known as *twill* in Scottish;
later associated with Tweed,
Scotland, where the fabric was
first made

TWILIGHT: lit., two light, but
probably meaning "half light";
related words: twin, twine
TYCOON: Chinese-Japanese *tai*, great
+ *kun*, monarch; term of respect
for an emperor; see *typhoon*
tympan: drum
tympan, tympani, tympanic,
tympanites, tympanitis,
tympanum, tympany
typ-e: a figure, model
≈typ-e: type, typecast, typical
≈typi-: typify
≈typo-: typographical,
typography, typology
- type: with prefixes: allotype,
antetype, antitype, ectype,
haplotype, holotype,
monotype, prototype
- type: with combining forms:
archetype, auxotype, cerotype,
collotype, graphotype,
logotype, phenotype,
phonotype, somatotype,
stenotype, stereotype
- typic: heterotypic, homeotypic,
polytypic
- typical: atypical, stereotypical
- typy: allotypy, amphitypy,
autotypy, entypy, homotypy,
lithotypy, monotypy,
phonotypy, phototypy,
stenotypy, thermotypy
typh: vapor, fever
≈typh: typhus
≈tyhp-: typhoid
- typhoid: arthrotyphoid,
paratyphoid, pharyngotyphoid,
pleurotyphoid, posttyphoid,
tonsillotyphoid
TYPHOON: Chinese: *tai-fung*: great
wind; see *tycoon*
tyran-ni: tyrant, an absolute ruler
≈tyrann: tyrannical, tyrannize,
tyrannous, tyranny
≈tyrant: tyrant

≈tyranni-: tyrannicide
≈tyranno-: tyrannosaur
TYRO: beginner, novice; from *tiro*,
   young soldier

U

uber: to bear abundantly; from
   "udder"
   exuberance, exuberant,
   exuberate
   [variant form: udder]
ubi: where
   ubiety, ubiquitous, ubiquity
   [phrases: ubi sunt, ubi supra]
U-BOAT: German for *Unterseeboot*,
   or "under sea boat"; a German
   submarine used in World War II
UKASE: Russian: in czarist Russia, an
   imperial order or decree, having
   the force of law; edict
UKULELE: Hawaiian: lit., leaping
   flea; a musical instrument
uln: elbow
   ulna, ulnar; ulnoradial
ulo^1: gums
   ulocarinoma, uloglossitis,
   ulorrhagia, ulotomy—one
   meaning, ulotripsis
ulo^2: scar
   ulotomy—one meaning
ULULANT: howling, wailing
ULCER, ulcerous: abscess, wound
ulo: woolly
   ulotrichous—having woolly or
   tightly twisted hair
ult: see s-ult for exult
ult-im: beyond
≈ult: ulterior, ultimate,
   ultimately, ultimatum, ultimo
≈ultimo-: ultimogeniture
- ult-: penult, penultimate
≈ultra: ultra, ultraism
≈ultra-: ultrabasic, ultracapacitor,
   ultracentrifuge, ultraertia,
   ultramarine, ultramontane,

ultramundane, ultrasonic,
   ultraviolet, ultravirus
   [variant forms: outrage,
   outrageous, outrance, outré]
   [phrases: ne plus ultra; ultima
   Thule]
{word note: outrage: an extremely
   vicious act; from outré:
   exaggerated, eccentric, bizarre}
umbel-l: shade
≈umbel-l: umbel, umbellate,
   umbellic, umbellule
≈umbelli-: umbelliferous,
   umbelliform
≈umbr: umbra, umbrage,
   umbrageous, umbrella
≈umbri-: umbriferous
- umbra-te: penumbra; adumbrate
- umbrella: subumbrella
   [variant forms: ombré, somber,
   sombrero, umber]
{word notes: <u>somber</u>: with *sub-*,
   under, *subumbrare*, to shade; thus,
   dark and gloomy; <u>sombrero</u>:
   Spanish for "under the shade";
   <u>umbrella</u>: Italian for "small shade}
umbilic: navel
≈umbilic: umbilic, umbilical,
   umbilicate, umbilication,
   umbilicus
≈umbil-: umbilectomy
≈umbili-: umbiliform
≈umbilico-: umbilicoplasty
≈umbo: umbo
UMIAK, UMIAQ: Eskimo: a large open
   boat
UMPIRE: lit., not equal; one who is
   not for either side; a referee
un-: not, negative
≈unadorned, unabridged,
   unaltered, unapt, unassuming,
   unattached, unattended,
   unbalance, unbalanced
   unbecoming, unbowed
≈unceremonious, uncertain,
   uncivil, uncomfortable,
   unconcern, unconcerned,

undeclared, unconditional,
unconformable, unconsidered,
unconscionable,
unconstitutional,
unconventional
≈undeceive, undecided,
undeniable, unequal,
unequivocal, unfamiliar,
unfilial, unfocused,
unimpeachable, unkempt,
unkind, unknown
≈unlettered, unlimited,
unmannerly, unmitigated,
unnatural, unnecessary,
unplumbed, unpopular,
unprincipled, unpublished
≈unqualified, unrealistic,
unrequited, unsaturated,
unscrupulous, unseasoned,
unsociable, unsocial,
unspeakable, unstable, unstep,
untenable

uncate: a hook
aduncate—curved or hooked, as
a parrot's beak

unct: to smear
unction, unctuous; inunction
[variant forms: ointment, anoint,
unguent]

und-ul: a wave
≈undul: undulant, undulate,
undulation, undulatory
- undance: abundance
- undant: abundant, inundant,
redundant, superabundant
- undate: inundate
[variant forms: abound, redound,
superabound, surround; sound—
one meaning]

ungu-l: hoof, nail
ungula, unguiculate, unguis,
ungulate; unguilograde;
notoungulate
[phrase: ad unguem]

un-i: one
≈uni: Uniate, union, unique

≈unit-e: unit, Unitarian, unitary,
unite, united, unitive, unitize,
unity
≈un-: unanimous
≈uni-: uniaxial, unibody,
unicameral, unicapsular,
unicellular, uniclinal, unicorn,
unicornate, unicostate,
unicycle, unidimensional
≈unifiable, unifilar, unifoliate,
unifoliolate, uniform, unify,
unijugate
≈unilateral, unilineal, unilingual,
unilocular
≈uniparous, unipersonal,
unipetalous, uniplanar,
unipolar, unipotent
≈uniramous, unisex, unisexual,
unison
≈univalent, univalve, universal,
universe, university, univocal
- un-e: coadunate; triune
- unify: reunify
- union: disunion, reunion
- unite: disunite, reunite
- unity: disunity
[variant forms: onion, ounce]
[phrase: e pluribus unum]

uran-o: heaven
uranium; uranography,
uranology, uranometry

urb: city
≈urb: urbia, urban, urbane,
urbanize
- urban-e: exburban, interurban,
suburban; inurbane
- urbation: conurbation
- urbia: exurbia, suburbia
[phrase: urbi et orbi]
- urbs: exurbs, suburbs
URDU: from Hindi *zaban-i-urdu*, lit.,
language of the camp; a Hindi
language, spoken mainly by
Pakistanis; the base of *Urdu* also
yields *horde*, a great number of
soldiers in a camp

ured-o: to burn, **blight**
uredinium, uredo;
uredophobia, uredospore
urge: to press hard
urge, urgency, urgent
-urgy words: see ergo
ur-o[1]: **urine**
≈ur: urea, ureter, urethra, uretic
≈urin-e: urinal, urinary, urinate
   urine
≈ur-: uremia
≈ureo-: ureotelic
≈urethr-: urethritis
≈uretero-: ureterostomy
≈urethro-: urethroscope
≈uri-: urinalysis [urine + analysis]
≈urico: uricosuric, uricotelic
   [urico=uric acid]
≈urini-: uriniferous
≈urino-: urinogenital
≈uro-: urocele, urochrome,
   urocyst, urogenital, urogenous,
   urokinase, urolith, urolithiasis,
   urology, uroscopy
- uresis: anuresis, diuresis,
   eneuresis
- uretic: diuretic
- uria: with prefixes: anuria,
   dysuria, polyuria
- uria: with combining forms:
   aciduria, adiposuria,
   albuminuria, bradyuria,
   cyanuria, erythruria, lipuria,
   nocturia, glycosuria,
   hematuria, hemoglobinuria,
   ketonuria, oliguria, opsiuria
ur-o[2]: **tail**
≈uro-: urochord, uropod,
   uropygial
- uran: anturan, xiphosuran
- ure: cynosure
- urous: anurous, brachyurous,
   macrurous
- urus: coenurus
   [variant forms: adulate, squirrel]

{word note: adulate: orig., to wag the
tail; to praise too highly or flatter
servilely; to admire intensely or
excessively}
usher: see or-al
ursi: **bear**
   ursine; ursiform;
   Ursa Major, Ursa Minor
urtic: **nettle**, to itch
   urticaria, urticate, urtication
us-e: **to use**
≈us: usage, usance, usual
≈use: use, useable, used, useful,
   useless, user
≈usur: usurer, usurious, usury
≈usurp: usurp, usurpation
≈usu-: usufruct, usufructuary
- use: abuse, disabuse, peruse
- usive: abusive
≈utensil: utensil
≈util-e: utile, utilitarian, utility,
   utilities, utilize
- util-e: disutility, inutile
ust-ul: **to burn**
   ustulate, ustulation; combust,
   combustion, combustor,
   combustible, incombustible
uter: **uterus**
≈uter: uterine, uterus
≈uter-: uterodynia
≈utero-: uterocele, uterocervical,
   uterogenic, uteroglobin,
   uterography, uterolith,
   uterometer, uteroplasty,
   uterotomy
- uterine: extrauterine,
   intrauterine
UTOPIA: a place or state of ideal
   perfection; from Sir Thomas
   More's *Utopia*, lit., not a place
uv: **to put on**
   exuviae, exuviate
   [variant form: omentum]
uv-e: **grapelike**; from *uva*, grape
   uvea, uvula, uvular; uveitis;
   uvulectomy, uvulitis

uxor-i: wife
≈uxor: uxorial, uxorious
≈uxori-: uxoricide, uxorilocal

V

vac: empty
≈vac: vacancy, vacant, vacate,
vacation; vacuity, vacuous,
vacuum
≈vacuol-e: vacuolate,
vacuolation, vacuole
- vacu-: evacuant, evacuate,
evacuation, evacuee
≈vain: vain, vainglorious,
vainglory, vainly
≈van: vanish, vanitas, vanity
- vanesc-e: evanesce,
evanescence, evanescent
≈vast: vast, vastitude, vasty
- vastate: devastate
≈void: void, voidance, voided
- void: avoid, devoid
[variant form: vaunt]
[phrase: in vacuo]
vaccin-e: from *vacca*, **cow**
vaccinal, vaccinate,
vaccination, vaccine, vaccinia
[Spanish: vaca—cow;
vaquero—cowboy; carne de
vaca—lit., meat of the cow;
beefsteak]
vacill: to sway back and forth
vacillant, vacillate
[variant form: varus—bent]
vad-e: to go
≈vad: vadose
- vade: evade, invade, pervade
- vasion: evasion, invasion
- vasive: evasive, invasive,
pervasive
[variant forms: wade; American
Spanish: old slang: vamoose—
from *vamos*, let us go; to leave
quickly; go away from hurriedly]

[phrase: vade mecum, lit., go with
me; a handbook; manual]
vag-a: to wander
≈vaga: vagabond, vagabondage,
vagal
≈vagar: vagarious, vagary
≈vagu-e: vague, vagus
≈vagr: vagrancy, vagrant
- vagal: vasovagal
- vagan-: extravagance,
extravagant; extravaganza
- vagate: divagate, extravagate
[variant form: rave]
vagin: sheath, vagina
≈vagin-a: vagina, vaginal,
vaginate, vaginismus
≈vagin-: vaginitis, vaginosis
≈vagino-: vaginocele,
vaginogram, vaginography,
vaginolabial, vaginopathy,
vaginopexy, vaginoscope,
vaginotomy, vaginovesical,
vaginovulvar
≈vago-: vagolysis, vagotomy,
vagotonia, vagotropic
- vaginate: evaginate, exvaginate,
invaginate
[variant form: vanilla, from its
elongated fruit]
VALANCE: may be from Valence,
France, center of textile
manufacturing; short drapery
val-e: valley
vale, vallecula, valley;
intervale; reveal—one meaning
{word note: reveal: that part of the
side of an opening for a window
or door which is between the outer
edge of the opening and the frame
of the window or door; jamb}
VALGUS: from "to turn"; clubfoot in
which the foot is turned outward;
orig., bowlegged
**val-id: to be strong, to be worth,
to be well**
≈val: valence, valetudinarian,
valiant

≈valid: valid, validate, validation, validity

≈valor: valor, valorization, valorize, valorous

≈valu-e: valuable, valuate, value, valued, valuta

≈vale-: valediction, valedictorian, valedictory

- valence: ambivalence bivalence, covalence, equivalence, trivalence, univalence

- valent: bivalent, divalent, equivalent, hexavalent, monovalent, multivalent, pentavalent, polyvalent, prevalent, quadrivalent, quinquevalent, tervalent, tetravalent, trivalent, univalent

- valesc-e: convalesce, convalescence, convalescent

- valiant: pot-valiant

- valid-: invalid—two meanings, invalidate, invalidism, revalidate

- valuable: invaluable, unvaluable

- valuate: evaluate, revaluate, reevaluate

- valuation: devaluation, evaluation, reevaluation

- value: disvalue, misvalue, transvalue, undervalue

- vail-: avail, countervail, prevail, prevailing; unavailing

- vailable: available, unavailable
  [phrase: ad valorem—according to the value, as *ad valorem tax*]

val-l: wall, palisade
contravallation, interval
{word note: interval: orig., the space between two palisades or walls; gap; distance; in mathematics, the set containing all numbers between two given numbers; in

music, the difference in pitch between two tones}

valv-e: leaf of a folding door
≈valv-e: valvate, valvule, valve
- valve: bivalve, inequivalve, thermovalve, univalve
VAMPIRE: from Slavic folklore: a corpse that becomes reanimated and leaves its grave at night to suck the blood of sleeping persons
VANDA: Hindi: mistletoe; an orchid
VANDALISM: from the Vandals, an East Germanic people that ravaged Gaul, Spain, and North Africa and sacked Rome; malicious or ignorant destruction of public or private property

vane: small flag, pennon
vane, paravane
vanish: see vac
vantage: see ante

vap: moisture, vapor, steam
≈vapid: vapid, vapidity
≈vapor: vapor, vaporetto, vaporing, vaporizer, vaporous
≈vapori-: vaporific, vaporiform, vaporimeter
- vapo-: evapotranspiration
- vapor-: evaporate, evaporite

var-i: to vary, change
≈vari: varia, variable, variance, variant, variate, variation
≈varie-d: varied, variegate, variegated, variegation, varier, varietal, variety
≈vario-us: variorum, various
≈vari-: varicolored, variform
≈vario-: variocoupler, variogram, variometer
- vari-: covariance, invariable, invariably, invariant
- variate: bivariate, covariate, multivariate, univariate
≈vary: vary
  [variant forms: vair, miniver; varistor—various + resistor]
  [phrase: varia lectio]

varic: **to straddle**
divaricate, divarication,
divaricator, prevaricate
{word note: prevaricate: lit., to walk
crookedl; to turn aside from, or
evade, the truth; equivocate; to tell
an untruth; to lie}

varic-o: **pustule**, **pimple**, **enlarged**
vein; raised area of skin [see
related var-i]

≈varic: variceal, varicellate,
varicose, varicosis, varicosity

≈varico-: varicocele, varicotomy

≈vario-: variolite

≈variol-e: variolate—one
meaning, variole

≈varix: varix, pl., varices

{word note: variolite: a basic rock
whose pockmarked appearance is
caused by the presence of
numerous white, rounded,
embedded spherules}

vario: **smallpox** [from *varius*,
speckled; see var-i; also, varic-o]

≈varic: varicella

≈vario: variola, variolate—one
meaning, variolous

≈variol-: varioloid—a mild form
of smallpox

VARNISH: from Berenike, now
Benghazi, ancient city in
Cyrenaica; a resin; as a verb, to
make superficially attractive or
acceptable, as by embellishing, as
to varnish the truth

VARVE: from Swedish *varv*, layer;
from *varva*, to bend; ultimately
from Old Norse *hverfa*; in
geology, a layer or series of layers
of sediment deposited in a body of
still water in one year

vas-cul: **vessel**

≈vas-e: vas, vascular, vasculum,
pl., vascula, vasculatur, vase

≈vas-: vasectomy

≈vasculi-: vasculiferous,
vasculiform

≈vasculo-: vasculocardiac,
vasculogenesis, vasculomotor,
vasculopathy

≈vaso-: vasoactive,
vasoconstrictor, vasodilator,
vasoinhibitor, vasopressin,
vasopressor, vasospasm,
vasotomy, vasovagal

- vasat-e: extravasate,
intravasation

- vascular: with prefixes:
avascular, circumvascular,
extravascular, hypervascular,
intravascular, microvascular

- vascular: with combining forms:
cardiovascular, dermovascular,
gastrovascular, myovascular,
neurovascular
[medical term: vas deferens]

VASELINE®: from German *Wasser*,
water + Greek *elaion*, oil + –*ine*,
arbitrary suffix; a petroleum jelly
manufactured by Chesebrough
Ponds

VATIC; vaticinal, vaticinate: prophet;
of a prophet; prophetic

vect: **to carry**, **bring**

≈vect: vector, vectored, vectorial,
vectorization

- vection: advection,
circumvection, convection,
evection, provection

- vective: advective, convective,
invective

≈veh: vehement, vehicle,
vehicular

- vey: convey, conveyance

- veigh: inveigh

≈vex: vex, vexation, vexatious

- vex: convex
[variant forms: convoy, veliation,
velites]

{word note: invective: inveighing;
using, inclined to use, or
characterized by strong verbal
abuse; as a noun, a violent verbal

attack; strong criticism, insults,
curses, etc.; vituperation}

veget: **to enliven**
vegetable, vegetal, vegetarian,
vegetate, vegetation,
vegetative; revegetate
veigle: see ocul for inveigle
veil: see vigil for reveille

vel[1]: **to cover, wrap**
≈vel-a: vela, velamen, velar,
velarium, velarize, velate;
velum
- velation: revelation
- velop-e: develop, development,
envelop, envelope
[variant forms: développé,
reveal—one meaning,
veil, veiled, veiling, voile]

vel[2]: **shaggy hair**; from "wool"
velure, velutinous;
velvet, velveteen, velvety
[variant forms: velour, or velours,
velouté]

vellic: **to pluck out**
vellicate, vellication
[variant form: svelte—French;
from Italian *svelto*; past participle
of *svegliere*, to pull out; slender
and graceful; lithe: used chiefly of
women; suave, polished]
VELLUM: a parchment made from
calfskin, lambskin, or kidskin;
from *veal*, calf

velo-ci: **speed**
velocity; velocimeter,
velocipede; velodrome

ven[1]: **to sell**
≈ven: venal, venality; venatic
≈vend: vend, vendee, vendible,
vendition, vendor, vendue

ven[2]: **to hunt**
venatic, venery, venison

ven-e[1]: **vein**
≈ven: venation, venose, venous,
venule
≈ven-: venectasia, venectomy

≈vene-: venepuncture, or
venipuncture, venesection,
venesuture
≈veni-: venipuncture, venisuture
≈veno-: venogram, venography
- venous: intravenous
[variant forms: vein, veined,
veining, veinule, veiny]
[medical term: vena cava]

ven-e[2]: **to come**
≈ven: venire, venue
- ven-: coven, souvenir
- venance: convenance,
prevenance, provenance
- venant: covenant, revenant
- vene: advene, convene,
contravene, intervene,
reconvene, subvene, supervene
- venience: convenience,
disconvenience,
inconvenience, intervenience,
provenience, supervenience
- venient: convenient,
inconvenient, intervenient,
prevenient, unconvenient
- vent: advent, convent, event,
invent, prevent
- ventitious: adventitious
- vention: convention, invention,
intervention, obvention,
prevention, subvention
- ventional: conventional,
unconventional
- ventive: adventive, inventive,
preventive
- ventor-y: inventor, inventory
- ventual-: eventual, eventuality,
eventually, eventuate
≈ventur-e: venture, venturesome,
venturous
- venture: adventure,
misadventure, peradventure
- venu-e: avenue, parvenu,
revenue, revenuer
[phrase: venire facias]

VENEER: from French *fournir*, to
furnish; to cover over with a thin
layer of more costly material
ven-er-eo: to love
venial, venerable, venerate,
venereal, venery; venereology
VENEZUELA: lit., Little Venice, from
the natives' houses being built on
stilts much like those of the
Venetian explorers
venge: see vict-or for revenge
venom: poison; orig., love potion
venom, venomous; envenom;
venin; antivenin
vent-il: wind
≈vent: vent, ventage, ventail
≈ventil: ventilate, ventilation,
ventilator, ventilatory
≈venti-: ventifact
- ventilation: hyperventilation,
hypoventilation,
overventilation,
underventilation
[variant forms: vol-au-vent;
Spanish: viento—wind]
vent-r: stomach
≈vent-r: venter, ventral, ventricle,
ventricose, ventricular,
ventriculus
≈ventri-: ventriduction,
ventriflexion, ventriloquial,
ventriloquist
≈ventro-: ventrodorsal,
ventrofixation, ventrolateral,
ventroptosis, ventroscopy,
ventrotomy
- ventriculus: proventriculus
[variant form: Gros Ventre: big
belly; a member of a western tribe
of the Arapaho]
VERANDA: Hindi: balcony; in
America, an open porch or portico
verb: to lash, whip
reverb, reverberant,
reverberate, reverberation,
reverberatory

verb-i: word
≈verb: verb, verbal, verbalism,
verbalist, verbalize, verbatim;
verbiage, verbid; verbose
≈verbi-: verbigeration
- verb: adverb, proverb
- verb-: deverbative, proverbial
[variant form: verve]
[phrases: sub verbo, ipsissima
verba]
VERBOTEN: German: forbidden;
prohibited
verd-i: green
≈verd: verdant, verderer, or
verderor, verdure, verdurous
≈verdi-: verditer [second root is
terr, earth], verdigris [second
root is *Greece*]
≈viresc: virescence, virescent
≈virid: viridescent, viridian,
viridity
- verdin: biliverdin
[variant forms: verjuice; vert,
terre-verte; Vermont]
{word note: verderer: in medieval
England, a judicial officer who
maintained law and order in the
king's forests}
ver-e: to fear, to be in awe
revere, reverence, reverend,
reverent, reverential;
irreverence
verge: see vers-e
ver-i: true
≈ver: veracious, veracity, veriest,
verily, verism
≈verit-y: veritable, verity
≈ver-: verdict
≈veri-: veridical; verifiable,
verification, verify, verisimilar,
verisimilitude
- ver-: aver, inveracity
[variant forms: verismo, vérité]
[phrases: in vino veritas, voir dire]
{word note: verdict: lit., a thing said;
true saying; in law, the formal
finding of a judge or jury}

verm-i: worm, interpreted as "red worm"

≈verm: vermeil; vermicelli, vermilion

≈vermicul: vermicular, vermiculate, vermiculation, vermiculite

≈vermin: vermin, vermination, verminous

≈vermi-: vermicide, vermiform, vermifuge
[variant form: varmint]
{word note: vermicelli: lit., little worms; very thin spaghetti}
VERMOUTH: from French *vermout*; from German *Wermut*, wormroot; a white wine flavored with wormroot

vern: belonging to spring
vernal, vernalize, vernation
VERNACULAR: orig., belonging to home-born slaves; using the native language

verruc: wart
verruca, verrucas; verruciform

vers-e: to turn, bend

≈vers-e: versant, versatile, verse, versed, versicle, version, verso, versus

≈versi-: versicolor, versification, versifier, versify

- vers-: diversionary, revers
- versal: reversal, universal
- versary: adversary, anniversary
- versate: tergiversate
- versation: conversation, malversation
- verse: averse, adverse, converse, diverse, inverse, obverse, perverse, reverse, traverse, transverse, universe
- versi-: diversification; diversify
- versible: eversible, reversible, irreversible
- versity: diversity, perversity, university

- rse of *verse*: dextrorse, extorse, intorse, retrorse, sinistrorse
- s-e of *verse*: prosaic, prosaism, prose, proser, prosy
- version: with prefixes: aversion, ambiversion, anteversion, conversion, diversion, extroversion, inversion, introversion, obversion, perversion, retroversion, subversion
- version: with combining form: animadversion
- versive: aversive, conversive, eversive, extraversive, extroversive, introversive, inversive, perversive, reversive, subversive
- versy: controversy

≈vert: vertex, vertical, verticil, verticillaster, verticillate

- vert: avert, advert, antevert, convert, controvert, divert, evert, extrovert, invert, introvert, obvert, pervert, revert, subvert
- vert-: advertise, divertimento, diverting, divertissement, evertor, inadvertent
- verted: extroverted, introverted, perverted
- vertible: convertible, inconvertible, incontrovertible, indivertible

≈vertebra: vertebra, pl., vertebrae, vertebral, vertebrate: backbone

- vertebrate: invertebrate
- verticul-: diverticulitis diverticulosis, diverticulum

≈vertig: vertiginous, vertigo

≈verge: verge (two related meanings)

- verge: converge, diverge
- vergence: convergence, divergence

- vergent: convergent, divergent,
  nonconvergent
- vorce-: divorce, divorcé,
  divorcée, divorcement
≈vort: vortex, pl., vortexes, or
  vortices, vortical, vorticella,
  vorticism, vorticose,
  vortiginous
  [variant forms: varsity,
  bouleversement]
  [phrase: vers libre—free verse]

vesic: bladder, blister
  vesica, vesical, vesicant,
  vesicate, vesication, vesicle,
  vesicular, vesiculate
  [variant form: vessel]

vesp: wasp
  vespiary, vespid, vespine

vesper: evening
  vesper, vespers, vesperal,
  vespertine; vesper sparrow—
  so called from its singing in the
  evening
  [vespertilionid: a family of
  long-tailed bats]
VESPUCCI, Amerigo (1454-1512),
  Italian navigator and explorer;
  eponym of America

vest: to clothe
≈vest: vest, vested, vestiary,
  vesting, vestment, vestry,
  vesture
- vest: devest, divest, invest
- vest-: investitive, travesty,
  transvestite
- vestiture: divestiture, investiture
- vestment: investment
VESTAL: pertaining to Vesta, the
  goddess of the hearth; short for
  vestal virgin; a chaste woman
VESTIBULE: an entrance hall; in
  anatomy and zoology, any cavity
  or space serving as an entrance to
  another cavity or space

vestig-e: trace, footprint
  vestige, vestigial; investigate,
  investigation

veter: old
  veteran, veterinarian,
  veterinary; inveterate
  {word note: veterinarian: orig., one
  who treated "old" animals}
VETO: a one-word Latin sentence: I
  forbid
vex: see vect

vexill-o: a standard, flag; from
  "veil"
  vexillar, vexillary, vexillate,
  vexillation, vexillum, pl.,
  vexilla; vexillographer,
  vexillology

vi-a: way, road
≈via: via, viatic, viaticum
≈via-: viaduct
- via-l: trivia; trivial, triviality,
  trivialize
- viant: deviant
- viate: deviate, obviate
- vious: devious, obvious,
  pervious, previous, impervious
- vium: quadrivium, trivium
  [variant forms: envoi, invoice,
  voyage, voyageur, envoy, foy]
  [phrase: via media]

vibr-a: to shake, vibrate
  vibraculum, vibrancy, vibrant,
  vibrate, vibratile, vibration,
  vibrative, vibrato, vibrator,
  vibratory, vibrio; vibrissa
  [variant form: veer]

vic-ar: substitute, change
≈vic: vicar, vicarage, vicarial,
  vicariate, vicarious, vicissitude
≈vice-: vicegerency, vicegerent,
  vice-president, vicereine,
  viceroy
≈vis-: viscount, viscountess

vic-e: vice, fault
≈vic-e: vice, vicious
≈vit: vitiable, vitiate, vitiligo
≈vitu-: vituperate, vituperation
  [terms: vice squad, vicious
  circle]

VICHYSSOISE: from Vichy, a city in France; a smooth, thick soup

vicin: **near**, **group of houses**, **village**; see ec-o
vicinage, vicinal, vicinity
[Spanish: vecindad— vicinity]

VICTIM, victimize: orig., a person or animal killed as a sacrifice to a god in a religious rite

vict-or: **to conquer**, **overcome**

≈vic: victor, victorious, victory
- vict-: convict, evict
- viction: conviction, eviction
- victive: convictive, evictive
≈vincible: vincible
≈vin-: vindicable, vindicate, vindictive
- vinc-e: convince, evince; convincing
- vincible: convincible, evincible, invincible, inconvincible
≈venge: vengeance, vengeful
- venge-: avenge, revenge, revengeful
[variant forms: vanquish; revanchism, vendetta]

VICUÑA: Quechan: a small llama

vid-eo: **to see**

≈video: video
≈video-: videography
- vid-e: invidious, provide, providing
- vidence: evidence, providence
- vident: evident, provident, improvident
- vident-: evidentiary, evidently, providential
≈vis-ion: visa, visage, visibility, visible, vision, visional, visionary, visor
- visible: invisible
≈visit: visit, visitable, visitant, visitation, visitatorial, visitor
≈visual: visual, visualize
- vis-: envisage; improvisation, invisible, proviso

- visable: advisable, inadvisable
- vise: advise, improvise, previse, revise, supervise
- vision: envision, prevision, provision, revision, television
- vision-: provisional, revisionist
- visit: revisit
- visory: advisory, provisory, revisory, supervisory
≈view: view, viewing, viewless, viewy
- view: counterview, interview, overview, preview, purview, review
- vey-: purvey, purveyance, survey, surveyor
[variant forms: advice, envious, vide, videlicet, vide post, envy, gazebo, prudence, prudent, vista, voilà, videlicit; revue; voyeur, voyeurism, voyeuristic; clairvoyant]
[phrases: vide ante, vide infra, vide supra, quod vide (Q.V.); vis-à-vis, déja vu]

vid-e: **to separate**

- vid-e: divide, divided, dividend, divider
- divide: subdivide
- vidual: individual, individualism, individuality, individualize, individually
- viduate: individuate
- vis-e: divisive, divisor; devise
- visible: divisible, indivisible
- vision: division, subdivision
[variant form: device]
{word note: individual: that which cannot be divided; not separable}

VIETNAM: a Chinese compound meaning "those strangers to the south" of China

vigil: **to watch**, **to arouse**

≈vigil: vigil, vigilant, vigilante, vigilantism
- vigilate: invigilate

- veil: surveil
- veill-e: reveille, surveillance,
  surveillant
{word note: reveille: a trumpet call
  to awaken soldiers and sailors; the
  first formation of the day in the
  military}
vigor: **to be strong**
≈vigor: vigor, vigorous, vigoroso
- vigor-: invigorate, invigorating
VIGORISH: Yiddish, or Russian:
  winnings, profit
vil-e: **cheap, base**; from "venal"
  [see ven¹]
  vile, vilification, vilify,
  vilipend
vill: **fleece, wool**
≈vill: villosity, villous, villose,
  villus
≈villi-: villiform
- villus: microvillus
  [variant form: velvet]
villa: **farm house** [see ec-o]
≈villa-ge: villa, village, villager;
  villatic
≈villain: villain, villainous,
  villainy
≈villan: villanella, villanelle
≈villein: villein, villeinage
{word note: villain: orig., a farm
  servant; then, a serf; the
  boorishness of such a servant
  came to mean a knave, a
  scoundrel; thus, a villain
[Note: Hundreds of place names end
  in –ville.]
VIMEN: in botany, a long flexible
  shoot or branch
vin-e: **vine**
≈vin-e: vinaceous, vinaigrette,
  vinic, vinous; vine, vinery,
  vineyard
≈vine-: vinegar, vinegaroon,
  vinegary [second root is acrid]
≈vini-: viniculture, vinifera,
  viniferous, vinification, vinify
≈vint: vintage, vintager, vintner

[variant forms: alegar, vignette,
  vinyl; vino, vin rosé; vise, vitta,
  viticulture, wine]
VINCULUM: that which binds; bond;
  fetter; tie; from *vincere*, to bind; in
  anatomy, a band or connecting
  fold; in *mathematics*, a line drawn
  over two or more terms of a
  compound quantity to show that
  they are to be treated together
viol: **to use force or violence**
≈violat-e: violate, violation,
  violator, violent
- viol-: inviolable, inviolate
vir: **man, worth**
≈vir: virago
≈viril-e: virile, virilism, virility
≈virtu-e: virtu, virtual, virtually,
  virtue, virtuoso, virtuous
≈viri-: virilocal—same as
  patrilocal
- vir: decemvir, duumvir,
  triumvir
- viral: decemviral, septemviral,
  triumviral
- virate: centumvirate,
  decemvirate, duumvirate,
  quadrumvirate, septemvirate,
  sextumvirate, triumvirate,
  viginitivirate
  [phrase: toga virilis]
{word note: virago: a quarrelsome,
  shrewish, nagging woman; a
  scold}
virg: **twig**
  virga, virgate; virgin, virginal,
  virginity: maiden; akin to "twig";
  virgulate, virgule; verge—one
  meaning
virid: see verd-i
viron: **a circuit**; from "to turn"
  environ, environment, environs
vir-us: **poison**
≈vir-us: viral, virion, virulence,
  virulent, virus
≈vir-: viroid, virosis
≈viro-: virology

≈viru-: virucide
- viral: antiviral, enteroviral
- virus: with prefixes:
  polyomavirus, retrovirus,
  ultravirus
- virus: with combining forms:
  calcivirus, coltivirus,
  myxovirus, oncovirus,
  poliovirus, rhabdovirus,
  rhinovirus

visc[1]: **an inner part of the body;
intestines**
  viscus, pl., viscera, visceral;
  eviscerate

visc[2]: **birdlime: stickiness**
  viscid, viscoid, viscose,
  viscosity, viscous; inviscid

vit: **to shun**
  evitable, inevitable

vit-e: origin obscure; possibly
  means "to hunt"
  invitation, invitational,
  invitatory, invite, inviting;
  disinvite
  [variant form: vie]

vitell: **egg yolk**
  vitellin, vitelline, vitellus

vitr-i: **glass**
≈vitre: vitreous, vitrescent
≈vitri: vitric, vitrics, vitrine
≈vitriol: vitriol, vitriolic,
  vitriolize
≈vitri-: vitriform, vitrify
- vitrify: devitrify
  [variant form: verglas]
  [phrase: in vitro]
  {word notes: vitrine: a glass-paneled
  cabinet or glass display case for
  art objects, curios, etc.; vitriol:
  sharpness or bitterness of feeling,
  as in speech or writing}

viv-e: **life**
≈vi: viable, viand
≈vi-: viper, viperine, viperous
≈viv: vivacious, vivacity,
  vivarium, vivid, vividity

≈vivi-: vivify, viviparous,
  viviparum, vivisect,
  vivisection, vivisectionist
- viable: inviable
- vival: revival, survival
- vive: revive, survive
- vivi-: antivivisection, revivify,
  reviviscent
- vivial: convivial
- vivor: survivor, survivorship
- vivus: redivivus
≈vital: vital, vitalism, vitality,
  vitalize
- vitalize: devitalize, revitalize
≈vitamin: vitamin
- vitamin: antivitamin,
  decavitamin, hexavitamin,
  megavitamin, multivitamin,
  oleovitamin, provitamin
  [variant forms: victual, victualer]
  [phrases: viva voce, vive, in vivo,
  inter vivos, savoir-vivre, aqua
  vitae, arbor vitae, qui vive?,
  speculum vitae, taedium vitae]

voca: **to call**
≈voc: vocable, vocabulary
≈vocal: vocal, vocalic, vocalise,
  vocalism, vocalist, vocalize
≈vocat: vocation, vocational,
  vocative
≈voci-: vociferant, vociferate,
  vociferous
- vocable: evocable, revocable,
  irrevocable
- vocacy: advocacy
- vocal: equivocal, univocal
- vocalic: intervocalic, prevocalic
- vocate: advocate, equivocate
- vocation: avocation,
  convocation, evocation,
  equivocation, invocation,
  provocation, revocation
- vocative: evocative,
  provocative
- vocator: equivocator

≈voice: voice, voiced, voiceless
- voice: revoice
[NB: invoice; see vi-a]
- voke: evoke, convoke,
  equivoke, invoke, provoke,
  revoke
- voque: equivoque
≈vouch: vouch, voucher
≈vow-el: vow, vowel, vowelize
- vow-: avow, avowed, disavow,
  disavowal
- vox: Magnavox®
[phrases: sotto voce, sub
  voce, viva voce, vox populi]
VODKA: Russian *voda*: water; brandy
VOGUE: fashion; from "rowing of a
  ship"
vola: to fly
volant, volatile, volatilize,
vole—one meaning; volitant,
volitation; volley, volleyball;
volplane
[variant form: vol-au-vent]
VOLAR: in anatomy, the palm of the
  hand or the sole of the foot [see
  palm]
volcan: a vent in the earth's crust;
from Vulcan, Roman god of fire
and metalworking
volcanic, volcanism, volcanize,
volcano; volcanologist,
volcanology
[variant form: vulcanization]
vol-i: to wish, to be willing
≈voli: volition, volitive
- volence: benevolence,
  malevolence, unbenevolence
- volent: benevolent, malevolent
≈voluntar-y: voluntarism,
  voluntary, voluntaryism
- voluntary: involuntary
≈volunteer: volunteer,
  volunteerism
≈volupt-: voluptuary, voluptuous
[variant forms: velleity, volupté]
[phrase: nolens volens]

VOLKSLIED: German: folk song
VOLOST: Russian: peasant
volt: an electrical measure; from
Italian physicist Alessandro Volta
(1745-1827)
volt, voltage, voltaic, voltaism;
voltmeter; voltameter
volu-me: to roll
≈volu-me: voluble, volume,
  voluminous
≈volu-: volumeter, volumetric
≈volut-e: volute, volution
- volute: convolute, evolute,
  involute, obvolute, revolute,
  supervolute
- volution: convolution,
  devolution, evolution,
  involution, macroevolution,
  obvolution, revolution
- volution-: evolutionist,
  revolutionize; revolutionary
≈volv: volva, volvox, volvulus
- volve: circumvolve, convolve,
  devolve, evolve, involve,
  intervolve, revolve
- volv-: convolvulus, involved,
  revolver, revolving
≈volt-: volt—one meaning
- volt: archivolt, revolt, revolting
- voluc-: involucel, involucrate,
  involucre: wrapper, case,
  envelope
≈vulv: vulva, pl., vulvas, or vulvae,
  vulval, vulvismus, same as
  vaginismus
≈vulv-: vulvectomy, vulvitis,
  vulvodynia
≈vulvi-: vulviform
≈vulvo-: vulvocrurual,
  vulvovaginal, vulgovaginitis,
  vulvopathy, vulvorectal
[variant forms: vault, vaulted,
  vaulting, volte-face; cavort]
{word note: cavort: to leap about;
  prance; to romp about happily;
  frolic}

VOMER: lit., plowshare; in anatomy, the flat bone separating the nasal passages

vomit: to discharge, **vomit**
vomit, vomitive, vomitory, vomitous, vomiturition, vomitus
[phrase: nux vomica]

vor-e: **to eat**
≈vor: voracious, voracity
- vore: carnivore, detritivore, frugivore, herbivore, insectivore, mucivore, nectarivore, omnivore, pollinivore, verbivore
- vorous: algivorous, amphivorous, apivorous, arachnivorous, baccivorous, calcivorous, carnivorous, equivorous, frugivorous, fucivorous, fungivorous, graminvorous, granivorous, herbivorous, insectivorous, lactivorous, lignivorous, limivorous, omnivorous, piscivorous
[variant form: devour]

vot: **a wish**, **vow**
≈vot-e: votary, vote, voter, votive
- vot-e: devote, devoted, devotee, devotion
[phrase: ex voto]

vulg-e: **common people**
≈vulg: vulgar, vulgarian, vulgarity, vulgarization, vulgarize, Vulgate
- vulg-e: divulge, divulgence
[variant forms: Vulgar Latin; promulgate]

vulner: **wound**, **injury**
vulnerable, vulnerary; invulnerable
[variant forms: vulture, vulturine, vulturous]
VULPINE: like a fox; clever, cunning, sly

vuls-e: **to pull**, **pluck**
convulse; avulsion, convulsion, divulsion, evulsion, revulsion
vulva: see volum-e

W-Z

WADI: Arabic: dry riverbed
WAFER, WAFFLE: Dutch
WAIF, WAIVE, WAIVER: to abandon
WALNUT: lit., "foreign nut" as perceived by the British
WANDERJAHR: German: wander year
WAPITI: Shawnee: one with a white rump; the elk
WAPPENSCHAWING: Scottish: weapon-showing
ward: see gar-r
ware: see gar-r
WARLOCK: Anglo-Saxon: orig., faith or oath breaker; now, a male witch
WEDNESDAY: orig., Woden's Day; in Germanic mythology, Woden was the chief deity; identified with Norse Odin
WELCOME: orig, a welcome or pleasure-guest; from *willa*, pleasure + *cuma*, guest
WEREWOLF: IE *wiros*, man + Old English *wulf*, wolf; in English folklore, a person changed into a wolf, or one capable of assuming the form of a wolf at will; a lycanthrope
WHISK: from Old Norse *visk*; orig. referred to a wisp; came to mean brush, broom
WHISKEY: Irish and Scottish *usquebaugh*, lit., water of life
WINDOW: Norse *vindra*, wind + *auga*, eye; *vindauga*, wind eye
WINNEBAGO: Fox: person of dirty water in reference to muddy waters of a nearby river
WINNEPEG: Cree: body of muddy water

WISTERIA: after Caspar Wistar (1761-
1818), U.S. anatomist; a flower
WORDHOARD: Anglo-Saxon:
vocabulary; stored or hoarded,
words
wright: Old English *wyrhta*, maker,
worker
boatwright, millwright,
playwright, shipwright,
wainwright, wheelwright
WUNDERKIND: German; lit., wonder
child; a child prodigy
WYOMING: the state was named after
Wyoming Valley, a valley of the
Susquehanna River; the valley was
named from German *Wayomick*, a
transliteration of Munsee (a
Delaware language) *chwewamink*,
large river bottom
xanth-o: yellow
≈xanth: xanthate, xanthein,
xanthic, xanthous
≈xanth-: xanthoma
≈xantho-: xanthochroid,
xanthoderma, xanthogenic,
xanthophyll
xen-o: stranger, foreign
≈xen: xenia, xenon
≈xen-: xenorexis
≈xeno-: xenobiotic, xenoblast,
xenocryst, xenogamy,
xenogenesis, xenograft,
xenolith, xenophilia,
xenophobia
- xene: pyroxene
- xenic: axenic, antixenic,
holoxenic, monoxenic,
pyroxenic, synexenic
- xenite: cacoxenite, euxenite,
pyroxenite
xer-o: dry
≈xer: xeric; Xerox®
≈xer-: xerarch, xerophthalmia,
xerosis
≈xero-: xerochilia, xerocyte,
xeroderma, xerography,

xerophagy, xerophilous,
xerophyte, xerophytic,
xerosere, xerothermic
- xera: phylloxera
[variant form: serene]
xiph-os: sword
≈xiph: xiphidium
≈xiph-: xiphoid, xiphodon
≈xipho-: xiphocostal,
xiphophyllous, xiphosternum
≈xiphos-: xiphosuran
xyl-o: wood
≈xyl: xylan, xylem, xylene
≈xyl-: xyloid, xyloma
≈xylo-: xylograph, xylophagous,
xylophone, xylotomous,
xylotomy
- xylem: metaxylem, protoxylem
YACHT: Dutch; short for *jaghtschip*,
"pursuit ship" against pirates
YAKUZA: Japanese: gangster
yard: see gird
YAM: a West African native name for
a variety of sweet potato
YODEL: from German *jodeln*
YOGA, YOKE: Sanskrit: union
YOGURT: Turkish
YOLK: Middle English: yellow part
YOM KIPPUR: Hebrew: *yom*, day +
kiper, atone; day of atonement
YURT: Turkish; orig. meaning:
dwelling, home; a circular tent
used by the nomads of Mongolia
ZAFTIG: from East Yiddish *zaftik*,
juicy, succulent; slang for a full,
shapely figure: said of a woman;
buxomy
ZAIBATSU: Japanese; *zai*, wealth +
batsu, family; the few families
who dominate Japanese finance,
commerce, and industry
zeal: zeal, emulation
zeal, zealot, zealous
[variant forms: jealous, jalousie]
ZENITH: Arabic: *samt*, road; the
highest point
ze-o: to boil
zeolite, eczema

ZEPHYR: Greek: the west wind: a gentle breeze

ZERO: Arabic *sifr*; cipher, none

zes: to settle down
synizesis, lit., to sink in; collapse; contraction of two syllables into one by uniting in pronouncing two adjacent vowels

zeug, zeux: yoke, to join
zeugma, epizeuxis

ZIGGURAT: from Akkadian *zaqru*, high, massive; a terraced pyramid with successively receding stories; Akkadian: an extinct Semitic language of the Mesopotamian region

zinc-o: point, prong
zinc, zincite; zincography

ZINNIA: after J. G. Zinn (d. 1759), German botanist; a summer flower

ZOMBIE: Congo zumbi: fetish; a person held to resemble the so-called walking dead

zon-e: to gird
≈zon-e: zonal, zonary, zonation, zonule, zone
- zone: evzone
- zonal: azonal, diazonal, interzonal, intrazonal

zo-o: animal
≈zo-o: zodiac, zoea, zooid; zoo [short for zoological garden]
≈zo-: zoanthropy
≈zoo-: zooflagellate, zoogamete, zoogenic, zoogeography, zoogloea, zoography, zoolatry, zoology, zoometry, zoomorphic, zoomorphism, zoonosis, zooparasite, zoophagous, zoophilia, zoophobia, zoophyte, zooplankton, zoosporangium, zoospore, zoosterol, zootomy
- zoa: with prefixes: azoa, ectozoa, endozoa, entozoan, epizoa, mesozoa, metazoa, microzoa, monozoa, polyzoa, protozoa

- zoa: with combining forms: bryozoa, hydrozoa, malacozoa, oozoa, protozoa, spermatazoa, sporozoa
- zoan: with prefixes: ectozoan, mesozoan, metazoan, parazoan, protozoan
- zoan: with combining forms: anthozoan, bryosozoan, heliozoan, mycetozoan, scyphozoan, sporozoan
- zoarium: polyzoarium
- zoic: Cenozoic, epizoic, Mesozoic, Paleozoic, Phanerozoic, Proterozoic, saprozoic
- zoid: spermatozoid
- zoism: hylozoism
- zoite: merozoite, sporozoite, trophozoite
- zoology: protozoology
- zoon: entozoon, epizoon, hematozoon, spermatozoon
- zootic: enzootic, epizootic
- zote: azote

zyg-o: to join, yoke
≈zyg: zygote
≈zyg-: zygapophysis, zygoid, zygoma
≈zygo-: zygodactyl, zygogenesis, zygomorphia, zygophyte, zygospore, zygotene
- zygosis: heterozygosis, homozygosis, prozygosis
- zygote: heterozygote, hemizygote, homozygote, merozygote
- zygotic: dizygotic, monozygotic
- zygous: azygous, autozygous, cryptozygous, dizygous, gynecozygous, hemizygous, heterozygous, homozygous, monozygous
- zygy: syzygy [variant forms: yoga, yoke]

zym-o: fermentation

≈zym: zymase, zymotic

≈zym-: zymosis, zymurgy

≈zymo-: zymogenic,
   zymogenesis, zymology,
   zymolysis, zymometer
      -   zym-e: enzyme,
          enzymology

Part Two
English to Roots

abnormal: dys-, terat-o
above: super
acute infectious disease: tetan
abundance: cop
accept: dect
accompany: comit
accomplish: form^2
account: calc-i
accustomed (to become): custom,
   sue
acetate: keton
achieve: hent
across: dia-, trans-
act: able, agog, agon
action: drama-t
active (to be): play
actor: histrion, mim-e, person
additional: extr-a-
adult: puber
afar: tele-
after: meta-, ob-, post^2
again: re-
against: anti-, cont-r-ar, ob-
age: ev, secul
age (of ripe): puber
agitate: rit
agree: gru
aid: ancil, jut
air: aero, aria, pneuma-at
algae: algo^3
all: omni-, pan-, tot-al
allot: trib-e^2
almond: amygdal
almost: pen^1
alone: mon-o, sol-i
alongside: para-^{1}
along with: meta-
always: semper
amass: cumul
ammonia: amine
among: meta-
ancient: archa, pale-o
angle: ang-le, gon-io
angry: ir
animal: zo-o
animals of an area: faun-a
anklebone: astragal, tars-o
announce solemnly: calend
anointing oil: chris-m-a
ant: myrmeco
anterior: ep-i

anther: andr-o
anus: ann-u, cul, proct-o
apart: chori, for-, se-
ape: pithec
appear: phaner-o
appearance: ide, schem-a
appease: pi
applaud: plaud
apple: mel^1, pom-e
apply oneself: stud
appoint: leg^1
appraise: est, tax
arch: forni
arched: campylo
arch (part of Gothic): og
arise: orient
arm: brace, brachi-o
armpit: axill
around: amb^2, circ-a, per-i-
arouse: vigil
arrange: chicane, ord, para-^{2}, range,
   tax-i
arrow: fletch, sagitt
arsenic: arsen
art: ert
artery: arter-io
ashamed (to be): pud
ashes: ciner, lixiv, tephr-a
as if: quasi-
ask: quest-ion, rog
ass: as-i
assembly: agora, eccles-io
assign: trib-e^2
assume: lemma^1
asunder: dicha
at: ob-
atone: pi
attach: fix
attack: fest
attain: ept
attempt: conat, try
auger: om-i
away: ab-, abs-, apo-, de-, ex-, for-
away from: sunder
awe: ceremon, ver-e
awn: ather-o
awry: liqu-e^2
ax: hach
axis: ax, pol-e^1
babble: lal
back (adverb): palin, re-, retro-

back of: meta-
back (the): dors, noto, terg-i
backward: palin, re-, retro-
bacterium (berry-shaped): cocc-id
bad: cac-o, dys-, male-, mis-
bad-smelling vapor: meph
bag: asc-o, marsup, sac-c
baggage: plunder
bald: calv, glab-r
ball: glob-e, plot, spher-e
band: fasc
bar, barrier: bar-r, cumb
bare: nud-e, psilo
barren: steril-e
barter: camb
base: bas-e^2, vil-e
basin: pelv, pyel
basket: peddl
battle: machy
battle (line of): phalan-ge
be: essen, futur-e, sens
beam: bauch, trab
bear (noun): ursi
bear (verb): fer-e, ger^1, lat-e, pher-o,
    phor-e, probr, toler
bear abundantly: uber
beard: barb
beast: best, brut, ther-io
beat: bat-t, fut-e, pav-e, tund
beautiful: bell
beauty: bell, calli, char-isma
becoming (process of): -esence
bed: cub-e
bees: api
befit: dece
before: ante-, fore-, pre-, prim-e, pro-
begin: ord
beginning: archa
beginning (process of): -esence
behind (adverb): opistho, post^2
being: ont-o, presence
belch: ruct
belief: doc-t
believe: cred-it
bell: campan-o
bellows: foll, phys-o
below: hyp-o, infer-o, sub-
belt: cinc-t
bend: ang-le, flect, pli, sin-e, vers-e
bent: campylo, curv-e
bereft: orphan

berry: bacc-i
beside: ep-i, juxta
besides: extr-a-
best: aristo
better: melior
between: enter, entre-, inter-, meta-
bewitch: charm, fascin
beyond: extr-a, hyper-, meta-, preter,
    super, ult-im
bile: bil-e, chol-era
bill: rhynch-o
billion: giga
bind: desm, lig-e, nex, string
bird: avi, ornith-o
birdlime: visc^2
birth: gen-e, nat-e
birthmark: nev
bite: mord
bit piece: frustu
bitter: acerb, amar, picr-o
black: melan-o, nigr-o
blade: spatul
bladder: asc-o, cyst-i, phys-o, vesic
blame: culp-a
blank: blanc
bleeding: crud-e
blemish: macul
blight: ured-o
blind: amaur, ciego
blindly: temer
blister: pustul-e, vesic
blood: hemat-o, sang-uin-e
blood clot: throm-o
blot out: del-e
blow (noun): coup
blow (verb): flat-e, fum-e, munc,
    phys-o
blue (color): cyan, glauc-o
blunt, blunted: amblyo, hebet, muti
board: tabl-e
boat (small): bar-k, cymb
bodily fluid: ser-um
body: corp-or, soma-t
body cavity: coel-o, visc^1
body (dried-up): skeleton
body fluid: lyph-o
body (part of the): member
body (upper part): corn-i
boil: bull^1, ferment, ferv, ze-o
bold: audac
bone: oss-i

bones (between fingers or toes): phalan-ge
book: bibl-io, libel-l, teuch
border: limit
bore (verb): trepan
born (to be): nat-e
both: amb[2]
bottom: fund-a
boundary: fin-e
bounds (to set): term-in-e
bow: ar-c-h
bowl: cymb
boy: puer-ile
braid: plect-o
brain: cerebr-o, encephal
branch: clad-o, ram
brass: chalc-o
brave: gall
bread: pan-n
break: clast, frac-t, quash, rupt
breast: mamma-l
breastbone: sternum
breastplate: thorax
breathe: hal-e, pneuma-at, spir-e
bridge: pons
bridle: frenu-m
brief: brev-i
bright: clar-i
bring: vect
bring about: chicane
bring forth: par-e[1], phys-i
bristles: chaet-o, horr-i, set-ac
broad: eury-, plac-e
brother: adelph, frater
bud: gem-m, germ-i, graft
build (verb): edi, moli, struct, techn
bulge: gib-b, tuber
bulk: onco
bull: taur-o
bump: tuber
burial vault: tomb
burn: arg, brand, caus-t, ether, flam-e, neal, ured-o, ust-ul
butterfly: pap-il
buttocks: cul, pyg
buy: deem, emp-li, merc-e
buy victuals: opson-i
by: per-
cabbage: cali
call: ban-n, calend, concil-e, voca
call forth: cit-e

calm: seren-e
cancer: canc-r, carcin-o
car: charg-e
carbon: carb
carbuncle: anthrac-x
card: cart-o
care: cult-i, cur-e, sur-e
carpet: tap-e
carrot: caroten
carry: fer-e, lat-e, phor-e, port[2], vect
cartilage: chondr-o
carve: glyph-o, sculpt
casing: fuse[1]
castle: castell
cat: ailuro, feli
cause: caus-e
cave, cavity: alveolo, celi, coel-o, cotyledon, grot-to, spele, trog-lo
cease: lectic
cell (of body): cyt-o, gon-o, ont-o
center: centesis, centr, foc-us
central point: omphal-os
ceremony: ceremon
cervix: cervic
chaff: ather-o
chain (link of): caten
chair: cathedra-l, h-edr
chamber: camer-a, thalam
chance: fortu, sort-i
change: camb, meta-, mogri, mut-a, trop-e, var-e, vic-ar
charm: fascin
chart: cart-o
channel: can-e, solen-o, stria
character: eth-o
chatter: garrul
cheap: vil-e
checkmate: matad
cheek: bucc, malar
cheese: case
chemistry: chem-o
chest: pector, stetho
chew: mastic
chicken: poult
chief: archa
child: ped-o[1]
childbirth: toc-o
chin: ment[2]
choke: anxi-o, strangl-e
choose: leg[3], opt
chord: cord

chorus: chor-eo
church: clesia, eccles-io
chyle: chym
chyme: chym
cilia: trich
circle: circ-a, cycl-e, gird, gyr-o
circuit: viron
cistern: lacco
citrus: citr-o
city: civ-il, poli-s, urb
claim: sump
clap: plaud
claw: chela
clay: argill
clean: pur-e
cleanse: put-a
clear: clar-i
clear, to make: argu-e
cleave: fiss
clerg: cler
clever: soph-o
climb: scal-e[1]
cloak: chlamy-do, mant
close (verb): claus-e, my, opercul
closed: clav-i[2]
clot (blood): throm-o
cloth: nap
cloth (piece of): pane-l
clothe: vest
cloud, cloudy: nepho
club: clav-i[1]
cluster of grapes: racem-e
coal: anthrac-x
coarse: scurril-e
coast: coast
coat: chlamy-do
cock (rooster): gallin
code: cod-e
coin (a small): stip
cold: algo-[1], frig, psychro
cold (extreme): cryo
color: chromat, color-i
column: colon, pil-e[2]
comb: pect[2], kempt
come: ven-e[2]
comfort: sol-e
common: cen-o[2], mun
common people: pleb-e-i, vulg-e
compact: dens-e
companion: heta, soci
complain: quer

complete: sat-i
completely: per-
comprehend: know
compress: pil-e[2]
condition: -osis
condition (resulting): -mony
cone: con-e
confine: erec
congeal: pect[1]
conquer: vict-or
consider: sul-t
construct: edi
contain: ampl
contend: cert
contest: cert
contrivance: machin-e
control: check
cook (verb): coc-t
copper: chalc-o, cupr
cord: chord, cord, funic, fuse[1]
cork: phell-o, suber
corn (on foot): corn-i
corner: cant-h, gon-io
cotton: bomba
cough: tuss
counselor: medi-c
count: numer
country: agr-i, chor, pag, rust
country house: villa
couple: copul
cover: calyptr-o, ceil, cover, mant,
   scur-e, teg-u, vel[1]
covering: aril-l, elytron, ilemma,
   tunic
cow: bov
crab: canc-r
cram: stip
crane: gree
craving for: mania
crawl: rept, serp
creep: rept, serp
crest: lopho
crooked: ankyl-o, campylo, prav-e
cross: cruci
crosswise: chiasm
crown: cor-n
cruel: atr-a
crumb: mic-a
crush: machi
crust: crust
crust (vent in the earth's): volcan

cry out: clam, cry, ech-o, plain-t,
    plor-e
cup: cup, scyph, tass[1]
cure: cur-e
curl: cirr
curve: sin-e
curved: ar-c-h
cushion: pulvi-n
custody (to keep in): bail, custod
custom: eth-o, moral
cut: cide, put-a, sciss, sect[2], tail-le,
    tom-e
cut further (that which cannot be):
    atom
cut into: entom
cutting out (a): ectomy
cycle: cycl-e
cylinder: cylind-r
damn: dam-ni
dance: chor-eo, orchestr-a
dare: audac
dark: crep[2], fusc, scot-o, temer
daughter: fili
day: dia, diurn, h-emer, jour-nal
deaf: surd
dear: car, preci
death: leth-al, mort, necro, than-ato
deceive: apat, fall
declaim: rhetor
deep, depth: bath-o
deep sleep: coma-t
deity: dei, num
delay: mora
deliberate (verb): sul-t
delta: delt
depth of the sea: benthos
defend: alex, phylac
delight in: terpsi
deliver: bail
demand: postul
dense: pyen, spiss
deserving: dign-i
desire: covet, cupid, pet-e
desolate: hermit
destroy: bezzle, del-e
devil: demon
devise: fict
dig: foss-il-i
digest: peps
dignity: hon
dinner: cena, prandial

dip: merg-e
disc: disc
discharge: vomit
discover: heuristic
disease: mor-bid, nos-o, pathos
disgust: fast, ted
disorder: chao, turb-id
distribute: noma
disturb: tara
ditch: foss-il-i
divide: clast, des, hor-iz, part-e
divider: sept[1]
divination: -mancy
divine law (of): farious
divine spirit: demon
do: act, agog, agon, deed, dim, fac-e,
    ger[1], practic-e, say
dog: can, cyn-o-s
doll: pup-il
dominance: hegemon
donkey: as-i
door: port[1]
doors (God of): jan-itor
double: diplo
doubt: dub
down: cat-a-, de-, infer-o
drain (verb): haust
drama: drama-t
draw: haust, spasm, tir-e, tract
draw together: sphincter, string
dream: oneir-o, rave
dregs: fec
dress up: pol
dried-up body: skeleton
drink: bib-e, pot
drink (strong): tem
drink (without): sob-r
drive (verb): puls-e
drop (noun): gutt, still
drug dosage: poso
drum: tympan
drunk, drunkenness: crapul, ebri
dry: sicc, xer-o
dull: amblyo, hebet, surd
dung: copr-o, sterc-or-i
dusky: fusc
dust: conidi-o, pulver
dwell: col-e, quil
dye: reg-o, tinct
each: per-
eagle: aquil

ear: aur-ic, ot-o
ear of millet: pan-ic
earn: merc-e
early: eo-sin-o
earnest: sever-e
earth: cham, chthon, ge-o, hum-e,
   ped-o^2, tellur, ter-r
earthquake: seism
earthworm: lumbric
ease: oti, palli-at-e
eat: ed^2, phag-o, vor-e
edge: cant-h
egg: oo, ov-a
egg yolk: lecith, vitell
eggs (bearing): oophor
eight: oct-o
elbow: uln
elephant: elephant
eleven: hendeca
else: ali^2
embryo: amnio
empty: ceno, fatu, jejun-e, vac
emulation: zeal
enchantment: glam
encircle: cinc-t
enclose: erc, gird, phragm
enclosed place: court
enclosure: sept^1
end: fin-e, pause, tel-eo, term-i-ne
enemy: hosp
engraving: grave
engraving instrument: character
enjoy: fruct-i
enliven: veget
enough: sat-i
ensnare: lect
enter: penetr-o
entice: lect, lure
environment: ec-o
equal: emulat-e, equ-a, h-om-o,
   par-e^2
equal (to strive to): imitat-e
erase: del-e
esteem: hon
eustachian tubes: salping
even: artio, equ-a
evening: seren-e, vesper
examine: scop-e
excel: emulat-e
excessive: hyper-
exchange: mut-a

excite: rit, tice
excrement: copr-o, scato, ster-cor-i
exercise: asc
existence: ont-o
expel: munc
experiment: pir
explainer: interpret
extend: pand
external: ecto-
extravagance: lux-e
eye: ocul-o, opto
eyelash: cili-o
eyelid: blephar-o
face: prosop
fall (to cause to): sphalt
fall in drops: stax
fallopian tubes: salping
fasten: apt-i, fix, paci, s-er-t
fall (verb): cad-e, cide, gru, lab^2,
   laps-e, pet, pto-m
false: pseud-o
family establishment: famil-y
fan (breeze): flabell
fat: adipo, greas-e, lip-o, stear-o
father: abb, pater-n
fault: vic-e
favor: fav-or, grat-i
fear: tim-id, ver-e
fear of: phobia
feather: pen-n, plum-e, pter-o
feces: fec, scato, sterc-or-i
feed: nourish, past, troph
feel: pass^2, sens-e
feeling: esthe, pathos
female: fem-in, gyn
fermentation: zym-o
fern: pterido
fertile: fec-und
fetal membrane: chori-on
fetus: fet-e
fever: caus-t, febr, phlog, pyr-o, typh
few: olig-o, pauro
fiber: fiber
field: agr-i, camp, champ, pamp-a
fierce: atr-a
fig: syc-o
fight: pug-n
figure: form^1, typ-e
fill: plen-t
filter: filt-r
filth: scen-e, sord

find: triev-e, trov-e
fine (penalty): pen[2]
fine skin: membran-e
finger: dactyl-o
fingernail: onych-o
fire: pyr-o
fire (to set on): ign
fireplace: foc-us
firm: firm, stut
first: archa, prim-e, prote-in, prot-
first principle: element
fish: ichthy, pisc
fit out: orn
fitting: dign-i
fitting together: harmon
five: cinque, pent-a, quin-t
fix (verb): paci
flagella: trich
flag (noun): vexill-o
flagrant: flam-e
flame: flam-e
flame (expose to): broil[1]
flammable gas: methan-e
flat: equ-a, plac-e, plan-e, platy
flat land: champ
flat of the foot: tars-o
flaw: mend
flax (long-fiber): line[1]
flee: fug-e
fleece: vill
flesh: carn-i, creas, omo, sarc-o
flint: silic-a
float: flot
flood: lav-a
floor: sol-i
flora: phyto
flow: flu-c, man[1]
flower: anth-o, flor
fly (insect): musc
fly (verb): vola
foam: spum-e
fog: nebul-a
fold: fold, pli, ptych
follow: sect[1]
following: aco
food: fora, sit-o
foolish: fatu, mor-e
foot: ped[1], pod
foot (flat of the): tars-o
footprint: ichno, vestig-e
force: fort-i, venge

force (to use): viol
foreign: xen-o
foreskin: film
forest: silv
forgetful: leth
fork: furc
form: fict, form[1], ide, mold,
    morph-o, plasm-a, schem-a
fortification: muni-t
forth: pro-
forty: quadr
forward: pro-
fossil: foss-i, tapho
foul: fil-e[2]
four: quadr, tetr-a
free: franch, liber-al
free will: spontan
freeze: gel-at-o
frenzy: estrus, mania
frequent: frequen-t
friend: ami
frighten: terr-i
front: front-i
front (in_of): ob-, fore-
frontier: limit
fruit: carp-o, fruct-i
fruit stone: karyo
full: bry-o, plen-t, sat-i
funeral rites: cedium, funer
fungus: agar, fung, myc-o
furnish: form[2]
furrow: sulc
gadfly: estrus
gain: lucr-e
game: jeu
gap: gulf
gape: hi
garden: horti
garlic: ali[1]
gas: man[3]
gate: port[1], pyl-e
gather: leg[3]
gear: quip
general: mun, strat[2]
generation: sei (Japanese), secul
germ: sperm
giant: giga
gift: dor-a, muni
gills: branch-io
gird: cinc-t, zon-e
girl: pup-il

give: dat-e
glad: fain, hilar
gland: adeno, gland
glass, glassy: hyal-o, vitr-i
gleam: splend-i
glide: gliss, man[1]
globe: glob-e, spher-e
glory: glor-y
glow: can-d-el, ferv
glue: coll-a, gli-a, glutin
gnaw: rod-e
go: bas-e[2], cede, ion-o, it, vad-e
go directly toward: ithy
god, God: dei, the-o
gold: aur-i, chrys-a, or
go: cede, ion-to, it
goat: chevr-e, hirc
gold: gild
good: ben-e, bon-a, eu-, prob-e
goose: anser
govern: govern
grace: char-isma
grain: chondr-o, farin, frument, gran, mic-a, sit-o
grain of wheat: pyren-e
grainy: ather-o
grape: acin, uv-e
grapelike: staphylo
grapes (cluster of): racem-e
grasp: apt-i, eresis
grass: gramin, herb-i
gray: polio
great: grand-i, magn, mega
greater: maj, mayor
greatest: maxim
great honor: glor-y
greed, greedy: avar
green: chlor-o, verd-i, virid
grief: dol-e, penthe
grind: mol, pestle, trit-e
gristle: cartilag-e
groin: inguin
groove: can-e, stria, sulc
ground: cham, hum-e, sol-i
ground (nesting on the): gallin
grounds: fec
groundwater: phreat-o
group of houses: vicin
grow: cresc, olesc, phu, phys-i
grow up: al
guard: cust, phylact

guard (to be on one's): caut
guilt: culp-a
gulf: chas-m, gulf
gullet: fauc, rum
gums: gingiv, gum-m, ulo[1]
hair: capill, chaet-o, com-a, crin[2], hevel, pil-e[1], trich, vel[2]
half: demi-, hemi-, semi-
half (more than; one and a): sesqui
hammer: malle
hand: chir-o, mand
hand down: lob-e
hang: pend
happy: felic
hard: crac-y, dur, scler-o, stere-o
hardened: call
hare: lepor
harm: dam-ni, noc
harp: arp
harrow: hears-e
harsh: auster
hate: fiend, loath, mis-o, odi
have: able
head: cap-it, cephal-o, corn-i, crani-o
heal: acea, iatr-o
health: salv
healthy: san-e
heap: acerv
hearing: acousto, aud-i-o
heart: cardi-o, cord-i
heat: caus-t, thalp, therm-o
heaven: celest, coelo, uran-o
heavy: bar-i, grav-e
heel (of foot): cal-c
height: acro, alti, hyps
helmet: galea
helper: ancill, jut
hen: gallin
herb: herb-i
herd: greg
hernia: -cele
hero: hero
heroic: gall
hide (noun): cor-i
hide (verb): clan, cond, cover
hidden: crypt
high: acro, alti
highest: sum
hill: mont
hindrance: tric
hip: cox, ischi, sciat

hiss: sibil
hitch: choat-e
hold: able, cap, choat-e, e-ch, hab-it,
   lab-e, ten-t
hole: fora, tremat
hollow: cav-e, chas-m, coel-o, cotyledon
holy: hagi-o, hier-o, h-ol-o, sacr-al
home: ec-o
honey: mel-li
honeycomb: fav-eol
honor: celebr
hoof: ungu-i
hook: ang-le, cros, unct
hope: sper
horn: cer-at, kerat
horse: caval, equ-i, hipp-o
hot: cald
hour: horo
house: cas, dom-e
hovering in the air: eor
how much: quant-i, quot-e
hue: color-i
human: human-e
humor: chym, phlegm
hump: gib-b
hundred: cent, hect
hundredth: centi-
hunger: fam
hunt: ven^2, vit-e
hurry: festin
husk: lemma^2
I: ego
ice: glac-io
idea: ide
ileum: ile-o
imitator: mim-e
immerse: bapt
ill: dys-
image: form^1, icon-o, ide, imag-o
impulse: hormone, osm-o
in: en-^{2}, in-^{1}
incense: thur
increase: auct, cresc
inferior: aster
inflammation: -itis, phlog
in front of: ob-
inhabit: col-e
inherit: her-ed
injure: lid-e, sphalt, trauma-t, vulner
insect: entom-o

insensible: surd
insensitive: call
inside: intra-, intro-
intensive: in-^{3}
intestine: enter-o, hernia, visc^1
intestine (lower part of):
   col-on
into: eso-, intro-
iris: irid
iron: fer-r, molybd, sider^2
island: insul, isl, nesia
itch: prur, urtic
jaundice: chol-era
jaw: gnath, mandib
jaw (upper): maxill-a
jest: faceti, joc, scherz-o
join: jug, s-er-t, techn, zeug, zyg-o
joint: arthr-o, art-ic, genic
joke: joc
joy: joy
joyful: fain, fest-iv-e, gaud
judge: cens, cert-i, crit, judic
judgment (sound): prud
juice: chym
jump: salt
justice: dic
keeper: custod
kernel: cocc-id, karyo, nuc-le-o
key: clav-i^2
kidnapping: plagiar
kidney: nephro, ren-i
kill: cide, cton, matad
kind (what): quale
kindness: char-isma
knee: genic
kneecap: pate-ll-a
knife: cultr
knob: tass^2
knot: nod-e, tass^2
know, knowledge: gnom-e, know,
   sci^1
knowing: histor-ic
label: tit-le
lack of: penur
ladder: scal-e^1
lake (marshy): limn-o
lance: lance
language: ling
large: ampl, gross, large, macro,
   mega
larynx: laryng

lash: verb
lasting: dur
late: opsi
laugh: ri-d
law: leg⁴, nom-o
layer (thin sheet): lamell, strat¹
lead (verb): agog, duc, leit, men
lead weight: plum-b
leaf: foli-o, phyll-o
leaf of a folding door: valv-e
leap: lop-er
learn: mathemat
leave: linqu
leave off: lectic
leaf: foli, frond
leaflet: pen-n
leafstalk: petiol-e
lean (to): clim
leap: salt
learned: histor-ic
leather: cor-i
leave: leip
left side: levo, sinist-ro
leg: gamb, scel-o
lend: prest
length: meco
lens: lenti, phaco
lentil: lenti, phaco
less: mei, min-im
letter: liter
level: equ-a, plan-e
lice: pedicul
lie down: cub-e
life: anim-a, bi-o, viv-e
limb (of body): mel²
light: luc, photo, pyr-o
light (in weight): lev-y
lightning: fulmin
like (adjective): h-om-o
likeness: imag-o
lily: crin¹
limbs (condition of): melia
limestone: calc-i
line: line²
line of poetry (measurement of):
    meter, stich-o
liquid (to be): liqu-e¹, ner
little: para-³
lizard: lacer, saur-o
limit: fin-e, term-in-e
line: fil-e¹

link of chain: caten
lip: chilo, lab¹
listen: auscult
literary thief: plagiar
live (verb): viv-e
lively: scherz-o
liver: hepa-t-o
load a wagon: charg-e
loathing: fast
locked: ser
log: caud²
loin: lumb-o
long: dolicho, long
look at: theor-em, tui
loose: lax, rar-e
loosen: solv-e
loosening: -lysis
love: amat, ero-t, phil, ven-er-eo
lot: sort-i
low: bas-e¹, infer-o
lump: mass²
lung: pneum-at, pulmon
lure: lure
lust: lagn
luxury: lux-e
lye: lixiv
lying nearby: eas-e
machine: machin-e, mechan
madness: mania, rab
maim: muti
mainland: epeiro
make: fac-e, po
maker: wright
malformed: terat-o
man: andr-o, anthrop-o, h-om,
    human-e, mascul, vir
manhood (early): epheb-e
manifest (to make): del
manner: guis-e
manners: moral
many: multi-, plural, poly-
map: cart-o
mark: hil, marc, not-e, sign
mark off: hor-iz
marketplace: agora
marriage: gam-ete, mar-it
marrow: myel-o
marry: nub
marvel: mir-e
mask: masque
mass: mass², mol-e, onco

master: magist
matter: hylo
mature: coc-t, matur-e
maze: labyrinth
measure: mensu, meter, mod-e,
  rhythm
measurement, art of: arithm
measuring device: meter
meat: carn-i
medicine: acea, pharmac
melt: fund[2], liqu-e[1], tectic
membrane (fetal): chori-o, film,
  membran-e, mening
memory: mne-m
menstruation: men-o
merciful: clemen
merry: gall
messenger: angel
metal: metal, mine-r-a
mid: meri
middle: med, mes-o-
mild: clemen, leni
milk: galact-o, lact, muls
millet: mili
mind: ment, no-u, phren-o, psych-e,
  thym[1]
mine: metal
minimum: min-im
mint (of a): mone-t
miracle: thauma
mist: nebul-a
mite: acaro
mix: misc-e
mix in proportion: temper
mixing: crater
mob: ochlo
model: typ-e
moist, moisture: hum, hygr-o, nepho,
  vap
moisten: taint
mold: fict, mold, muci-l, plasm-a
mollusks: malaco
money: pecun
money basket: fisc
monster: terat-o
month: men-o
moon: cyn-th, lun-e, men-o, seleno-
moral: moral
more than: extr-a-, hyper-, pleio
moss: bryo
mother: matr-i, metr-o

mountain: mont, or-o
mouth: bucca, or-al, stom-a
mouth (roof of): palat-e
move: mot[2]
move from one place to another:
  migra-te
movement: kine
movies: cine
much: quant-i
mucus: myx-o
mud: pel
muscle: myo
mushroom: fung
music: mus
musket: fusil-l
nail (of the body): onych-o
naked: gymn, nud-e
name: nomen, onomast
narrow: anxi-o, sten-o
narrow passage: isthm
nation: ethn-o
native soda: nitr-o
natron: nitr-o
nature: phys-i
navel: omphal-os, umbilic
near: juxta, ob-, pleio, prop, vicin
neck: cervic, col-l, trachel
need (to be in): indig
needle: acer, obel
negative: ab-, dis-, in-[2], negat-e, non-
negotiator: interpret
nerve: nerv-e, neur
nest: nid-i
net: ret-ic
nettle: urtic
neutral: neutr-o
new: cen-o, neo-n, nov
night: noct, nyct
nine: non
nipplelike: pap-ill-a, thelium
nod: nut
north wind: borea-l
nose: nas-o, rhin-e
not: an-, en-[1]
notched: cren, serra
note: not-e
not either: neutr-o
nothing: nihil
nourish: ali, nourish, nutri, troph
nude: gymn, nud-e
numb: torp-or

number: numer, pleth-ora
nut: karyo, nuc-le-o
oak: querc, rob
oar blade: pilot, rem-e
obelus: obel
observe: skept
obstruction: cumb
odor: odor-i
off: ab-, abs-, de-
offense: crim-in
offensive: ted
offspring: gon-o, prol-e
oil: ol-e
oil (anointing): chris-m-a
old: ger[2], pale-o, presby, sen, veter
on: ep-i
one: hen-o, mon-o, sol-i, uni
one's own: idio, prop-ri
open: aper, pat-ent
opening: fora, or-al, port[1]
opening from the stomach: pyl-e
opposite: cont-r-ar
orbit: orb-it
orchid: orchi-d
order: ord
ore: mine-r-a
organ: organ
organism: ont-o
origin: gen-e, nat-e
orphan: pup-il
other: ali[2], allo, alter, heter-o, meta-
our, ours: nost-r
out: ex-
outdoors: for[2]
outer: ex-
outer sea: ocean-o
outfit (verb): couter
outside: ecto-, ep-i-, exo-, extr-a-,
    for[2], hors
outside territory: provinc-e
over: ep-i, hyper-, meta-
overflow: rheo
overlapping: imbric
ovum: oo, ov-a
ox: bov
oxygen: ox-y
owe: deb-t
pack (verb): spiss, stip
pad: mattress
pain: algo[2], dol-e, odyn-e
pale: och

pale (to grow): pal-l
pale yellow: och
palm: palm
pan: pate-ll-a
paper: papyr-o
papyrus: papyr-o
paralysis: -plegia
parasite: parasit-e
part (noun): mer, par-e[1], piece
part (verb): sunder
part of the body: member
partly: semi-
pass: man[1]
passage: por-e
passage (narrow): isthm
past: preter-
paste: coll-a, past-e
pasture (wooded): nemo, noma
patch: plaque, sartor
pea: pis
peace: fray, paci
peace (goddess of): iren
peacock: pav
peak: con-e, culmin, ocre
peasant: pag
pebble: psamm
peculiar: priv-e
penalty: pen[2], pun-i
penis: pen-i, phall-o, puce
people: dem-o, ethn-o, lai, liturg,
    popul
people (common): pleb-e-i, vulg-e
perceive: aesth, esth, no-u, sag-e
perform: funct-ion
permitted (to be): licen-se
perplexity: trig
person: person
physician: medi-c
phylum: phyl-o
piece of cloth: pane-l
pig: porc
pillar: colon, styl-e[1]
pillow: pulvi-n
pimple: pap-ill-a, varic-o
pine, pineapple: pin-a
pipe: aul, fistul, pip-er, syring
pistil: gyn
pit for storage: sil-e
pity: miser-i
place (noun): chor, loca-l, -orium,
    pos-e

place (verb): sit-u, thesis, top-o
place marked out: templ-e
plague: pest-i
plain: pamp-a
plait: trec
plant: botan-i, phyto
plant disease: ergot
plaque: plaque
plate: scu-te
plate (a thin metal): bract-eo
play: lud-e
pleasant: eu-
please: plac
pleasing: grac-e, grat-i
pleasure: hedon, libid
pledge: gag-e, pledg-e, spond, tru-e
pluck (verb): carp-o, vellic, vuls-e
plunder: pred
plunge: merg-e
pod: sili
poetry (measurement of line of):
    meter
poison: pharmac, tox, venom, vir-us
point, pointed: acer, acro, apic-o,
    apti, centesis, cusp, omphal-os,
    prick, spic, styl-e[1], zinc-o
point (verb): dex, punct
point out: mon-it
pole: staff
polish: pol
pollution: myso
pome: pom-e
ponder: cogitat-e, muse
poor (to be): pover
pore: por-e
post (noun): stel-e
pot: test
potash: potas
pottery: ceram
pouch: marsup
poultry: poul-t
pound (verb): pestle
pour: fund[2], libat
power: dyna-m, may, poss
praise: laud
pray: or-al, prec
precious stone: gem-m
prepare: h-opl, para-[2]
preserve: sote-rio
press: pres-s
press hard: urge

pressure: piezo
prey: pred
price: preci
prick: pica, stigma, s-tinct
prickly: echin-o
priest: cler
primary: archa, prote-in
principal (main): cardin
private property: pecun
procreation: gon-o
productive: fet-e
project: cel-l, men
promise solemnly: spond
prong: zinc-o
property: fee
property (private): pecun
prophet: manti
prostate: prostat-e
prostitute: porn
protect: arm-a, gar-r , para-[2], phylact
prove: dic
prune: put-a
pubic region: episio-
public: mun
public treasury: fisc
pull: spasm, tract, vuls-e
pulse: crot
puncture: centesis
punishment: pen[2], pun-i
punishment in kind: tali
pure: pur-e
pure (to make): cathar
purple: porphyry, purpur-e
pursue: ept
pus: pustul-e, py-o
push: osm-o, puls-e
pustule: varic-o
put: dim, pos-e
put in order: ray
put on: dus, uv
putrefaction: sep-s
quantity: pleth-ora
quarrel: broil[2]
quarry: metal
quartz: silic-a
quiet: qui-es
rabbit: cone
rage: fur, rab
rain: hyet-o, ombro, pluvi
rainbow: irid
raise: lev-y

ram (verb): pav-e
ram down: pil-e[2]
rank (to be): ranc
rare: rar-e
rash: temer
rasping sound: strid-ul
rattle: crep[1]
rave: hallucin-o
raven: corac
raw: crud-e
ray: actini, radi-o
reach: orex
read: leg[2]
real: real
reason: caus-e, rat-e
recent: cen-o[1]
reckon: count[1], put-a, tax
red: erythr-, rhod, rub-e
red lead: mini
reed: calamus, can-e, syring
regular: ortho
rein: frain
remain: man[2]
remember: memor
repeat: iterat-e
report (verb): nunci
reproduction (sexual): gam-ete,
    gon-o
repute: hon
restraint: check
resulting condition: -mony
retire: chor
return: nost-o
revel: com
reverent rite: ceremon
rib: cost, pleur-e
ribbon: cest, fet-a, taenia
riches: lucr-e, opu-s
riddle: griph
right: dext-r, rect-i
right of seizure: sylum
rim: cant-h
rind: lemma[2]
ring: annu
ripe: matur-e
rise: cel-l, surg-e
rival: riv-al
river: potam
riverbank: riv-al
road: h-od-e, vi-a
roam: rave, spac-e

roar: streper
rob: spol
rock: lap-id, lith-o, petr-i, sax-i
rod: bacill-i, ferul, radi-o, rhabo,
    staff
roll: cylind-r, velop, volu-me
roof: fastigi
roof of mouth: palat-e
room: camer-a, cell-o
root: rad, rhiz-o, s-tirp
rope: cord, funic
rose: rhod
rotation: dino[1]
rotten: putr-, sapr-o
rough: asper, crud-e, lep-ido, rud-e
row: line[2], stich-o, tire
row (set in a): range
rub: fric, trib-e, trib-e[1], triv-e
rule (noun): norm, rect-i
rule (verb): arch, crac-y
run: cur, drom-e
rush at: pet-e
rustic: pag
S (the letter): sigma
sac: cyst-i, sac-c
sack: sac-c
sacred: sacr-al
safety: salv
sail: plius
saliva: saliva, sial
salt: hal-o, sal
same: ident-i, iso-, simil, taut-o
sanctuary: templ-e
sand: aren-i, psamm
sash: fasc
satisfy a desire: dulg-e
sausage: allanto
save: sote-rio
saw (noun): serra
sawed (something): prism-at
say: dict, locu
scab: scab-r
scaffold: falque
scale: squama
scales (of fish): cten-o
scales (weighing): libra
scalloped: cren
scaly: lep-ido
scar: cicatr, eschar, hil, ulo[2]
scarce: olig-o, pauro
scatter: spor-e

school: schol
scorn: temn
scrape (verb): rad-e
scratch: scari
sea: mar-in, nau, ner, ocean-o, pelag,
    thalass
seal (an animal): phoco
seal (to enclose): bull[2]
sea nymph: ner
second: deuter-o
secret: clan, crypt, myst-er
see: scop-e, skept, speci, vid-eo
seed: cocc-id, gon-o, semen, sperm,
    spor-e
seek: pet-e, quest-ion
seer: manti
seize: agra, cap, lemma[1], prehen-s,
    pris, rap-t
self: auto, ego, ipsi, locu, sam
    (Russian), sui
self-denying: asc
sell: pol-e[2], ven[1]
semen: gon-o
send: heter, leg[1], miss, stal
sense: sens-e
sepal: sepal
separate: cert-i, crit, priv-e, sever,
    sunder, vid-e
serf: helot
sermon: homil
serpent: herp-eto
servant: ancill
serve: lat-r, minister, serv-e[1]
service: con
set: stem-o
set in motion: esis
set in a row: range
set in order: par-e[1], per
set on fire: ign
settle down: zes
seven: hebdomad, hept-a-, sept[2]
sew: couter, rhaps
sexual immorality: forni
sexual love: ero-t
sexual reproduction: gam-ete
shade: umbel-l
shadow: sci[2]
shady: opa-c
shake: cuss, donet, quash, vibr-a
shape: eid-o, form[1], morph-o
sharp: acid, ox-y

sharp point: mucro
sheath: cole-o, elytron, vagin
shell: conch, crust, ostrac, scal-e[2],
    test
shield: arm-a, pelt, scu-te
shine: can-d-el, fulg-ur, lamp,
    splend-i
shiny: glac-io
ship: nav-e, quip, scaph-o
shirt: camis
shoe: calc
shoot (of a plant): blast-o, clad-o,
    germ-i, graft, thall-o
shore: riv-al
short: brachy, brev-i, curt
shoulder: om
shout: clam
show (verb): dic, mon-it
shrub: frut
shudder: horr-i
shun: vit
shut: opercul
sickle: falc-i
side: cost, h-edr, later, par-e[1]
sift: cert-i, crit
sight: ocul-o
sign (noun): sema, tit-le
sign (verb): sign
silent (to be): siopesis, tac-it
silica: silic-a
silk: seric
silver: argent, platin
similar to: -ine, -oid
simple: simpl-e
sin (verb): pecc-a
sing: can-t, charm, ed[1], od-e
singers: chor-eo
single: h-apl-o
sink: merg-e
sister: soror-i
sit: h-edr, h-izesis, sed-ent
six: hexa-, sex-t
sketch: scari
skill: ert
skillful: soph-o
skin (noun): cor-i, cut, derm,
    membran-e, pel-l
skull: crani-o
sky: coelo
slab: stel-e
slander: calumn

slanting: loxo, plagio

slave: dul-e, helot, lat-r, thrall

sleep (deep): coma-t, dorm, hypn, somn-i, sopor-i

slime: pel

slippery: lubric

slope: clim, fastigi

slow: brady, stult, tardi

small: demi, mei, micr-o, min-im, olig-o, pet-t

smallpox: vario

smell: fragr, odor-i, ol, osm, ozo-n-e, savor

smoke: fum-e

smooth: lev, lubric

smother: stifl-e

snail, snail shell: cochl

snake: colubr, ophi-o

snare: lace

snout: rhynch-o

snow: niv

so: item

soap: sapon

soft: leni, mit

soil: hum-e, sol-i

soldier: milit

solemn procession: pomp

solid: stere-o, sol-i³

song: mel-o, psalm

sorghum: sorg

sorrow: mourn

sound: ech-o, phon-e, phthong, son-e

sound judgment: prud

sour: acid, sauer (German)

south: austral

sow: spor-e

space: lacu, spac-e

spare: pars

spark: scinti

spasm: spasm

speak: fab, lex, locu, loqu, or-al, phras-eo, rhetor

speak in riddles: enigma

spear: cusp

speech: phasia

speed: velo-ci

sphere: glob-e

spice, sweet: aroma

spider: arachn

spike: spire

spindle: fuse¹

spine: rach, spin-e

spiny: echin-o

spiral: helic

spirit: anim-a, pneum-at, thym-ia

spit (noun): obel

spit (verb): pty-al

spleen: splen

split: cide, fiss, schiz-o

spoil: spol

spoke of a wheel: radi-o

spot: macul, plaque

spread: pand, strat¹

spread out: pat-ent, petal

spring (of water): fount

spring back: elastic

spring (pertaining to): vern

sprinkle: past-e, sperg

sprout: blast-o, cym, plan-t

square: quadr

staff: bacill-i

stake: pal-e, tach

stalk: rach, s-tip-ul-e

stamens (number of): adelph, andr-o

stammer: hesit

stand: post¹, stand, stem-o, trust

star: astr-o, galact-o, sider¹, stell-i

stare at: muse

starch: amyl

steal: klep-t, pilfer, ro-be, steal

steer a ship: govern

stem: caud², stel-e, trunc-h

step: grad-e, pass¹

stick (noun): ferul, fust

stick (verb): here

stickiness: visc²

stiff: rig¹, torp-or

stomach: gastr, stom-a, vent-r

stomach (opening from the): pyl-e

stomach (third__in ruminants): omasum

stone (precious): gem-m, -ite, lith-o, scrup

stone (small): coral-l

stop: stop

storage (pit for): sil-e

straddle: varic

straight: ithy, ortho, rect-i

strain (verb): col, filt-r

strange: allo

stranger: hosp, xen-o

strangle: strangl-e

strap: ament
straw: s-tip-ul-e
strength: crac-y, dyna-m, sthen-o
stretch: tens-e, ton-e
stretching out: ectasis, strat[2]
strew: sperg
strike: bat-t, coup, crot, cus-e, cuss,
   fend, fer-e, flict, fut-e, paci, pinge,
   puls-e, ract, tund
strike out: cancel
string: chord
strive to equal: imitat-e, nis (nit)
stroke (paralysis): -plegia
stroke (verb): mulc
strong: bil, firm, fort-i, poll, rob, val-
   id, vigor
struggle: athlet-e, luct
study: stud
study of: -logy
stuff (verb): farc-e, frequen-t, gav
stunned (to be): stup-e
stupid: stult
stupor: narc-o
stylus: grave
suck: fellat-e, suc-t
sugar: gluc-o, sacchar
suitable: apt-i
subdue: damant
substitute: vic-ar
such: tal
suck in: sorb
suffer: pass[2], pathos
sulfur: sul-f, thio
summer: there
summit: culmin
summon: ban-n, cit-e
sun: heli-o, sol
surrender: tradit-e
sustain: toler
swallow (verb): glut, gorg-e
sway: vacill
swear: judic
swear (to make one): orc
sweat: hidr, s-ud-e
sweet: dulc, gluc-o, suas
swell (verb): bry-o, gemm, gib-b,
   tum, turg
swelling: gangli-o, pan-ic
swift: tachy
swim: nata
swing: oscill

sword: gladi, xiph-os
swift: celer
symbol: icon-o
table: disc, mensa, tabl-e
tablet of laws: cod-e
tail: caud[1], cerc, pen-i, ur-o[2]
tailor: sartor
take: cap, emp-li, eresis, heres-i, pris
take up: sump
talk: lal, par-l
tallow: seb
tape, tapeworm: taenia
taste: gust, sap, savor
tax: cens
tax (exemption from further): atel
teach: didac-t, doc-t
tear (drop): dacry-o, lachryn
tear (verb): lacerat-e
teeth: cten-o, dent-i, odont-o
tell: count[2], narrat-e
temple: fan-e
ten: dec
tension: ton-e
terrible: dino[2]
terrify: stern
territory (outside): provinc-e
test (verb): tempt
testicle: orchi-d
thick: crass, dens-e, greas-e, gross,
   hadron, pachy, pycno
thick: spiss
thief: furt
thigh: mer
thin: lepto-n, maciat, rar-e
things in the air: meteor
think: opin-e
third: ter
thirst: dipso, torr
this side of: cis-
thorn: acantho-
thong: ament
thousand: chili, kilo, mil-l, myria-d
thread: fil-e[1], mit-o, nemat-o
threaten: men
three: tri-
throat: fauc, garg, guttur, pharyngo,
   rum
throb: sphygm-o
through: dia-
throw: bal-l, esis, jac, sip
thrust: trud

thunder: bronto, ton
thus: item
thymus: thym^2
thyroid: thyr
tie (verb): nex
time: chrono, temp-or
tin: stann
tinge: tinct
tire (verb): fatig
tissue: histo
title: tit-le
to, toward: ad-, ob-, pros
toe: dactyl-o
toenail: onych-o
together: com-, sym-
tolerate: toler
tomb: comb, tapho
tomorrow: cras
tongue: gloss, ling
tonsil: amygd
tool: organ, teuch
tooth: dent-i, odont-o
toothlike: pect^2
topmost: acro
touch: mass^1, palp, tact, thigm-o
tower: turr
town: civ-il, muni
trace: vestig-e
track: orb-it
trade: merc-e
translate: hermeneut
transparent: hyal-o
trap: lace
trash: plunder, crut
treasury (public): fisc
treatment: iatr-, therap-y
tree: arbor, dendr-o, silv
tree trunk: bauch
tremble: trem
trial: pir
trickery: calumn, dul
true: ver-i
true (to think): dogma
true sense of a word: etymo-n
trumpet: salping
trunk: trunc-h
trust: fid
try: peril, tempt
tub: cup
tube: aul, fistul, fuse^1, salping,
  siphon, tub-e

tuff: lopho
tumor: -cele, oma, onco
turmoil: clonus
turn: rhomb-o, spir-o, stroph-e, tort,
  triv-e, trop-e, vers-e
twelve: dodeca
twice: di-, semi-
twig: clon-e, plan-t, virg
twin: didym, diplo, gemin
twist: strangl-e, strepto, tort
two: bi-, di-, didym, diplo, du-o
two (in): dicha
tyrant: tyran-ni
ulcer: fistul
uncertain: dub
unction: chris-m-a
under: hyp-o, sub-
undertake: conat
unequal: aniso
unite: copul
universe: cosm-os
unmarried: celib
unredeemed: dentist
upright: ortho
upside down: supin-e
urge: hort, suas
urinate: mictur-i
urine: ur-o^1
use: chresis, us-e
uterus: hyster-o, metr-o
utter: thegm
uvula: staphylo
vaccine: vaccin-e
vagina: cole-o
valley: thal, val-e
value: cens, est
vapor: atmo, nebul-a, typh, vap
vapor (bad-smelling): meph
vary: var-i
varying: poikilo
vault: forni
vault (burial): tomb
vegetation: phyto
vein: nerv-e, neur, phleb-o, varic-o,
  ven-e^1
vent in the earth's crust: volcan
vertebra: astragal, spondyl
vessel: angi-o, vas-cul
vibrate: vibr-a
vice: vic-e
view: -orama

village: vicin, villa
villain: felon
vine: vin-e
vinegar: aceto
violence: viol
violet: iod-o
virgin: partheno
viscera: splanchn
visible (to be): par
voice: phthong
volt: volt
vomit: eme, vomit
vote: vot
vow: vot
vulgar: scurril-e
wail: cry, lament, plor-e
waiver (in opinion): dub
walk: amb[1], pate, spac-e
wall: mur-al, parie-t, val-l
wander: err, il-e, vag-a
wander mentally: hallucin-o
want (need): penur
wantonness: libid, prur, ribald
war: belli, mart, polemic
ward: pup-il
warm: cald, for[1]
warm (slightly): tep-e
warm (to keep): forment
warn: mon-it
warranty: pledg-e
wart: verruc
wash: clys, lav-a
wasp: vesp
watch (verb): vigil
watch (to keep): serv-e[2]
water: aqu-a, hydr-o, rig[2]
water animal: nutria
wave: cym, und-ul
wax: cer-a
way: guis-e, h-od-e, por-e, vi-a
weak: debil, feeble
wealth: pluto
wear away: mor-bid, trypano
weary: fatig, langu, ted
weave: plect-o, techn, text
wedge: con-e, cune, sphene
week: hebdomad
weigh: libra, pend
well: ben-e
well (noun): phreat-o
well-known: nob-le

well (to be): val-id
wet: tinct
whale: cet-o
what kind: quale
wheat (grain of): pyren-e
wheel: rota, troch-ee
where: ubi
whip: flagell-i, verb
whirl: gyr-o, turb-id
whistle: sibil
white: alb, blanc, leuko
who: quo-d
whole: h-ol-o, sol-i[3], tot-al
wide: eury-, later
wife: uxor-i
wife (young): nymph-o
wild: fer
will (free): spontan
willing (to be): vol-i
wind (noun): anem-o, vent-il
window: fenestr
windbag: foll
winding passage: labyrinth
windpipe: bronch-o, trach-ea
wine: oeno
wing: alat
wink (verb): nict
winter: cheim, hibern
wipe: terg-e
wise: soph-o
wish: vol-i, vot
with: com-, sym-
witchcraft (to practice): pharmac
wither: marce
within: endo-, ento-, intim, intra-,
    intro-, intus
witness: test-i
without: an-, sans (French), sine
without drink: sob-r
witness: martyr-o
wolf: lyc
woman: gyn
womb: cole-o, hyster-o
wonder (noun): mir-e
wood: dar, hylo, lign-i, xyl-o
wooded pasture: nemo
wooden shoe: sabot
wooden tower: falque
wool: floc-c, lan-i, vill
woolly: ulo

word: dict, ep-o, lex, -logy, mot^2,
   verb-i
word (true sense of): etymo-n
work: arg, ergo, oeuvre, opu-s,
   orphan, pone
worker: wright
work with the hands: surg-ery
workman: fabric
work performed: muni
world: cosm-os, mund
worm: helminth-o, scol-ex, verm-i
worm (intestinal): ascar
worse: pejor, pessim
worship of: lat-r
worth: val-id
worthy: axio-m, dign-i
wound: trauma-t, vulner
wrap: vel^1
wrench: spasm
wretched: miser-i
wrinkle: rhyt, rug
wrist: carp
write: gram, scrib-e
wrong: mis-
yawning: chas-m
year: ann-i
yellow: flav-on, fulv, xanth-o
yield: cede, dulg-e
yoke: zeug, zyg-o
yolk (egg): lecith, vitell
young man: epheb-e, hebe, jun,
   neo-n
young wife: nymph-o
youth: hebe
zeal: jealous, zeal
zone: zon-e